Behavior and
Classroom Management
in the Multicultural Classroom

I would like to dedicate this book to the memory of my sister,
Lisa Shepherd Scott (1959–2013).
She was an education paraprofessional, and we had a
number of conversations
about behavior and intervention strategies.
Her love for others will transcend time.

Terry L. Shepherd

I dedicate this book to my parents, Bernice and Theodore Linn,
and to my children, Máximo and Sandra.

Diana Linn

Behavior and Classroom Management in the Multicultural Classroom

Proactive, Active, and Reactive Strategies

Terry L. Shepherd

Indiana University South Bend

Diana Linn

Texas A&M International University

Los Angeles | London | New Delhi
Singapore | Washington DC

Los Angeles | London | New Delhi
Singapore | Washington DC

FOR INFORMATION:

SAGE Publications, Inc.
2455 Teller Road
Thousand Oaks, California 91320
E-mail: order@sagepub.com

SAGE Publications Ltd.
1 Oliver's Yard
55 City Road
London EC1Y 1SP
United Kingdom

SAGE Publications India Pvt. Ltd.
B 1/I 1 Mohan Cooperative Industrial Area
Mathura Road, New Delhi 110 044
India

SAGE Publications Asia-Pacific Pte. Ltd.
3 Church Street
#10-04 Samsung Hub
Singapore 049483

Acquisitions Editor: Theresa Accomazzo
Associate Digital Content Editor: Rachael Leblond
Editorial Assistant: Georgia McLaughlin
Production Editor: Libby Larson
Copy Editor: Judy Selhorst
Typesetter: C&M Digitals (P) Ltd.
Proofreader: Theresa Kay
Indexer: Sylvia Coates
Cover Designer: Glenn Vogel
Marketing Manager: Terra Schultz

Printed in the United States of America

Library of Congress Cataloging-in-Publication Data

Shepherd, Terry L.

Behavior and classroom management in the multicultural classroom : proactive, active, and reactive strategies / Terry L. Shepherd, Indiana University South Bend, Diana Linn, Texas A&M International University.

pages cm.
Includes bibliographical references and index.

ISBN 978-1-4522-2626-2 (pbk. : alk. paper)

1. Classroom management—Social aspects. 2. Behavior modification. 3. Culturally relevant pedagogy. I. Linn, Diana. II. Title.

LB3013.S515 2015

371.102′4—dc23   2014012083

This book is printed on acid-free paper.

14 15 16 17 18 10 9 8 7 6 5 4 3 2 1

BRIEF CONTENTS

DETAILED CONTENTS

PREFACE

PURPOSE OF THIS BOOK

Behavior and classroom management has been a critical issue facing teachers for nearly 40 years. With the increasing numbers of culturally and linguistically diverse students in our schools, teachers often do not feel prepared to handle many of the behavioral problems they face in their classrooms today. The purpose of this book is to provide teachers with the knowledge, skills, and strategies they need to create learning environments that will benefit children from all backgrounds and experiences.

This book is designed differently from many other textbooks. It introduces the concept of a universal design for classroom management, which is a proactive approach to developing a behavior and classroom management plan that considers the needs of students with disabilities, culturally and linguistically diverse students, struggling learners, and students of all ability levels. As part of the universal design for classroom management, behavior and classroom management programs must include proactive, active, and reactive interventions to be successful in the classroom. This book addresses all facets of these interventions: basic classroom management plans, functional behavioral analysis, functional behavioral assessments, behavior intervention plans, response-to-intervention, and school-wide positive behavior support. The book also provides overviews of developmental theories of behavior and the legal issues related to behavior management. The inclusion of developmental theories is especially crucial: These theories provide teachers with some understanding of behavior and serve as a basis for practical applications.

Additionally, this book goes beyond traditional classroom management strategies and behavior interventions, including chapters on teacher collaboration with students' parents and other family members, the role of the teacher in developing and implementing behavior strategies, and social skills training. The book also explores the effects that culture and language have on the behaviors of children from diverse backgrounds and how these might influence the strategies teachers use when implementing behavior and classroom management interventions. The overall goal of the book is to provide information on the major facets of behavior and classroom management that will help teachers create safe and secure environments that promote the learning of all students.

This book is designed for undergraduate and graduate courses in classroom management, behavior management, and applied behavior management. It can also be used by general education teachers, elementary education teachers, secondary education teachers, special education teachers, school administrators, school counselors, and education paraprofessionals.

FEATURES

Several pedagogical features are incorporated in the content of this textbook:

- Objectives at the beginning of every chapter highlight the important issues in the chapter.
- Review questions and activities at the end of each chapter test students' understanding of the content and concepts of the chapter.
- In a tribute to the Dick and Jane stories from our youth, we include in each chapter a case study involving Ricardo, Jane, Kale, or Timothy. Each case study emphasizes an important issue covered in the chapter.
- "What Would You Do?" vignettes are included in all chapters to encourage readers to formulate responses to classroom situations.
- Contemporary educational issues are discussed, including the needs of culturally and linguistically diverse students, at-risk students, and students with disabilities.
- Practical applications of research-based practices are offered, such as social skills instruction and teacher collaboration with diverse families.
- A glossary provides definitions of key terms, each of which appears in the text in boldface type on its first substantive mention.

ANCILLARIES

Instructor Teaching Site

A password-protected site, available at www.sagepub.com/shepherd, features resources that have been designed to help instructors plan and teach their courses.

These resources include an extensive test bank in Word and Respondus formats, chapter-specific PowerPoint presentations, and links to SAGE journal articles and web resources.

Student Study Site

A web-based study site is available at **www.sagepub.com/shepherd**. This site provides access to several study tools including mobile-friendly eFlashcards and web quizzes as well as links to SAGE journal articles and web resources.

ACKNOWLEDGMENTS

A s with the creation of any textbook, a number of individuals have given a lot of personal and professional time in the completion of this book. We would like to thank Theresa Accomazzo and Reid Hester for their patience, constructive criticism, and emotional support. We would also like to thank our families, who allowed us to spend an inordinate amount of time at home staring at the computer.

Terry would like to thank his wife, Melanie, who read through every draft without complaint and offered a number of valuable edits and suggestions. He would also like to acknowledge his children, Shaun, Bessie, Tony, Patty, Jared, and Samuel. Again, he promises not to engage in another major project for at least 3 months.

Diana would like to thank her family, friends, and colleagues who supported her during the writing of this book. She would also like to acknowledge Clarissa Riojas, graduate assistant, for her help with the research for the book.

We and SAGE would like to gratefully acknowledge the following peer reviewers for their editorial insight and guidance:

Christopher B. Denning, *University of Massachusetts–Boston*

Mike F. Desiderio, *Texas A&M University–Kingsville*

Maryann Gromoll, *Daytona State College*

Andrew Knight, *University of North Dakota*

Cynthia Miller, *Fort Hays State University*

Arnold Nyarambi, *East Tennessee State University*

Christine R. Ogilvie, *University of West Florida*

Jessica A. Scher Lisa, *St. Joseph's College*

Karen Schmalz, *Geneva College*

Judy Stuart, *Furman University*

CHAPTER 1

BEHAVIOR AND CLASSROOM MANAGEMENT BASICS

After reading this chapter, you should be able to do the following:

- Explain the importance of understanding developmental theories of behavior.
- Describe the similarities and differences among major developmental theories.
- Understand how culture plays a role in the development of behavior and classroom management plans.
- Explain the premise of a universal design for behavior management.
- Understand the principles of culturally responsive behavior and classroom management.
- Describe how the goals of behavior and classroom management influence behavior strategies and interventions.

FOUNDATIONS OF BEHAVIOR MANAGEMENT

Behavior and classroom management has always been one of the predominant concerns of all teachers, administrators, and other education professionals. Behavior and classroom management consumes an inordinate amount of teachers' and administrators' time, and while well-developed management plans are effective with a majority of students, a small percentage of students still refuse to "follow the rules." That is why it is extremely important for education professionals to remember that students who behave appropriately choose to behave in such a manner because it is often in their best interest to do so. Because of this crucial axiom in behavior and classroom management, it is essential that teachers develop management plans based comparatively on the needs of their students. Teachers need to understand behavior and the factors that affect it.

It is certainly understandable that teachers and administrators are interested in the practical application of behavior and classroom management; however, behavior and classroom management is no longer a simple matter of establishing five rules, five consequences, and five rewards. Today's teachers need to understand developmental theories, examine the various facets of behavior and classroom management, and recognize the impact of culture on student behavior.

Teachers need to consider many aspects of behavior and classroom management when they are developing and implementing classroom management plans. In addition to rules, consequences, and rewards, teachers need to develop relevant curriculum, consider the needs of culturally and linguistically diverse students, and implement proactive, active, and reactive strategies. They also need to examine their own perceptions and assumptions that might affect their development of effective behavior management programs.

With the increasing numbers of culturally and linguistically diverse children entering today's classrooms, teachers also need to understand the impact that culture has on behavior. Before they can understand the diverse cultures of their students, teachers first need to understand their own cultures and how their perceptions affect the ways in which they interact with students and students' family members. Through authentic understanding of the various aspects of culture, teachers can develop culturally responsive behavior and classroom management programs.

DEVELOPMENTAL THEORIES OF BEHAVIOR

Developmental theories are often dismissed as a component of behavior management, but there are two important reasons teachers need to understand developmental theories. First, understanding the development of children and adolescents affects the interpretation of childhood and how children are treated. Second, developmental theories provide the basis for practical applications that can improve the behavior of students (Thelen, 2005).

The developmental theories that explain the behavior of children are diverse and often contrary to one another, yet many of these theories form the foundation of behavior and classroom management. These theories include classical conditioning, operant conditioning, social cognitive theory, ecological systems theory, sociocultural theory, and moral development theory, each of which is discussed in turn below.

Classical Conditioning

Classical conditioning involves the repeated pairing of a neutral stimulus with an unconditioned stimulus to produce a conditioned response. A stimulus is an external event that affects an individual's behavior or response. An unconditioned stimulus is a stimulus that triggers an unconditioned response. An unconditioned response is a naturally occurring reaction to a stimulus. Unconditioned responses are generally not learned. For example, the smell of homemade pizza in the oven (an unconditioned stimulus) triggers the feeling of hunger in an individual (an unconditioned response). Generally, unconditioned stimuli and unconditioned responses are instinctive, reflexive behaviors, such as eye blinking or sneezing.

Pavlov

The Russian physiologist Ivan Pavlov (1849–1936) is considered the father of classical conditioning. During his research on the physiology of the digestion system in dogs, Pavlov noted that the dogs in his experiments naturally salivated (an unconditioned response) in response to food (an unconditioned stimulus). Pavlov also observed that the dogs began salivating with the appearance of his assistant, who was responsible for providing food for the dogs.

In his now classic experiment, Pavlov repeatedly paired the sound of a bell with food for the dogs. The bell was a neutral stimulus—that is, a stimulus that does not naturally occur in conjunction with an unconditioned stimulus. In other words, dogs normally do not associate the sound of a bell with food. After a period of time, the dogs began to associate the sound of the bell (a neutral stimulus) with food (an unconditioned stimulus) and began salivating (an unconditioned response) even when there was no food present.

In an extreme example, if a person is repeatedly exposed to the sound of a cell phone's text message alert paired with the smell of homemade pizza, the cell phone's sound may trigger hunger in the person even when the smell of pizza is absent. When a neutral stimulus elicits an unconditioned response, the neutral stimulus becomes a conditioned stimulus and the response becomes a conditioned response, or the learned behavior of a previous neutral stimulus. In classical conditioning, when a neutral stimulus (sound of text message alert) is repeatedly paired with an unconditioned stimulus (the smell of pizza), a conditioned response (hunger) is produced.

Watson

Building on the work of Pavlov, psychologist John B. Watson (1878–1958) viewed conditioning as the basis for most human learning. He advocated a radical approach to psychology through the measurement of observable behavior and reactions and the exclusion of the emotional and mental states of individuals. Watson (1914, 1925) referred to this objective study of behavior as **behaviorism**.

In the classic study of an 11-month-old boy named Albert B., Watson and his assistant, Rosalie Alberta Rayner, conducted an experiment based on classical conditioning. Albert was allowed to play with a white laboratory rat. Initially, he did not show any fear toward the rat and eagerly played with the animal. Watson and Rayner then began pairing a loud clang, a sound that frightened Albert, with his touching of the rat. After being exposed to repeated pairing of the two stimuli, Albert began to cry when he saw the rat even when no sound was present. Thus the neutral stimulus (the loud clang) became the conditioned stimulus, which produced a conditioned response (Albert's fear of the rat). This fear also generalized to other white furry objects, such as a white rabbit and Santa Claus (Watson & Rayner, 1920). Unfortunately, Albert moved away before Watson could decondition him, which left many to question what ever happened to the boy. Despite the questionable ethics involved in the research, the "Little Albert" study is among the experiments most frequently cited in psychology textbooks (Beck, Levinson, & Irons, 2009).

While human behavior is complex and individuals often do not respond to classical conditioning as expected, there are some practical applications for classical conditioning in the classroom. For example, elementary teachers have used classical conditioning methods such as the following to teach students to be quiet. Before conditioning, the teacher instructs the class to be quiet and then raises her hand and counts one, two, three, both with her fingers and verbally. During conditioning, the teacher raises her hand and counts one, two, three with her fingers and then instructs the class to be quiet. Finally, after conditioning, the teacher simple raises her hand and counts one, two, three with her fingers, and the class gets quiet.

Operant Conditioning

Classical conditioning deals with behaviors that are reflexive, or responses that are involuntary. For example, if the smell of homemade pizza triggers hunger in an individual, hunger is an automatic response. Conversely, operant conditioning deals with behaviors that are voluntary. Operant conditioning is a method of learning in which the probability that an individual's behavior will increase or decrease is manipulated through the use of reinforcements that are pleasurable or not pleasurable. Psychologist Edward L. Thorndike (1874–1949) was one of the first to apply the principles of operant conditioning in his research on animal behavior. In his book *Law of Effects* (1905) he surmised that if a behavior is pleasurable, the likelihood of the behavior being repeated is increased. This principle of reinforcements became the basis for operant conditioning.

Skinner

American psychologist B. F. Skinner (1904–1990) found that classical conditioning does not explain all behaviors, especially those that have no apparent cause. He believed that thoughts and emotions also affect behavior. By including thoughts and emotions as facets of behavior, Skinner developed a *radical behaviorism*, which sought to study all behavior. Unlike classical conditioning, in which the behavior is caused by an antecedent event, *operant behavior* is affected by consequences. For example, if a student does not study for a history test (behavior) and then fails the test (consequence), the student studies for the next test to avoid failing the test (alternative behavior).

The environment also plays an important role in operant conditioning, and the consequences of the behavior can strengthen the relationship between the environment and the behavior. Skinner (1969) believed that any relationship between an individual and the environment must include the event that elicits the behavior, the behavior itself, and a consequence that reinforces the behavior. This three-term contingency is often referred to as the ABCs (antecedent, behavior, and consequence) of functional behavioral analysis. The antecedent is the event that occurs before the behavior, and the consequence is the stimulus that occurs following the behavior. This behavioral analysis is one of the most common methods of evaluating behavior used in schools today.

CASE STUDY   **Timothy and Dennis**

A fifth grader at Brantwood Middle School, Timothy has an unstable home life. He is being raised by a single mother who has had difficulties maintaining a job and is seldom home at night. He has not seen his father in 3 years. His home environment has affected his academic and behavior performance at school. He is failing several classes and his behavior is often inappropriate.

Lost in thought, Timothy enters his fifth-hour mathematics class with the other students. Mrs. Cantu, the teacher, is writing math problems on the board as the students start taking their seats in anticipation of the tardy bell.

Dennis Baker, a popular football player, comes up behind Timothy. "Hey, Tim," he says softly and with a grin, "I heard that your mom was at the Roundup with three guys." The Roundup is a notorious bar on the fringe of town.

Bristling, Timothy hisses, "Shut up."

Grinning, Dennis responds, "Or maybe it was four guys . . ."

"Shut up," Timothy repeats, raising his fists.

"You might have a new baby brother soon," continues Dennis.

Hearing a commotion behind her, Mrs. Cantu turns in time to see Timothy shove Dennis, who falls to the floor.

"Timothy!" Mrs. Cantu orders sternly, "Go to the office!"

Angry and frustrated, Timothy walks past a grinning Dennis as he leaves the classroom. What are the antecedent, behavior, and consequences of this event?

In operant conditioning, the environmental event (antecedent) influences the behavior, but unlike in classical conditioning, the environmental event does not cause the behavior. It is actually the consequence that influences the behavior. For example, the smell of fresh-baked pizza may influence the individual to eat the pizza, but the individual eats the pizza because eating pizza is a pleasurable experience. The consequence, or reinforcer, increases the probability that the behavior will occur again and with increased frequency (Skinner, 1953). It is the consequence that causes the individual to eat the pizza, and the consequence increases the probability that the individual will repeat the behavior.

It is important to realize that individual humans respond differently to similar situations. Environmental factors, personal characteristics, cultural attributes, and other elements can influence how a person responds to an event. Thus a consequence that works for one student may not work for a different student displaying the same type of behavior. Sometimes a student's response may be entirely unexpected. Teachers need to be familiar enough with their students to be able to take into consideration all the different variables that may affect any given student's response to a consequence.

Social Cognitive Theory

Social cognitive theory states that an individual can gain knowledge by observing others. Psychologists Neal E. Miller and John Dollard (1941) suggested that individuals could learn behavior by observing the behavior of others. If the imitation of the observed behaviors is reinforced, the probability that the observed behavior will be repeated is increased. For example, an infant learns to say "mama" and "dada" by hearing the parents say the words repeatedly. When the infant imitates the words, she is rewarded by the joyful response of the parents, which encourages the infant to say the words again.

This social learning theory was subsequently expanded to include cognition. This emphasis on thoughts and cognition merges the principles of operant conditioning, social interaction, and cognitive developmental theories, which form the basis of social cognitive theory.

Bandura

Albert Bandura, an American psychologist, is a major proponent of social cognitive theory. He believes that most human behavior is learned through the observation of the behavior of others (Bandura, 1986). Children observe and imitate the behaviors of their parents, siblings, and others, including individuals in the mass media.

Observational learning occurs when an individual observes the behavior of another person and how the consequences of the behavior are reinforced (Bandura, 1997). For example, Ricardo has to stay in the classroom instead of going out to play at recess because he is constantly talking in class. Jane observes Ricardo's behavior and the consequence of that behavior and learns that if she talks in class, she will not be allowed to have recess.

An individual must have the ability to retain an observed behavior in order to imitate or repeat the behavior, especially if the person who modeled the behavior is absent. Children with intellectual disabilities may have a difficult time learning through observation because they may not be able to remember the target behavior. If an individual can retain an image of the target behavior, he or she must also be able to repeat, or reproduce, the target behavior. Again, children with intellectual and physical disabilities may have difficulty performing the target behavior. Finally, the individual must be motivated to imitate the behavior. For example, Jane does not want to miss recess like Ricardo, so she will not talk excessively in class.

An important component of social cognitive theory is self-efficacy—that is, the individual's belief in his or her abilities to perform specific tasks despite difficulties, obstacles, and initial failures. Self-efficacy can affect students' beliefs in their cognitive and physical abilities, their motivation, and their behavior (Bandura, 1993; Briones, Tabernero, & Arenas, 2007). For example, a student who does not believe she has the ability to do well in algebra will most likely do poorly in the class. Students with a high sense of self-efficacy are likely to do well in school despite any difficulties and display intrinsic reinforcement/motivation when performing tasks. Conversely, students with a low sense of self-efficacy are less likely to do well in school and experience failures even more acutely (Prat-Sala & Redford, 2010). For example, Emily does not believe she has the ability to do well in algebra. When she takes the unit test in algebra, she does not believe she can pass the test, and she fails. Her belief that she will not succeed contributes to her failure. As a result of failing the test, Emily is less likely to try harder the next time. It is unlikely that Emily will develop a strong sense of self-efficacy because "self-efficacy beliefs are developed and strengthened by mastery experiences, social modeling, and persuasive forms of social influences" (Bandura, Caprara, Barbaranelli, Gerbino, & Pastorelli, 2003, p. 769).

Cultural expectations can also affect self-efficacy. For example, Hispanic females may be discouraged from doing well in school, pursuing higher education degrees, or considering certain occupations due to conflicting familial expectations. Mayra has already earned her degree in teaching and is currently working on an advanced degree at the university. As a result, she has classes two nights a week and hours of studying at home. This has created conflict between Mayra and her husband because her husband expects her to be home taking care of the house and the children. Mayra's husband may question her ability to complete an advanced degree and may berate her for neglecting her responsibilities at home. Such perceived cultural barriers may influence Hispanic females' development of self-efficacy (Rivera, Chen, Flores, Blumberg, & Ponterotto, 2007).

Ecological Systems Theory

Ecological systems theory provides a theoretical framework for understanding how a child's development and behaviors are influenced by the complex interactions of environmental factors. This theory assumes that the child cannot be separated from the many complex social systems surrounding the child, and any behavior interventions must involve the child, the environment, and the beliefs of those within the child's ecological system (Apter, 1977; Apter & Conoley, 1984).

Bronfenbrenner

Noted psychologist Urie Bronfenbrenner (1917–2005) developed an ecological systems theory for understanding children's interactions with their environments. A child's environment is "a set of nested structures, each inside the next, like a set of Russian dolls" (Bronfenbrenner, 1979, p. 3). The interactions that occur between the child and the separate structures are bidirectional and reciprocal, and affect the growth and the development of the child. The child's ecological system includes five components: microsystem, mesosystem, exosystem, macrosystem, and chronosystem (see Figure 1.1; Bronfenbrenner, 1979, 2005). Each component contains its own set of rules, roles, and expectations that influence the child's development.

The child's development, especially in the early phases of life, hinges on the child's interactions with individuals in his environment on a regular basis and over a long period of time. The family is at the epicenter of this system. All members of the family are active participants in this system, and they influence one another through their behaviors. The relationship between the child and the family can result in a nurturing foundation of love and trust or a nightmarish environment of violence and abuse leading to mistrust. For example, 5-year-old David has autism, and as a result his parents devote more time to David because of his unique needs and less time to their younger daughter, Andrea. Andrea feels that her parents do not love her as much as they love David because they spend less time with her. She even pretends to have characteristics of autism in order to vie for her parents' attention. The parents become upset with Andrea because she is copying David's behaviors, and they ignore these behaviors. Over time, such reciprocal interactions can become established and can affect the child's development (Bronfenbrenner, 1995).

The child's interactions with all the components of her environment create interconnections among the various systems. When the child interacts with school, peers, and the neighborhood, the family members develops relationships with these environments through the child (see Figure 1.2). These relationships can affect the child's academic performance and behavior in school. For example, Strayhorn (2010) found that African American students whose parents were involved in their children's education through attending school meetings and checking their children's homework had higher math achievement scores than did students whose parents were not so involved.

Figure 1.1 Bronfenbrenner's Ecological System

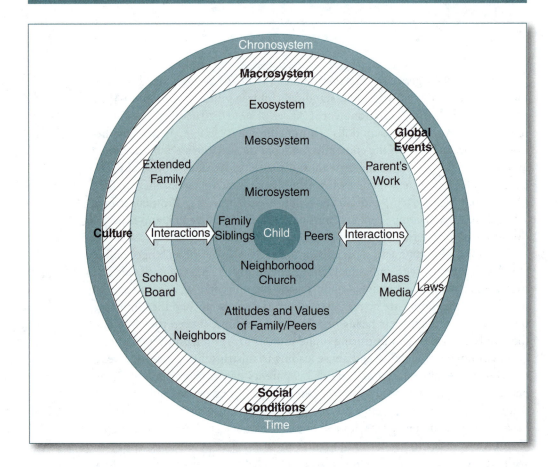

Ecological systems theory also takes into account the characteristics of cultures and subcultures, which include beliefs, cultural values, laws, political trends, ideologies, and global events. For example, school climate and peer interaction are significantly affected by the culture of the community. If the school has an accepting and tolerant community and peer culture, the child is likely to perceive the school climate as positive. If the school's cultural norms do not include tolerance of differences or if acceptance is based on individuals' activities and social status, then the child may perceive the school climate as hostile (Lee, 2011). In this type of environment, bullying may be encouraged by the macrosystem, sometimes with dire results. For example, it has been reported that Eric Harris and Dylan Klebold were victims of frequent bullying by school athletes before they carried out the 1999 shootings at Columbine High School

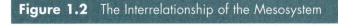

Figure 1.2 The Interrelationship of the Mesosystem

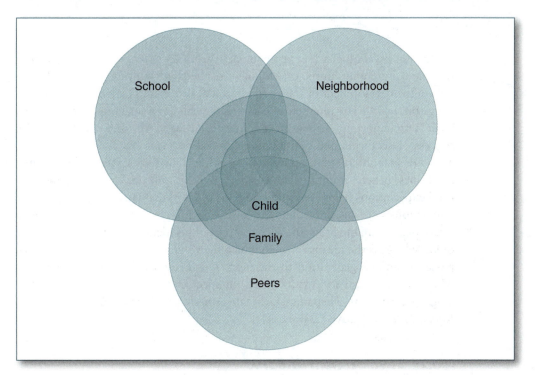

in Colorado. Harris and Klebold did not fit in with the cultural vision of masculinity in the dominant "jock culture" in this macrosystem, and the frequent bullying they endured because they were different could have been a factor leading to the shootings (Hong, Cho, Allen-Meares, & Espelage, 2011).

According to ecological systems theory, when the relationship between the child and the environment is appropriate and compatible, the child and the ecosystem are balanced. When the child and the ecosystem are not balanced, the child displays unacceptable behavior. Teachers developing classroom and behavior management plans based on this theory need to strive to balance the interactions between ecosystem and child.

Sociocultural Theory

Culture and moral development are two factors that affect the behavior of children. It is important for teachers to understand these factors so that they can determine whether the behaviors that children display are appropriate or inappropriate before they develop any behavior management strategies.

Vygotsky

Russian psychologist Lev Semyonovich Vygotsky (1896–1934) investigated the role culture plays in the development of the child. Culture is a central variable in the development of the child (Calzada, Brotman, Huang, Bat-Chava, & Kingston, 2009). The interaction between the child and his immediate environment is an important element in enculturation (Liu & Matthews, 2005), or the process of acquiring and maintaining cultural norms and values (Kim, 2007). Through such interaction, referred to as cultural mediation, the child acquires the values, beliefs, traditions, and language of his culture. Understanding cultural expectations helps the child know his place in the world, and through his interactions with his immediate environment, the child gains knowledge and internalizes it, making this knowledge a part of his identity. This internalization of knowledge is the means through which the values and beliefs of a culture are passed from one generation to the next. This is especially true for groups in which sociocultural identity is based on specific history, oral traditions, and language, such as Hispanics, African Americans, Native Americans, and *Kanaka Maoli* (Native Hawaiians).

Moral Development Theory

Moral development theory is generally not included in discussions of classroom and behavior management because it does not comply with the facets of behavioral psychology. According to behaviorism, behavior is observable and measurable and does not consider intrinsic motivation; however, just like classical and operant conditioning, moral development occurs through interactions between the child and the environment. Additionally, the child acquires morals from the values and beliefs of the cultural community. Moral development involves a system of beliefs, values, and fundamental judgments about the rightness or wrongness of human acts and how these relate to societal expectations (Zimbardo & Gerrig, 2004). The engagement of prosocial behaviors and the inhibition of antisocial behaviors are aspects of moral development. Both types of behaviors have impacts on the school environment (Koenig, Cicchetti, & Rogosch, 2004). It is important that teachers and administrators understand the cultural community when developing classroom and behavior management plans.

Piaget

Swiss developmental psychologist Jean Piaget (1896–1980) is known for his cognitive developmental theory, but he also developed a two-stage theory of moral development. According to this theory, moral development takes place in two stages: heteronomous morality and autonomous morality. The first, *heteronomous morality*, occurs between the ages of 5 and 10. During this stage, children see morals as absolutes: A behavior is either right or wrong. Children regard rules as having been handed down by authority and view them as unchangeable. The wrongness of an act is determined by the amount of damage that results, not by the motivation behind the behavior (Piaget, 1932/1997). For example, 7-year-old Natalie wants to make breakfast for her parents, but when she pulls the eggs out of the refrigerator, she drops the carton and breaks five eggs. Natalie sees the accidental breaking of five eggs as a greater offense than that of another child who intentionally breaks one egg. The wrongness of the behavior is determined by the amount of damage (five broken eggs), not the reason behind the behavior (making breakfast for her parents, accidentally breaking the eggs).

Piaget's second stage, *autonomous morality*, occurs about the same time as early adolescence. Older children and adolescents view rules more critically than do younger children. They realize that rules are not absolute and can be revised based on circumstances and the requirements of fair reciprocity, or treating others as they want to be treated. They realize that the consequence for breaking five eggs accidentally should not be the same as that for breaking one egg intentionally.

For better or worse, moral judgment is taught in school. It is important that children understand right and wrong so that they can grow up and function as adults in the real world; however, schools should not indoctrinate students with societal expectations. Given the principle of fair reciprocity, older students should be involved in the development of classroom rules and consequences.

Self-determination is also a factor in a child's transition to autonomous morality. Self-determination fulfills the adolescent's needs for autonomy, relatedness, and competence, and also leads the adolescent to more autonomous moral judgments (Weinstock, Assor, & Broide, 2009). When students are involved in determining rules and consequences, they need to understand the importance of rules and how certain rules and consequences relate to their lives. Well-constructed classroom and behavior management plans maintain the classroom environment, but allowing students the opportunity to participate in the development of these plans gives students a sense of ownership, fairness, and self-determination.

Kohlberg

American psychologist Lawrence Kohlberg (1927–1987) organized his theory of moral development into preconventional, conventional, and postconventional levels (see Table 1.1). Each level contains two stages that an individual experiences from infancy to adulthood (Kohlberg, 1975; Kohlberg & Hersh, 1977).

Kohlberg believed that moral principles are universal and common to various cultures. While some research has supported the universality of Kohlberg's moral development stages (Gibbs, Basinger, Grime, & Snarey, 2007), other researchers do not agree that there is a universal set of moral principles common to various cultures (Partington, 1996–1997). Some have asserted that Kohlberg's theory of moral development is gender biased (e.g., Gilligan, 1982). However, having some understanding of the different moral stages can assist educators in developing classroom and behavior management plans. For example, understanding that children may comply with rules to gain a teacher's approval would lead the teacher to develop plans that support the moral development of students. Conversely, adolescents who understand that rules should be fair and consistent should be involved in the development of classroom rules and consequences.

Table 1.1 Kohlberg's Theory of Moral Development

Level	Stage	Description
Preconventional	Punishment and obedience orientation	Child follows rules to avoid punishment.
	Instrumental relativist orientation	Child follows rules to satisfy his own needs.
Conventional	Good boy–nice girl orientation	Child behaves to gain approval.
	Law-and-order orientation	Child follows rules and laws, which are absolute.
Postconventional	Social contract, legalistic orientation	Person values general individual rights.
	Universal ethical principle orientation	Person values universal principles of human rights and dignity.

Gilligan

American social psychologist Carol Gilligan argues that Kohlberg's moral development theory underestimates the complexity of women's moral reasoning abilities. The study on which Kohlberg based his moral developmental theory included only European American males as participants. Gilligan (1979, 1982) asserts that men and women approach and solve ethical problems differently, and thus Kohlberg's theory does not represent the morality of women. She believes that women speak in a "different voice." This voice, unlike men's voice, is not based on individual rights and societal order; rather, it is based on care, responsibility to others, and interdependent relationships. Gilligan asserts that this *ethic of care* influences the way in which women approach and solve moral conflicts. Women try to solve "moral dilemmas through negotiation and communication, through attempts to make the facts clear in a dilemma situation" (Driver, 2005, p. 184). Gilligan's theory of moral development involves a sequence of three levels (orientation toward self-interest, goodness as self-sacrifice, and morality of nonviolence) and two transition stages (see Table 1.2).

Many researchers, including Kohlberg, have been critical of Gilligan's theory. Tulviste and Koor (2005), for example, found all children in their study to be more justice oriented than care oriented. Additionally, Vikan, Camino, and Biaggio's (2005) research indicates that moral development may not be gender related but, instead, culturally specific. When developing classroom and behavior management plans, however, teachers may find that Gilligan's theory of moral development accounts for the differences in behaviors between girls and

Table 1.2 Gilligan's Theory of Moral Development

Stage	Level	Characteristics
Preconventional	Orientation toward self-interest	Concerned with survival; cares for self.
Transition 1	**Self-Interest to responsibility to others**	
Conventional	Goodness as self-sacrifice	Puts interests of others above self-interests.
Transition 2	**Goodness to truth**	
Postconventional	Morality of nonviolence	Does not hurt others or self.

boys. In comparison to girls, boys tend to engage in activities that are more aggressive and contain more conflicts. Because society still expects girls to follow a morality of caring, their play activities seldom involve conflict (Tulviste & Koor, 2005). As a result, boys tend to display acting-out behaviors in school, while girls tend to avoid conflict. Many teachers base their classroom and behavior management plans on the covert behaviors of boys, but such plans might be inappropriate for girls. Again, it is important for teachers to consider all students when creating their classroom and behavior plans, just as they must consider the needs of all students when developing a curriculum. The universal design for classroom management considers the differential needs of students of both genders as well as all cultures, languages, and ability levels in the development of a behavior and classroom management plan.

Table 1.3 Developmental Theories of Behavior

Theory	Major researchers	Important characteristics
Classical conditioning	Pavlov Watson	Shows that pairing a neutral stimulus with an unconditioned stimulus produces a conditioned response. Represents the beginning of behaviorism.
Operant conditioning	Thorndike Skinner	Serves as the basis for applied behavior analysis and the use of positive and negative reinforcement.
Social cognitive theory	Bandura	Asserts that individuals can learn behavior by observing the behavior of others. Focuses on self-efficacy, or an individual's belief in his or her ability to perform specific tasks despite difficulties, obstacles, and initial failures.
Ecological systems theory	Bronfenbrenner	Asserts that a child's development and behaviors are influenced by the complex interactions of the child's various environmental factors.
Sociocultural theory	Vygotsky	Asserts that culture and moral development are two factors that affect the behavior of the child.
Moral development theory	Piaget Kohlberg Gilligan	Describes a system of beliefs, values, and fundamental judgments about the rightness or wrongness of human acts and how these relate to societal expectations. Notes that self-determination fulfills an individual's needs for autonomy, relatedness, and competence.

UNDERSTANDING BEHAVIOR MANAGEMENT

Even if teachers are very knowledgeable about academic content and pedagogy, teaching and learning cannot occur unless a positive learning environment has been established in the classroom. Students cannot learn if peers disrupt the classroom or if they do not feel safe in the classroom. One of the most important jobs of the teacher is to manage the classroom effectively, and the primary purpose of classroom management is to create a positive and safe environment in which learning can take place.

However, given the diverse needs of today's students, classroom management needs to go beyond the simple matter of establishing five rules, five consequences, and five rewards. When developing behavior and classroom management plans, teachers must take into account a number of considerations, including the management of content, conduct, and covenant.

Teachers manage content before the students enter the classroom. One of the most important aspects of content management is a rigorous and relevant curriculum (Kraft, 2010). Teachers need to create lessons that are well prepared and have some meaning to students' lives. If students perceive that lessons are not important to their lives, they are more likely to demonstrate off-task behaviors. Appropriate materials can enhance lessons and prevent off-task behavior. For example, using manipulatives to teach basic math concepts to younger students is more effective than using only pencil and paper to teach these lessons. Management of content also involves the physical environment of the classroom, which includes how the room is arranged in relation to the teaching style and personality of the teacher (see Chapter 5).

Management of conduct encompasses the handling of day-to-day student behavior as well as discipline problems. Teachers establish classroom rules and hierarchies of consequences and rewards to assist in managing student behavior. Again, when developing behavior and classroom management plans, teachers should take the needs of their students into account. Once they have developed and implemented their plans, teachers need to be consistent in following them. If students perceive that their teacher is not consistently adhering to the classroom management plan, they are more likely to engage in inappropriate behaviors. Remember, teachers cannot control student behaviors, which is why it is important for teachers to develop plans that meet the academic, behavioral, emotional, and social needs of their students.

Management of covenant involves the social dynamics and interpersonal relationships in the classroom. The life experiences and culture of the teacher affect covenant management. It is also important that teachers understand the cultural backgrounds of the students they teach and how these may affect behavior in the classroom.

Since schools are expected to serve all students, it has become necessary for teachers to develop differentiated discipline strategies to meet the needs of a diverse student population. As a result, teachers should move beyond the need to "manage" behavior and create positive environments in which learning can take place, but also environments that promote student self-efficacy. To achieve this goal, teachers need to employ the principles of **universal design for classroom management (UDCM)**, a proactive approach to developing behavior and classroom management plans that meet the needs of a diverse student population. A teacher using UDCM considers the needs of students with disabilities, ethnically and linguistically diverse students, struggling learners, and students of all ability levels and then develops a behavior and classroom management plan that can meet the academic, behavioral, emotional, and social needs of each student.

Finally, a successful behavior and classroom management plan will include proactive, active, and reactive strategies. Proactive strategies include the development of a universal design for classroom management and management of content, active strategies include the maintenance of a positive learning environment, and reactive strategies include management of conduct and covenant.

Postulations of Behavior

Teachers need to consider several suppositions about behavior and classroom management when they are developing and implementing behavior strategies in the classroom. Most teachers and other education professionals believe that behaviorist theories are the most appropriate theories on which to base the development of classroom management plans. Behaviorists believe that behavior can be measured through observation and precludes the emotional and mental states of individuals. In fact, many of the strategies used in behavior and classroom management today, and in applied behavior analysis, are based on the interactions of the antecedent, behavior, and consequence. However, behavior and classroom management is a complex construction and goes beyond the five rules–five consequences/reinforcement approach. Behavior is also influenced by the child's environment, cognitive ability, and social and cultural backgrounds, which is why teachers should have some knowledge of multiple theoretical perspectives.

Behavior is also a social construct—that is, it is based on societal norms, cultural expectations, and political responses to these expectations. Social construction influences how individuals or groups are perceived, and this social reality must be maintained or reaffirmed to continue. Simultaneously, social constructs are dynamic; they change if they are not maintained. Teachers need to understand how social constructs affect behavior and classroom management. For example, 40 years ago corporal punishment was socially acceptable as a means of behavior management, but today society has deemed corporal punishment to be an inappropriate means of managing student behavior.

Behaviorists believe that behaviors are learned and can be taught. Many behavior management strategies are based on this premise, which focuses on applied behavior analysis and reinforcements. Behavior and classroom management plans based on these tenets of behaviorism are very successful and should not be discarded because they are limited in scope. These strategies help teachers define target behaviors that are observable and measurable, which is important when they are trying to enable students develop alternatives to unacceptable behaviors.

Assumptions of Behavior Management

There are several divergent assumptions regarding behavior and classroom management. Many teachers and other education professionals believe that providing students with reinforcements for appropriate behavior is a form of bribery. Students should behave appropriately because it is expected of them, not because they will be rewarded for such behavior. However, all behavior is reinforced in some manner, and most of us behave in the ways we do because we will be rewarded for our efforts. In the world of economics, reinforcements promote effort and performance, so it is not unreasonable for teachers to use reinforcements to encourage appropriate behavior and academic achievement in students.

Conversely, there are those who believe that students should work for intrinsic reinforcements (the self-gratification individuals get from successfully completing tasks) instead of extrinsic reinforcements (external rewards). Some studies have indicated that extrinsic reinforcements can conflict and interfere with intrinsic reinforcements; however, the success of both intrinsic and extrinsic reinforcements is correlated to students' levels of self-efficacy (Prat-Sala & Redford, 2010). For example, if a student is confident that she can do well in history, she is more likely to extract deeper meanings from the history lessons and complete assignments in that subject area for her own self-satisfaction. However, if the same student is not as confident in her math skills, she is more likely to complete math assignments because of extrinsic reinforcements (e.g., she will earn a poor grade if she does not study). This is one reason a teacher should have multiple behavior and classroom management strategies in place—one size does not fit all.

However, some teachers and other education professionals believe that all students should be treated equally. Many teachers adopt a "diversity-blind" ideology when working with students in an honest attempt to treat all students the same. Diversity-blind teachers try to convince themselves that all students are the same despite their culturally, ethnically, racially, and linguistically different backgrounds. As a result, these teachers may not recognize discriminatory practices directed toward some students. Traditional behavior and classroom practices are then presented in education preparation programs and in classrooms as a culturally unbiased concept instead of as a middle-class European American construction. Best practices would suggest that teachers should treat all students equitably instead of equally. By treating students equitably, teachers provide each student with whatever that individual needs to be successful in school. Again, to be successful, behavior and classroom management plans should include a number of strategies to meet the unique behavior needs of every child in the classroom.

Misconstructions of Behavior Management

A prevalent fallacy is that teachers can control students through effective classroom and behavior management strategies. Teachers can develop classroom and behavior management strategies that serve as guidelines for students and provide for positive learning environments, but they cannot control their students' behaviors. Students are individuals with their own needs and wants, and they tend to behave based on those needs and wants. Students will follow classroom rules only if they choose to follow the rules. Fortunately, the majority of students follow classroom rules because they see that it is in their best interest to do so. Generally, 5–10% of students in a classroom simply refuse to follow the rules. Unfortunately, in terms of behavior management, teachers spend about 80% of their time dealing with these students.

One of the most difficult lessons a teacher must learn is that not all students will be successful in school, and, despite the laudable goal that all students can learn or that all students can behave appropriately, some choose not to. For example, 14-year-old Timothy does not want to go to school. Every morning, when he arrives at school, he commits an action that results in his suspension or expulsion. No intervention or strategy has been successful with Timothy.

He chooses not to follow the behavior expectations of the school community, and at this point the school does not have the resources or the ability to provide him with what he needs to be successful in school. However, teachers should never give up on a child. Every teacher must make every effort to help students achieve their potential. This is the ultimate goal of all teachers.

CULTURAL INFLUENCE ON BEHAVIOR

With the increasing numbers of culturally and linguistically diverse children entering today's classrooms, it is important that teachers have some understanding of their students' cultures and how these affect the students' behaviors. Unfortunately, the overwhelming majority of teachers in classrooms across the United States are female European Americans who do not fully understand how the diversity among their students affects the ways in which they interpret the students' behaviors and the ways in which they interact with these students (Cartledge, Singh, & Gibson, 2008). Teachers' biases toward students who are culturally and linguistically different from themselves are often based on misperceptions and stereotypes (Cartledge, Gardner, & Ford, 2009). For example, when an African American student talks back to a teacher, the student may not be acting out of disrespect or malice, but rather may be responding in a way he sees as necessary for his own survival—the student may not want his friends to see him as being weak (Milner & Tenore, 2010).

Non–European American students have higher rates of discipline referrals than do European American students (Drakeford, 2006; Dray & Wisneski, 2011; Imler, 2009). African American and Hispanic students are also more likely than European American students to be suspended or expelled (Achilles, McLaughlin, & Croninger, 2007; Krezmien, Leone, & Achilles, 2006; Skiba et al., 2011). Additionally, these students are more likely to be referred for special education services. Hispanic and African American males are also more likely than European American males to be identified as having emotional and behavioral disorders (Billingsley, Fall, & Williams, 2006; Zewelanji, Hayling, Stevenson, & Kem, 2013).

Enculturation and Acculturation

Teachers need to remember that children acquire the values, beliefs, traditions, and languages of their cultures through interactions with their environments. Culturally and linguistically diverse students experience two types of cultural processes: enculturation and acculturation. Enculturation is the process through which the child acquires and maintains the cultural norms and values of her family, or the culture of her heritage (Kim, 2007). Enculturation occurs through interactions between the child and her immediate environment. Acculturation is the process through which the child adapts to and adopts the values, beliefs, and traditions of another culture. Acculturation occurs when the child is exposed to cultures and values outside her immediate environment.

Enculturation and acculturation interact at four different levels (see Table 1.4). Low enculturation, or rejection of the heritage culture, combined with high acculturation, or acceptance and participation in the new culture, results in assimilation. Assimilation is the strategy endorsed by groups who value the concept of society as a "melting pot" in which subcultures adopt the traits of the dominant culture and all become subsumed in one cultural society. High enculturation, or maintenance of the heritage culture, combined with low acculturation, or rejection of the new culture, results in separation, in which subcultures are separated into racial or ethnic groups. Low enculturation combined with low acculturation results in marginalization, in which culture is excluded from society. High enculturation combined with high acculturation results in integration. With integration, subcultures maintain their heritage cultures while adopting traits of the dominant culture. Integration promotes multiculturalism, which is the acceptance and appreciation of multiple cultures in a society (Sam & Berry, 2010).

Understanding the effects of enculturation and acculturation may give teachers some insight into the cultures of their students and help them to develop appropriate behavior and classroom management plans. It also may help teachers when they interact with parents of students who are culturally

Table 1.4   Interactions of Acculturation and Enculturation

	Low acculturation: Rejection of new culture	**High acculturation: Acceptance of new culture**
Low enculturation: Rejection of heritage culture	Marginalization	Assimilation
High enculturation: Maintenance of heritage culture	Separation	Integration

and linguistically different from themselves. While high acculturation of diverse students to the dominant European American culture increases the risk of inappropriate behaviors in school, the high acculturation of parents also plays a role in increased inappropriate behaviors of diverse students in the classroom (Wang, Kim, Anderson, Chen, & Yan, 2012). Many cultures emphasize the cooperation of individuals and the needs of the whole, but because European American culture stresses individualism and winning at any cost, many high-acculturation parents no longer encourage their children to respect authority figures or behave appropriately (Dumka, Gonzales, Bonds, & Millsap, 2009). Additionally, because European American culture rewards individual accomplishment, acculturation is a statistically significant predictor of whether students of non–European American heritage go on to college (Castillo, López-Arenas, & Saldivar, 2010).

Culturally Responsive Classroom Management

Abstract knowledge of the diverse cultures of students is insufficient to enable teachers to develop successful behavior and classroom management plans. It is crucial that teachers understand the cultural backgrounds of their students, but they must also understand how these backgrounds affect students' behaviors, students' interactions with others, and even the ways in which academic content is best presented. To be culturally responsive in their behavior and classroom management, teachers must adhere to the following five principles:

1. Recognize their own ethnocentrism

2. Gain knowledge of their students' cultures

3. Be aware of the broader social, economic, and political context in education

4. Use culturally appropriate management strategies

5. Develop caring classroom communities (Weinstein, Tomlinson-Clarke, & Curran, 2004)

Awareness of Ethnocentrism

Cultural self-awareness is a key element of culturally responsive classroom management (Blanco-Vega, Castro-Olivo, & Merrell, 2008; Cartledge & Kourea, 2008), but for many European American teachers, understanding their own ethnocentrism is fraught with complex contradictions. Part of the problem lies in the difficulty of understanding ethnocentrism and culture. Ethnocentrism is generally defined as the evaluation of the cultures of other groups from the perspective of one's own cultural experiences, but this description is too simple for such a multifaceted concept. For example, given that ethnocentrism often leads to misunderstandings about the cultures of others, it could be defined as "the inability to view other cultures as equally viable alternatives for organizing reality" (Gollnick & Chinn, 2013, p. 6).

Culture is an extremely difficult concept to define. It is often described in relation to the race or ethnicity of a group, but culture has multiple dimensions. It includes a multitude of values, traditions, languages, artistic and musical expressions, foods, attitudes, and religious beliefs inherited from past human activity, which guide acceptable ways of behaving (Cole & Packer, 2011).

Adding to the difficulty of understanding ethnocentrism and culture is the lack of training in cultural awareness that preservice teachers receive at universities. American university education programs currently provide minimal knowledge about culturally and linguistically diverse students through courses taught by European American professors or discussions on multicultural education. One course or a course discussion may improve teacher candidates' awareness of multicultural education, but it cannot change their cultural beliefs. Additionally, education programs do not provide the experiences that teachers need to gain sufficient understanding of different cultures. Preservice teachers need to be immersed in cultures different from their own to fully understand multiculturalism. Unfortunately, universities today often do not have the resources to make this happen, and European American teachers often have their first immersion experiences with children from different cultures when they start teaching. Without fully understanding their own ethnocentrism and without experiencing different cultures prior to teaching culturally and linguistically diverse students in the classroom, new teachers find it difficult to develop a universal design for classroom management.

When asked to describe their culture, many European American teachers are confused by the question. They are unaware of their own cultural identity and how their culture affects others. Teachers must begin using self-reflective practices to examine their own culture and to develop cultural awareness. Teachers need to reflect on their personal values, beliefs, and biases and examine how these can affect how they treat their students (Dray & Wisneski, 2011; Imler, 2009). By understanding their own cultures, teachers can become less likely to misinterpret the behaviors of diverse students and more likely to treat all students equitably (Weinstein et al., 2004).

It is important to remember that treating students equitably is not the same as treating them equally. Treating students equally means treating all students the same. This is not necessarily the best practice in academics or behavior management. For example, Anthony has an emotional and behavioral disorder. Because of his disability, he is easily frustrated with academic work and, once frustrated, refuses to complete assignments. If the teacher applies her classroom management plan equally to all students, Anthony will most likely end up in the principal's office for refusing to complete his assignment. Anthony may eventually be suspended for continually refusing to complete his work, and he could end up in a self-contained classroom. While many teachers believe that students with emotional and behavioral disorders should be relegated to self-contained classrooms and do not recognize emotional and behavioral disorders as disabilities, this method of classroom management is not best practice. In treating students equitably, the teacher provides what is necessary for each student to succeed in school. Special education teachers have learned to treat students equitably through differential instruction and meeting the individual needs of students. For a teacher developing a universal design for classroom management, this is an important concept: meeting the needs of all students in a diverse student population. The teacher could develop a strategy to defuse Anthony's frustration that would allow him to complete his assignments and to be successful in the general education setting. For example, when Anthony gets frustrated with his assignment, he could be allowed to go to the back of the classroom and do some toe touches for a few minutes before returning to his desk. He might be the only student in the class with this strategy, but it is fair and equitable because it provides him what he needs to be successful in school.

Knowledge of Students' Cultures

In using culturally responsive practices in behavior and classroom management, teachers also need to understand the cultural backgrounds of their students. While this may be a daunting task, it can also become a fascinating journey for the teacher. Teachers gain knowledge about the cultures of others, which helps them interact with their students. This interaction is essential for teachers to teach students from diverse backgrounds, but is also essential for successful behavior and classroom management. The student–teacher relationship is the impetus for the teacher's understanding of the cultures of the students, but this also means that students gain an understanding of their teacher's culture. Students who have positive relationships with their teachers have fewer behavior problems, greater social skills, and better academic performance than students who do not have such relationships (Holt, Hargrove, & Harris, 2011; Murray & Greenberg, 2006). Positive teacher–student relationships are beneficial for teachers as well. Positive relationships with students can contribute to the well-being of the teacher, while consistent negative interactions with students, or behavioral conflicts with a few students in the classroom, may lead to burnout (Spilt, Koomen, & Thijs, 2011).

To understand the cultural backgrounds of their students, teachers must immerse themselves in the students' worlds. They can do this by finding out about their students' interests, such as what musical artists they like, what sports teams they follow, what television shows and movies they enjoy, and what kinds of foods they like. For example, *Kanaka Maoli* students might revere Israel Kamakawiwo'ole, who was a well-known musician who promoted Hawaiian rights and Hawaiian independence through his music.

Teachers and students should also share information about their cultural traditions and beliefs. For example, in the spring, a European American teacher might discuss the tradition of the Easter egg hunt, and some Hispanic students might share their tradition of breaking *cascarones* (hollowed-out eggshells filled with confetti) on their heads as part of the celebration of Easter. It is believed that breaking a *cascaron* on your head will bring you good luck, and the broken eggshell is symbolic of the Resurrection of Christ.

Teachers should also understand cultures in terms of individualism versus collectivism. These cultural dimensions can influence how students behave in the classroom. Individualist cultures emphasize the needs of the individual, independence, and individual initiative and accomplishment. Collectivist cultures stress group consciousness, group identity, and the needs of the group. In a collectivist culture, the individual's sense of self is understood in relationship to others within the community. The predominant European American culture (and the cultures of Canada, Australia, and Western European countries) is individualist in nature. This kind of culture lauds the accomplishments of the individual, and the American education system is based on the success of the individual. The cultures of Asian countries, South American countries, and Mexico, as well as Native American culture, are predominantly collectivist (Klassen, 2004). This kind of culture is concerned with the welfare of the group.

With the increasing numbers of students from diverse cultures entering schools today, it is important that teachers understand the multifaceted nature of culture and how culture affects behavior and classroom management. Many behavior conflicts that arise between teachers and students in the classroom are the result of teachers' lack of knowledge about or misunderstanding of the socioeconomic, cultural, racial, and ethnic characteristics of diverse students, as well as teachers' failure to understand how their own cultural backgrounds contribute to these conflicts.

Awareness of the Broader Context

European American culture also contributes to the perpetuation of discriminatory practices toward diverse students (Weinstein et al., 2004). Discipline problems in the classroom are often resolved through detentions, suspensions, and expulsions, and disproportionate numbers of socioeconomically disadvantaged students, special education students, males, and African American students are referred for exclusionary discipline (Dray & Wisneski, 2011; Imler, 2009; Milner & Tenore, 2010). Instead of examining how their own cultural beliefs affect the way they view students, teachers attribute students' inappropriate behaviors and academic failures to the students, the students' home lives, and the students' parents, who the teachers believe do not value education (Garcia & Guerra, 2004). Such misinterpretation of students' cultures can lead to behavioral conflicts in the classroom. For example, African American males may engage in a form of verbal sparring. Because this behavior may appear aggressive and inappropriate to culturally unaware teachers, misunderstanding of this ritual has resulted in high numbers of referrals of African American males to the principal's office. In another example, maintaining eye contact when talking to another individual is expected in European American culture. If a student does not maintain eye contact with the teacher, the teacher may conclude that the student is not paying attention, or that he is being disrespectful; however, in certain Hispanic cultures, it is considered disrespectful for a student to look directly into the eyes of someone who is older and in a position of authority.

The institutional nature of schools also makes it difficult to implement culturally responsive behavior management. Behavior management is reliant on the support of principals, who take their cues from superintendents, who follow national and state guidelines. As a result of institutional expectations, teachers try to develop behavior and classroom management strategies that encourage a system of "oppression and voicelessness among students" (Milner & Tenore, 2010, p. 570). In such a system, students naturally challenge behavior and classroom management strategies that dismiss their cultures, values, and beliefs. This approach is not conducive to a safe and secure learning environment in which students can be academically successful. As a result, schools have set up barriers that prevent the academic success of sociologically, racially, ethnically, and linguistically diverse students (Lindsey, Robins, Lindsey, & Terrell, 2009). Schools need to reexamine policies that unintentionally dismiss the cultures of diverse students and create environments where students behave inappropriately in reaction to these policies.

Use of Culturally Appropriate Management Strategies

Self-reflection is the most important tool for teachers to use when developing and implementing behavior and classroom management plans. Teachers need to reflect on their own ethnocentrism, how their cultural biases affect how they respond to diverse students, and how institutional cultures may create barriers for diverse students. Through self-reflective practices, teachers can develop cultural proficiency—that is, an understanding of their own culture and how it affects their interactions with other individuals. Culturally proficient teachers are willing to listen to students, and they are willing to make accommodations to meet the needs of students who are different (Dray & Wisneski, 2011). Again, teachers need to treat students equitably, providing what is necessary for each student to succeed in school.

Teachers need to reflect on whether their "traditional" behavior and classroom management strategies are effective with diverse students. They should ask themselves if these strategies are in conflict with the cultural backgrounds of their students, and if they are, they should take steps to change the strategies. Conversely, there are times when students should function within the culture of the school. For example, in some cultures, fighting may seem to be an acceptable way to settle one's differences, but this type of behavior will never be appropriate at school.

Development of Caring Communities

The final principle of culturally responsive behavior and classroom management is the development of a caring and nurturing classroom environment. In essence, behavior and classroom management is really about the interactions and relationships between the teacher and students. Caring about students is one of the prevalent characteristics of highly effective teachers. These teachers are described as warm, friendly, and caring (Colker, 2008). They take a personal interest in students, share experiences with them, and connect with students at a personal level. More important, caring teachers find a way of making students feel wanted and comfortable in the classroom (Walker, 2008). They listen to students, view students as individuals with unique needs, and have an understanding of students' backgrounds and cultures. Yet caring teachers also expect students to do their best in school, and they implement classroom management plans characterized by respect, equality, comfort, and fairness. Caring communities enhance the quality of teacher–student relationships, increase student learning outcomes, and improve classroom behavior.

WHAT WOULD YOU DO?   Ricardo

You are a third-grade teacher in a rural school district, and you are beginning your first lesson in reading. The class will read *Judy Moody* orally, have a classroom discussion after reading certain sections, and then complete related worksheets and activities. However, every time the class begins reading the book, Ricardo disrupts the reading by making animal noises (birds, dogs, and so on). Ricardo generally does not have behavior difficulties, so you inform him that the class would like to read the book, and he needs to be quiet. Students then take turns reading sections of the book, but after a few minutes, Ricardo begins making noises again.

What would you do about Ricardo's behavior?

GOALS OF BEHAVIOR AND CLASSROOM MANAGEMENT

The systems-based approach and the principle-centered approach are two basic strategies of behavior and classroom management. In the systems-based approach, teachers and schools have a set of prescribed rules and consequences that are administered to all students equally without regard to the students' situations or cultural backgrounds. In the principle-centered approach, a set of principles and values are established for behavior strategies, which are based on the situation and the individual student (Laursen, 2003). Many practitioners believe that these two approaches are mutually exclusive, but both are key ingredients in an effective behavior and classroom management plan.

According to the principles of positive behavior support, which is a multi-level prevention and intervention system, behavior and classroom management plans should have three tiers of interventions. The primary or universal level (Tier 1) provides classroom management for all students. This level includes basic rules, consequences, and reinforcements. No matter which approach the teacher prefers, traditional rules and a hierarchy of consequences and reinforcements are a part of the behavior and classroom management plan. This structure provides an important learning process for students who live in a nation where breaking the law results in consequences. Rules and consequences are the foundation of behavior and classroom management. While many students will be successful in school following a systems-based approach, other students will not be successful. These students will receive additional support at the secondary or individualized level (Tier 2). The tertiary or comprehensive level (Tier 3) provides extensive, individualized support for students who are still having behavior difficulties despite the strategies used in Tiers 1 and 2. At this level, a functional behavioral assessment should be used to analyze the student's behavior and to develop strategies to address identified needs (Sayeski & Brown, 2011).

Based on the principles of developmental theories, culturally responsive classroom management, and systems-based and principle-centered approaches, three basic goals of behavior and classroom management emerge:

1. Provide a safe and positive environment that recognizes and respects diversity and in which students are treated equitably and learning can take place.

2. Provide opportunities for students to learn reasonable rules and consequences, as well as the reasons for them.

3. Teach students to manage their own behaviors while providing opportunities for them to learn social skills.

Perhaps the most important goal of behavior and classroom management is to provide students with a safe and positive environment in which learning can take place. As discussed previously, the classroom environment should provide opportunities for teachers and students to develop awareness of their own ethnocentrism and to explore the cultures of others. Teachers and students can explore cultures and cultural assumptions in a safe and secure learning environment. Such an environment allows teachers to teach and students to learn, which is, after all, the main purpose of schools.

SUMMARY

Behavior and classroom management is one of the biggest concerns among preservice teachers, teachers, and administrators. While it is understandable that teachers and administrators are interested in the practical application of classroom management, developing and implementing strategies and plans is a complex process. Classroom management is not as simple as establishing five rules, five consequences, and five rewards. Understanding how students' ability levels and their cultural, social, ethnic, and socioeconomic backgrounds can affect behavior is crucial to developing practical behavior and classroom management plans.

Developmental theories help explain the behavior of students and form the foundation of behavior and classroom management. Familiarity with classical conditioning, operant conditioning, social learning theory, ecological systems theory, and moral development theory may help teachers understand behavior and apply that knowledge to the development of effective behavior and classroom management plans.

To be successful, a behavior and classroom management plan must include proactive, active, and reactive strategies. Examples of proactive strategies are the development of a universal design for classroom management and strategies for the management of content. Active strategies include the maintenance of a positive learning environment, and reactive strategies include management of conduct and covenant.

Teachers also need to be knowledgeable about their students' cultures and how these affect behavior in the classroom. An understanding of the effects of enculturation and acculturation may give teachers some insight into the cultures of their students and help them to develop culturally responsive behavior and classroom management plans. For teachers to be successful in developing culturally responsive behavior and classroom management, they must recognize their own ethnocentrism; gain knowledge of their students' cultures; be aware of the broader social, economic, and political context in education; use culturally appropriate management strategies; and develop caring classroom communities. A safe and secure classroom environment provides opportunities for teacher and students to explore cultures and cultural assumptions. Most important, such an environment allows teachers to teach and students to learn.

REVIEW ACTIVITIES

1. How might each of the major developmental theories affect the development of behavior and classroom management plans?

2. Describe the antecedent, behavior, and consequences of the behaviors of Timothy and Dennis in this chapter's case study.

3. How would you develop a universal design for classroom management? What strategies would you include?

4. Describe your culture. How might your culture be different from the cultures of students in your classroom? How might your culture affect the way you interact with diverse students in your classroom?

5. Kale is a 10-year-old *Kanaka Maoli* whose family adheres to a cooperative *'ohana* (extended family) structure. As Kale's teacher, what cultural factors should you consider when developing a classroom management plan that meets Kale needs?

Visit the Student Study Site at **www.sagepub.com/shepherd** to access additional study tools including mobile-friendly eFlashcards and web quizzes as well as links to SAGE journal articles and web resources.

CHAPTER 2

LEGAL ISSUES OF BEHAVIOR AND CLASSROOM MANAGEMENT

After reading this chapter, you should be able to do the following:

- Explain the proactive, active, and reactive strategies of successful behavior and classroom management.
- Describe the major differences between the Individuals with Disabilities Education Act and Section 504 of the Rehabilitation Act.
- Explain how inclusion applies to all students.
- Explain when school districts can invoke the "same treatment" rule for students with disabilities.
- Understand the procedures for expelling or suspending students with disabilities.
- Explain when a manifestation determination should take place.
- Describe how court cases have affected the development and implementation of behavior and classroom management.

RESPONSIBILITIES OF TEACHERS

The ultimate purpose of schools is to provide children the opportunity for an education. It is important to remember that no one, not even the best teachers, can guarantee anyone an education, because various factors can affect a person's educational progress, including the predisposition to learn. However, schools *can* provide every child the opportunity to learn. Thus, it is important that teachers and administrators provide a safe and secure environment in which learning can take place, and behavior and classroom management is the means by which teachers and administrators create this positive learning environment.

Beyond the ethical considerations of providing a safe environment for children in classrooms, teachers and administrators have legal rights and responsibilities for managing student behaviors. The responsibilities include not only disciplining students but also teaching students appropriate behavior. The legal rights are granted by a society that entrusts children to schools to be educated and protected while under the schools' care.

Over the years, court decisions and legislation have established a set of laws that provide teachers and administrators sufficient latitude to create safe learning environments for all students. Indeed, much of the authority granted teachers and administrators is inherent to the nature of their positions and not based in statutes. Much of this authority comes from the common law principle of *in loco parentis.*

In loco parentis (the Latin term translates as "in place of a parent") is based on an old English common law that gave schoolmasters nearly absolute authority over students and their behaviors. Today, under in loco parentis, teachers and administrators have the responsibility to provide students with a safe learning environment. In loco parentis gives schools the authority to manage student behavior so that potentially disruptive behaviors do not interfere with the educational process; however, the consequences students face for inappropriate behaviors must be reasonable and restrained. For example, in 1980, a teacher at Piscataway High School in Middlesex County, New Jersey, discovered two girls in the restroom, one of whom was caught smoking and admitted to the offense. The second girl, identified in court records as T.L.O., denied that she was smoking. Since smoking in the restroom was a violation of school rules, both girls were taken to the principal's office, where the assistant vice principal searched T.L.O.'s purse. During the search, the assistant vice principal found a pack of cigarettes in the purse. Examining the purse further, the assistant vice principal found rolling papers, a small amount of marijuana, and evidence that T.L.O. was selling marijuana at the high school. T.L.O. was taken to the police station and was later convicted and placed on probation by a juvenile court. The New Jersey Supreme Court overturned the conviction, stating that the school had violated T.L.O.'s Fourth Amendment rights by unlawfully searching her purse. However, the U.S. Supreme Court overturned the lower court's ruling, stating that because school officials have a responsibility to maintain a safe and secure school environment, a child's Fourth Amendment rights are limited. As such, teachers and administrators can search a student if they have a reasonable suspicion that the search is necessary (*New Jersey v. T.L.O.*, 1980). Teachers or school officials have reasonable suspicion when they suspect that a search of a student will reveal evidence that the student has violated school rules, district policy, or the law. Reasonable suspicion cannot be based on a hunch or a rumor, and searches are limited to the school setting and off-campus settings where school-related activities are taking place.

Development and Implementation of Behavior Management Policies

Teachers have an ethical and legal responsibility to teach students. Successful classroom and behavior management creates a safe environment in which learning can take place, and a crucial part of this is the development and implementation of effective discipline policies. Often, when teachers begin their careers, they find they must follow and enforce the discipline policies that have already been established by the school district. In some districts, school-wide behavior and classroom management models have been adopted, which may limit individual teachers' involvement in developing management plans. A school-wide management plan provides rules and consequences that are consistent across classrooms; however, these plans should have the flexibility to meet the needs of culturally and linguistically diverse students, students with disabilities, students from diverse socioeconomic backgrounds, and students with different ability levels. With the numbers of diverse students in today's classrooms, the traditional hierarchy of rules and consequences may no longer be an effective means to manage the behaviors of all students.

Rules and Consequences

Many teachers working in the United States today most likely attended public schools that used the traditional hierarchy of rules and consequences. This classroom management plan is familiar and comfortable, and while many teacher education programs at universities currently offer teacher candidates some training in differential instruction, any courses and discussions regarding classroom management usually focus on the layout of the classroom and on rules and consequences.

The traditional hierarchy of rules and consequences is based on the behaviorist model of behavior and classroom management. Plans based on the hierarchy usually include five simple rules written in a positive manner, five consequences, and, sometimes, five rewards. The consequences and rewards are reinforcers designed to increase the probability that the appropriate behavior will occur and with increased frequency. While such a plan is likely to be effective with the majority of students in the classroom, it may not be effective for students with behavior difficulties. Additionally, traditional rules and consequences are often disproportionately applied to culturally, linguistically, and ethnically diverse students (Dray & Wisneski, 2011; Imler, 2009).

It is important for today's teachers to remember that the traditional hierarchy of rules and consequences is not the end of behavior and classroom management, it is the beginning. A behavior and classroom management plan needs to meet the needs of all students in the classroom. It should combine the consistency of rules and consequences with the flexibility necessary to meet the differential behavior needs of diverse students. Achieving a balance between consistency and flexibility is important in developing a universal design for classroom management, which should include proactive, active, and reactive strategies.

Proactive, Active, and Reactive Strategies

Successful behavior and classroom management should be based on a universal design for classroom management and should include proactive,

Table 2.1 The Proactive, Active, and Reactive Strategies of the Traditional Hierarchy of Rules, Consequences, and Rewards

Types of strategies	Examples
Proactive	Developing rules and reinforcements prior to the first day of school
	Considering the needs of diverse students when developing rules and reinforcements
Active	Revising rules and reinforcements with student input
	Implementing rules and reinforcements
	Maintenance: Reminding students of rules and reinforcements
Reactive	Providing consequences and reinforcements for behaviors

active, and reactive strategies. As noted above, many behavior and classroom management plans in today's schools are based on behaviorist theories and strategies, which generally incorporate a one-size-fits-all traditional hierarchy of rules, consequences, and rewards. In such strategies, teachers apply reinforcements to behaviors in the hope of reducing the probability that inappropriate behaviors will occur again. While these strategies are important components of successful behavior and classroom management plans, they represent only one part of classroom management. The increasing numbers of diverse students in today's classrooms necessitate a paradigm shift in classroom management that also includes proactive and active strategies. Proactive, active, and reactive strategies often overlap and should be incorporated into a UDCM.

Table 2.2 Strategies for a Universal Design for Classroom Management

Proactive	Active	Reactive
Development of a hierarchical behavior management plan	Implementation of a hierarchical behavior management plan/classroom rules	Enforcement of consequences for behaviors
Cultural competence/ development of culturally responsive strategies	Implementation of culturally responsive strategies	Management of conduct
Development and implementation of a school-wide positive behavior support system	Use of universal interventions (Tier 1) and individualized interventions (Tier 2)	Use of comprehensive interventions (Tier 3)
Management of content		
Student instruction regarding routines and expectations		Management of covenant
	Implementation of functional behavioral analysis/behavior intervention plan	Implementation of functional behavioral analysis/behavior intervention plan
	Response-to-intervention	Referral for special education services
Equitable treatment	Equitable treatment	Equitable treatment

Proactive Strategies

Proactive strategies can prevent behavior difficulties from occurring in the classroom (Niesyn, 2009; Stormont & Reinke, 2009). Teachers should develop and implement such strategies before students enter the classroom, and the strategies should include the development of a universal design for classroom management. A UDCM considers the differential needs of students of both genders; of all cultural, linguistic, and socioeconomic backgrounds; and all ability levels. In addition to the development of the traditional hierarchy of rules, consequences, and rewards, the UDCM should include the development of alternative behavior strategies for culturally and linguistically diverse students, students with disabilities, and students from socioeconomically disadvantaged backgrounds.

Proactive strategies also include the development and implementation of a school-wide positive behavior support system, which is a three-tiered prevention and intervention system designed to increase adaptive, prosocial behaviors in the schools. Students are instructed to exhibit socially acceptable behaviors, and the school environment is arranged to prevent inappropriate behaviors. A well-developed positive behavior support system includes management of content, student instruction regarding routines and expectations, and reinforcement of appropriate behavior (Reinke, Herman, & Stormont, 2013). Management of content includes the development of lessons that actively engage students and are relevant to the students. Appropriate and relevant lessons can prevent off-task behaviors that lead to disruptions in the classroom. This management of content is an important aspect of maintaining effective behavior and classroom management. Additionally, when the teacher is prepared, she is able to move around the room while providing instruction. Even when students are working at their desks, the teacher should monitor student progress using the "tennis shoe method" of teaching. That is, the teacher should metaphorically put on tennis shoes to walk around the classroom, circulating among students to monitor their progress and behavior (Shepherd, 2010). Management of content also includes arrangement of the physical environment of the classroom, which should be designed to support the learning outcomes of students.

Active Strategies

Active strategies maintain student behaviors and preserve a positive learning environment. Maintaining a positive learning environment includes the implementation of the traditional hierarchy of rules, consequences, and rewards. The majority of students will comply with well-written and relevant classroom rules without the need of consequences. Usually these students are intrinsically motivated to behave in a certain manner, and active strategies encourage this behavior.

Similar to positive behavior supports, response-to-intervention is a broad conceptualization of a multitier prevention and intervention system designed to improve students' academic performance (Sugai & Horner, 2009). Response-to-intervention is described in the Individuals with Disabilities Education Act as a method of identifying students with learning disabilities. However, it can and should be incorporated as a strategy to provide interventions for students who are having behavior difficulties (see Chapter 12). As part of a positive behavior support program, response-to-intervention should be incorporated as specialized support for students with identified needs. Response-to-intervention strategies for students with behavior difficulties might include social skills training, school counseling programs, and peer tutoring.

Functional behavioral assessment and behavior intervention plans should also be used as active strategies to identify behaviors and develop alternative or replacement behaviors in the general education setting, and not as a strategy for students in special education. Functional behavioral assessments are used to identify the facets of a student's inappropriate behavior (see Chapter 8), while behavior intervention plans implement strategies intended to reduce or eliminate inappropriate behavior (see Chapter 10). Unfortunately, functional behavioral assessments and behavior intervention plans are often used as reactive strategies—that is, they are not used until after a student begins receiving special education services.

Reactive Strategies

Reactive strategies will always be an important component of any behavior and classroom management plan. Such strategies provide the most intensive interventions for student behaviors. They include enforcing consequences and giving reinforcement for behaviors based on the traditional hierarchical behavior management plan. Reactive strategies also include referring a student for special education services when interventions in the general education setting have been ineffective.

Proactive, active, and reactive strategies should all incorporate the equitable treatment of all students. By treating students equitably, the teacher provides what is necessary for each student to succeed in school; this goal should be part of any behavior management strategy. Special education teachers have learned to treat students equitably through differential instruction and meeting the individual needs of the students. This is also an important concept in the development of a UDCM: meeting the needs of all students in a diverse student population.

CASE STUDY   Mrs. Cox and Timothy

Mrs. Cox is a third-grade teacher at McKay Elementary School. On the first day of school, she had her students complete an interest survey. The survey asked students about their favorite television shows and movies, activities or hobbies, foods, and other interests. The purpose of the survey was twofold: It would allow Mrs. Cox to get to know her students, and it would help her to develop a list of reinforcers to use to modify student behavior.

Timothy was a particular challenge for Mrs. Cox. He had been diagnosed with attention-deficit/hyperactivity disorder, and he had difficulty keeping on task and completing assignments. On his interest survey, he had listed computer time, model building, and drawing as favorite activities. Trying to improve his on-task behavior, Mrs. Cox developed a positive reinforcement strategy in which Timothy would receive 5 minutes of computer time for every five questions he completed on his in-class assignments. While Timothy was agreeable to the strategy, it was ineffective. Timothy could not seem to focus on his assignments.

One day, Mrs. Cox noticed that Timothy seemed to be staying on task. Since it was routine for Mrs. Cox to walk around the class to monitor her students' progress during in-class assignments, Timothy did not pay any attention to her when she walked past his desk. Mrs. Cox noticed that Timothy was drawing in the margins of his paper, but she also saw that he had half of the assignment completed. Instead of reprimanding him for drawing on his paper, she kept silent.

At the end of class, Timothy handed in his assignment. He had completed all but one question. When Mrs. Cox graded his paper, she decided to also make positive comments on the drawings he had made in the margins.

Timothy responded positively to Mrs. Cox's notes on his drawings, and during the next several assignments he continued to draw in the margins while working on his assignments. His on-task behavior continued to improve.

Mrs. Cox continued to observe Timothy closely as he worked on his assignments. She began to notice that when his focus began to waver, he began drawing in the margins. After a few minutes of drawing, he returned to the assignment. Mrs. Cox realized that Timothy had developed his own strategy for on-task behaviors. Had she reprimanded him for drawing in the margins, an effective behavior strategy would have been discarded.

LEGISLATION AFFECTING BEHAVIOR AND CLASSROOM MANAGEMENT

Teachers and administrators should be aware of all laws that affect the development and implementation of behavior and classroom management. Noncompliance with such laws can result in legal issues for schools and school personnel. The three most important pieces of legislation with which teachers and administrators should be familiar are the Individuals with Disabilities Education Improvement Act (2004), the Americans with Disabilities Act (1990), and Section 504 of the Rehabilitation Act (1973). The Individuals with Disabilities Education Improvement Act was specifically created to guarantee the provision of educational services for children with disabilities in public schools. Section 504 of the Rehabilitation Act basically prevents discrimination toward individuals with disabilities by any program receiving federal financial assistance, and the Americans with Disabilities Act protects individuals with disabilities from discrimination in the workplace or at any public program or activity and guarantees accessibility at public places for those with disabilities. Together, these laws ensure that students with disabilities are treated equitably—that is, the laws require schools to provide what each student needs to be successful.

Individuals with Disabilities Education Improvement Act

In 1975, Congress passed the Education for All Handicapped Children Act, which provided federal funding for states delivering services for students with disabilities in the public schools. This act guaranteed the right of children with disabilities to receive a free and appropriate public education in the least restrictive environment (LRE). In 1990 the act was renamed the Individuals with Disabilities Education Act (IDEA), and in 2004 it became the Individuals with Disabilities Education Improvement Act (still known as IDEA). According to the IDEA (2004, § 300.114[a][2]) definition of LRE, children with disabilities are to be educated as much as possible with children who are not disabled. In other words, the first consideration for educational services for students with disabilities is inclusion in the general education classroom; however, the law does not mandate that all students with disabilities receive services in the general education classroom. Placement decisions should always be based on the needs of the students with disabilities.

Inclusion is not mentioned in IDEA, but the law's definition of least restrictive environment provides the impetus for the inclusion movement because it mandates that students with disabilities be educated alongside their peers without disabilities who receive their education in the general education classroom. Teachers and administrators often do not support inclusion because they do not fully understand it (Sindelar, Shearer, Yendol-Hoppey, & Liebert, 2006); however, inclusion is an equitable concept that encompasses *all* students, not just students with disabilities. Inclusion involves providing the necessary support to promote the learning of every student in the general education setting within the neighborhood school. While it is obvious that inclusion applies to students with disabilities who need support to be successful in the general education classroom, it can also apply to struggling learners, linguistically and culturally diverse students, and even gifted students. For example, a teacher may have a student who has an advanced understanding of mathematics. To meet the needs of this student, the teacher must challenge her by providing supplementary materials and lessons. Teachers incorporate inclusion into their behavior and classroom management plans by providing supports for students with behavior difficulties.

Because federal law requires that students with disabilities be educated in the least restrictive environment, teachers and administrators need to consider the needs of these students when developing and implementing behavior and classroom management plans in the general education classroom. Today, it is not uncommon for a teacher to have a minimum of five students with disabilities in a class of thirty. These students could have a range of disabilities, including learning disabilities, intellectual disabilities, emotional and behavioral disorders, autism, and physical disabilities. This does not include an additional two or three students with attention-deficit/ hyperactivity disorder (ADHD), who are protected under Section 504 of the Rehabilitation Act.

With the renaming of the Education for All Handicapped Children Act as the Individuals with Disabilities Education, the term *handicapped* was replaced with *disability*, using people-first language. In other words, a child was no longer described as a *learning disabled child*, but as a *child with learning disabilities*. The child or individual comes before the descriptive disability.

The reauthorizations of IDEA in 1997 and 2004 added several provisions that directly affect behavior and classroom management that require further discussion. These provisions include positive behavior support (see Chapter 13); manifestation determination, which involves suspension and expulsion; functional behavioral assessments; and behavior intervention plans.

Behavior Management of Students with Disabilities

In comparison with disciplining other students, disciplining students with disabilities involves a more complex set of regulations and procedures; however, in many instances, students with disabilities can receive the same consequences as students without disabilities. Teachers and administrators need to understand when students with disabilities can receive the same consequences as students without disabilities and when they must use alternative disciplinary approaches. One of the key considerations in the behavior and classroom management of students with disabilities is whether the consequence of a behavior results in the student's change of placement.

Short-term disciplinary removal. Based on the U.S. Supreme Court ruling in *Honig v. Doe* (1988) and administrative rulings by the U.S. Department of Education's Office for Civil Rights (1988) and the Office of Special Education Programs (1995), students with disabilities can be suspended up to a maximum of 10 school days in an academic year without this being considered a change in placement. During that period, students with disabilities can receive the same consequences as students without disabilities unless the inappropriate behavior is related to the student's disability. For example, Avery, who is a high school student with a learning disability in mathematics, got into a fight during lunch period with Dennis, who does not have a disability. Based on Avery's past and current school records, disciplinary referrals, and current individualized education program (IEP), Avery's behavior was not related to his learning disability. As a result, Avery could receive the same disciplinary action as Dennis, which, according to the school's behavior management plan, was a 3-day suspension. It is important to remember that under the "same treatment rule," a student with a disability can receive the same discipline as a student without disabilities for the same infraction of school rules. However, if Avery had previously been suspended for a total of 8 days due to other offenses, the additional 3 days of suspension would have exceeded the 10-day restriction and would have been considered a "change in placement."

A school must convene a manifestation determination review within 10 days of any decision to change the placement of a student with disabilities. Under IDEA, the team conducting the manifestation determination must decide whether the student's behavior was related to the student's disability or if the behavior was a direct result of the school's failure to implement the student's IEP appropriately (Arnberger & Shoop, 2006). The team conducting the determination is made up of school personnel, the student's parents, and other relevant members of the student's IEP team as determined by the school and the parents. The team reviews all relevant information regarding the student, including evaluations and diagnostic results, pertinent information provided by the parents, teacher observations of the student, the student's IEP, the student's behavior intervention plan (BIP), and any previous records of the inappropriate behavior (Arnberger & Shoop, 2006). For example, if Avery did not understand the impacts or consequences of his behavior or could not control his behavior because of his disability, then the behavior is a manifestation of his disability. If the behavior is directly related to the student's disability, a team must conduct a

Figure 2.1 Manifestation Determination Procedures

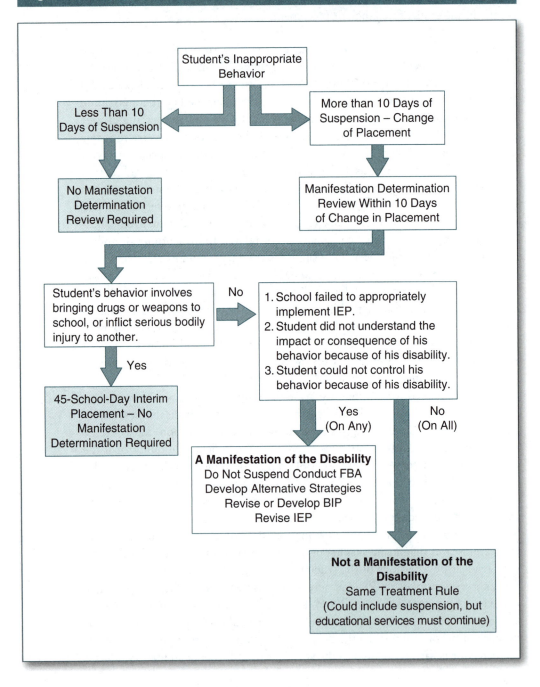

functional behavioral assessment and develop a BIP. Additionally, an alternative behavior and classroom management strategy needs to be implemented.

Long-term disciplinary removal. In some instances students with disabilities can be removed for more than 10 days. Students with disabilities can be unilaterally removed to an interim alternative educational setting for a maximum of 45 school days for possession of a weapon, possession of illegal drugs, or the infliction of serious bodily injury on another while at school, on school premises, or at a school function. Interim alternative educational settings are settings in which students receive educational services on a temporary basis. Such settings include schools set up by districts for students who have committed severe behavior infractions.

Students with disabilities who bring drugs or weapons to school or inflict serious bodily injury on others can be removed from the school setting without a manifestation determination. The parents need to be notified and provided a copy of the school's safety procedures once the decision to remove the student has been made. The 45-school-day interim alternative setting provides an equitable option to expulsion for students with disabilities by providing a balance between the least restrictive environment and safeguarding other students.

Zero-tolerance policy. As a result of the shootings at Columbine High School in 1999, many schools have adopted zero-tolerance policies regarding threatening and potentially dangerous behaviors by students. Zero-tolerance policies have gained momentum due to provisions in the No Child Left Behind Act and the Elementary and Secondary Education Act, which requires schools to suspend for one year any student who brings a gun to school (Shah, 2011). However, a number of professionals have criticized these policies as resulting in harsh punishments for innocent and minor infractions. In Texas, thousands of students are receiving Class C misdemeanor tickets each year for minor misbehaviors that are not threatening or dangerous (Fowler, 2011b). Often, the consequences for these actions are prescribed without consideration of the circumstances. For example, a middle school student was awarded with a pocketknife for earning the most merit badges at a weekend Boy Scout camping trip. Forgetting that he had left the knife in his jacket pocket, he returned to school on Monday, and an administrator discovered the knife. Without considering the circumstances or whether the boy's possession of the pocketknife posed a danger to others, the school immediately placed the student in an interim setting for 45 days (Shepherd, 2010). Additionally, research has shown that African American students and students with emotional and behavioral disorders are twice as likely as other students to be expelled under rigid zero-tolerance policies (Achilles, McLaughlin, & Croninger, 2007; Fowler, 2011a; Kaplan & Cornell, 2005; Shah, 2011). Because of the inflexibility of such policies, U.S. Secretary of Education Arne Duncan has begun discussions to reshape discipline policies that unfairly place students in the juvenile justice system (Shah, 2011).

With metal detectors at every door, surveillance cameras in hallways and classrooms, and the threat of arrest for minor infractions, students in many school districts feel under siege in hostile learning environments that more closely resemble prisons than schools (Thompson, 2011). While the purpose of zero-tolerance policies is to protect students from threatening and potentially dangerous behaviors of others, the application of these policies should not result in a paradigm shift toward criminalizing student behaviors and outsourcing the consequences from the principal's office to the courts (Fowler, 2011a; Turner & Goodner, 2010).

Functional Behavioral Assessment

The purpose of a functional behavioral assessment is to identify a problem behavior, determine the antecedent that prompts the behavior, and identify the consequence that maintains the behavior (Erickson, Stage, & Nelson, 2006). Once the aspects of the target behavior are identified, alternative or replacement behaviors can be developed.

Functional behavioral assessments have existed since the 1960s, when they were conducted in psychological laboratories or clinical settings (Couvillon, Bullock, & Gable, 2009). When the 1997 revision of IDEA mandated the use of functional behavioral assessments and behavior intervention plans, the usage of these two specific interventions increased in public school settings. Unfortunately, most of the research on functional behavioral assessments has been conducted by researchers in restrictive settings with students identified as having emotional and behavioral disorders. A majority of general education teachers do not know if their schools provide functional behavioral assessment and intervention planning (Stormont, Reinke, & Herman, 2011). General education teachers seldom receive any training in the implementation and interpretation of functional behavioral assessments, and even when training is provided, teachers generally disregard information gained from functional behavioral assessments when developing BIPs (Couvillon et al., 2009; Van Acker, Boreson, Gable, & Potterton, 2005). Additionally, many school districts are still engaged in reactive behavior strategies in which consequences are determined by "the nature of the offense, with little or no effort to determine the reason a student might engage in the specific behavior" (Van Acker et al., 2005, p. 36).

Functional behavioral assessments are not required for all students with disabilities. For example, such an assessment is not required for every student whose behavior is inappropriate and interferes with the learning process or disrupts the learning environment. The IEP team needs to consider whether a functional behavioral assessment is appropriate in such a case, but an assessment is not required. However, a functional behavioral assessment must be conducted when the school is considering a disciplinary change of placement and if the student's disruptive behavior is due to the student's disability (Zirkel, 2009). If the behavior is unrelated to the student's disability, or if the student does not have a disability, a functional behavioral assessment is not required.

Unfortunately, functional behavioral assessments are often used as a last resort (Moreno, 2010), when a student has been identified for special education services and after the student's behaviors have prompted a change in placement. This is a reactive behavior strategy that would be more beneficial as an active strategy. For example, Timothy continuously refuses to follow teachers' redirection, and the basic traditional hierarchy of rules, consequences, and rewards has not been effective in managing his inappropriate behavior. If the typical, reactive pattern of behavior management continues, Timothy will be sent to the office several times, suspended, expelled, or maybe referred for special education services. Instead, a team of teachers could conduct a functional behavioral assessment and try to determine the antecedent and consequences of Timothy's behavior. If the team members can determine what triggers the behavior and what reinforces the behavior, they may be able to develop an alternative or replacement behavior for Timothy. Once the team has developed a replacement behavior, a behavior intervention plan can be implemented.

Behavior Intervention Plans

The purpose of the behavior intervention plan is to take the information obtained through a functional behavioral assessment and implement strategies that will reduce or eliminate the inappropriate behavior. BIPs should be individualized based on students' functional behavioral assessments and should include positive behavioral strategies (Etscheidt, 2006). Once a student's BIP has been implemented, teachers need to monitor the student to determine whether the plan is effective in reducing or eliminating the inappropriate behavior (Etscheidt, 2006; Maag & Katsiyannis, 2006).

As with functional behavioral assessments, a school district is required to develop and implement a behavior intervention plan only when a school is considering a change of placement for a student and when the student's behavior is due to a disability. Implementing BIPs before considering special education services may actually reduce the number of students placed in special education and promote the learning of students in the general education classrooms. Additionally, BIPs may reduce the numbers of students who receive office referrals, suspensions, and expulsions, especially among students from diverse backgrounds.

The development and implementation of behavior intervention plans may be arduous for teachers and administrators. Teachers often do not have the necessary training to conduct a functional behavioral assessment, which is an important element in the development of a BIP. Also, the ever-increasing demands placed on teachers by administrators, parents, and state and federal laws prevent teachers from having the time they need to implement assessment procedures and develop BIPs (Killu, Weber, Derby, & Barretto, 2006).

General education teachers often refer students who need more assistance for special education services instead of considering alternative interventions in the general education classroom. However, many schools today are adopting systems of school-wide positive behavior support, which establishes three tiers of support with increasing levels of intensity to prevent or reduce inappropriate behaviors (Horner et al., 2009). Functional behavioral assessments and behavior intervention plans can be integral parts of such positive behavior support.

Students Not Yet Eligible for Special Education Services

Under certain circumstances, students who are not yet eligible for special education services may be protected from disciplinary action for some kinds of behaviors if the school has knowledge of the child's disability. The school is deemed to have that knowledge if

a. the student's parent has expressed concern in writing to the principal, teacher or other administrator that their child is in need of special education and related services;

b. the parent has requested an evaluation of the child; or

c. the teacher of the child, or other school personnel had expressed specific concerns about a child's pattern of behavior to administrators or other supervisory personnel. (IDEA, 2004)

If any of these three conditions is met, then the child is treated in the same manner as a student identified as having a disability and is subject to the same disciplinary protections. For example, a third grader with ADHD who had not been identified for special education services had been receiving interventions for 2 years. Her current teacher reported that the child's increasing behavior difficulties were having negative impacts on her academic performance. The response-to-intervention team recommended that the student undergo a mental health evaluation but did not refer her for special education evaluation. A month later, the child was suspended and then expelled for threatening behavior. The parents filed for due process, but the school maintained that a manifestation determination was not required because the student had not yet been eligible for special education services under IDEA. The court ruled, however, that the school had known about the student's disability and had violated IDEA by failing to conduct a manifestation determination prior to suspending and excluding the student for disciplinary reasons. The court recommended that the suspension and expulsion be removed from the student's records and that the student be provided with compensatory education for the time she was excluded (*Jackson v. Northwest Local School District*, 2010).

WHAT WOULD YOU DO? Michael

Michael is a student in your fifth-grade class. His father passed away in an automobile accident last year. Before his father's death Michael always did well in school and never had behavior difficulties, but since the accident his grades have been poor. He has been receiving academic interventions developed by the school district through a response-to-intervention model, but his behavior difficulties have been increasing. He has been prone to verbal outbursts, threatening other students, and hitting the top of his desk with his fists.

You expressed your concerns about Michael to your principal and your school's at-risk team. The at-risk team met to discuss Michael's case and recommended some behavior strategies for him. The team also recommended that Michael meet with the school counselor once a week to discuss his behaviors. Yesterday, Michael once again threatened another student, and then he punched a hole in a wall. The principal immediately suspended Michael and began the paperwork to have him suspended for the remainder of the semester.

Do you agree that this was the appropriate course of action to address Michael's behavior? Did Michael's case raise any legal issues that needed to be considered? What would you have done if you were Michael's teacher?

Bullying and Discriminatory Harassment

Bullying has become a major concern for many schools districts, and more than 44 U.S. states have passed laws requiring school districts to implement anti-bullying programs and policies (Espelage & Swearer, 2010). However, when the target of bullying behavior is a student with disabilities, the action could be construed as discriminatory harassment. Discriminatory harassment occurs when a student is harassed because of "race, color, national origin, sex, or disability" in a manner "sufficiently serious that it creates a hostile environment and such harassment is encouraged, tolerated, not adequately addressed, or ignored by school employees" (U.S. Department of Education, Office for Civil Rights, 2010, p. 1). Thus, if a student with a disability is bullied, this action could be considered discriminatory harassment, and the school is responsible for immediately addressing any incidents of such harassment about which it is aware. For example, the case of *Hemet California Unified School District* (2009) involved a student with ADHD who was on medication that caused the student to have facial tics and to produce noises. The student was subjected to derogatory disability-related name-calling by another student and was able to describe what happened. The school district made a good-faith effort to resolve what it viewed as a typical dispute between students, but it was not successful, and the harassment continued. The Office for Civil Rights concluded that the school was guilty of discrimination because it did not adequately respond to an instance of disability-related harassment (Katsiyannis, Losinski, & Prince, 2012).

Section 504 and the Americans with Disabilities Act

Section 504 of the Rehabilitation Act (1973) was the first major federal legislation to protect individuals with disabilities against discrimination. Under Section 504, any program receiving federal financial assistance may not discriminate against students with disabilities. Section 504 applies to K–12 public schools and to private and parochial schools that receive any federal financial assistance. Passed by Congress in 1990, the Americans with Disabilities Act protects individuals with disabilities from discrimination in the workplace and at any public program or activity and provides a guarantee of accessibility at public places (Bowman, 2011). Thus, this law prohibits discrimination against students with disabilities in private schools that do not receive federal funding. Both Section 504 and the Americans with Disabilities Act define a person with a disability as one who has a physical or mental impairment that substantially limits one or more of the major life activities of the individual, has a record of such an impairment, or is regarded as having such an impairment. Major life activities are those activities that need to be adversely affected for someone to be considered as a person with a disability; they include caring for oneself, performing manual tasks, walking, seeing, hearing, speaking, breathing, learning, and working.

However, two U.S. Supreme Court cases have significantly restricted the definition of a person with a disability under Section 504 and the Americans with Disabilities Act. In *Sutton v. United Air Lines, Inc.* (1999), the Supreme Court ruled that the "substantially limits" requirement for defining a person as having a disability is not met if mitigating or corrective measures reduce the impairment to a negligible or moderate limitation instead of a substantial limitation (Zirkel, 2009). For example, if a student with ADHD takes medication that reduces his hyperactive behaviors and helps him focus on tasks, then the child would no longer be covered under Section 504 because the ADHD no longer substantially limits any of the child's major life activities.

In *Toyota Motor Manufacturing v. Williams* (2002), the Supreme Court narrowly defined a major life activity as an activity of central importance. This decision required a "demanding standard" in the determination of whether an individual has a disability. For example, a student with dysgraphia (a learning disability that affects spelling, handwriting, and writing thoughts on paper) may no longer be considered as a person with a disability under Section 504 if computers, word-processing programs, spell checkers, and grammar checkers can provide the student with enough support that the dysgraphia no longer affects the student's learning activity.

An additional series of court cases resulted in amendments to the Americans with Disabilities Act in 2008 that effectively reversed previous judicial interpretations of the definition of an individual with a disability. These amendments also include a "conforming amendment" to Section 504, which means that expanded coverage added to the Americans with Disabilities Act also applies to Section 504 (Bowman, 2011; Zirkel, 2009).

Changes to the Americans with Disabilities Act and Section 504

The Americans with Disabilities Act Amendments (ADAA, 2008) did not change the definition of a person with a disability; rather, this legislation expanded the criteria for the definition. Under the ADAA, a broader standard must now be applied in the determination of whether a person has a disability. For example, children with ADHD, diabetes, asthma, cancer, or AIDS may not qualify for special education services under the categories of IDEA, but they are protected under Section 504. Schools must make appropriate accommodations to ensure that these students receive education opportunities.

The Supreme Court had previously established that mitigating or corrective methods had to be considered in the determination of whether a person's disability substantially limits a life activity. The ADAA reversed this trend. Currently, the determination of whether a person has a disability has to be made without regard to any ameliorative effects of mitigating or corrective treatments (Bowman, 2011). Additionally, the list of mitigating measures to be disregarded has been expanded. In the educational setting, this list includes medication, low-vision devices (except contact lenses and eyeglasses), hearing aids, cochlear implants, mobility devices, assistive technology, reasonable accommodations or services, and behavioral and neurological modifications (Bowman, 2011; Weber, 2010). This expanded list is especially pertinent when teachers are considering accommodations for students with behavioral and emotional difficulties in the classroom.

Previously, the Americans with Disabilities Act defined major life activities as caring for oneself, performing manual tasks, walking, seeing, hearing, speaking, breathing, learning, and working. Under the ADAA, the list of major life activities has been expanded to include reading, thinking, concentrating, sleeping, bowel functions, bladder functions, digestive functions, and eating. The addition of major bodily functions as major life activities will have a profound effect on students with serious medical conditions, even if mitigating measures have alleviated or corrected their conditions.

Under the Americans with Disabilities Act, a person had to prove that he or she had a disability. Under the ADAA, a person only has to show that he or she is perceived as having a disability. For example, if teachers have discussions in which they speculate that Johnny may have ADHD because they have observed his hyperactive behaviors, Johnny is then perceived to have a disability and is entitled to accommodations under the ADAA.

Finally, a person who has an impairment that is episodic or in remission may be considered as having a disability if the impairment would substantially limit a major life activity when active. For example, a student who has AIDS may not exhibit any symptoms, but he is considered a person with a disability because the disease may affect his educational performance in the future.

Select Court Cases Affecting Behavior and Classroom Management

A number of court cases have directly or indirectly affected how teachers manage student behaviors. Teachers need to consider the findings in these cases, as well as the policies of school districts, when developing and implementing behavior and classroom management plans.

One of the most influential court cases to affect behavior and classroom management is *Tinker v. Des Moines Independent School District* (1969). In 1965, students wore black armbands to school to protest the Vietnam War. When they refused to remove the armbands after school officials instructed them to do so, the students were suspended. The U.S. Supreme Court stated that students and teachers do not give up their constitutional rights to freedom of speech or expression when they enter the school; however, these rights must be balanced against the school's need to maintain a learning environment. The Court ruled that as long as students' actions do not disrupt classwork or school activities, those actions are acceptable. This proviso has been called the "disruption test," and since 1969 the courts have relied on *Tinker* in rulings on school attire, vulgar language, and inappropriate expression.

In *Honig v. Doe* (1988), "John Doe," a student who was identified as emotionally disturbed under the Education for All Handicapped Children Act (later IDEA), choked a peer after the peer had taunted Doe. As he was being escorted to the principal's office, Doe kicked out a school window. Doe was suspended for five days, but on the fifth day, the San Francisco Unified School District notified Doe's mother that it was recommending that her son be expelled. Additionally, Doe's suspension would be extended until the expulsion proceedings were concluded. This violated the Education for All Handicapped Children Act provision that children with disabilities must remain in their current placement pending the completing of any proceedings unless the parents and school officials agree to the contrary. The Supreme Court ruled that under the act, (a) students with disabilities had a substantive right to an education, (b) school officials could not unilaterally exclude students with disabilities from school for dangerous or disruptive actions that were manifestations of the students' disabilities, and (c) students with disabilities could not be suspended for more than 10 days. The only exception to the "stay put" provision under IDEA (2004) was that students with disabilities could be unilaterally removed to a 45-day interim placement if they are in possession of weapons or drugs, or if they inflicted serious bodily injury. Additionally, *Honig v. Doe* does not prevent school districts from using time-out, detention, restriction of privileges, or suspensions.

The Fifth and Fourteenth Amendments to the U.S. Constitution state that no one can be deprived of life, liberty, or property without due process. While these provisions, known as the due process clauses, originally applied to judicial proceedings, they were eventually applied to disciplinary proceedings in school settings. In the case of *Goss v. Lopez* (1975), nine students were suspended for 10 days for destroying school property and disrupting the learning environment. While state law required the school to notify the parents and afford a student a hearing if expelled, it did not provide such assurances if a student was suspended. The U.S. Supreme Court ruled that since education is a fundamental right, students who are suspended are entitled to due process. While school districts can still suspend students, they have to notify a student's parents of a suspension and provide a hearing if one is requested by the student or the parents.

In *Melissa S. v. School District of Pittsburgh* (2006), the Third Circuit Court ruled that placing a student in time-out does not violate IDEA if educational services are continued and if the time-out is a normal procedure for managing students who are endangering themselves or others. Melissa, a student with Down syndrome, had serious problems controlling her behavior, which included kicking and screaming, refusing to go to class, spitting at the teacher, grabbing the breast of the teacher, and running out of the school building. The school placed Melissa in a time-out area in an unused office where the classroom assistant and others would give her work and encourage her to return to class. The court ruled that in treating Melissa in this way the school district had not violated IDEA, the Rehabilitation Act, or the Fourteenth Amendment's due process clause.

While many states and school districts no longer condone corporal punishment as a disciplinary measure, the courts have upheld the use of corporal punishment in schools. In *Ingraham v. Wright* (1977), the U.S. Supreme Court ruled that corporal punishment administered by schools does not violate the Eighth Amendment, which prohibits cruel and unusual punishment. The Eighth Amendment was designed to protect criminals from inhumane punishment, not to protect students who misbehave in school. However, the lower courts have established a "shocking to the conscience" standard, in which any substantive due process inquiry is based on the severity of the punishment and whether the punishment was administered maliciously.

In *Vernonia School District v. Acton* (1995), the parents of 12-year-old James Acton refused to let their son submit to a drug test as a condition of trying out for his school's football team. Since drug testing was required of all student athletes, James was not allowed to try out for the football team. The parents argued that mandatory drug testing without cause violated the unreasonable search provision of the Fourth Amendment. The Supreme Court ruled that strict adherence to the requirement that searches be based on probable cause would undermine schools' ability and responsibility to maintain a safe and secure environment. Additionally, students who voluntarily participate in school athletics subject themselves to a degree of regulation even higher than

Table 2.3 Legislation and Court Findings Affecting Behavior and Classroom Management

Law/Court Case	Issue	Impact
Individuals with Disabilities Education Improvement Act (2004)	Students with disabilities	Provides a guarantee of educational services for students with disabilities.
	Least restrictive environment/inclusion	Students with disabilities must be educated with students without disabilities to the maximum extent possible.
	Same treatment rule	Students with disabilities can be disciplined in the same manner as students without disabilities if the behavior is not associated with the disability.
	Suspensions	Students with disabilities can be suspended for up to 10 days.
	Expulsions	Students with disabilities can be unilaterally expelled for 45 days for possession of drugs or weapons, or for inflicting serious bodily injury.
	Manifestation determination	If a student with a disability is suspended for more than a total of 10 school days, it must be determined if the behavior that prompted the suspension was the result of the disability. Exceptions are the possession of drugs or weapons and the infliction of serious bodily injury.
	Functional behavioral assessments/behavior intervention plans	A school must conduct a functional behavioral assessment and implement a behavior intervention plan if a student with a disability undergoes a change of placement and if the behavior in question is related to the student's disability.

(Continued)

Table 2.3 (Continued)

Law/Court Case	Issue	Impact
Americans with Disabilities Act (1990)	Protection of individuals with disabilities from discrimination	Prohibits discrimination against students with disabilities in private schools.
	Definition of person with disability	Recent changes expand the criteria for the definition of a person with a disability. Directly affects Section 504.
Section 504 of the Rehabilitation Act (1973)	Protection of individuals with disabilities from discrimination	Prohibits discrimination against students with disabilities in schools receiving federal financial assistance.
	Definition of person with disability	Recent changes to the Americans with Disabilities Act have expanded the criteria for the definition of a person with a disability in Section 504.
Jackson v. Northwest Local School District (2010)	Disciplinary actions	A student who is not yet eligible for special education services may be protected from disciplinary action if the school had knowledge of the child's disability.
Hemet California Unified School District (2009)	Discriminatory harassment	A school can be held accountable for not responding to disability-related harassment.
New Jersey v. T.L.O. (1980)	School searches	A student can be searched at school if there is a reasonable suspicion that the student has violated school rules, district policy, or the law.
Tinker v. Des Moines Independent School District (1969)	Freedom of speech at school	Protects students' freedom of speech at school unless it is disruptive to classroom or school activities.
Honig v. Doe (1988)	"Stay put" provision	Students with disabilities cannot be excluded for behaviors related to their disabilities.
Goss v. Lopez (1975)	Due process	Students who are suspended or expelled are entitled to due process.

Law/Court Case	Issue	Impact
Melissa S. v. School District of Pittsburgh (2006)	Use of time-outs	Students with disabilities can be placed in time-out if it is a normal procedure and if educational services are continued.
Ingraham v. Wright (1977)	Corporal punishment	Schools can use corporal punishment as long as the procedure is not "shocking to the conscience."
Vernonia School District v. Acton (1995)	Drug testing	Schools can require drug testing as a condition of student involvement in extracurricular activities.
JGS by Sterner v. Titusville Area School District (2010)	Physical restraint	Schools can use physical restraint if there are justifiable reasons and excessive force is not used.
Gottlieb v. Laurel Highlands School District (2001)	Physical restraint	Established a four-pronged test for the use of physical restraint.

that imposed on students in general, and student athletes have even fewer privacy rights. When a student joins a team, he or she must generally have a physical examination, obtain insurance, maintain a specific grade point average, and be willing to shower and change in a locker room. The Supreme Court ruled that drug testing for student athletes is reasonable and constitutional. The Court would later rule that a public school's mandatory drug testing of all students involved in extracurricular activities is also reasonable and does not violate the Fourth Amendment (*Board of Education v. Earls,* 2002).

Legal and Ethical Issues Related to Restraining Students

Sometimes it becomes necessary to restrain a student to protect the student from himself or to protect others from injury. Restraint is generally defined as any physical method of restricting an individual's freedom of movement (Mohr, LeBel, O'Halloran, & Preustch, 2010; Van Haren & Fiedler, 2004). Federal and state legislatures and courts allow physical restraint of students for therapeutic and risk prevention or as a response to imminent danger (McAfee, Schwilk, & Mitruski, 2006). The Council for Children with Behavioral Disorders has recommended that a student should be restrained only as a last resort, when the physical safety of the student or others is in immediate danger, and mechanical or chemical restraints should not be used; the council also notes that policies regarding the restraint of students should not be limited to special education but should be applied to all students (Peterson, Albrecht, & Johns, 2009). In order to minimize any potential for harm and any possible legal ramifications, teachers should be provided adequate training, supervision, and support to ensure that restraint procedures are used appropriately.

Restraint should be used as a protective procedure, and only in extreme circumstances, to prevent injury to students and teachers. Teachers "must use the safest method available, using the minimal amount of force necessary" when restraining students, and the restraint should be "discontinued as soon as possible" (Ryan & Peterson, 2004, p. 164). Excessive or prolonged restraint of a student is likely to be found illegal by the courts (Van Haren & Fiedler, 2004). However, courts are likely to uphold the use of more extreme or aversive interventions if there is justification for such actions. In *JGS by Sterner v. Titusville Area School District* (2010), JGS was a first grader with autism who had a history of verbal and physical outbursts that included screaming, profanity, threats of physical harm and violence, kicking, biting, and spitting on teachers and students. In February 2006, JGS stood up in the classroom and began screaming obscenities at other students. The class's paraprofessional tried to instruct JGS to stop yelling and return to his previous activity. When that was not successful, the paraprofessional put her hand over JGS's mouth for one or two seconds and instructed him to be quiet. When this failed, the paraprofessional removed the other students from the classroom while the teacher physically restrained JGS. Following the restraint, the teacher did not notice any ill effects in the child, such as choking or coughing, and JGS calmed down and took a nap. However, JGS's parents later contended that the paraprofessional had put hand sanitizer in her hand and held it over JGS's mouth and forced him to ingest it. The paraprofessional denied the allegation that she forced JGS to ingest liquid hand sanitizer, although she admitted that she used hand sanitizer through the day for sanitation purposes. The U.S. district court applied the four-pronged test established in *Gottlieb v. Laurel Highlands School District* (2001):

1. Was there a pedagogical justification for the use of force?

2. Was excessive force used to meet the legitimate objective in this situation?

3. Was the force applied in a good-faith effort to maintain or restore discipline, or maliciously and sadistically for the very purpose of causing harm?

4. Was there a serious injury?

The court determined that there was justification for the use of force, that excessive force was not used, that the paraprofessional and the teacher did not use force to cause harm, and that there was no serious injury. While the court maintained that forcing a student to ingest hand sanitizer could represent excessive force, there was insufficient evidence to support this claim. The teacher and the parents both maintained that JGS did not suffer any physical ill effects after the incident. As a result, the court ruled in favor of the school.

SUMMARY

Teachers have legal and ethical obligations toward the students in their classrooms. Teachers have the responsibility to teach children and to provide safe and secure environments in which learning can take place. Teachers have the responsibility not only to discipline students but also to teach students appropriate behavior. Beyond the traditional hierarchy of rules and consequences, teachers need to develop and implement behavior and classroom management plans that meet the behavior needs of all students in the classroom. A universal design for classroom management includes proactive, active, and reactive strategies for considering the different needs of students of both genders; students of diverse cultural, linguistic, and socioeconomic backgrounds; and students of all ability levels.

A number of laws and court decisions directly and indirectly affect the development and implementation of behavior and classroom management. The Individuals with Disabilities Education Improvement Act establishes procedures for disciplining students with disabilities and requires functional behavioral assessments and behavior intervention plans in certain instances. The Americans with Disabilities Act protects individuals with disabilities from discrimination in the workplace and at any public program or activity and guarantees accessibility at public places. Changes to this law have recently also affected Section 504 of the Rehabilitation Act, which protects students with disabilities from discrimination in any program receiving federal financial assistance. Additionally, a number of court decisions have balanced the rights of students against the needs of schools to maintain safe and secure learning environments.

It is important for teachers to understand the legal issues that may affect their development and implementation of effective behavior and classroom management. Noncompliance with the laws discussed in this chapter could result in violations of the rights of students, which do not end when they walk through the school door. Teachers' failure to adhere to these laws could also result in legal issues for schools and school personnel.

REVIEW ACTIVITIES

1. What are the advantages and disadvantages of developing and implementing a universal design for classroom management?

2. How are proactive, active, and reactive strategies different? Give examples of each.

3. What is the difference between treating all students equally and treating all students equitably?

4. How are IDEA, the Americans with Disabilities Act, and Section 504 similar? How are they different? How do these laws affect behavior and classroom management plans?

5. When does the "same treatment" rule apply to students with disabilities?

6. Under what conditions can a school suspend a student with disabilities? Under what conditions can a school expel a student with disabilities? Support your responses by citing legislation and court decisions.

7. Johnny, a high school senior, is wearing a shirt that says "All sinners will burn in hell" at school to protest the school district's decision not to include a brief prayer at the beginning of the commencement ceremony. Can school personnel require Johnny to remove his shirt? What court decisions support your response?

Visit the Student Study Site at www.sagepub.com/shepherd to access additional study tools including mobile-friendly eFlashcards and web quizzes as well as links to SAGE journal articles and web resources.

CHAPTER 3

COLLABORATING WITH PARENTS AND FAMILIES

After reading this chapter, you should be able to do the following:

- List some of the strategies teachers can use to establish positive relationships with students' parents and families.
- Describe the four interrelated elements of the family systems model.
- Describe the three concepts of family interaction and functioning levels.
- Summarize the eight family functions.
- Explain the family life cycle.
- Differentiate between family involvement and family engagement.
- List strategies for working with the parents and families of diverse students.
- Describe how academic optimism applies to teachers, families, and students.
- List the standards for professional relationships with students' parents.

UNDERSTANDING TODAY'S FAMILY

"It takes a village" is a phrase that is used extensively in connection with education, emphasizing the importance of teachers, administrators, parents, and community service providers working together to ensure the academic success of children in public schools. While the overuse of this African proverb has resulted in its diminished impact, the idea the phrase represents is still a crucial component of behavior and classroom management. Both Bronfenbrenner's ecological systems model and Bandura's social cognitive theory stress that a child's family and environment influence the child's behavior. Additionally, the concepts of universal design for classroom management, school-wide positive behavior support (Chapter 13), and wraparound services (Chapter 13) stress the involvement of the child's "village." Thus, it is important that teachers develop collaborative relationships with students' parents and other family members early on, even prior to the beginning of the school year. It is often too late for a teacher to develop a positive relationship with a student's parents if the teacher waits until that first parent–teacher conference or until an academic or behavioral concern arises.

The best strategy is for teachers to build parent–teacher relationships before they have a need to contact parents to address academic concerns or students' infringement of behavior expectations. When a teacher contacts parents for the first time because of a perceived problem, the parents may view the school as an unwelcoming and negative setting. Future phone calls may go unanswered, parents may not attend parent–teacher conferences, and the child's academic and behavior difficulties may be blamed on the teacher.

Demographics

Students in American schools today are increasingly diverse. It is predicted that by 2035, children of non–European American heritage will make up the majority of students in U.S. schools, and by 2040 they will represent 62% of the school population (National Center for Education Statistics, 2010). Hispanics make up both the largest and the fastest-growing group. The number of Hispanic children in the United States increased from 5.3 million in 1980 to 17.4 million in 2010 (Children's Defense Fund, 2012). Additionally, the number of English language learners increased from 4.1 million students in the 2002–2003 academic year to 4.7 million in the 2010–2011 academic year (National Center for Education Statistics, 2013).

Poverty has a significant impact on the emotional and behavioral development of children (Yoshikawa, Aber, & Beardslee, 2012). The proportion of children living in poverty in the United States increased from 15% in 2000 to 22% in 2013, and the proportion living in extreme poverty in 2013 was 9.8% (Amatea, Cholewa, & Mixon, 2012; Children's Defense Fund, 2013). With 12.4% of European American children, 39.1% of African American children, and 35% of Hispanic children living in poverty (Children's Defense Fund, 2012), teachers need to understand how poverty can affect academic performance and behavior.

Cultural Issues

With the increasing numbers of culturally and linguistically diverse students in today's classrooms, it is more essential than ever for teachers to establish relationships with their students' families. Teachers need to understand the cultural expectations of students' families and how to respond to the families in a culturally sensitive manner. Teachers need to remember that children acquire the values, beliefs, traditions, and languages of their cultures through interactions with their environments. Understanding the effects of enculturation and acculturation (see Chapter 1) may help teachers understand the cultures of their diverse students and help them to interact with students' parents. For example, Tom Yu, a first-generation Asian American student, is having academic difficulties in several of his classes. Many Asian American families take a collectivist view, focusing on the well-being and the needs of the whole rather than the individual. If an Asian American student is having academic difficulties, this may seem to be an affront to the family. In discussing Tom's academic difficulties with his parents, the teacher needs to be culturally sensitive. For example, the teacher may want to focus first on Tom's strengths: He participates well during group activities and always contributes to the group projects; he is always respectful and is especially helpful to other students needing assistance. Teachers should also keep in mind that the enculturation and acculturation of their diverse students' parents also play a role in the students' behaviors in the classroom.

ESTABLISHING RELATIONSHIPS WITH FAMILIES

Teachers can use a number of different strategies to establish positive relationships with the families of their students. Whatever strategies a teacher uses, it is a good practice to begin establishing these relationships prior to the beginning of the school year. Sending a postcard or an introductory letter two weeks prior to the start of school is a good way to lay the foundation for successful relationships with families. A postcard might simply give the teacher's name and include a message stating how much the teacher is looking forward to having the child in her classroom. An introductory letter could provide a little more information about the teacher and the goals for the year. By introducing themselves through postcards or letters in this way, teachers can take the first step in establishing what will become ongoing communication and collaboration with parents throughout the year (Dardig, 2005).

Establishing communication with parents at the start of the school year is only the beginning of the process. Teachers must engage in ongoing communication with their students' families. A teacher might create a monthly newsletter of class activities to keep parents and families informed about what is going on in their children's classroom. The teacher could also use the newsletter to share information about scheduled school events, such as conferences, and school activities in which students from the class are involved. The primary focus of the newsletter, however, should be the teacher's class and not the school.

Teachers should also send notes home when students are doing well academically (e.g., informing parents that their child received a good grade on a test or completed all assignments for the week) and when students have exhibited expected behaviors (e.g., praising students for never being late for class or for helping other students with assignments). Teachers might also make personal phone calls to parents or guardians to let them know how well their children are doing—this is an exceptional strategy for developing relationships with parents.

Teachers can also use electronic media to establish and maintain communications with students' parents and families. Many school websites provide space for teachers to set up their own home pages. Teachers might use these to post lists of assignments that are due for class as well as information about upcoming events and activities. Teachers should also provide parents with their school e-mail addresses. This is particularly important because many school websites are not very user-friendly, often requiring codes to access directories; some do not even make staff and faculty directories available. By giving students' parents their e-mail addresses, teachers enable the parents to contact them at the parents' convenience. Also, e-mails are a relatively nonintrusive, neutral means of facilitating communication between home and school.

CASE STUDY Jane and Mr. O'Neill

Jane is a third grader at Abydos Elementary School. Her teacher, Mr. O'Neill, recently noticed that Jane has not been completing her assignments, has not been interacting with peers, and seems withdrawn. Mr. O'Neill tried the basic intervention strategies (i.e., nonverbal and verbal interventions, redirection, and reinforcements), but nothing was effective in reducing Jane's academic and behavior difficulties.

Mr. O'Neill had previously established a good relationship with Jane's mother, Mrs. Gage, through positive communications (notes sent home, a classroom newsletter, e-mails, and phone calls), but now he felt that a face-to-face meeting was necessary. Unfortunately, from feedback he had received from Mrs. Gage, he knew it was going to be difficult to set up a face-to-face meeting with her because she was working two jobs: a day job at a grocery store and a night job at a fast-food restaurant. Mr. O'Neill decided to have dinner one night at the restaurant, hoping that he could talk to Mrs. Gage during her break.

Mr. O'Neill carried out his plan and was able to meet with Mrs. Gage at the restaurant. After he informed her about the change in Jane's academic performance and behavior, Mrs. Gage explained that Jane had been "feeling down" lately because of a number of school events. Earlier in the month, the school had held a father–daughter banquet, and next week students were to bring in parents to talk about their jobs during Parents' Day. These activities reminded Jane that she did not have a father—her dad, a marine, had died in a war 2 years ago.

As Parents' Day approached, Mr. O'Neill thought about what he could do to help Jane. As he tried to develop a strategy, he was in constant communication with Mrs. Gage. Finally, he thought he had a way to help Jane feel part of Parents' Day.

On Parents' Day, when the last of his students' parents had talked about her job, Mr. O'Neill went to the front of the classroom and opened the door. Three marines, wearing dress uniforms, and Mrs. Gage walked in. The marines stood at attention at the front of the classroom while Mrs. Gage sat in a chair near the front of the room that had been saved for her.

Mr. O'Neill called Jane to the front of the room. One of the marines came forward and crouched beside Jane. He addressed the class: "Jane's father was a soldier. He died 2 years ago in a war. He died protecting the freedom that we all have. He died so that parents could be here with their children today." The second marine came forward and presented Jane with a glass case containing a picture of her father in uniform and a folded American flag. A third marine, who had known Jane's father, came forward and told a couple of stories about Private Gage. Finally, the marines fell back in line and saluted Jane. Mr. O'Neill felt that on that day, Jane's father had attended Parents' Day.

With the increasing numbers of culturally and linguistically diverse students in today's classrooms, it is important that teachers quickly understand the backgrounds of their students. For example, if Maria's parents speak only Spanish, then sending home letters, notes, and newsletters in English will not help establish a relationship with Maria's family. Teachers should make every effort to have all such materials translated into the home languages of their students.

Teachers' strategies for building relationships with students' families need to go beyond the classroom setting. When teachers see their students and their families out in the community, they should make an effort to engage the parents in brief and friendly conversation. On these occasions there should be little to no discussion regarding the children's progress at school. These are opportunities to build rapport with parents.

If teachers are successful in establishing relationships with their students' parents from the beginning of the school year, when they need to contact the parents about academic or behavioral concerns, the parents are more likely to be receptive to the communication. When a student's behavior difficulties occur with some frequency, the teacher needs to involve the parents and the family in developing an intervention plan. Parents need to feel that their input is valued and that the teacher is as concerned about their child's academic success as they are. Parents need to know that the teacher cares.

There are times when no matter what strategy a teacher uses to establish rapport with parents, the parents will be unresponsive. Sometimes this is due to the parents' own experiences with schools when they were students. They remember schools as uninviting and inhospitable places. This does not mean that the teacher should quit trying to establish a relationship with the parents. Sometimes the teacher just needs to try harder. For example, Roberto's father never liked school. He was always in trouble as a student, and he never felt that anyone at school really cared about him. Now Roberto seems to be experiencing the same difficulties as his father. However, Mr. Salyers, Roberto's high school history teacher, continues to send positive notes home regarding Roberto's progress, even to the point of recommending certain colleges for Roberto, who is interested in a career in computer science. When he sees Roberto's father in the grocery store, Mr. Salyers approaches him and tells him how much he likes Roberto's creativity and spirit. Because of Mr. Salyers's repeated positive attempts, Roberto's father begins responding to the teacher. Communication is further expanded when Mr. Salyers encourages Roberto's other teachers to reach out to Roberto's father.

Again, there will be times when a teacher cannot establish a collaborative relationship with a student's parents no matter what strategy the teacher uses. Yet the teacher needs to continue to try. It is possible that the teacher's attempts may have a ripple effect, influencing a later relationship. For example, Mrs. Daily tried to communicate with Mayra's mother the entire academic year, but she never received any responses to her attempts. However, 2 years later, Mrs. Daily had Mayra's sister, Erika, in her class. Again, Mrs. Daily tried to establish positive communication with the mother. Remembering the communications she received from Mrs. Daily when Mayra was in her class, the mother was more open to communicating with Mrs. Daily regarding Erika.

Teachers need to realize that many of their diverse students' parents are dealing with a number of difficult conditions. Aside from issues of cultural identity, they may be socioeconomically disadvantaged, may have health problems, and so on. As in the ecological systems model, these factors influence how parents interact with their children's environment. These factors cannot be taken in isolation, and teachers need to understand the conditions from which their students come. While many of these factors are beyond teachers' ability to improve, by gaining an understanding of them, teachers may be better able to understand their students' families and, by extension, the students themselves.

A FAMILY SYSTEMS MODEL

The idea of teacher collaboration with students' families is aligned with Bronfenbrenner's (1979, 2005) concept of the mesosystem, in which home, school, neighborhood, and peers interact with one another. When the child interacts with school, peers, and neighborhood, the family develops reciprocal relationships with these environments through the child. Thus, the family is an interactive social system, and teachers need to take a family systems approach to working with families.

In the family systems model, the family is seen as an interrelated and interactive social system in which the events and experiences of each member of the family unit affect other members of the family. The model "considers communication and interaction patterns, separateness and connectedness, loyalty and independence, and adaptation to stress in the context of the whole as opposed to the individual in isolation" (Christian, 2006, p. 13). The family systems model can be illustrated as a mobile, a kinetic sculpture with a number of moving objects hanging from rods that take advantage of the principle of equilibrium. When one object in the mobile moves, it affects the other parts of the system, and they also move. This system will also pull the moving object back to the way it was before. Like family members, the objects in the mobile do not exist in isolation from one another.

Understanding family systems can help teachers better understand the interactions between students and their families and thereby meet the academic and behavior needs of their students and work collaboratively with families. A working knowledge of family systems can also enable teachers to understand the family dynamics of their culturally and linguistically diverse students.

The family systems model has four interrelated elements: family characteristics, family interaction, family functions, and family life cycle (Turnbull, Turnbull, Erwin, Soodak, & Shogren, 2011).

Family Characteristics

Definitions of *family* are as diverse as families themselves. The traditional, normative view of the family in the United States has been described as conjugal; this is the family that includes a husband, wife, and children. In some cultures, the common family form is consanguineal; these families include parents, children, and other related members. Such extended families are common among Hispanics, whose families may include grandparents, parents, and children living together in one household. Blended families—in which divorced parents remarry, bringing children from two former families together to form a new family—have become increasingly common. Family characteristics include all those qualities that make a family special and unique.

Each family member has a specific role and is expected to behave in a certain manner. The father may be the strong leader who guides the family through difficult times. The mother may be the nurturing member of the family, the person the children go to when they are upset or hurt. The older brother may be the responsible one, watching over his younger siblings and doing well in school. The sister may be the extrovert of the family, outgoing and friendly to everyone she meets. Another brother may be the athlete, and the youngest brother may be the "clown" of the family, always making everyone laugh. No matter what roles the various family members play, they affect each other, and if one member does not play his or her expected role, the family becomes imbalanced. Roles are also dynamic. As family members go through the various stages of the life cycle, their roles change; family members age, and children become adults and form their own families.

Family characteristics also include socioeconomic factors, cultural and linguistic backgrounds, the health of family members, family size, the presence of members with substance abuse problems, and the presence of members with disabilities. All of these factors can affect how a child interacts within the family, community, and school. For example, 9-year-old Randall has an older brother who has an intellectual disability. Randall's parents feel that somehow they are to blame for his brother's disability, so they spend an inordinate amount of time taking care of the brother. As a result, Randall feels neglected and unloved. He exhibits inappropriate behaviors at school to get attention from peers and teachers. School personnel inform Randall's parents of his behavior difficulties at school, which increases the stress level at home. The parents complain to Randall that they have enough problems taking care of his older brother, and that Randall should do what the teachers tell him to do. This leaves Randall feeling even more isolated at home, and his behavior at school escalates. The characteristics of the family affect the functioning level of the family members and how they interact with others both within and outside the family structure.

Family Interaction

Like the mobile with its many parts, the family as a whole is affected by the behaviors and characteristics of individual family members. The family members' reciprocal interactions contribute to the functioning level of the family. There are three basic concepts for understanding family interaction and functioning levels: family cohesion, family flexibility, and family communication.

Family Cohesion

Family cohesion is the emotional bonding or closeness that family members have toward each other (Ide, Dingmann, Cuevas, & Meehan, 2010; Olson, 2011). Three levels of family cohesion have been described: disengaged, balanced, and enmeshed. Families that are disengaged experience little emotional bonding. Children from disengaged families have difficulty trusting or respecting others and thus have difficulty developing healthy relationships.

Families that are at the other extreme of family cohesion are enmeshed. These families experience an excessive amount of emotional closeness. The parents may appear overly protective, and the children have little autonomy or independence. They may not have friends outside the family.

In families that have balanced cohesion, members develop caring and trusting relationships with one another and with individuals outside the family. Time with the family is important, but family members also have time with friends. Families that have balanced cohesion tend to be more functional than either disengaged or enmeshed families.

Family Flexibility

Family flexibility is the amount or degree of change that takes place in family leadership, role relationships, and relationship rules (Olson, 2011). Three levels of family flexibility have been described: rigid, balanced, and chaotic.

Families that are rigid have strictly enforced rules with no exceptions. Usually, one family member is in charge and wields nearly absolute control over other family members. For example, Samantha was late for dinner because she stayed after school to receive some tutoring in fractions, a subject in which she was having some difficulties. However, the family rule states that if anyone is late for dinner, that person does not receive a meal. Even though Samantha had a legitimate reason for being late, she did not have dinner that night. Families that are rigid have difficulty adjusting to changes and may become dysfunctional under stressful situations (Michael-Tsabari & Lavee, 2012).

Conversely, families that are chaotic have rules, but they are not consistently enforced. The parents do not set guidelines, and the roles in the family are unclear and constantly changing. For example, Jack is a very active 9-year-old. He is constantly in motion, from the moment he wakes up until he goes to bed. His younger brother, Daniel, is quiet and does not tax his parents' energy or patience. While Jack is required to go to bed at 8:00 p.m., which is the boys' established bedtime, Daniel is allowed to stay up 10:00. However, on many nights the parents do not enforce bedtime even for Jack.

In families that have balanced flexibility, rules are firmly enforced for all members of the family, but they are negotiated when circumstances require it. Family members are treated equitably. Family roles are adjusted to best meet the needs of the family in different situations. As with balanced cohesion, families that have balanced flexibility are more functional than families in which flexibility is rigid or chaotic.

Family Communication

Family communication encompasses the talking, listening, and understanding skills that family members use in facilitating levels of family cohesion and flexibility (Olson, 2011). Families at the extremes of cohesion and flexibility have poor communication skills. Communication in these families ranges from critical and harsh (rigid) to very little communication of any kind (disengaged). Families that have good communication skills generally fall within the balanced dimensions of cohesion and flexibility.

As we have noted, families that are balanced in their cohesion and flexibility are more likely to function well than are families in which extreme levels of cohesion and flexibility exist; children from the latter kinds of families may have difficulties interacting with family members and with people outside their families. The implication for teachers is that by gaining some understanding of their students' family dimensions, they may be able to develop strategies for engaging families in their children's education.

For example, if a teacher is dealing with a family displaying rigid flexibility, discussing the student's academic or behavior concerns with the parent who is not in charge may not yield any support from the family. The teacher will need to determine which parent is in control and specifically invite that individual to a conference.

Family Functions

Family functions are the routines, tasks, and activities individual family members perform to meet the members' diverse needs as well as those of the family as a unit. Aberrations of family functions can result in unmet familial needs and affect the development of children, resulting in academic and behavior difficulties

Figure 3.1 Family Interactions

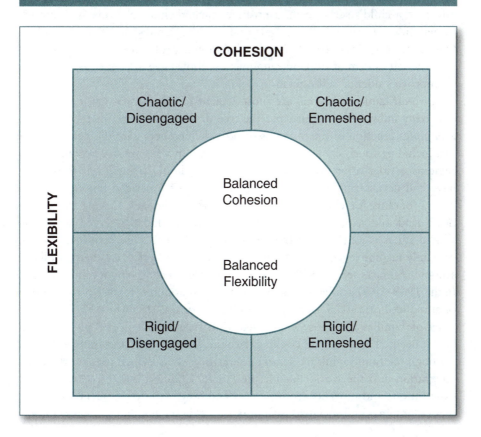

in school. Family functions may be broken down into eight types: affection, self-esteem, spiritual, economics, daily care, socialization, recreation, and education (Turnbull et al., 2011).

Affection is the emotional support family members receive from one another. A child's development is predicated on the interactions that occur between the child and the child's immediate environment. Families in which members show affection for one another provide children with a warm and nurturing environment. Affection can provide a foundation of love and trust that children will carry with them throughout their lives. Parental warmth and affection significantly affect children's psychological adjustment, development of positive dispositions across cultures, and development of prosocial skills (Khaleque, 2013). Children who experience parental affection are able to build positive relationships with peers and adults. *Self-esteem* is a sense of worth, or how an individual judges him- or herself. For students, self-esteem is a critical factor in academic achievement, behavior, and relationships with peers and adults. Just as a positive parent–child relationship can have a good affect on a child's self-esteem, a positive teacher–child relationship (support, availability, or approval) can also affect the child's self-esteem (Leflot, Onghena, & Colpin, 2010). Many educational professionals are concerned with the self-esteem of students, and many schools have implemented strategies to improve students' self-esteem.

Spiritual family functions are those related to religious or spiritual beliefs. For many individuals, culture and the role of the church are intertwined. The *economics* function of the family is to provide members with the necessities of life, including food, shelter, and clothing. Children who are not provided with these necessities often do not perform well in school. Rising levels of poverty have had devastating effects on the functioning of American families. School meal programs for children in need reflect these changes. During the 2011–2012 academic year, 59% of the five billion school lunches served across the United States were provided free of charge to children who qualified because of family income level; 9% were provided at reduced price. Of the two billion school breakfasts served, 84% were provided free of charge or at reduced price. In the 1969–1970 academic year, only 15% of school meals were provided free or at reduced price (U.S. Department of Agriculture, 2013). The *daily care* functions of families are those concerned with meeting members' physical and health needs. These include cooking, cleaning, health care, and transportation. Through the family, children learn *socialization* skills, which prepare them for integration into the world outside the family. Children initially learn societal expectations and morality from parents and other family members, preparing them to interact and socialize with others outside the family unit. *Recreation* is a quality-of-life component of family functioning. Families involved in recreational activities provide opportunities for members to interact positively with one another and with people outside the family. Families that provide opportunities for children to develop personal hobbies aid them in growing in multiple ways: expanding their knowledge, enabling them to feel the satisfaction and pride associated with developing skills, and creating opportunities for them to interact socially with others who have like interests. Children from families that engage in recreational activities are also more likely than other children to be involved in extracurricular activities in school. Finally, through their *education* function, families provide children with the knowledge, skills, and experiences to be successful in life.

Many family functions affect students' academic performance and behavior in school. Teachers have the opportunity to influence the well-being of students by supporting and encouraging many family functions. They may also be able to help families that are having difficulties with some family functions. By developing positive relationships with students' families, teachers might find that they can provide some families with needed resources and thus improve the children's academic performance and school behavior. For example, a teacher could provide information about an organization that provides free services in reading development for a parent with reading difficulties.

WHAT WOULD YOU DO? Ana

Ana is a student with mild intellectual disabilities in your seventh-grade English class. You have been following the accommodations listed in her individualized education program, and Ana has been making modest progress; however, recently she has had academic difficulties, and you are concerned about her behavior. Ana has begun bringing a doll to school, and she gets upset when you try to take it from her. She has been defecating in the classroom, and you have had to call her mother several times to bring clean clothes for Ana. After a conference with Ana's mother, it has been decided that some additional clothing for Ana will remain at school, and when she has one of her "accidents" she will go the laundry room with a paraprofessional and wash her clothes. However, this has not alleviated the problem, and Ana has developed new atypical behaviors. She has begun isolating herself increasingly, and she no longer likes being patted on the back. At another conference, the team members ask Ana's mother if anything has changed at home, but the mother adamantly denies that anything is different. One of the team members asks if the father is involved in Ana's life. The mother responds that he works all the time and doesn't have time to deal with Ana's problems at school.

Considering the family systems model, what do you think needs to be done to help Ana?

Family Life Cycle

Every family goes through a life cycle. According to Carter and McGoldrick (1999), the **family life cycle** is composed of developmental stages that families pass through, from childhood to retirement. At each stage, family members gain knowledge, skills, and experiences that prepare them for the challenges of life. If individuals do not gain the skills, knowledge, and experiences associated with a given stage, they can transition to the next stage, but they are more likely to have difficulties with relationships and subsequent transitions to the later stages. Additionally, individual development can occur only through strong emotional relationships with significant individuals. The family is often where these significant relationships begin (McGoldrick, Carter, & Garcia-Preto, 2011).

The family life cycle is influenced by a number of factors, one of which is culture. Extended family forms are common in many cultures, and this factor can affect the framework of the developmental stages of the family. However, through acculturation—that is, adoption of the values, beliefs, and traditions of another culture—the family cycle is altered after several generations.

The family life cycle is also influenced by the time in which the individual lives. The attitudes, beliefs, and values of individuals who grew up during the 1960s are profoundly different from those of individuals growing up today. For example, interracial marriages are more commonplace and accepted today than they were in the 1960s.

The family life cycle has the following eight developmental stages (see Figure 3.2):

1. Childhood

2. Leaving home

3. Unattached adult

4. New couple

5. Family with young children

6. Family with adolescents

7. Launching children

8. Later life

The transitions from stage to stage are unique for every individual who traverses the life cycle.

Figure 3.2 Family Life Cycle

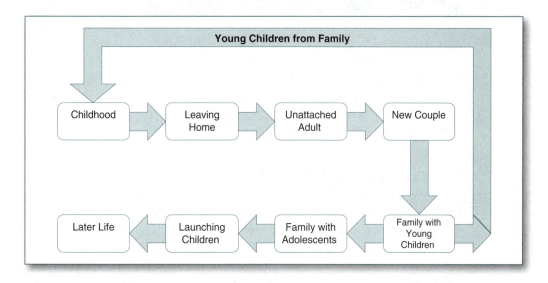

Family Life Cycle Stages

The *childhood* stage reflects the microsystem in ecological systems theory (Bronfenbrenner, 1979, 2005). The family is the epicenter of the child's life, and the child's development hinges on the interactions that occur within the family. It is through the childhood stage that children learn concepts, rules, boundaries, and expectations of the family. At the *leaving home* stage, the individual becomes independent from the family and develops adult relationships with parents. It is at this stage that the individual begins a career and develops financial independence. The *unattached adult* develops adult and intimate relationships with peers. When two individuals decide to marry, they enter the *new couple* stage. The couple learn to live together, and the relationships of each with family members, adult friends, and childhood friends are adjusted to include the spouse. When the couple decide to have a child, the family system is adjusted to make space for the child. The *family with young children* changes the dynamics of the extended family to include child-rearing roles for parents and grandparents. As the children grow older, the family transitions into the *family with adolescents* stage. At this stage, the relationships between the parents and the children change to allow adolescents to have more autonomy but still retain the support of the family. Parents begin to shift their focus from their children to their spouses and their careers. They also begin providing more care and attention to their own parents, their children's grandparents.

The adult children leave during the *launching children* stage and begin their own lives. The parents now have adult relationships with their children and their children's spouses, as well as relationships with their grandchildren. Additionally, the parents have to adjust to being a couple again, and they may have to contend with the deaths of their own parents.

In the final stage of the family life cycle, *later life,* parents have to cope with their own declining physical and mental functions, and also experience the loss of spouses, siblings, and peers. Parents at this stage often reflect upon their lives and begin thinking about death. Their children become the center of the family unit (McGoldrick et al., 2011).

FAMILY INVOLVEMENT AND ENGAGEMENT

Family involvement and family engagement are two different approaches that teachers can take in working with students' families (Ferlazzo, 2011). **Family involvement** tends to be one-sided: Teachers inform parents about how they can contribute to fulfilling their children's academic and behavior needs, and parental response or feedback is seldom necessary. For example, a teacher contacts parents about homework assignments and asks parents to make sure time is set aside at home for students to complete their homework. The family involvement approach is often not conducive to reciprocal communication between teachers and families.

In contrast, **family engagement** encourages reciprocal communication between teachers and families. Teachers actively seek input from families regarding the children's academic and behavior needs. In most instances, parents are the experts on their children. For example, when an individualized education program is being developed for a student, the parents need to be engaged in the process. The parents need to provide input regarding what they see as their child's strengths and needs, and they should help to determine the goals that will be set forth in the IEP. At these types of meetings, school personnel need to listen to parents' concerns and seek to understand the dreams the parents have for their children.

Teachers can take a family engagement approach in many other instances as well. For example, when meeting with parents on parent–teacher night, teachers often inform parents how their children are succeeding in school, but many do not also seek parental feedback. At these meetings, teachers could encourage parent engagement by asking questions and actively listening to the parents' responses. The teacher's goal in taking the family engagement approach is to gain collaborative partners (Ferlazzo, 2011).

Teachers do not have to choose either family involvement or family engagement. Each has its place in working with families, and many schools generally pursue both approaches. Teachers need to know which approach is the best practice to use in communicating and working with parents in different situations, and which approach is appropriate for obtaining the desired outcomes from interactions with parents.

WORKING WITH DIVERSE FAMILIES

Currently, 83% of teachers in the United States are European American females (National Center for Education Statistics, 2010)—a proportion that is hardly reflective of today's student population. Many of these teachers have little understanding of the lives of families that are culturally and linguistically different from themselves, or of the lives of families living in poverty. Efforts to address the academic and behavior concerns of diverse students are likely to be ineffective unless teachers understand the impact of poverty (Wiley, Brigham, Kauffman, & Bogan, 2013). They often view these families as dysfunctional and blame them for their children's academic and behavior problems (Hyland & Heuschkel, 2010). Given that students whose families are involved in their education often have higher academic achievement and fewer behavior difficulties than do students whose families are not so involved, it is imperative that teachers engage the families of culturally and linguistically diverse students. Teachers need to be culturally responsive to their students' families.

For some European American teachers, becoming culturally responsive to the families of their culturally and linguistically diverse students can be difficult. They often do not understand how their perceptions of diverse families, or of families of low income, affect how they interact with parents. Teachers first need to understand their own culture; however, many European Americans seldom evaluate their own culture. Cultural self-awareness is a key element in a person's consideration of the cultures of other groups. Teachers then need to have some knowledge of their students' cultures and, by extension, the cultures of their families. While teacher education programs try to prepare new teachers for working with diverse students and families, many preservice teachers give little thought to interacting with diverse families (Uludag, 2008). Once teachers have explored their own culture and how their beliefs affect their interactions with the families of diverse students, they can use several strategies to help engage parents of diverse students. We discuss some of these below.

Maintaining High Expectations

Some teachers perceive culturally and linguistically diverse students as lacking intelligence, having little interest in academics, and causing behavior problems.

They blame diverse students and their parents for the students' poor academic achievement and behavior difficulties (Amatea et al., 2012). Parents expect teachers to care about their children and want the best for them. If parents perceive that teachers do not think their children are capable of success in school, this sets up a barrier that makes it very difficult for teachers to establish collaborative relationships with the parents. Teachers should demonstrate to both students and their parents that they have high expectations of *all* students.

Avoiding Stereotypes

Teachers need to discard their preconceived notions of diverse students and families and see beyond the stereotypes. It is important for teachers to gain an in-depth understanding of the cultures of students and their families so that they can avoid the misconceptions of stereotypes. Teachers often do not understand the lack of involvement or lack of communication skills they observe in some of the parents of diverse students. For example, while most European Americans speak in a straightforward manner to convey information, many Asian Americans engage in more indirect communication. This is simply a form of politeness. Additionally, many Asian American cultures prefer to maintain harmony with others. Filipino Americans practice *pakikisama* to create group harmony. *Pakikisama* is getting along with others even if it conflicts with one's own desires. Chinese Americans also prefer to maintain harmony by conforming to societal expectations. Both groups often use shame or a sense of propriety as a means of creating conformity (Van Campen & Russell, 2010). Teachers may sometimes view these cultural differences in communicating as parents' lack of concern for their children's education, when in fact Asian American parents view their children's educational success as extremely important.

A Family Affair

The families of children from some cultures may view parent–teacher conferences, school activities, and even special education conferences as invitations to participation by all family members and friends. It is not unusual for aunts and uncles to show up with the parents at a conference to discuss a child's individualized education program or for close family friends to accompany parents to a parent–teacher conference. Teachers should make sure that there are enough chairs and materials to accommodate these extended families (Christian, 2006).

Family Engagement

Teachers need to build partnerships with parents by engaging them in school activities. Establishing culture afternoons at school, where parents are invited to talk about their cultures, is one strategy for encouraging engagement. Such gatherings might include the sharing of information on what kinds of foods the participants eat that are unique to their culture, or what activities their families take part in that are culturally based. For example, a breakfast taco blends the American breakfast of eggs, potatoes, and bacon with Mexican tortillas, cheese, and salsa. In some parts of Texas, this is called a breakfast taco, while in other parts it is called a breakfast burrito, and in Laredo, it is called a mariachi (Vine, 2011).

It is crucial for teachers to involve and engage parents in their children's education. Research has shown that students whose parents are involved in their education—including culturally and linguistically diverse students—have higher academic outcomes and fewer behavior difficulties. Teachers need to make the effort to understand their own cultures and beliefs, learn about the cultures of their students, and develop strategies for interacting with diverse families.

FAMILY INVOLVEMENT IN ACADEMIC OPTIMISM

One of the most important—but often ignored—dispositions of highly effective teachers is academic optimism. **Academic optimism** encompasses a teacher's belief that he or she can make a difference in the academic performance of students, academic emphasis, and trust between the teacher and family (Hoy, Tarter, & Woolfolk Hoy, 2006; Woolfolk Hoy, Hoy, & Kurz, 2008). The first component of academic optimism, teacher self-efficacy, has always been an important factor in students' academic achievement. When teachers believe that they can successfully affect student learning, even with students who have behavior difficulties, they are more effective teachers, and students' academic achievement increases. Teachers with a high sense of self-efficacy also are more resilient; they are more likely to continue to be effective teachers despite minor setbacks.

The second component of academic optimism is academic emphasis, which includes high academic expectations of students and a safe and secure classroom environment in which learning can take place (Hoy et al., 2006)—the mantra for behavior and classroom management. Academic emphasis is the implementation of innovative teaching strategies designed to increase student engagement in appropriate academic tasks (Beard, Hoy, & Woolfolk Hoy, 2010). Teachers with a high sense of self-efficacy are more likely to use innovative strategies, which generally result in higher academic achievement of students, which intrinsically reinforces teachers' self-efficacy.

The final component of academic optimism is trust between the teacher and the family. Trust is an essential element in the development of positive relationships among teachers, students, and parents. Students trust teachers to provide a safe environment in which they can learn, express opinions and beliefs, and receive needed academic and behavior support. Teachers trust students to do the best they can on assignments and activities, respect others, and behave in a manner that promotes learning in the classroom. Parents trust teachers to have the best interests of their children at heart. Parents want their children's teachers to care about their children and want their children to succeed. Teachers trust parents to be involved in their children's education at school and at home. High levels of perceived teacher caring, parent educational involvement, and perceived student potential result in higher teacher–family trust (Bower, Bowen, & Powers, 2011).

The three components of academic optimism interact and reinforce one another (see Figure 3.3). Academic optimism is one of the few organizational

Figure 3.3 Elements of Academic Optimism

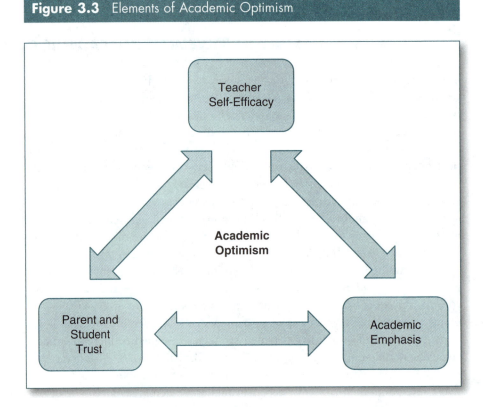

characteristics that affects student achievement when socioeconomic status is considered, promoting high levels of achievement and appropriate behavior (Beard et al., 2010).

STANDARDS FOR FAMILY RELATIONSHIPS

The Council for Exceptional Children (2008) has established the following professional practice standards for relationships between teachers and their students' parents. While these standards were developed specifically for special education teachers, they can easily be adapted for use by all teachers.

1. Teachers develop effective communication with parents, avoiding educational terminology, using the primary language of the home, and other modes of communication when appropriate.

2. Teachers involve parents in all aspects of the education of their children.

3. Teachers maintain communications between parents with appropriate respect for privacy and confidentiality.

4. Teachers provide opportunities for parent education by providing educational information through materials, workshops, and online resources.

5. Teachers inform parents of the educational rights of their children and of any proposed or actual practices that violate those rights.

6. Teachers recognize and respect cultural and linguistic diversities that exist in some families.

7. Teachers recognize that the relationship of home and community environmental conditions affects the behavior and outlook of students. (p. 3)

SUMMARY

Working with students' parents and families is a critical component of behavior and classroom management. The best strategy is for the teacher to begin developing positive parent–teacher relationships before the need arises to contact parents in regard to any academic or behavior concerns. With the increasing numbers of culturally and linguistically diverse students in U.S. schools today, it is more essential than ever that teachers establish positive relationships with their students' families.

There are a number of strategies that teachers can use to establish positive relationships with the families of students in their classrooms, and these strategies need to go beyond the classroom setting. They should include proactive and reactive strategies aimed at developing collaborative relationships.

Understanding the family systems model can help teachers better understand the interactions between students and their families. The four interrelated and interactive elements of this model are family characteristics, family interaction, family functions, and family life cycle. Family characteristics define the family in terms of roles and factors that affect how the student interacts within the family, community, and school. Family interaction—which includes family cohesion, family flexibility, and family communication—contributes to the functioning level of the family. Family functions are the routines, tasks, and activities that meet the needs of the family. The family life cycle includes developmental stages that families pass through, from childhood to retirement.

Family involvement and family engagement are two approaches that teachers can take in working with parents and families. Family involvement is usually a one-sided approach in which teachers inform parents how they can contribute to their children's education, with little reciprocal communication from parents. Family engagement, in contrast, encourages parents and families to participate more actively in their children's education. Both approaches are useful in increasing parental involvement.

Teachers need to use culturally responsive strategies when communicating with families of diverse students. Cultural self-awareness is a key element in teachers' efforts to consider the cultures of their students and their students' families. Teachers need to maintain high expectations for all students, avoid stereotypes, include extended families in various student-related activities and events, and engage diverse parents in school activities.

An important disposition of highly effective teachers is academic optimism, which encompasses a teacher's belief that he or she can make a difference in the academic performance of students, academic emphasis, and trust between the teacher and family. Trust is an essential element in the development of positive relationships among teachers, students, and parents. Parents want their children's teachers to care about their children and want their children to succeed.

By understanding the characteristics and the diverse needs of families, and by maintaining professional standards for family relationships, teachers can develop positive, reciprocal relationships with their students' parents and other family members, and this in turn can improve the academic performance and behavior of all students. By taking a proactive approach to developing family and parent relationships, teachers can establish effective partnerships between themselves and their students' families.

1. Develop a plan for establishing positive relationships with the families and parents of your students. Remember to consider the different aspects of culture, including socioeconomic status, in your plan.

2. Generally, the parents who attend parent–teacher nights are those whose children do not have any academic or behavior difficulties. What could you do to encourage the parents of children with difficulties at school to attend parent–teacher nights?

3. Examine your own culture, and then examine your preconceptions of the culturally and linguistically diverse students in your classroom.

Visit the Student Study Site at **www.sagepub.com/shepherd** to access additional study tools including mobile-friendly eFlashcards and web quizzes as well as links to SAGE journal articles and web resources.

CHAPTER 4
ROLE OF THE TEACHER

After reading this chapter, you should be able to do the following:

- List and describe some of the responsibilities of the professional teacher.
- Analyze the importance of ethical behavior from the viewpoints of teachers and the community.
- Describe how behavior and classroom management programs can affect the professional self-esteem of teachers.

Since colonial times, when only the privileged attended schools, and since the creation of truly inclusive one-room schools, the ultimate goal for teachers has been to educate children—to provide them with the skills and knowledge they need to be successful in life. While curricula and strategies have changed over the centuries, behavior and classroom management has always been a concern of teachers. Early headmasters administered strict discipline for minor infractions of school rules and expectations. Corporal punishment was the accepted norm until the late 20th century (31 U.S. states have now abolished corporal punishment in public schools, while 19 still allow it; Morones, 2013). It has long been understood that a setting conducive to learning is necessary for education to be successful. As a result, teachers have always had the legal, moral, and ethical responsibility to maintain an environment in which learning can take place.

During the past 50 years, behavior and classroom management has become a major concern for teachers, administrators, and students' families. With the increase in aggression and violence in today's schools, creating and maintaining a safe and secure school environment is an even more urgent issue. In fact, during school shootings, many teachers have risked their own lives to protect the children under their care (see Table 4.1).

Simply put, teachers are responsible for maintaining the behaviors of their students. In many ways, this is an oxymoron. No one can control the behavior of others, which would seem to indicate that behavior and classroom management plans are doomed to fail by the very nature of human behavior. Human beings will behave in a certain manner only if they deem it to be in their best interest to do so; this includes complying with the rules and expectations of society. This is why it is crucial that teachers employ effective behavior and classroom management plans.

Understanding the theoretical aspects of behavior is the foundation for developing applications and strategies for modifying an individual's behavior. For example, Jesse knows that if he runs a stoplight, he may receive a ticket for violating the law. If he does not pay the ticket, he may lose his driver's license or go to jail. Thus, logically, Jesse will not run the stoplight and risk the chance of getting a ticket or going to jail. Yet people often run stoplights despite the possible consequences. Why? To answer this question, we must understand the function, or cause, of the behavior.

Behavior and classroom management has changed considerably since the days when headmasters slapped the back of a student's hand with a ruler for minor infractions. Today's teachers need to have an understanding of behavior theories and strategies and consider the needs of students from cultural and

Table 4.1 Some Recent School Shootings

School	Date	Outcomes
Taft Union High School	January 10, 2013	1 student injured Shooter convinced to surrender by teacher
Sandy Hook Elementary School	December 14, 2012	20 students killed Staff members killed trying to protect students
Perry Hall High School	August 27, 2012	1 student injured Shooter subdued by guidance counselor and teachers
Chardon High School	February 27, 2012	3 students killed, 2 injured Shooter chased from school by teacher/coach
Deer Creek Middle School	February 23, 2010	2 students injured Shooter subdued by teacher
Pine Middle School	March 14, 2006	2 students injured Shooter subdued by teacher
Columbine High School	April 20, 1999	12 students and 1 teacher killed; 21 injured Shooters committed suicide
Frontier Middle School	February 2, 1996	2 students and 1 teacher killed Shooter subdued by gym coach

linguistically diverse backgrounds, students with physical disabilities, students with learning disabilities, and gifted students. Today's teachers need to use a universal design for classroom management to develop effective behavior and classroom management programs that meet the academic and behavior needs of all students. Without such programs, teachers have difficulty teaching students the skills and knowledge they need to be successful in life. Without effective behavior and classroom management plans, teachers cannot carry out their primary function: teaching.

RESPONSIBILITIES OF THE PROFESSIONAL TEACHER

The responsibilities of teachers are contingent on the many different roles of teachers. Obviously, the first and foremost responsibility of teachers is to teach. Teachers are expected to be proficient in the content areas in which they teach. However, teaching is more than just conveying subject matter to students. Teachers are facilitators of learning, and pedagogy is the method through which they provide students with the information and the strategies they need to master the subject. Teachers who act as facilitators share some of the decision-making process with students, in contrast to autocratic teachers, who control everything that occurs in the classroom (Harmer, 2007). Pedagogy is the art of teaching. Teachers need to establish reciprocal communication with students, understand the different modes in which learning takes place, and teach lessons that are relevant to the students (Löfström & Poom-Valickis, 2013). The pedagogical approach to teaching also requires teachers to consider how culture, linguistics, cognitive abilities, socioeconomic status, and home environment affect student learning.

Disciplinarian is another role that teachers play, and while the term is a bit archaic, parents, politicians, and others outside education see the maintenance of discipline as a major responsibility of teachers. Generally, a disciplinarian strictly enforces rules and hands out punishment to students who break those rules. However, rather than disciplinarians, today's teachers need to be behavior managers. Teachers establish classroom rules and a hierarchy of consequences and rewards to assist in managing student behavior. Teachers also need to consider the academic and behavior needs of all students within their classrooms when developing behavior and classroom management plans. A universal design for classroom management should consider the differential needs of students of both genders, students of diverse cultures and languages, and students of all ability levels.

Another responsibility of teachers as behavior managers is to create safe and secure environments in which learning can take place. Without effective behavior and classroom management plans, teachers would be unable to meet their primary responsibility, which is to teach. Teachers should also create environments where students feel safe to express their opinions and where they are not afraid to try and fail. Behavior and classroom management plans should be designed to meet the academic, behavioral, emotional, and social needs of all students, using proactive, active, and reactive strategies.

CASE STUDY   Kale and Mrs. Fisher

Mrs. Fisher was standing outside her classroom door monitoring the hallway at Lili'uokalani Elementary School when Kale, one of her third-grade students, walked past her. Mrs. Fisher greeted her cheerfully, but Kale, who was usually friendly and upbeat, did not respond. She seemed dejected. Before Mrs. Fisher could pursue the matter with Kale, Kaiko and Tua came around the corner, walking toward Kale. The two boys were also third-grade students in Mrs. Fisher's class, and while they were sometimes rambunctious, they were generally polite and followed classroom expectations.

When the paths of the three children converged, Kaiko crossed his eyes at Kale and said, "Dork!" Tua laughed at the remark. Kale quickened her pace and continued around the corner toward the cafeteria. Kaiko and Tua, still laughing, approached Mrs. Fisher's classroom.

When the boys reached her, she firmly instructed them to go into the classroom. When they had seated themselves at their desks, Mrs. Fisher asked why they had called Kale names. Looking slightly embarrassed, Tua responded, "We were just kidding with Kale."

"Yeah," agreed Kaiko. "Kale just got glasses, and we were just giving her a hard time."

"Do you know how that probably makes her feel?" Mrs. Fisher asked the two boys. "You probably hurt her feelings terribly."

Kaiko and Tua stated that they did not mean to hurt Kale's feelings—they were just playing around. Mrs. Fisher reminded them that everyone in school wants to feel safe and accepted. Did they think that Kale felt safe and accepted?

Both boys admitted that Kale probably did not feel safe and accepted, and they agreed to apologize to her. After the boys left to find Kale, Mrs. Fisher knew she also needed to talk to her. Kale had gotten glasses for the first time just a couple of days ago, and she was sure that Kale was feeling very self-conscious about wearing them. Mrs. Fisher pulled her own glasses out of her desk drawer and decided she would talk to Kale about how cool it is to wear glasses.

Bullying has become a growing concern is today's schools and can create a climate of fear and intimidation (Mehta, Cornell, Fan, & Gregory, 2013). Bullying is defined as any unwanted, aggressive behavior with the intent to harm that involves a real or perceived power imbalance (Olweus, 1993). In addition to physical attacks, bullying can include name-calling, making threats, spreading rumors, and excluding individuals from a group on purpose. Cyberbullying is an extension of bullying. Cyberbullying has been defined as aggressive behavior carried out repeatedly through electronic means by an individual or group against a victim who cannot easily defend him- or herself (Smith et al., 2008). Cyberbullying can include mean text messages, rumors posted on social networking sites, and embarrassing pictures and videos.

In both bullying and cyberbullying, a power imbalance exists. Because bullying results from this power imbalance instead of from deficits in social skills, it is difficult to implement interventions to reduce or eliminate bullying in schools (Whitted & Dupper, 2005).

Strategies to prevent bullying must include interventions designed to change the culture and climate of the school (Whitted & Dupper, 2005). This can be accomplished through the development and implementation of a school-wide positive behavior support program (see Chapter 13). Schools need procedures in place that can guarantee a safe and positive environment for all students. As part of a universal design for classroom management, strategies should be in place to prevent bullying and cyberbullying. School personnel need to take the following steps:

1. Establish a culture of inclusion and respect for all students.

2. Make sure students interact safely. Teachers and staff need to supervise areas throughout the school, including those in which bullying is likely to take place (bathrooms, playgrounds, and cafeteria).

3. Become actively involved in the prevention of bullying.

4. Set a tone of respect in the classroom. (U.S. Department of Health and Human Services, n.d.)

Planning is another responsibility of teachers. Teachers need to create engaging lessons with appropriate materials that are well prepared and relevant to students' lives. By considering the interests and instructional needs of all students, teachers can create lessons that meet the academic need of students and prevent off-task behaviors. Managing content is a component of effective behavior and classroom management.

Teachers also assess student assignments and tests; however, grading papers is only the beginning of the process. Teachers should analyze the results of assignments to determine whether the lessons are conveying the information students need to complete their assignments successfully. Upon reflection, teachers may discover that they need to alter some lessons to better meet the needs of their students. Teachers should also evaluate their behavior and classroom management plans for effectiveness. For example, if the consequences for violating a classroom rule are not effective in reducing the inappropriate behavior, the teacher should consider why it is not effective and then change the consequences accordingly.

Teachers need to remain current in the field by attending professional development workshops, taking classes, and reading professional journals. Unfortunately, due to time and financial restraints, this is an often-ignored responsibility of teachers. Teachers must recognize that through professional development, they can learn the latest best practices, strategies, and interventions for teaching and behavior management. Teachers have a responsibility to be lifelong learners. They should not use the same lesson plans, the same activities, or the same books over and over again for a number of years. Teachers have a responsibility to be dynamic in their field. School districts and state legislators have the obligation to provide teachers with the resources and funding they need to help them remain current in the field through school-based teacher training and professional development at conferences for educators.

Teachers have the responsibility to understand their students' cultural backgrounds. Understanding students' cultures may help teachers develop meaningful lessons and appropriate behavior and classroom management plans. It may also help teachers interact with the families of diverse students. Understanding the cultural backgrounds of students and how diversity affects behavior and academic performances is the first step toward developing culturally responsive teaching and culturally responsive classroom management.

Many teachers focus on nurturing and protecting their students (Thomas & Beauchamp, 2011), filling the role of counselor or surrogate parent. Many of today's students are raising themselves and their siblings because their parents are working two or more jobs, or one parent is absent from the home. Positive adult contact is crucial to the development of well-balanced children, and teachers can often provide such contact (Bullough, 2011).

In addition to the responsibilities noted above, teachers take on duties such as serving as chaperones at extracurricular activities and monitoring student behavior during lunch and recess periods. However, many of these duties are extensions of their two primary responsibilities: teaching and behavior management.

ETHICAL CONSIDERATIONS

Teachers live in glass houses. Whether at school, the grocery store, church, or a restaurant, teachers are often viewed by parents and students as individuals who should be held to the highest ethical and moral standards. Teachers' behaviors are often scrutinized, especially outside the classroom setting. While they may complain about the lack of privacy, teachers are public figures who are trusted with children of the community, and this public scrutiny is part of the job. Therefore, it is interesting that despite this public trust, there is no formal code of ethics for teachers.

While organizations such as the National Education Association, the Council for Exceptional Children, and the Association of American Educators have developed codes of conduct for teachers, these codes are very general and not enforceable. Additionally, most U.S. states have developed codes of ethics for their teachers. Teacher candidates are introduced to and encouraged to familiarize themselves with the codes of ethics for teachers in their states during their teacher preparation programs.

A code of ethics for professional educators should ensure high standards of practice, protect the public, and guide educators in making decisions (Barrett, Casey, Visser, & Headley, 2012). Extrapolating from the codes of ethics for teachers published by the three organizations noted above, a professional educator code of ethics might include the following:

- The professional educator creates a safe and secure learning environment that helps students reach their full potential.
- The professional educator treats all students equitably.
- The professional educator protects students from conditions harmful to learning, health, or safety.
- The professional educator will not intentionally expose students to embarrassment or disparagement.
- The professional educator will not use professional relationships with students for private advantage.
- The professional educator will make efforts to understand and respect the values and traditions of the diverse cultures of students, students' parents and families, and the community.
- The professional educator will comply with written local school policies, applicable laws and regulations, and codes of ethics.
- The professional educator will maintain a high level of competence and integrity in the classroom, the school, and the community.
- The professional educator will be a lifelong learner and remain current in the latest best practices, strategies, and interventions for teaching and behavior management. (see Association of American Educators, 2013; Council for Exceptional Children, 2008; National Education Association, 2013)

Social networking has changed how many individuals communicate and has become a normal part of social life. However, many preservice teachers and current teachers do not fully understand the possible consequences of publishing personal information on social networking sites (Foulger, Ewbank, Kay, Popp, & Carter, 2009). Teachers and administrators have also been struggling with the ethical and moral implications associated with social networking. Teachers have been disciplined and even dismissed from their positions for posting negative comments on social networking sites. Again, teachers need to realize that their lives are scrutinized by students, parents, and community members who expect them to exhibit a high level of ethical behavior both within and outside the classroom. Teachers need to be careful what they publish, as well as what others publish, on their social networking pages. For example, one preservice teacher was denied a teaching certificate because of a photo posted on MySpace depicting her as a "drunken pirate" (Read, 2007). At one university, more than 75% of elementary education majors who had public profiles posted inappropriate materials on Facebook (Olson, Clough, & Penning, 2009). It is becoming commonplace for prospective employers to check out the social network pages of job applicants.

Further, because of the nature of social networking, it can make it easy for teachers to cross boundaries of intimacy in teacher–student relationships (Preston, 2011). This can lead to ethical and legal ramifications for the teacher and reflects poorly on the profession as a whole. While there are many academic benefits to using social networks for communication among teachers, students, and parents, teachers need to be careful to keep these relationships strictly professional. One course of action a teacher might take is to not allow any student access to any of the teacher's personal social network accounts. A teacher might set up a dedicated account to help students with academic questions or concerns, but only if this is allowed under written school policies governing social networking.

WHAT WOULD YOU DO? Storm

Storm is an eighth-grade student at Hammond Middle School. She has been having academic difficulties in her algebra class and has been receiving one-on-one instruction from Mr. Thomas. During these sessions, she has confided to Mr. Thomas that as an adopted child, she often feels unwanted by her parents. She has told him that sometimes she feels very much alone. Mr. Thomas, who knows that Storm's adoptive parents are very concerned about her well-being, suggested that she try talking to them and explaining how she feels. Storm's response was that her parents do not understand her as well as Mr. Thomas understands her.

Like half of the people in the United States, Mr. Thomas has a personal Facebook account. While on Facebook one night after he and Storm talked, he received a request from Storm asking him to accept her as a friend.

If you were Mr. Thomas, what would you do about Storm's request?

PROFESSIONAL SELF-ESTEEM OF THE TEACHER

Professional self-esteem is an individual's belief in his or her worth and acceptance in a work-related position. High professional self-esteem is extremely important for teachers because it provides them with a higher purpose and creates an enthusiastic attachment with their profession (Tabassum & Ali, 2012). Teachers with high self-esteem are more optimistic, resilient, and effective than teachers with lower self-esteem. Teachers with high professional self-esteem are not discouraged by isolated incidents of failure. In contrast, teachers with low professional self-esteem perceive their value as insignificant and believe that colleagues do not accept them. Lack of respect and acceptance by colleagues is a factor associated with stress and burnout in teachers. Teachers experiencing burnout try to get by with doing the bare minimum (Leiter & Maslach, 2005).

Low professional self-esteem can lead to depersonalization and reduced personal accomplishments. **Depersonalization** is sometimes expressed as a detached attitude that teachers feel toward their job, students, and other teachers. Teachers who suffer from **reduced personal accomplishments** feel that they cannot accomplish anything, believe they cannot make a difference in the lives of their students, and feel incompetent (Fernet, Guay, Senécal, & Austin, 2012).

Problems with classroom management affect teachers' professional self-esteem and contribute to teacher stress and burnout. When teachers do not have effective behavior and classroom management plans in place, off-task behaviors increase and teachers spend a considerable amount of time trying to manage student behavior instead of teaching. Additionally, reactive classroom management strategies significantly increase teacher stress (Clunies-Ross, Little, & Kienhuis, 2008).

While developing a universal design for classroom management may increase a teacher's preparation time prior to and during the academic year, the proactive and active strategies of the UDCM will increase teacher efficacy in classroom management. This efficacy will lead to an increase in the teacher's professional self-esteem and a reduction in the kinds of stress that can lead to depersonalization, reduced personal accomplishments, and burnout. An effective behavior and classroom management plan will also reduce off-task behaviors and allow the teacher to spend more time teaching.

SUMMARY

Today's teachers have many roles and responsibilities. Their primary responsibility is to educate students; they need to be proficient in the content areas in which they teach and understand how to teach these areas. Today's teachers are expected to maintain appropriate behavior in their classrooms and to provide safe and secure environments in which learning can take place. They need to have an understanding of behavior theories and strategies, and they need to consider the needs of all students, including culturally and linguistically diverse students, students with physical disabilities, students with learning disabilities, and gifted students. Teachers need to be able to create engaging lessons that consider the interests and instructional needs of all students in their classrooms. Teachers need to be reflective practitioners. They need to evaluate their lessons and classroom management strategies for effectiveness. Teachers also need to be lifelong learners and maintain expertise in their field of education. Finally, teachers have the responsibility to understand their students' cultural backgrounds and develop culturally responsive lessons and classroom management plans.

Teachers' behaviors, both inside and outside the classroom setting, are often scrutinized by students, parents, and the community. Despite the lack of a formal code of ethics for teachers, teachers are held to high ethical and moral standards. The use of social networking has become a growing source of concern for teachers and administrators, and teachers need to be careful what they and others publish on their social networking sites.

Teachers with high professional self-esteem competently fulfill their roles and their responsibilities to students and parents. Teachers with low professional self-esteem may experience stress and burnout due to depersonalization and reduced personal accomplishments. Effective behavior and classroom management plans allow teachers to spend more time teaching and help them to maintain a sense of high self-worth and accomplishment.

REVIEW ACTIVITIES

1. Write your own code of ethics for teachers.

2. Develop a policy for social networking for teachers. Explain your rationale for your policy.

3. Is it fair for students, parents, and communities to hold teachers to a higher ethical and moral standard than they apply to other professionals, even for behavior outside the classroom setting? Support your position.

4. What are the responsibilities of the professional teacher?

Visit the Student Study Site at **www.sagepub.com/shepherd** to access additional study tools including mobile-friendly eFlashcards and web quizzes as well as links to SAGE journal articles and web resources.

CHAPTER 5

THE LEARNING ENVIRONMENT

After reading this chapter, you should be able to do the following:

- Identify what factors should be considered in decisions regarding the physical setup of a classroom.
- Distinguish between rules and routines and describe how each contributes to an effective learning environment.
- Describe a variety of ways to arrange student desks and the benefits of each arrangement.
- Explain the importance of classroom schedules and transitions to the learning environment.
- Summarize the behavioral models developed by Canter, Ginott, Kounin, and Jones.
- Understand how effective teaching behaviors can have a positive impact on the learning environment.

Creating a safe and secure classroom environment that is welcoming to students and conducive to their learning is one of the most critical tasks for a teacher. As part of a universal design for classroom management, it is a task that begins before students enter the classroom. Planning for the learning environment involves both the physical setup of the classroom and the establishment of rules and routines that enhance student learning.

PHYSICAL SETUP OF THE CLASSROOM

Students spend a majority of their day in the classroom, often spending more time at school than at home. The classroom needs to be a welcoming and stimulating place, and an environment that fosters student learning. This begins with the planning of the physical arrangement of the classroom. The teacher needs to plan for setting up and organizing the classroom. Specifically, the teacher needs to consider the physical arrangement of the teacher's desk and supplies, student desks (including students' access to their supplies), technology and other equipment (computers, whiteboards, projectors, and so on), other furniture (such as cabinets and bookcases), and any other spaces, such as library/reading corners or rugs for circle time.

In the planning of classroom space, the locations of the teacher's desk, storage cabinets, and bookcases are important, because supplies and books need to be readily available to both the teacher and the students. The supplies that are used most often should be placed closest to the teacher and students. Other materials that are used less often can be stored in closets and bookcases that are farther away.

The placement of the teacher's desk should be considered carefully. It needs to be easily accessible to children, but it should be in a nonprominent place, such as off to the side or in the back of the room. Remember, highly effective teachers are not seated at their desks very often; rather, they are walking around the room interacting with students and providing feedback. This proximity control allows teachers to move closer to students displaying behavior difficulties, which is sometimes all that is needed to redirect these students to the task at hand. However, during those moments when teachers are seated behind their desks, they should have an unobstructed view of the classroom so they can monitor student progress and behavior.

Some classroom environmental variables, such as temperature and lighting, may not be directly under the teacher's control. Working with the principal and the custodial staff, the teacher needs to make sure that students come into a classroom that has a comfortable temperature and adequate lighting for the activities in which they will participate.

One feature that a teacher most definitely has considerable influence over is the physical arrangement of furniture and spaces in the classroom. When arranging the classroom environment, the first things the teacher needs to consider are the parts of the classroom that cannot be moved. For example, whiteboards/chalkboards may be permanently attached to walls, and computers may need to be in certain places because of the locations of electrical outlets.

Four factors should help the teacher determine the spatial layout of the classroom: visibility, movement, minimization of distractions, and personal spaces. *Visibility* means that the teacher can see all of the students and all of the students can see the teacher. Also, the teacher needs to ensure that students are seated in such a way that they can see lesson presentations. Materials that are posted should also be in plain view for all students. Teacher proximity is a part of visibility as well. The teacher needs to make sure that she is close enough to students to provide assistance to those who need it or to redirect potentially inappropriate behavior.

Movement means that both the teacher and students can move easily around the classroom when necessary. The teacher needs to make sure that areas that receive a lot of traffic (e.g., the teacher's desk, the wastebasket, assignment boxes, the pencil sharpener) can accommodate larger numbers of students. The classroom should have ample walkways so that students and teacher are not bumping into each other or interrupting students working at their desks. This "bump" factor can be a catalyst for potential behavior difficulties (Trussell, 2008).

Minimization of distractions means the elimination of attention-diverting elements so that students can remain actively involved in the academic task. Potential distractions include windows and doors through which students may see movement. The teacher needs to consider how to arrange the classroom so as to minimize such distractions.

Finally, the teacher and students need their own *personal spaces*. These may take the form of desks or study carrels. Students should be taught to respect the personal spaces of other students, including the belongings within those spaces, as well as the personal space of the teacher's desk. Likewise, the teacher should respect students' personal spaces. The concept of personal space also applies to the amount of space individuals need between themselves and others in order to feel comfortable, and teachers should be aware that these amounts vary among cultures. For example, for most European Americans, the amount of personal space needed for comfort is about two feet; some Native Americans, in contrast, require a greater amount of personal space. Maintaining a respectful distance when communicating with Native Americans is important, and Native Americans may feel insulted or uncomfortable if their need for personal space is disregarded.

The teacher should arrange the physical environment of the classroom in a way that supports the goals of providing a safe and secure learning environment, preventing a number of inappropriate behaviors, and promoting the learning of all students. A well-structured classroom can improve the academic and behavior outcomes of students, and an important part of such a classroom is the seating arrangement. The arrangement of students' seating in the classroom deserves the teacher's attention because research has found that students' seating locations are related to academic achievement and classroom participation; further, they influence interactions between students and teachers (Fernandes, Huang, & Rinaldo, 2011).

Advantages of Rows, Clusters, and Semicircles

The effectiveness of classroom seating arrangements depends on the nature of the interactions that teachers plan to have with their students. As part of the management of content, the physical environment of the classroom should be arranged to reflect the academic task and the desired behavior (e.g., independent work, class discussion). When arranging student desks and the teacher's desk, the teacher needs to keep in mind that the teacher should be able to make eye contact with every student and have easy access to each student.

No single arrangement of student desks is better than any other, but it is important for teachers to remember that seating arrangements can have a significant impact on student behavior, so they should consider carefully how student desks are placed (Wannarka & Ruhl, 2008). This may be of particular importance in inclusive settings where students have a wide variety of academic, behavioral, and social characteristics. Seating arrangements should be designed in accordance with the needs of the students and the teaching style of the teacher. Room logistics, students' personalities, and amounts and types of interactions should also be considered. Further, seating arrangements should take into account the size of the classroom; the numbers and ages of students; the types of chairs, desks, and tables available; and the activities planned.

Student desks might be arranged in rows, clusters, or semicircles (often called U shapes). The most traditional approach to classroom seating is to organize student desks in rows and columns (see Figure 5.1). This arrangement increases "on-task behaviour and/or decrease[s] off-task behaviour when students [are] expected to work on their own" (Wannarka & Ruhl, 2008, p. 90). Teachers may be able to manage inappropriate behavior more effectively during independent seatwork by arranging students in rows and columns (Bicard, Ervin, Bicard, & Baylot-Casey, 2012). This arrangement also facilitates the introduction of new materials and testing (Betoret & Artiga, 2004). While rows and columns may facilitate the monitoring of independent student work, this arrangement may not facilitate whole-class discussion because students seated in the front of the classroom will have a harder time hearing the contributions of their peers seated at the back. Finally, if students seated in rows are asked to engage in discussion or an activity with peers in pairs or small groups, this arrangement may result in a disruption of the lesson because students are not sure with whom they should work (Bonus & Riordan, 1998).

Other possible arrangements involve setting student desks in groups. These include clusters of groups (see Figure 5.2) and semicircular or U-shaped arrangements (see Figure 5.3). These types of arrangements are most appropriate when the academic tasks involve high levels of interaction between teacher and students and among students. Cluster seating arrangements allow for

Figure 5.1 Rows and Columns Seating Arrangement

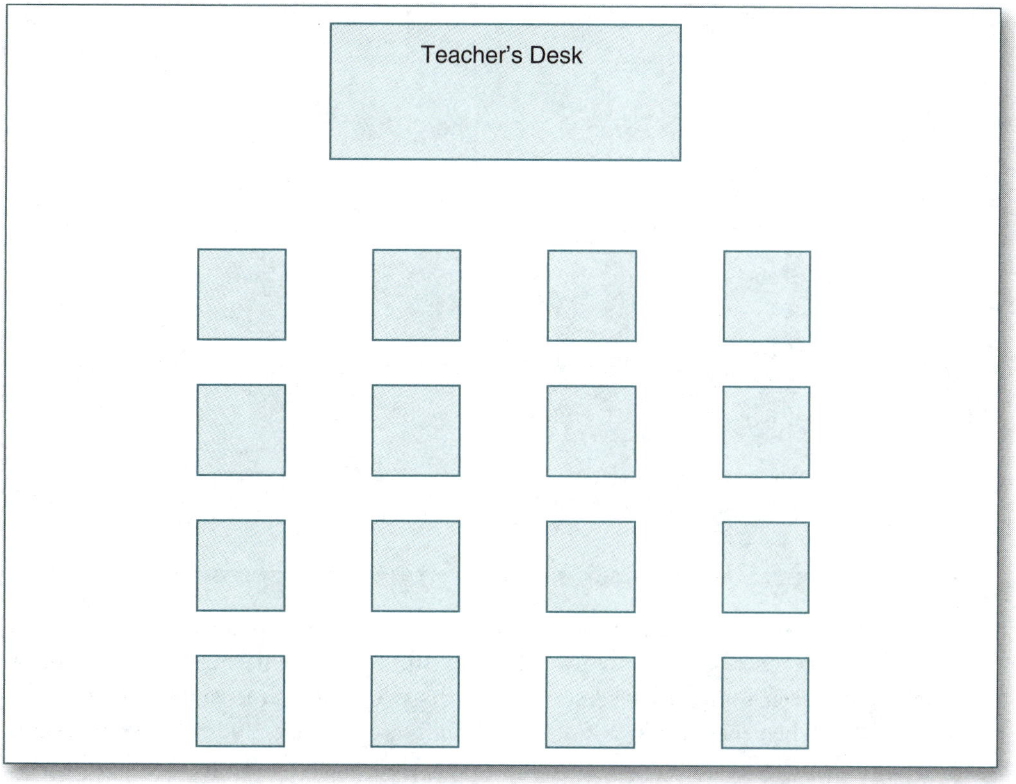

Figure 5.2 Cluster Seating Arrangement

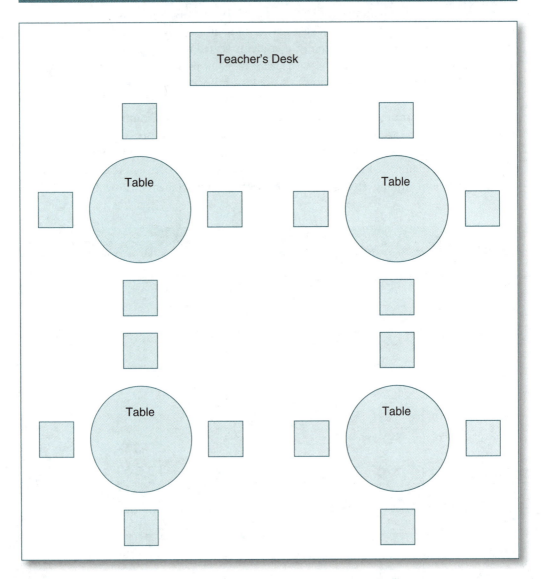

student–student interaction, while semicircle seating arrangements allow for both teacher–student interaction and student–student interaction. Students have been found to ask more questions when they are seated in semicircles than when they are in rows (Marx, Fuhrer, & Hartig, 2000). Students seated in semicircles and rows produce work that is of the same quality, but the quantity of completed work increases when students are seated in rows

Figure 5.3 Semicircle/U-Shaped Seating Arrangement

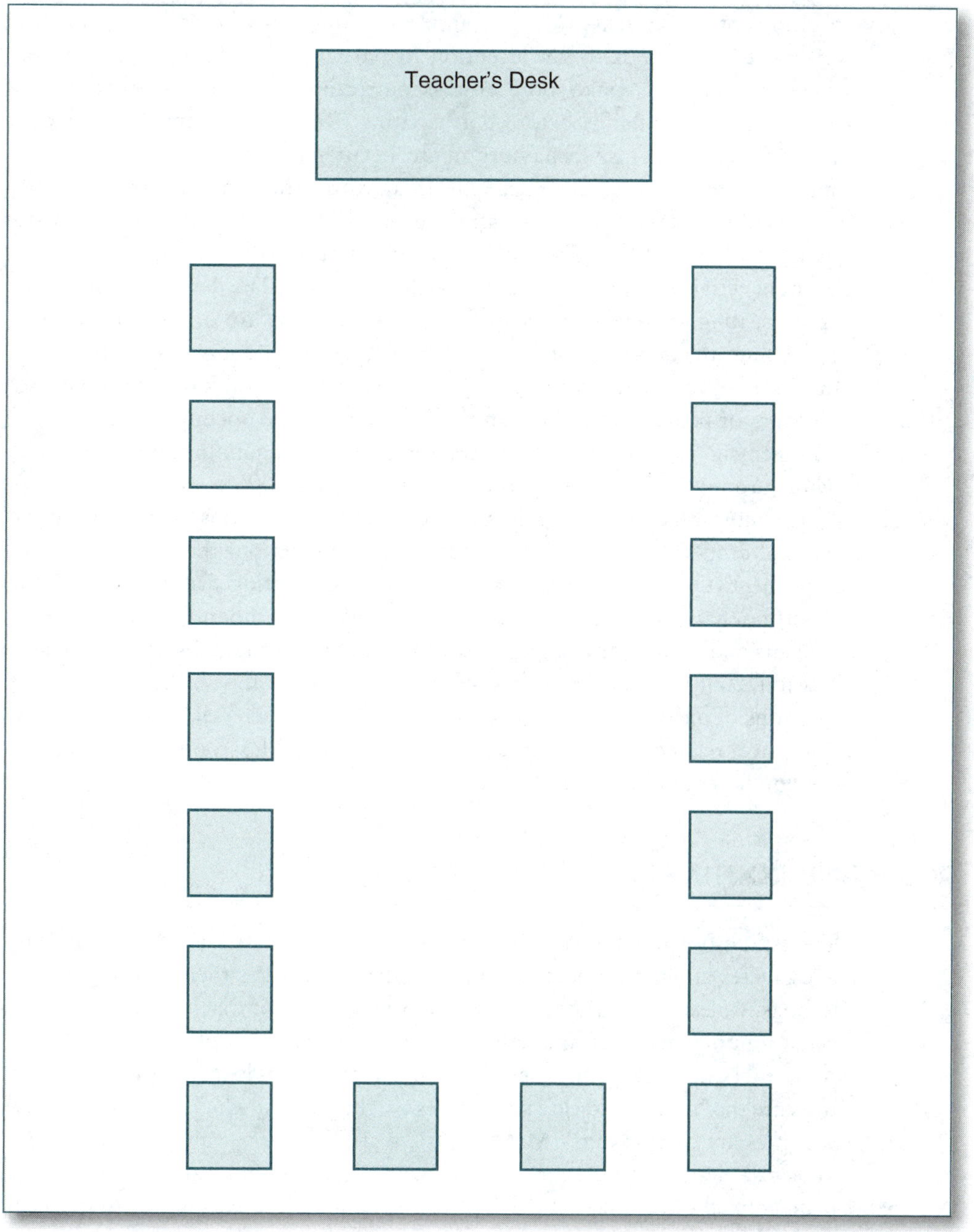

(Bennett & Blundell, 1983). Clustered desks and semicircle groups are useful when the task requires brainstorming, collaboration, or asking questions because these arrangements facilitate interaction due to the proximity and positions of the students (Marx et al., 2000). Students who are seated in clusters raise their hands to get attention to participate in discussions, whereas those in semicircles make more on-task out-of-order comments—that is, they do not raise their hands before participating (Rosenfield, Lambert, & Black, 1985). Finally, off-task behaviors might occur more frequently with cluster and semicircle seating arrangements than with other seating arrangements; however, in these arrangements students can hear one another during discussions and have adequate space to work with each other during cooperative learning activities and share materials (Bonus & Riordan, 1998). Additionally, group seating arrangements help the teacher to be aware of movement while still being able to promote student participation and discussion (Kaya & Burgess, 2007). Finally, small groups offer students social interaction with set numbers of people (only those in their groups), while opening up the seating arrangement to a semicircle allows for increased communication with the whole group (Betoret & Artiga, 2004; Marx et al., 2000).

The most effective seating arrangement for a classroom is dependent on the types of academic tasks and the nature of the interactions the teacher plans to implement. Once the types of activities and the seating arrangement of the classroom have been determined, the teacher needs to monitor the behavior of students and modify or change the seating arrangement if necessary (Wannarka & Ruhl, 2008). Regardless of the seating arrangement the teacher chooses, the locations of individual students should be considered as well, as "seating locations are related to academic achievement and classroom participation" (Fernandes et al., 2011, p. 66).

RULES AND ROUTINES

The establishment of rules and routines allows the classroom to run smoothly and creates an environment for students that maximizes their learning opportunities. Rules and routines are part of a proactive approach to behavior and classroom management and can help prevent behavior problems in the classroom (Shook, 2012). Rules serve as guidelines for student behavior, and routines are the "daily operating procedures . . . the ways in which noninstructional activities are carried out" (Meese, 2001, p. 102). As integral components of a universal design for classroom management, rules and routines should be planned well in advance of the first day of school. The teacher should discuss these rules and routines with students on the first day of class, asking for their input to give students ownership in what occurs in their classroom. The students should then practice these rules and routines during the first weeks of the school year.

While **rules** are an essential element of behavior and classroom management, they must be integrated as part of a comprehensive plan (Little & Akin-Little, 2008). Generally, the number of rules should be kept to a minimum; a maximum of five rules is recommended. Rules should be stated simply and positively; that is, they should tell students what to do rather than what not to do. They should be very specific and should describe behavior that is observable and measurable (Little & Akin-Little, 2003). For example, "Respect others" is a better rule than "Don't hit anyone." The teacher should introduce the rules to students and explain what behaviors each rules encompasses. For example, "Respect others" would elicit a discussion about the types of behaviors students and teacher use (or do not use) when they show respect for each other. Next, the teacher should post the rules (along with the lists of rewards and consequences for compliance and noncompliance) in a visible place in the classroom. Students should be given many opportunities to practice following the rules, especially during the first weeks of the school year, and should be rewarded for doing so. A classroom without clear and consistent rules and expectations is likely to encourage behavior difficulties.

Routines, or procedures, help create an orderly environment in the classroom. Like rules, they should be planned in advance by the teacher and taught and practiced by students. Teachers should establish routines in the following areas: beginning and ending the day (e.g., taking attendance and copying homework), distributing and collecting materials, handing in work, using the restroom and water fountain, requesting help, and finishing work early (Meese, 2001). Additionally, routines should establish how students work independently in small groups and during whole-class activities.

SCHEDULES AND TRANSITIONS

While rules and routines help students know what is expected of them, schedules help students know what to expect during the instructional day and during particular class periods. Transitions help students move through the schedule of activities effortlessly and with minimum distractions. Along with rules and routines, a predictable schedule and effective transitions enhance classroom management so that the teacher is able to teach and the students are able to learn.

Schedules

Scheduling is a proactive strategy that teachers can control to help maintain a safe and secure classroom environment. Schedules help structure the learning environment to support students so that they can function more independently in the classroom (Meadan, Ostrosky, Triplett, Micha, & Fettig, 2011). Unscheduled time can result in off-task and disruptive behaviors (Trussell, 2008). Students are more productive and their learning is enhanced if they are provided with a schedule of weekly and daily activities (Kamps, 2002). Schedules also allow teachers to convey to students what is expected of them, which helps them development greater independence and responsibility (Downing & Peckham-Hardin, 2001). Finally, schedules for students require teachers to use effective organizational skills in planning weekly and daily activities (Short, Short, & Blanton, 1994).

An effective classroom schedule fuses basic structure with flexibility. Flexibility in the schedule permits the teacher to respond to unforeseen events, such as a canceled computer class or an early dismissal (Downing & Peckham-Hardin, 2001). Weekly schedules should also include time slots for activities that take place outside the classroom, such as recess, lunch, and physical education. Daily schedules should include the activities that take place throughout the day and weekly activities. Having schedules helps students prepare, organize, and communicate about their day and its activities, both in school and at home (Downing & Peckham-Hardin, 2001). Teachers should post daily and weekly schedules in accessible and visible places in their classrooms, and students should be advised of any changes to schedules ahead of time (Reutzel & Clark, 2011).

For students with exceptionalities, schedules may be very individualized. Daily schedules may have to be broken down into smaller periods, such as morning and afternoon schedules. If students participate in activities or classes outside the inclusive classroom, such as speech therapy or resource room, these need to be addressed in their schedules. In such cases, teachers might find it helpful to tape individual students' schedules to the students' desks. Schedules for students with exceptionalities may utilize real objects, photographs, or drawings, or they may be part of students' notebooks (Meadan et al., 2011). Some students will require portable schedules to take with them as they move throughout the school day. Finally, teachers may want to consider using schedules that are integrated into technology such as iPods or tablets.

Regardless of the form a weekly or daily classroom schedule takes, students may need verbal and nonverbal reminders about schedules as they progress through the day or week. Such reminders encourage students to maintain on-task behavior and to manage their time wisely. Finally, smooth transitions from one activity to another will ensure that students complete tasks in a timely manner so as to adhere to the schedule.

Transitions

Transitions are intervals of time during which students move from one lesson or activity to another, usually after the teacher has given the indication to do so. Successful transitions between lessons or activities are fast, with clear beginnings and endings, and they reduce the amount of downtime between activities. Effective transitions help the teacher to minimize disruptions, increase instructional time, and maintain optimal learning conditions (Cangelosi, 2000).

Several of the strategies previously discussed in this chapter can help to facilitate quick transitions. For example, if the teacher has planned the classroom's physical arrangement so that it facilitates student movement, a transition that requires students to move from one area of the classroom to another will be carried out efficiently. Additionally, if the teacher has carefully considered where supplies are stored in the classroom, so that needed materials are close at hand and students can access them quickly and easily, transitions between activities or lessons can be achieved with a minimum of disruption. Likewise, if the teacher has a routine for taking attendance in place, then the transition from taking attendance to the first lesson of the day will be accomplished smoothly. Also, if there is a rule concerning the use of "inside voices" in the classroom, then potential disruptions might be avoided because students are quietly getting out the materials for the next lesson or moving quietly to the next learning center. Finally, if the daily schedule is posted, students will know which activity is next and will probably know how to transition to it. Thus, the teacher can manage effective transitions through careful planning of the physical environment of the classroom and through the establishment of rules, routines, and schedules.

Teaching students when and how to perform transitions helps to alleviate the issues that sometimes surround transitions, such as students not knowing where to go or what to do (McIntosh, Herman, Sanford, McGraw, & Kira, 2004). Teachers should model the appropriate way for students to transition between activities and then have students practice it. Teachers might also consider giving students a consistent signal when it is time to transition. As with routines, visual supports or cues, such as pictures, symbols, or tape on the floor, help students move from one activity to another (McIntosh et al., 2004;

Winterman & Sapina, 2002). The teacher should give the signal for a transition in advance, so that students have prior notice as well as enough time to wrap up what they are working on and prepare for the next task. Once the transition has started, the teacher should give students enough time to finish the transition so that they are ready for the next activity or set of instructions. The teacher should circulate among students during transition times to answer student questions, help them get materials ready for the next lesson or activity, and minimize any disruptions (Burden, 2003).

Active supervision is a technique that enables teachers to monitor students during classroom transitions and in nonclassroom settings. It encompasses three basic teacher behaviors: scanning, moving, and interacting. *Scanning* involves examining the overall classroom environment for both appropriate and inappropriate behaviors. *Moving* consists of walking around the classroom or other setting—making the teacher's presence known to the students. In *interacting*, the teacher engages with students by providing positive reinforcement and redirection (McIntosh et al., 2004).

CASE STUDY   Ms. Contreras

Ms. Contreras has just graduated from a teacher preparation program at her local university, and she is very excited about her first year as a third-grade teacher. She remembers from her course work and field experiences that she will need to first consider how she wants to set up her learning environment so that students are able to engage in the lessons. Ms. Contreras believes that students learn best through social interaction, and she knows that her students will spend the majority of their time in cooperative learning groups. She decides to arrange the student desks in small groups throughout the classroom. After she has organized the physical space in her classroom, she walks around it several times, ensuring that students can move about the classroom safely, have their own personal spaces, and can access materials readily.

Ms. Contreras also knows that she must set expectations for student behavior by establishing rules and routines for her classroom to run smoothly. For example, one of her rules is *Raise your hand for permission to leave your seat.* Likewise, she plans what her classroom's routines will be for passing out materials, handing in homework, lining up to leave the classroom, and getting ready to go home.

Finally, Ms. Contreras understands that the most effective component of a classroom management plan is the planning and delivering of engaging lessons that meet the academic, social, and emotional needs of her students. She carefully studies the content standards, curricula, and textbooks for all the subjects she will be teaching and plans lessons carefully.

BEHAVIORAL MANAGEMENT MODELS

Schools and classroom teachers have traditionally used several different behavior management models in addressing the behavior of students. The models examined here are those developed by Lee Canter, Haim Ginott, Jacob Kounin, and Fred Jones.

Lee Canter

Initially developed by Lee Canter and Marlene Canter (1992), assertive discipline is a systematic behavioral management plan that helps teachers be consistent with behavioral expectations and provides appropriate consequences for student behavior. The model has been modified throughout the years. The original model focused on the development and retention of teachers as strong leaders in the classroom; more recently, it has focused on student needs and on teaching students how to behave appropriately (Malmgren, Trezek, & Paul, 2005). This behavioral management model places great emphasis on "catching students being good" and then providing them with feedback and reinforcement (Canter & Canter, 2001). In other words, it is a teacher-centered model, because classroom discipline depends on how the teacher responds to inappropriate behavior. The model also states that teachers have a right to teach in well-managed classrooms and students have a right to learn in structured environments. To that end, teachers can be trained to manage behavior in a classroom setting.

Canter and Canter (1992) present five steps for teachers using assertive discipline. First, teachers must recognize that they can and do have an effect on student behavior in the classroom. Second, teachers should learn to display an assertive response style, which is the most effective style that they can have. Third, teachers should develop discipline plans that contain good rules and clear consequences. Fourth, teachers should provide students with instruction concerning their discipline plans. Finally, teachers should provide students with instruction on how to behave appropriately.

Teachers using the assertive discipline model should "establish a systematic discipline plan prior to the start of the school year and then communicate expectations and consequences to the students immediately" (Malmgren et al., 2005, p. 36). The four components of assertive discipline assist the teacher in the setup of the discipline plan. First, the teacher establishes a set of rules that are fair, firm, and consistent. Second, the teacher determines ahead of time the consequences for students who follow the rules. Along these lines, the teacher also predetermines consequences for students who do not follow the rules. Finally, the teacher determines how to implement the plan with students (Canter & Canter, 2001). Teaching the discipline model to students is approached in the same manner as any other academic content, with a series of lessons that teach the plan: First, the teacher explains the reasons for the rules; second, the teacher teaches the rules and checks for student understanding of the rules; third, the teacher explains the supportive feedback that students who follow the rules will receive and the consequences that students who do not follow the rules will receive; and finally, the teacher checks again for understanding on the part of the students (Canter & Canter, 2001).

The assertive discipline model can be applied to any classroom situation at any grade level. The teacher can decide on expectations and consequences that are appropriate for the ages of the students they serve. This model may be particularly suited to students in secondary classrooms, where some teachers may hold the erroneous belief that adolescents already understand what is expected of them and will choose to exhibit appropriate classroom behaviors (Malmgren et al., 2005).

WHAT WOULD YOU DO?   Mrs. Garza

You are a special education teacher for students with mild disabilities at Washington Middle School. Mrs. Garza, a math teacher, has complained to you that Avery, one of your students with a learning disability in reading, has been disrupting her classroom. Avery has not been a problem in other general education classrooms, so you have agreed to observe him in Mrs. Garza's class to determine the reason for his behavior difficulties.

During Mrs. Garza's class, you notice Avery talking to the girl seated at the desk next to his. Mrs. Garza warns Avery that if he continues to talk, he will have his name written on the board; she then continues with her lesson. A few minutes later, Avery is talking again. Mrs. Garza warns him a second time that if he continues to talk, he will get his name on the board. This pattern continues for another 10 minutes, with Mrs. Garza warning Avery each time he talks that he will get his name on the board. The fifth time it happens, you hear a student next to you mutter to another student that Avery should have had checkmarks by his name by now and sent to the principal's office.

What do you think is the reason for Avery's noncompliance? What would you say in discussing this with Mrs. Garza?

Haim Ginott

Haim Ginott was a clinical psychologist and parent educator. Among his publications are the books *Between Parent and Child* (1965), *Between Parent and Teenager* (1969), and *Teacher and Child* (1972). Ginott believed that teachers are an essential element in classroom management and that teachers who demonstrate self-discipline serve as models for students. According to Ginott (1972), the foundation of communication from teacher to student is for the teacher to talk to the situation, not to the student's character or personality. He illustrates this with an example of a child who spills paint. The teacher could respond in either of two ways: The teacher could attack the child, accusing her of clumsiness and reprimanding her for being careless, or, conversely, the teacher could acknowledge that paint has been spilled and suggest that it needs to be cleaned up. The second option addresses the situation and is the preferred form of communication. This kind of positive communication by teachers in dealing with students has been found to improve students' self-concepts, which in turn produces better classroom discipline (Martella, Nelson, Marchand-Martella, & O'Reilly, 2012). Finally, Ginott's (1972) work suggests that teachers can create classrooms with "congruent communication" by doing three things: modeling communication that is consistent with students' emotions and environment, using cooperative learning techniques, and using discipline instead of punishment.

Ginott's theories were very popular during the 1970s and are still influential today, as evidenced by the fact that he is still often quoted, as in a 2009/2010 issue of *Phi Delta Kappan*:

> I've come to a frightening conclusion that I am the decisive element in the classroom. It's my personal approach that creates the climate. It's my daily mood that makes the weather. As a teacher, I have tremendous power to make a child's life miserable or joyous. I can be a tool of torture or an instrument of inspiration. I can humiliate or humor, hurt or heal. In all situations, it is my response that decides whether a crisis will be escalated or de-escalated and a child humanized or dehumanized.

Jacob Kounin

Jacob Kounin (1970) developed a behavioral management model based on research he conducted in the late 1950s and the 1960s concerning early intervention and effective classroom management skills. His model is built around 10 concepts: the ripple effect, with-it-ness, momentum, smoothness, group alerting, student accountability, overlapping, avoidance of satiation, valence and challenge arousal, and seatwork variety and challenge. Brief definitions of these concepts are presented in Table 5.1.

Martella and colleagues (2012) suggest the use of Kounin's model for management of low-level behaviors, especially the concepts of with-it-ness and desists. Also, they point out that the effectiveness of this model and its components has been demonstrated through research. However, they consider the model to be incomplete, as it does not address the more severe behavior issues that some students may have.

Fred Jones

According to Fred Jones (1987), teachers need to learn two major skill clusters. The first of these involves body language, which accounts for 90% of

Table 5.1 Kounin's Concepts

Concept	Definition
Ripple effect	Reaction of students to teacher's actions, when teacher's actions are for another student
With-it-ness	Awareness of all that is going on in the classroom; the idea that teachers have eyes in the backs of their heads
Momentum	Appropriateness of pace and progress throughout lesson or activity
Smoothness	Ease and efficiency with which transitions between activities occur
Group alerting	Gaining students' attention before instructing them as to what is expected of them
Student accountability	Keeping students involved in the lesson
Overlapping	Teacher's ability to attend to two or more events in the classroom at the same time
Avoidance of satiation	Keeping lessons interesting to avoid boredom and frustration
Valence and challenge arousal	Teacher's enthusiasm for the lesson and use of a variety of activities
Seatwork variety and challenge	Teacher's ability to keep seatwork interesting to students

effective discipline. Body language includes eye contact, physical proximity to students, stance, display of appropriate facial expressions, and use of gestures, such as a thumbs-up to indicate approval of a behavior. The second skill cluster consists of the use of a group-based incentive system and the use of "Grandma's rule." The preferred activity time (PAT) incentive system allows a group of students to gain access to activities they enjoy. Grandma's rule is the idea of "Eat your vegetables, then you can have dessert." In the classroom, students finish less desirable tasks and then are rewarded with PAT. Jones also suggests that by having classrooms that are organized, including seating arrangements and rules and routines, teachers can minimize the need for interventions with students regarding behavior.

Regardless of the behavioral management model a teacher chooses, the classroom management system implemented in the classroom is one of the most important factors in successful teaching and learning. Although poor salary is the reason most often given by beginning teachers who leave the profession, student discipline problems are ranked second. In a recent survey, when beginning teachers (those who had been teaching for 5 years or less) who left the field of education were asked their reasons for doing so, 29% cited job dissatisfaction. While 78% of those who said they quit teaching because they were dissatisfied with the job cited poor salary, 84% listed four different working conditions, of which student discipline problems was number one, cited by 35% of respondents (percentages do not add to 100 because respondents could list three reasons why they left the field). Student discipline problems ranked ahead of poor administrative support and poor student motivation (Ingersoll & Smith, 2003). Student discipline, unlike salary, is an issue that teachers can address through the implementation of effective classroom management plans.

It is just as important for teachers to articulate their philosophies of classroom management as it is for them to articulate their overall philosophies of teaching. Teachers should educate themselves about the various classroom management models and then choose those that match their philosophies and teaching styles. This will ensure that teachers make rational, well-informed decisions about behavior problems when they arise, rather than reactive or unintended responses (Malmgren et al., 2005).

Without a doubt, the most effective classroom management plan begins with an effective teacher who delivers instruction so as to maximize learning outcomes. Lessons that actively engage students and are relevant to them maintain the students' focus. Appropriate and relevant lessons can prevent off-task behaviors that lead to disruptions in the classroom. Classroom management depends greatly on students' engagement in the learning activities taking place (Doyle, 2006). Students who are engaged in lessons and activities are less likely to misbehave. In other words, "students who are academically engaged cannot simultaneously be engaged in off-task behavior" (Ratcliff et al., 2010, p. 46). What makes a teacher effective as a classroom manager? The next section discusses what we know about what effective teachers do in the classroom.

CHARACTERISTICS OF HIGHLY EFFECTIVE TEACHERS

Standards for teacher preparation programs require that candidates possess the knowledge, skills, and dispositions, or personal characteristics, necessary to become effective teachers. Many studies have shown that instructional and management processes are key elements in the classrooms of highly effective teachers (Stronge, 2007). Teachers who are effective classroom managers create classroom environments that are conducive to desirable student learning outcomes. This includes forming instructional groups that meet students' academic and affective needs; making efficient use of learning time; optimizing student time on task; planning, organizing, and implementing effective instruction; and monitoring student progress (Cotton, 1995, 2000; Ratcliff et al., 2010; Stronge, 2007).

Engaging instruction, well-managed classrooms, and positive relationships with students are basic tools that teachers can use to prevent student behavior that is disruptive. "Approaches aimed at improving school and classroom environments, including reducing the negative effects of disruptive or distracting behaviors, can enhance the chances that effective teaching and learning will occur, both for the students exhibiting problem behaviors and for their classmates" (Epstein, Atkins, Cullinan, Kutash, & Weaver, 2008, p. 5).

Additionally, particular dispositions, often described as a teacher's personal characteristics, have also been identified as essential for successful teaching (Colker, 2008; Walker, 2008). In other words, teachers can have knowledge and skills, but unless they have the necessary dispositions, learning will not take place. Walker (2008) lists these dispositions as follows:

- Coming to class prepared
- Maintaining a positive attitude toward teaching and students
- Holding high expectations for all students
- Demonstrating creativity in teaching
- Treating students fairly
- Demonstrating a personal touch with students
- Cultivating a sense of belonging
- Showing compassion
- Having a sense of humor

- Showing respect for students
- Demonstrating forgiveness
- Admitting mistakes

Colker (2008) presents a similar list of characteristics of effective early child-hood teachers. In addition, her list includes passion, perseverance, patience, flexibility, and authenticity.

SUMMARY

When managing the learning environment, teachers need to consider such things as the physical setup of the classroom, the establishment of rules and routines, the development of schedules, and plans for smooth transitions. Teachers also need to consider their classroom management philosophies as carefully as they reflect upon their overall teaching philosophies. The strategies presented in this chapter are part of what Charles (2011) refers to as preventive discipline—that is, they are actions taken before problems arise that have the potential to prevent or minimize inappropriate behaviors in the classroom. Other kinds of discipline are known as supportive and corrective. Supportive discipline is aimed at assisting students to stay on task when they first show signs of inappropriate behavior. Corrective discipline involves stopping student misbehavior. Most of the remaining chapters in this book are dedicated to strategies that can help teachers apply supportive discipline, redirecting inappropriate behavior when it happens.

REVIEW ACTIVITIES

1. Design the physical environment of your classroom. Explain your teaching style and the types of interactions you want to have with students. Consult websites that provide teachers with help in planning classroom layouts, such as Classroom Architect at 4Teachers.org (http://classroom.4teachers.org) and the sample classroom floor plans at the University of North Carolina's School of Education site (http://www.learnnc.org/lp/pages/742).

2. List your classroom rules along with the corresponding consequences and rewards. Do your rules meet the characteristics of effective classroom rules? Are your consequences and rewards appropriate and manageable?

3. Design a routine for each of the following activities:

   a. Passing out materials

   b. Handing in homework

   c. Lining up for the cafeteria

   d. Moving to learning centers

   e. Getting ready to go home

Visit the Student Study Site at www.sagepub.com/shepherd to access additional study tools including mobile-friendly eFlashcards and web quizzes as well as links to SAGE journal articles and web resources.

CHAPTER 6

BASIC CLASSROOM MANAGEMENT STRATEGIES

After reading this chapter, you should be able to do the following:

- Identify nonverbal and verbal interventions for addressing inappropriate student behavior.
- Distinguish between positive and negative reinforcement and between extinction and punishment, and give examples of how each can be used in the classroom to address student behavior.
- Explain the use of time-out.
- Develop a contingency contract and a token economy.
- Analyze the impact culture can have on basic classroom management strategies.

TEACHER EXPECTATIONS

As noted in Chapter 5, teachers can communicate behavior expectations to students in several ways. Proactive management strategies can prevent behavior difficulties from occurring in the classroom (Niesyn, 2009; Stormont & Reinke, 2009). The first opportunity teachers have for conveying their expectations to students concerning appropriate classroom behavior is when they establish rules in their classrooms. As part of a universal design for classroom management, the establishment of classroom rules, discussion and practice of appropriate behaviors with students, and implementation of instruction that is relevant and engaging are paramount to providing students a clear understanding of behaviors that are expected of them. However, many students will continue to need the teacher to assist them as they strive to meet expectations for appropriate behavior throughout the school day. Active strategies maintain student behaviors and preserve a positive learning environment. Sometimes even with teachers' best efforts to employ proactive and active strategies, teachers will have to modify inappropriate behavior and help students act in a more appropriate way. Reactive strategies provide the most intensive interventions for student behaviors.

NONVERBAL AND VERBAL INTERVENTIONS

Nonverbal and verbal interventions are strategies that teachers can use to support students as they strive to exhibit appropriate classroom behavior. These strategies include planned ignoring, proximity control, signal interference, redirection, contingent praise, and tension reduction.

Planned Ignoring

Planned ignoring is a procedure designed to weaken, decrease, or eliminate an inappropriate behavior by abruptly withdrawing the reinforcer that is maintaining the behavior (Hester, Hendrickson, & Gable, 2009; Payne, Mancil, & Landers, 2005). The basic premise of planned ignoring is that when the reinforcement is withheld, the student will cease displaying the behavior (Gable, Hester, Rock, & Hughes, 2009). The kinds of behaviors for which planned ignoring may be an effective strategy are usually minor but are nonetheless annoying and may disrupt the learning environment, such as talking without permission or making noises. The reinforcer that is withdrawn is the teacher's attention.

It is important to note that planned ignoring is usually effective only if the student is seeking the teacher's attention. For example, it is unlikely that ignoring the behavior will be effective if the student is making noises at his desk because he is bored or restless. Determining the reason, or the function, of the behavior is important in developing an appropriate response.

If the student is seeking the teacher's attention, the teacher using planned ignoring must make every effort to ignore the inappropriate behavior completely. The teacher cannot tell the student that she is "not going to talk to him until he stops making noises" or make disapproving eye contact. Such reactions let the student know that the teacher is paying attention, which reinforces the inappropriate behavior (Payne et al., 2005). If planned ignoring is to be effective, the teacher must not provide any interaction with the student related to the inappropriate behavior. This may be difficult, especially if withdrawing attention initially increases the behavior, as the student tries harder to gain the teacher's attention. For planned ignoring to be effective in eliminating attention-seeking behavior, the teacher must consistently ignore the behavior, even when it escalates, or risk reinforcing the inappropriate behavior at a more intense level (Gable et al., 2009; Obenchain & Taylor, 2005).

Planned ignoring should be paired with a contingency strategy, in which the teacher ignores the inappropriate behavior but praises the student for an appropriate behavior that replaces the ignored behavior (Hester et al., 2009). For example, the teacher asks a question during a discussion of the causes of the American Civil War. Without raising her hand, Kale blurts out an answer. The teacher completely ignores Kale's behavior and thus reduces the probability that Kale will continue to respond to questions without raising her hand. Conversely, in those instances in which Kale does raise her hand in response to the teacher's questions, the teacher should take the opportunity to call on Kale. This "catch 'em being good" strategy increases the probability that the appropriate behavior will be repeated.

Planned ignoring is unlikely to be effective if the student is seeking attention from peers (Payne et al., 2005). For example, if Ricardo is making wisecracks during a discussion of the Civil War and the teacher chooses to ignore his behavior, the wisecracks are most likely to continue if the function of the behavior is to gain attention from peers. The teacher will need to consider another strategy to modify Ricardo's behavior.

Finally, planned ignoring should never be used with aggressive behaviors or behaviors that interfere with the instructional environment. Teachers have a responsibility to provide safe and secure environments for students in their classrooms.

Proximity Control

Proximity control is a nonverbal strategy that alters behavioral responses through the physical presence of an authority figure. For example, an individual is driving 15 miles per hour over the speed limit on the highway when he sees a state trooper in his rearview mirror. Immediately, the driver slows down. The state trooper, an authority figure, is affecting the behavior of the driver by being in a proximate position—that is, in the same vicinity as the driver. A similar phenomenon is at work in the classroom. Students typically engage in on-task behavior and demonstrate improved compliance when the teacher is nearby, in close proximity. Proximity control is generally appropriate for dealing with nonthreatening and minimally disruptive behaviors, such as talking out, note passing, and pencil tapping or other forms of fidgeting.

Proximity control is useful for helping students become aware of their behaviors. The main element of this technique is for the teacher to take a position in close proximity to students who are showing indications of getting off task. The idea is that once the students feel the presence of the authority figure, the behavior will stop. For example, during group activities, the teacher should circulate around the room to keep students focused. Also, if the teacher knows that a particular group of students is likely to interrupt class, he should try standing or sitting close to them while he leads an activity or provides directions. To hold an individual student's attention, the teacher stands near the student before giving directions or engaging in discussion. When the teacher walks near a student, it is the student's cue to focus on the task. The student automatically perks up, copies notes more intently, or stops talking.

In using proximity control, teachers should take the following factors into consideration (Allday, 2011). First, proximity control is a proactive strategy to increase on-task behavior. For example, Kale is talking to a friend instead of working on her history assignment. The teacher moves in her direction, which cues Kale to return to the task. However, if Ricardo is refusing to sit down at his seat, proximity control is not likely to be effective. Second, providing too much attention when using proximity control can exacerbate the behavior. If the teacher stands in front of the student with arms crossed and a raised eyebrow, for example, the behavior may increase. When using proximity control, the teacher should simply walk near the student while continuing the lesson. She should not provide any additional attention through hand gestures or eye contact. Once the behavior is diminished, she should walk away and continue the lesson (Allday, 2011).

Signal Interference

Signal interference is the use of nonverbal cues to remind students to redirect inappropriate behavior. These cues might include hand gestures, facial expressions, and eye contact. The following are some examples of signal interference techniques:

- Putting a finger to your lips to indicate quiet
- Shaking your head slowly to indicate disapproval
- Making eye contact with a student who is talking to a classmate
- Pointing to a seat when a student is wandering around
- Holding up a hand to stop a student from calling out
- Making a thumbs-up gesture for approval or a thumbs-down gesture for disapproval
- Holding up the number of fingers that corresponds to the number of a classroom rule being broken

To be effective, signal interference must be clearly directed at the off-task student without disturbing other students. There should be no doubt in the student's mind that the teacher is aware of what is going on and that the student is responsible for the behavior. Finally, teachers can use nonverbal signals, such as smiles and nods, to indicate approval of student behavior. Teachers should exercise caution in using signal interference techniques, however, because various signals may mean different things in different cultures.

In using signal interference, teachers must remember to consider the impact culture may have on behavior. For example, they should not insist on eye contact for all students, as making eye contact with authority figures may violate the cultural norms of some students.

Verbal Redirection

Although inappropriate behavior can often be redirected through signal interference such as a stern look from the teacher, redirection most often takes a verbal form. The effective classroom manager redirects minor infractions before they turn into major disruptions. This type of corrective discipline redirects misbehavior into positive directions and keeps students on task. For example, when students are off task, a teacher might say, "Be sure your group is working on the experiment." A teacher might redirect an individual student's behavior by getting the student's attention (usually by saying the student's name) and then asking the student to engage in the appropriate behavior. For example, a teacher might say, "Patricia, please return to your seat." A private redirection of this type is preferred because it is less likely to draw attention to inappropriate behavior or to interrupt a lesson.

CASE STUDY   Miss Fowler and Ricardo

Miss Fowler is a first-year science teacher at Lincoln High School. She is European American, and she grew up in a small rural community, where she had little interaction with culturally and linguistically diverse individuals. She attended a university not far from her hometown and completed her student teaching experience in the high school from which she graduated. Her ambition was to teach at the high school in her hometown or in a nearby community. However, since many teachers in those schools do not leave their positions until they retire, no positions were available for Miss Fowler when she graduated from her teacher education program. She was able to secure a position at Lincoln High School, an urban high school several hours away.

Lincoln High School has a large population of Hispanic students, and while Miss Fowler took a university course in multiculturalism and diversity, her perceptions of Hispanics are firmly based in the portrayals she has seen in television shows and movies. When she got the job at Lincoln, she expected that many of her students would be involved in gangs or drugs.

After enthusiastically providing a lesson in science one day, Miss Fowler had her students complete a worksheet for the remainder of the class time. While others students were working on their worksheets, Ricardo was talking to a friend who was sitting at the desk next to his. Miss Fowler asked Ricardo to finish his assignment. Ricardo smiled, shrugged his shoulders, and said, "My bad." Believing that Ricardo was being disrespectful, Miss Fowler sent him to the principal's office.

After school, Miss Fowler met with the principal and Mr. Garza, Ricardo's father. After Miss Fowler explained what had happened in her classroom, Mr. Garza leaned back in his chair and laughed good-naturedly. He told the principal and Miss Fowler that whenever he had to correct Ricardo for something he had done at home, Ricardo would smile, shrug his shoulders, and say "My bad" to show he understood and that things were good between the two of them. In behaving as he did, Ricardo was actually showing respect toward Miss Fowler.

Contingent Praise

One of the easiest and most effective strategies for modifying student behavior is the use of contingent praise. Contingent praise is an affirmative statement that immediately follows the completion of appropriate academic or social behaviors (Moore Partin, Robertson, Maggin, Oliver, & Wehby, 2010; Musti-Rao & Haydon, 2011). Contingent praise is based on the principles of operant conditioning (see Chapter 1) and applied behavior analysis in that a consequence that immediately follows a behavior results in increasing the probability that the student will engage in the behavior again. When used correctly, contingent praise has been shown to increase positive behavior, improve teacher–student relationships, and reduce inappropriate behavior (Allday, 2011; Gable et al., 2009).

Contingent praise can be categorized as non-behavior-specific praise or behavior-specific praise. With *non-behavior-specific praise,* the teacher praises the student without describing the behavior. For example, the teacher uses generic terms when praising a student, such as "nice job" or "I like that." With *behavior-specific praise,* the teacher specifies the behavior when praising the student (Musti-Rao & Haydon, 2011). For example, the teacher may tell the student that he "did an excellent job in completing his assignment on time." When using behavior-specific praise, the teacher identifies the behavior she is trying to reinforce.

Teachers should keep the following criteria in mind when using contingent praise:

1. Contingent praise should be linked to student behaviors that the teacher wants to reinforce.

2. Contingent praise should provide feedback of the specific behavior and performance.

3. Contingent praise should provide positive interactions between the teacher and students.

4. Teachers should consider the skill levels of students when using contingent praise.

5. Teachers who use contingent praise should evaluate its effectiveness. (Moore Partin et al., 2010)

While not used as often as non-behavior-specific praise, behavior-specific praise is more effective. Behavior-specific praise prevents any confusion as to which student behavior is targeted. For example, Jane raises her hand while working on a classroom assignment. To reinforce Jane's appropriate behavior of raising her hand, Mrs. Garza walks to her desk and says, "Good job, Jane." Yet, despite the many times Mrs. Garza praises Jane for raising her hand, the target behavior does not increase because Jane thinks she is being praised for her handwriting. Using behavior-specific praise, Mrs. Garza should have said, "Thanks for raising your hand, Jane."

Contingent praise should be used immediately and consistently to be effective. Providing praise immediately emphasizes that the student is completing a task correctly or recognizing an appropriate behavior. Using praise consistently and systematically is an important component of positive behavior support for all students and is a key element in teaching new behaviors (Hester et al., 2009).

Despite evidence that supports contingent praise as an effective strategy for managing student behavior, many teachers do not use praise frequently in their classrooms (Gable et al., 2009; Musti-Rao & Haydon, 2011). While teachers may believe that they use praise at an appropriate rate, they generally use negative feedback or reprimands three times more often than praise (Hester et al., 2009). Reprimands often provide immediate cessation of minor inappropriate behaviors, while praise takes longer to modify such behaviors. However, praise promotes positive teacher–student interactions, improves academic and nonacademic behaviors, and creates a positive classroom environment. It has been recommended that teachers use a ratio of praise to negative feedback of 4:1 (Kalis, Vannest, & Parker, 2007; Trussell, 2008).

Tension Reduction

Sometimes students can become tense, frustrated, or anxious because of behavioral expectations or learning tasks in the classroom. Physical activity is one strategy for reducing tension. For example, in today's high-stakes testing environment, many students may be anxious about their performance when faced with taking standardized tests. To alleviate some of this tension, just before administering the test the teacher could have the students stand at their desks and then run in place for a few minutes.

A teacher might also use humor to help defuse tension in students. Research has shown that the physiological benefits of humor include a reduction in stress, anxiety, and tension (Berk, 2008). A joke or a lighthearted comment can "act as a pressure release valve to allow the student to laugh off something without a negative response—to 'save face'" (Pierangelo & Giuliani, 2008, p. 18). Humor can also be used to create a healthy learning environment, an environment where students feel valued, emotionally safe, and free to participate in classroom activities (Skinner, 2010). A healthy learning environment promotes appropriate student behaviors. Of course, teachers must avoid using any kind of humor that marginalizes individuals or groups.

REINFORCEMENT

Reinforcement increases the probability that a behavior will occur in the future through attainment or avoidance of a consequence. For example, Alejandra tries a new recipe and serves it to her family for dinner one evening. Alejandra's family compliments the dinner, saying it is delicious. Alejandra relishes the compliments, and she is more likely to sustain or increase her behavior of preparing new dishes in the future (attainment of attention). In another example, a toddler, Keisha, is crying. Keisha's father is annoyed by the crying, so he gives Keisha a cookie. She stops crying. In the future, Keisha's dad is more likely to give her a cookie to stop her crying (avoidance of adverse interactions). In addition, Keisha's behavior has been reinforced. She is more likely to cry when she wants a cookie or a treat (attainment of reward). There are two types of reinforcements that increase behavior: positive reinforcement and negative reinforcement.

Positive Reinforcement

Positive reinforcement increases the probability that a behavior will be repeated when the behavior is followed by a preferred stimulus. For example, when a student gets a gold star on a spelling quiz for receiving a good grade, the gold star (reinforcer) increases the probability that he will do well on the next spelling quiz (behavior). Of course, the probability of the behavior occurring again is contingent on whether the student perceives the gold star as a desired consequence. Teachers need to understand the three basic tenets of positive reinforcement. First, it is the behavior that is reinforced. Whether it is an appropriate behavior, such as completing a math assignment, or an inappropriate behavior, such as talking without permission, positive reinforcement *strengthens* the behavior. Second, the behavior is reinforced by a *desired* stimulus. The stimulus should match the student's interests, or the reinforcement will be ineffective. For example, Johnny will receive 5 minutes of computer time for every five questions he answers on his history worksheet. Many students are interested in spending time on a computer, and computer time can easily be used as a reinforcer in the classroom. Finally, the student should receive the reinforcer only if he exhibits the behavior. For example, Johnny completes only four questions on his history worksheet, so he does not receive 5 minutes of computer time.

A positive reinforcement strengthens a behavior by adding an incentive or a stimulus. The following are additional examples of the use of positive reinforcement in the classroom:

- For every 20 math problems he completes, Harry receives a gold star on his worksheet. In the future he is more likely to complete more math problems.
- Susan is praised for participating in a group activity. In the future she is more likely to continue to participate in group activities.

Types of Reinforcers

In order to be effective as a reinforcer, a consequence must be contingent on the appropriate behavior and should be administered immediately when the student displays the appropriate behavior. There are two major types of reinforcers: primary and secondary.

Primary reinforcers are of biological importance to a person. They include food, water, sleep, and sex. Given their importance to sustaining life, these tend to be highly motivating to individuals. In the classroom, food and water are common and appropriate reinforcers. Also referred to as edible reinforcers, food and water are used mainly in teaching new behaviors to young students and students with severe disabilities. They are less appropriate for older students, general education students, and students with mild disabilities. For example, it may not be appropriate to offer a high school student a candy bar for finishing his biology experiment, but a pizza party might be appropriate for a group of students who have finished all their homework assignments for a given month.

Secondary reinforcers do not have biological importance to a person; their value is learned or conditioned. Money is an example of a secondary reinforcer. While money as a distinct item is not needed for survival, it is used to buy food, a primary reinforcer. Individuals learn to value secondary reinforcers through their pairing with primary reinforcers.

Secondary reinforcers can be classified as tangible reinforcers, activity reinforcers, or social reinforcers (Payne et al., 2005). Tangible reinforcers are preferred items presented after a behavior occurs, resulting in an increase of the behavior. Just about any items desired by the individual can serve as tangible reinforcers; for students, examples include stickers, books, and small toys. Activity reinforcers are probably the types of reinforcers most often used by teachers. These are any preferred activities presented to a student after a behavior occurs, resulting in an increase of the behavior. Examples include activities such as computer time or use of the arts and crafts center, and privileges such as being first in line or being hall monitor. Praise and other forms of recognition (e.g., smiles, attention) are examples of social reinforcers.

Negative Reinforcement

While positive reinforcement increases behavior followed by a desired stimulus, negative reinforcement also increases the probability that a behavior will be repeated by *removing an adverse stimulus* after the desired behavior has been exhibited (Skinner, 1953, 1994). As with positive reinforcement, the behavior is being reinforced by a stimulus. However, with negative reinforcement, there is a removal of some *aversive* consequence. Take the example of Keisha's crying. It is bothersome to her father, and he wants to remove this aversive consequence, so he gives Keisha a cookie. This presentation of the consequence of a cookie effectively removes the unpleasant stimulus, the crying. This increases the probability that the father will give Keisha cookies to quiet her in the future. Of course, the cookie might also serve as a positive reinforcement for Keisha's crying behavior, and it is likely that Keisha's crying will be maintained or increase as the behavior is reinforced with a cookie. The following are examples of negative reinforcement in the classroom:

- Rodrigo makes sure to complete all his work in class so that he does not have to take it home as homework.
- Xuesong is careful to finish her work because if she does not she will have to sit next to the teacher's desk.

Inadvertent Use of Negative Reinforcement

A teacher may use negative reinforcement unintentionally. For example, Jonathan refuses to do a math assignment. He disrupts the class by throwing a tantrum. The teacher removes the assignment, hoping that Jonathan will stop his behavior, which he does. The likelihood that Jonathan will be disruptive the next time he is given a math assignment increases because the aversive stimulus (the math assignment) was removed.

Students who see particular tasks as difficult, boring, or repetitive might engage in inappropriate behavior in order to avoid those tasks. Teachers can ensure that this does not happen by providing students with the necessary instruction, directions, and support during academic tasks.

Negative reinforcement is often confused with punishment. Positive reinforcement appears to "reward" behavior, and because negative is often considered the opposite of positive, negative reinforcement would appear to "punish" behavior (Sidman, 2006). However, teachers must remember that both positive and negative reinforcements increase the probability that a behavior will be repeated.

Schedule of Reinforcement

When using positive or negative reinforcements, the teacher needs to develop a schedule for delivering the reinforcer to the student. In **continuous reinforcement**, each instance of the desired behavior is reinforced. Continuous reinforcement is very effective for teaching students new behaviors, but it usually unsustainable as a behavior management technique. It is also not necessary. In **intermittent reinforcement**, only some incidents of the behavior are reinforced (Sarafino, 2012). The reinforcements are delivered according to ratio schedules and interval schedules.

Ratio schedules are based on numbers of correct responses. Ratio schedules can be fixed or variable. With a **fixed-ratio schedule**, reinforcements are delivered after certain fixed numbers of responses. For example, for every five math problems a student completes correctly, the student receives a gold star. On a **variable-ratio schedule** of reinforcement, an individual's behavior is reinforced after an average number of instances of the target behavior. Instead of receiving a reinforcer after every five math problems correctly solved, a student receives a gold star after solving seven problems, then four, then eight, then six—the number varies, but the target behavior is reinforced for an average of five occurrences.

Interval schedules are based on the passage of time since the last reinforcer was delivered. Like ratio schedules, interval schedules are either fixed or variable. A fixed-interval schedule delivers reinforcement after a fixed amount of time has passed. For example, most workers are paid on fixed-interval schedules; that is, every 2 weeks or every month. A **variable-interval schedule** involves an unspecified and changing amount of time. For example, to increase students' in-seat behavior, a teacher might set a timer for 9 minutes, then 13, 10, and 8 minutes and reinforce in-seat behavior at the end of each of these intervals.

EXTINCTION AND PUNISHMENT

Extinction and punishment are ways to decrease unwanted or inappropriate behaviors. **Extinction** reduces a target behavior by withholding the reinforcer that maintains the behavior. In the classroom, if teacher attention is serving as the reinforcer for certain inappropriate behaviors, such as calling out or acting as the class clown, then planned ignoring should be applied, as discussed above.

Punishment is another facet of operant conditioning. Unlike positive and negative reinforcements, **punishment** *decreases* the probability that a behavior will be repeated. Similar to reinforcements, punishment can be either positive or negative. **Positive punishment** decreases the probability that a behavior will be repeated when followed by an aversive consequence. Scolds and reprimands serve as positive punishers for many people. For example, if a student has to write 25 times "I will not talk in class" because she was consistently talking in class, this task (punishment) should decrease the future probability of the student talking in class (behavior).

Negative punishment decreases the probability that an inappropriate behavior will be repeated by withdrawing a desired reinforcement after the behavior is displayed. A negative punishment that is easy to use in the classroom is response cost, which is simply the removal of a positive reinforcer contingent on an inappropriate behavior (Little & Akin-Little, 2008). For example, a student really enjoys recess because he can be with his friends (a desired reinforcement). If the student receives detention during recess because he was consistently talking in class, the loss of recess (withdrawal of a desired behavior) decreases the future probability of the student talking in class (behavior). Response cost is often used to increase the effectiveness of a token economy.

Another reductive strategy is overcorrection, or the use of repetitive behavior as a consequence for exhibiting inappropriate behavior. The two types of overcorrection are restitutional and positive-practice. Restitutional overcorrection is the most adaptable form of overcorrection. The student must restore and improve the environment, leaving it in a better state than it was in before the inappropriate behavior. For example, a student caught writing on his desk would have to clean all the desks in the classroom. With positive-practice overcorrection, the student displaying an inappropriate behavior must repeatedly perform an appropriate behavior (Little & Akin-Little, 2008). For example, Mickey consistently leaves his empty lunch tray at the table when he leaves the cafeteria instead of taking it to the conveyor belt that delivers trays to be washed. As a result of this behavior, Mickey has to pick up his tray, scrape any remaining food from the tray into the trash can, and put the tray on the conveyor belt. Then he must take his tray back to the table and repeat the procedure ten more times.

The effectiveness of punishment has been debated. While reinforcement increases behavior, punishment focuses on decreasing behavior, which is more difficult to accomplish. Punishment can also evoke negative responses, such as anger, resentment, anxiety, and fear. Additionally, teachers may unintentionally use punishment procedures that are too severe for the behaviors they are seeking to diminish, especially if they determine the punisher at the time of the student's inappropriate behavior. Finally, the effects of punishment may be only transitory—that is, they may not have any lasting effects on behavior (Skinner, 1953).

TIME-OUT

Time-out is a form of negative punishment because it is the loss of opportunity to receive positive reinforcement. Time-out is a behavior modification procedure in which the student displaying inappropriate behaviors is removed from a reinforcing environment to an austere environment for a specified period of time

(Donaldson & Vollmer, 2011). Two conditions are necessary for time-out to be effective: First, the student must be receiving some type of reinforcement in the current environment; second, the student must prefer remaining in the reinforcing environment over removal to an environment without reinforcement (Kostewicz, 2010). For example, for time-out to be effective in correcting LeVar's behavior, LeVar must want to remain in the classroom with his peers instead of being isolated in the time-out room. If LeVar prefers to be in isolation instead of remaining in the classroom with his peers, time-out will have no effect on his behavior.

Teachers can use various forms of time-out, ranging from simply removing reinforcements from the student within the classroom to removing the student from the classroom. The three major types of time-out are inclusion time-out, exclusion time-out, and seclusion time-out.

Inclusion Time-Out

Inclusion time-out is the least restrictive form and the easiest to implement in the classroom. The student remains in her seat and observes classroom instruction but does not have the opportunity to participate or receive reinforcements (Ryan, Sanders, Katsiyannis, & Yell, 2007). There are three levels of inclusion time-out: removing the reinforcement, ignoring the student, and contingent observation. Removing the reinforcement might include asking the student to put his head on the desk or removing materials or objects from the desk. Planned ignoring can be used as an effective means of inclusion time-out. With contingent observation, the student moves to another location in the classroom, such as a corner or a time-out chair. The student observes the appropriate behaviors of peers but cannot participate or earn reinforcements.

With younger students, the use of a time-out ribbon can be an effective method of inclusion time-out. A time-out ribbon is a ribbon, wristband, or other item that is paired with a reinforcement that does not naturally lead to reinforcement (Kostewicz, 2010). For example, Ana is talking in class without permission. The teacher removes the time-out ribbon for a predetermined period of time. During this time, Ana cannot receive any type of reinforcement until the ribbon is returned.

Exclusion Time-Out

Exclusion time-out involves removing the student from a reinforcing activity or setting for a specified time. The student might be removed to a chair in the back of the room, a study carrel, the hallway, or another teacher's classroom, away from the work environment. During such a time-out, the student is not required to observe what is going on in the classroom.

Seclusion Time-Out

Seclusion time-out, the most restrictive form of time-out, is perhaps the most familiar. The student is removed from the classroom to a designated place, a secluded area or a time-out room, for a specified period of time. The student receives no reinforcements while in seclusion time-out. Seclusion time-out removes the disruptive student from the classroom and allows learning to continue for other students. Seclusion time-out is often used with students who are verbally or physically aggressive or who are destroying property. The time-out area should be well ventilated, well lighted, and quiet.

Duration of Time-Out

A common misapplication of time-out is exceeding the amount of time needed to reduce the inappropriate behavior by the student. A student should be in time-out for a specified period of time. The amount of time a student serves in time-out is dependent on whether it is a fixed-duration time-out or a release-contingency time-out. For a *fixed-duration time-out,* the amount of time should equal 1 minute for each year of the student's age. For example, 14-year-old LeVar's time-out should not exceed 14 minutes. In most instances, time-out should not exceed 12 to 15 minutes. Thus, 17-year-old Clayton's time-out would not be 17 minutes; rather, it should be restricted to the maximum of 15 minutes.

Release-contingency time-out can take different forms, including time-out in which the duration may be reset and interval-based time-out. For *resetting time-out duration,* release from time-out is contingent on the student's not exhibiting any inappropriate behaviors for the duration of the time-out. If the student displays inappropriate behaviors, the time-out duration is reset; this continues until no inappropriate behaviors are displayed (Donaldson & Vollmer, 2011). For example, LeVar can be released from time-out if he does not display any inappropriate behaviors for 5 minutes. If he displays any inappropriate behaviors, the time starts over, and he must again display no inappropriate behaviors for 5 minutes. With *interval-based time-out,* the student must not display any inappropriate behaviors at the end of the time-out (Donaldson &

Vollmer, 2011). For example, if LeVar does not display any inappropriate behaviors for 1 minute at the end of a 10-minute time-out, he can return to class. However, if LeVar displays inappropriate behaviors during the last minute of a 10-minute time-out, his time-out is extended until he has 1 minute of appropriate behavior.

CONTINGENCY CONTRACTS

A **contingency contract** is a formal, written agreement between the student and teacher that addresses the behavioral, academic, and social goals of the student and the reinforcers the student is to receive after achieving these goals. Contingency contracts are based on the Premack principle of reinforcement, which states that more probable behaviors will reinforce less probable behaviors. "First you eat your supper" (low-probability behavior) "and then you can have dessert" (high-probability behavior) is a common example of the Premack principle. The high-probability behavior is used to reinforce the low-probability behavior (Premack, 1965). For example, Jane will complete her math assignment (low-probability behavior), and then she can go out to recess (high-probability behavior).

Contingency contracts are fairly easy to develop and implement, and they have been found to be effective in reducing a variety of inappropriate behaviors (Mruzek, Cohen, & Smith, 2007; Navarro, Aguilar, Aguilar, Alcalde, & Marchena, 2007). The student should be actively involved in the development of the contingency contract, as this gives her ownership of her behavior. In developing a contingency contract, the teacher should take the following steps:

1. Define the target behavior in observable and measurable terms.

2. With the student, determine the reinforcer or reward that the student will earn after completing the contract.

3. Set the criteria for contract completion (the frequency of the behavior and the degree to which it is exhibited).

4. Write the contingency contract in age-appropriate language, and have all participants sign it.

5. Reinforce the behavior immediately upon completion of the contract.

6. Review the contingency contract on a regular basis.

For example, Jane talks in class without raising her hand seven times in a 45-minute math class. Jane and her teacher, Mrs. Cox, negotiate a contingency contract designed to reduce the number of times Jane talks in class without raising her hand. They determine that Jane's goal should be to raise her hand and wait to be called on five times in a 45-minute math class. If Jane achieves this goal, she will receive 5 minutes of computer time at the end of the class. Mrs. Cox and Jane will review the contract every Friday to determine Jane's progress toward her goal (see Figure 6.1).

The use of contingency contracts has several advantages. One is that the student's active participation in the development of the contract facilitates communication between the student and the teacher. In some instances, this results in improved relations between student and teacher (Mruzek et al., 2007). Students who have positive relationships with teachers have fewer behavior problems and better academic achievement (Holt, Hargrove, & Harris, 2011; Murray & Greenberg, 2006). Contingency contracts also take a minimal amount of time to develop and implement in the classroom setting—definitely

---

Figure 6.1   Contingency Contract for Jane

Contract

<u>Jane</u> will
Student's Name

<u>Raise her hand five times in math class and wait to be called on by Mrs. Cox.</u>

<u>Mrs. Cox</u> will
Teacher's Name

<u>Call on Jane when she raises her hand. When Jane raises her hand five times and waits to be called on, Mrs. Cox will give her 5 minutes of time on the computer at the end of class. Mrs. Cox will go over the contract with Jane every Friday to see how she is doing.</u>

Jane Anderson   Mrs. Cox
_____   _____
Student   Teacher

<u>October 2, 2014</u>
Date

an advantage for teachers who already have many responsibilities. Finally, contingency contracts have been found to be effective in reducing inappropriate behaviors and increasing appropriate behaviors (Garrick Duhaney, 2003; Walker, Ramsey, & Gresham, 2004).

TOKEN ECONOMY

A token economy is a contingency management system that allows students to earn tokens that can be exchanged for predetermined reinforcers (Kazdin, 1977). The tokens, which are also secondary reinforcers, can be any inexpensive items, such as play money, stickers, points, or checkmarks. They acquire symbolic value similar to money, and students can use them to purchase items or activities within the classroom. Because token economy programs are flexible and easy to implement, they have been widely used in classrooms to improve academic and social skills, attention, and appropriate behaviors (Maggin, Chafouleas, Goddard, & Johnson, 2011).

To implement a token economy program in the classroom, the teacher needs to take six steps:

1. Identify the target behavior or rules to be reinforced.

2. Identify the tokens that will be used for reinforcement.

3. With student input, develop a menu of reinforcers to reward appropriate behaviors (e.g., candy bars, pencils, computer time).

4. Create an explicit protocol for the exchange of tokens for reinforcers (the prices or numbers of tokens needed to purchase reinforcers, how and when purchases are to be made).

5. Design a system for monitoring tokens earned and spent.

6. Develop procedures for fading the use of the token economy program.

For example, every time Kristen finishes her math assignment in class, she earns $100 in play money. She also earns $50 for every time she raises her hand to ask a question. During math class, Kristen has earned $200. At the end of the day, Kristen exchanges $150 for a candy bar. The remaining $50 will carry over to the next day.

It should be noted that providing reinforcers for token economy programs can be problematic for teachers. School districts seldom provide funding for reinforcers, so many teachers purchase reinforcers from their own personal funds. Fortunately, some popular reinforcers are very inexpensive or even free (e.g., preferred activities and privileges).

Teachers also need to consider the impact of culture when developing token economy programs as part of behavior and classroom management. For example, some Hispanic parents find withdrawal strategies (e.g., response cost, time-out) to be more acceptable than reward techniques such as token economy programs (Borrego, Ibanez, Spendlove, & Pemberton, 2007). Teachers need to inform the parents of their culturally and linguistically diverse students of the purposes of behavior and classroom management strategies and work with them in developing plans that will be effective in modifying student behaviors.

While many educational professionals believe that token economy systems have been successful in reducing inappropriate behavior and improving academic performance, some studies indicate that there is insufficient empirical support for token economy systems as an evidence-based practice. To create successful token economy programs, teachers must be careful to develop explicit procedures (Maggin et al., 2011).

CULTURAL IMPACT ON BEHAVIOR STRATEGIES

Culture can influence the effectiveness of basic behavior management strategies, and teachers need to be culturally responsive in their choices of strategies. For example, many teachers use eye contact to reduce behavior difficulties (Kodak, Northup, & Kelley, 2007), but, as noted previously, some cultures perceive eye contact between student and teacher as disrespectful. In other cases, a teacher's staring at a student could be considered threatening. Teachers should remember that it is important to keep eye contact with students brief (Allday, 2011).

When asking students questions, many teachers generally wait 3 to 5 seconds for a response, which is a typical response time for most European American students. However, the typical response time of many Native Americans is 6 to 10 seconds. Native Americans value reflection, which is consistent with their global perspective for processing information. When asked questions, Native Americans think about responses that are compatible with their culture. Native Americans also may not respond to questions. They are comfortable with silence, since it serves many purposes. For example, in most American classrooms, students are expected to display their knowledge and skills openly to the teacher and their peers. They are also expected to be proud of their accomplishments. However, Native Americans value humility and the accomplishment of the group. The typical expectations of the classroom are in conflict with Native Americans' culture and may create an environment of shame for Native American students. A teacher might assume that a Native American student does not know the answer to a question, is noncompliant, or just does not care because the student takes too long to answer the question or does not answer the question at all (Hammond, Dupoux, & Ingalls, 2004). The teacher may then use a verbal or nonverbal behavior strategy to correct a behavior that does not need correcting.

Some African American students may prefer a more active engagement in classrooms, and so may call out comments during classroom discussion (Weinstein, Tomlinson-Clarke, & Curran, 2004). Many teachers would consider this behavior disrespectful and rude, and they may try using planned ignoring, proximity control, redirection, or other behavior strategies. Diversity requires that teachers take different approaches to behavior and classroom management. Teachers should not interpret the behavior of culturally and linguistically diverse students based on their own experiences and values. They should nurture behaviors that encourage and promote academic learning. Classrooms should be dynamic environments in which ideas and opinions are encouraged in a respectful manner. Classrooms do not necessarily have to be silent for learning to take place, and a noisy classroom does not necessarily mean that the teacher does not have an effective classroom management plan in place.

WHAT WOULD YOU DO?   Antonio

Antonio is an African American student in your U.S. history class. His grades in class are usually above average, but he consistently talks without permission. While you are teaching a lesson on George Washington's role in the American Revolution, Antonio keeps interjecting comments on the subject without raising his hand. The comments are generally appropriate, and there appears to be no malicious intent on Antonio's part, but he is continuing to violate the posted classroom rule of raising your hand for permission to speak. What would you do about Antonio's behavior?

SUMMARY

The most basic classroom management strategy is to ensure that students know what behaviors are expected of them. The teacher can accomplish this through the establishment of rules. The planning and delivery of engaging and relevant instruction is also paramount to the basic classroom management plan.

Teachers can implement several different nonverbal and verbal strategies to support students, including planned ignoring, proximity control, signal interference, redirection, and tension reduction.

The field of applied behavior analysis provides teachers with additional strategies for supporting and correcting student behavior. These include contingency contracting and token economy programs, which utilize several behavioral principles, most notably reinforcement.

Teachers also need to understand the impact of culture on basic behavior management strategies. Some strategies may be ineffective with linguistically diverse students because of their values and experiences. Teachers need to understand their students' cultures and develop or modify the behavior strategies used so that they are effective for all students in their classrooms.

REVIEW ACTIVITIES

1. Briefly describe the different verbal and nonverbal intervention strategies. Explain which you are more likely to use in your classroom and why.

2. Explain the advantages and disadvantages of inclusion time-out, exclusion time-out, and seclusion time-out.

3. Timothy is a third grader in your class who has a difficult time remaining in his seat. It is possible that he has undiagnosed attention-deficit/hyperactivity disorder, but his parents refuse to have him evaluated. However, you have noticed that he enjoys reading the *Stink* book series. Develop a contingency contract for Timothy.

Visit the Student Study Site at www.sagepub.com/shepherd to access additional study tools including mobile-friendly eFlashcards and web quizzes as well as links to SAGE journal articles and web resources.

CHAPTER 7

COGNITIVE
BEHAVIOR MANAGEMENT

After reading this chapter, you should be able to do the following:

- Define cognitive behavior management.
- Explain the importance of goal setting for a cognitive behavior management program.
- Describe the steps a teacher uses when training a student to self-instruct.
- Delineate the steps for implementing self-monitoring strategies with students.
- Describe how to teach students to use self-evaluation and self-reinforcement as part of a behavior management plan.
- Understand how teachers can use strategies to help students manage anger and stress.

DEFINING COGNITIVE BEHAVIOR MANAGEMENT

Cognitive behavior management is the use of intervention strategies designed to teach students to control their own behaviors. Through cognitive behavior management, students are taught how their behaviors create ripple effects that affect their relationships with others and their academic and behavior outcomes, just as dropping a pebble in still waters creates ripples emanating outward that affect everything in their path.

Under a universal design for classroom management, cognitive behavior management is a proactive strategy. Teaching students to manage their own behaviors can prevent the occurrence of behavior difficulties in the classroom. When students can manage their own behaviors, they do not rely on external controls (Rafferty, 2010) such as nonverbal and verbal interventions, reinforcements, and token economies.

IMPLEMENTING A SELF-MANAGEMENT PLAN

Self-management techniques may be effective alternatives to teacher-mediated interventions in reducing incidents of disruptive behavior (Briesch & Chafouleas, 2009). **Self-management** is an umbrella term that includes a number of techniques specifically designed to teach students to control their own behaviors (Chafouleas, Hagermoser Sanetti, Jaffery, & Fallon, 2012). Much of the research conducted on self-management has involved students with disabilities; however, self-management techniques have also been found to be effective for students without disabilities (Moore, Anderson, Glassenbury, Lang, & Didden, 2013). Self-management techniques vary in a number of ways, but common features among these techniques include identification of the target behavior, self-observation, and self-recording. Both general education students and students with disabilities can be taught to manage their own behavior.

Students can be taught to use any of several different techniques to change their behavior. Whatever techniques teachers choose, they need to take the following steps in implementing a self-management plan:

1. Identify the target behavior.

2. Determine the criteria for mastery of the appropriate behavior.

3. Discuss with the student the relevance of the appropriate behavior.

4. Introduce the self-management technique.

5. Model the technique.

6. Provide guided practice in the technique.

7. Practice the technique in authentic settings. (King-Sears, 2008; Patton, Jolivette, & Ramsey, 2006)

The first step in implementing a self-management plan is to identify the target behavior. Target behaviors are *observable, measurable,* and *repeatable,* and they are usually expressed in terms of action in a positive tone (see Chapter 8). For example, Charlie, a third grader, often pushes peers during transition times, when in line going to lunch or recess, and when the teacher is not looking. Since the inappropriate behavior is pushing peers, Charlie's target behavior would be to keep his hands to himself. Once the inappropriate behavior has been identified, the teacher needs to determine the criteria for mastery of the target behavior. Charlie's teacher monitored Charlie's behavior during transition times, while in line, during lunch, and during recess. The teacher noted that over a 2-day period, Charlie displayed his inappropriate behavior eight times.

The third step is to discuss the relevance of the appropriate behavior. Charlie needs to understand the benefits to himself for displaying the target behavior, such as developing positive relationships with his peers, being able to eat lunch in the cafeteria, being able to go to recess, and having positive notes sent home. Once Charlie understands the difference between the inappropriate behavior and the target behavior, the teacher selects a self-management technique and explains the technique to Charlie. The teacher provides a worksheet for Charlie to use in monitoring his behavior across settings and shows him how to mark the worksheet. For example, Charlie is to circle "yes" or "no" depending on whether he displayed the appropriate behavior in specific settings (see Figure 7.1). At the end of each day, if Charlie has answered yes four times on the worksheet, he rewards himself in a way that he and his teacher previously determined.

After a self-management technique has been chosen, the teacher needs to model how to use it. Charlie's teacher verbalizes her thought process while she models appropriate and inappropriate behaviors, and while she marks the self-management worksheet as yes, she did keep her hands to herself, or no, she did not keep her hands to herself. Then the teacher provides Charlie an opportunity to practice using the self-management worksheet. During guided practice, the teacher offers feedback and helps Charlie learn the self-management procedures. Finally, the self-management plan is implemented in "authentic" settings. In Charlie's case, this means he demonstrates appropriate behavior during transitions within the classroom, while in line, and during lunch and recess.

Figure 7.1   Self-Monitoring Worksheet for Charlie

Name of Student: *Charlie*	Date: *February 22*
Did I keep my hands to myself:	
When I was putting papers away after science	Yes No
When I was in line for lunch	Yes No
When I was putting papers away after reading	Yes No
When I was in line for recess	Yes No
When I was at recess	Yes No

SELF-MANAGEMENT TECHNIQUES

Teachers often use five common techniques of self-management to help students regulate their own behavior: goal setting, self-instruction, self-monitoring, self-evaluation, and self-reinforcement (Mooney, Ryan, Uhing, Reid, & Epstein, 2005).

Goal Setting

As part of ringing in the New Year, many adults begin self-improvement plans by engaging in goal setting. They may set goals for getting in shape, eating healthy, or learning a new hobby. Students can also set goals, and they can be taught how to do so. In the classroom, students set goals for performance in both academic and behavioral areas. Here we focus on student goal setting for behavior improvement.

In setting a behavior improvement goal, it is best to address a behavior that the student can already perform in some situations and that will result in positive outcomes when it is used in naturally occurring environments. It is also recommended that the student and teacher choose an emerging skill for the student and set a goal to increase the student's independent use of that skill, rather than set a goal that the student will acquire a new skill. It is useful for the teacher to have a discussion with the student about what the student would like to have happen with regard to his or her behavior. Finally, a student might select an individual behavioral goal that is aligned with a classroom or school-wide behavior expectation (Oakes et al., 2012).

Self-Instruction

Prior to teaching the student self-instruction strategies, the teacher should make sure that the behavioral goal chosen during goal setting is observable and measurable. In other words, the student needs to know what the target behavior looks like in order to be able to record when it happens. For example, if the target behavior chosen during goal setting is on-task behavior, then the student should understand that on-task behavior means that the student is either looking at the teacher or looking at and engaging with materials during a lesson.

Self-instruction involves self-talk that assists in regulating behaviors. It includes self-statements that students are taught to use to direct their own behavior. That is, students literally talk to themselves to help them finish tasks, solve problems, or mediate social situations (Menzies, Lane, & Lee, 2009). Most individuals have engaged in self-instruction at one time or another, talking themselves through difficult tasks or situations. When they do so silently, the self-instruction is covert.

Sometimes, however, people engage in overt self-instruction, speaking to themselves aloud, especially for the most difficult of tasks.

Most guidelines for teaching self-instruction to students have been adapted from seminal work by Meichenbaum and Goodman (1971). In teaching self-instruction to a student, the following steps can be used:

1. The teacher models the task for the student while talking aloud.

2. The student performs the task while the teacher talks aloud.

3. The teacher uses a quiet voice and the student talks aloud while performing the task.

4. The student whispers while performing the task. The teacher may mouth the words to the task or use body language or facial expressions to guide or prompt the student to complete the task.

5. The student performs the task while using silent self-instruction.

Self-Monitoring

During **self-monitoring**, students observe their own behaviors and self-record whether they are exhibiting particular behaviors (Rafferty, 2010). A student can record the occurrences of behavior to be decreased (e.g., talking without permission) or behavior to be increased (e.g., time on task). Examples of self-monitoring include crossing things off a to-do list and tracking how much water one drinks in a day. In the classroom, students can be taught to self-monitor just about any behavior, from completing homework tasks to speaking out inappropriately. Successful self-monitoring can enhance and improve academic and social performance. Although self-monitoring can be used in isolation, it is most often used in tandem with self-evaluation, in which the student compares the data collected from self-recording with an established performance standard (Briesch & Chafouleas, 2009).

Self-recording can be cued or noncued. In cued self-recording, students record their behavior when a signal is given. The signal is usually a recorded tone, such as a chime or bell. When students hear the tone, they indicate on a data collection sheet if they are engaged in a given behavior at that time. In noncued self-recording, students are asked to make a notation on a data collection sheet each time they perform the target behavior.

It is recommended that teachers take the following steps in implementing self-monitoring strategies with students:

1. Select a target behavior, if this was not done during the goal-setting phase of the behavior management plan.

2. Define the behavior in observable, measurable terms. Help the student recognize examples as well as nonexamples of the behavior. For example, the teacher may ask the student, "Belinda, are you on task or off task?"

3. Instruct the student in the use of an appropriate data collection system and its corresponding form. For example, for discrete behaviors (those with a clear beginning and end), event recording (recording each time the target behavior occurs) is most appropriate (see Figure 7.2). To self-record continuous behaviors, such as being on task, students might use time sampling or interval recording (see Figure 7.3).

4. Instruct the student how to self-monitor. The student should be able to determine the difference between engaging and not engaging in the target behavior.

5. Monitor the student during a practice data-recording time period. The teacher may want to keep her own record in order to compare accuracy.

6. Fade the use of the intervention, so that the student self-monitors without the intervention. (Rafferty, 2010)

Self-Evaluation

During **self-evaluation**, students compare their performance to a set criterion (Menzies et al., 2009). Examples of self-evaluation include a person's assessment of his own job performance and an athlete's determination of how well she ran a race or played a game. In the classroom, students may evaluate how well they

---

WHAT WOULD YOU DO?   Belinda

Belinda is a sixth grader in her first month at Sheffield Middle School. She is a good student and is thrilled to be in middle school. She has made a lot of friends and likes all her new classes and teachers. She particularly likes that she moves from class to class and has a different teacher for each class.

Belinda's teachers state that she does well in class. She is very attentive, her time on task is excellent, and she seems to learn new concepts quickly. The only thing that Belinda seems to be struggling with is remembering to bring her homework and the correct notebook and materials to each class. For example, when she arrives at math class, she has her English homework and her biology notebook, but not her materials for math. She also usually forgets her pencil, and the teacher does not accept work done in pen in math class.

As one of her teachers, what would you do to help Belinda remember to bring the correct homework and materials to each of her classes?

Figure 7.2   Self-Monitoring Chart for Class Preparedness

AM I PREPARED FOR CLASS?

NAME: _____   DATE: _____

Color a star for every class period your materials are ready. (Book, pen, pencil, notebook)

My goal for this week: _____

Period	Monday	Tuesday	Wednesday	Thursday	Friday
Math	☆	☆	☆	☆	☆
Reading	☆	☆	☆	☆	☆
Science	☆	☆	☆	☆	☆
Social Studies	☆	☆	☆	☆	☆
Writing	☆	☆	☆	☆	☆

Figure 7.3 Self-Monitoring Chart for On Task Behavior

NAME: _____   DATE: _____

When you hear the clicker put a [+] if you are on task with your_____worksheet. Put a [o] if you are NOT on task with your worksheet.

My goal for this week: _____

Monday	Tuesday	Wednesday	Thursday	Friday

did in a musical performance, or they may assess their participation in a group project. When a student uses self-evaluation, he compares his own behavior to a predetermined standard set either by the student himself or by the teacher. Self-evaluation occurs after the student has collected data during the self-monitoring phase of self-management of behavior. Additionally, self-evaluation determines self-reinforcement and therefore takes place before such reinforcement.

The self-monitoring charts presented in Figures 7.2 and 7.3 have been modified in Figures 7.4 and 7.5 to include self-evaluation components. The addition of the "my achievements" line allows the student to evaluate himself against the goal that was set at the beginning of the self-monitoring period.

Self-Reinforcement

With self-reinforcement, students manage their behaviors by rewarding themselves when they successfully complete self-prescribed activities (Bandura, 1976). Many of us have engaged in self-reinforcement in our daily lives. For example, you may buy yourself new clothes when you have lost 10 pounds or go out on a Friday night with friends after you have completed your workweek productively. The behavior management interventions described above are more effective when combined with self-reinforcement—that is, when students give themselves

Figure 7.4 Self-Evaluation for Class Preparedness

AM I PREPARED FOR CLASS?

NAME: _____   DATE: _____

Color a star for every class period your materials are ready. (Book, pen, pencil, notebook)
My goal for this week: _____

Period	Monday	Tuesday	Wednesday	Thursday	Friday
Math	☆	☆	☆	☆	☆
Reading	☆	☆	☆	☆	☆
Science	☆	☆	☆	☆	☆
Social Studies	☆	☆	☆	☆	☆
Writing	☆	☆	☆	☆	☆

Achievement Chart

4–5 daily stars/20–25 stars weekly	Great! I was almost prepared for class.
3 daily stars/15–19 stars weekly	Okay, I was usually prepared for class.
Fewer than 3 daily stars/fewer than 15 stars weekly	Not so good. I wasn't prepared for class today and this week.

My achievements for this week were: _____

Was my goal reached? **Yes** or **No**

Figure 7.5 Time Sampling or Interval Recording with Self-Evaluation

Name: _____   Date: _____

When you hear the clicker put a [+] if you are on task with your _____ worksheet. Put a [o] if you are NOT on task with your worksheet.

My goal for this week: _____

Monday	Tuesday	Wednesday	Thursday	Friday

Achievement Chart

3–4 daily/15–20 weekly [+]	Great! I stayed on task for most of the week.
2 daily/10–14 weekly [+]	Okay, I was usually on task.
Fewer than 2 daily/fewer than 10 [+]	Not so good. I wasn't on task.

My achievements for this week were: _____

Was my goal reached? Yes or No

reinforcers if they conclude they have met the standard for the target behavior. Reinforcers may be points, tokens, or activities—whatever the student decides.

When using self-reinforcement strategies with students as part of a behavior management plan, it is best to start with teacher-initiated contingencies with which students are already involved. Students may already be allowed to choose their own reinforcers, such as extra computer time after finishing a worksheet. The transition from teacher-mediated reinforcement of behavior to student-managed reinforcement is made easier when students are explicitly taught to use self-reinforcement. Self-reinforcement may involve the students choosing their own reinforcers, setting criteria for earning reinforcers, or both.

Goal setting, self-instruction, self-monitoring, self-evaluation, and self-reinforcement form the basis for effective cognitive behavior management interventions. The learning and behavior of students with and without disabilities in the general education classroom setting can be enhanced through the use of self-management techniques (Moore et al., 2013). Furthermore, self-management meets the criteria for being an evidence-based practice that can be used across age groups and settings (Rafferty, 2010).

CASE STUDY Jane and Ms. Daniels

Jane is a third grader at Abydos Elementary School. Her physical education teacher, Ms. Daniels, has recently noticed that Jane has been consistently arriving late at the gymnasium for class after changing into her gym clothes in the locker room. Ms. Daniels talks to Jane, and she finds out that Jane likes and can do the activities in the class. It seems to Ms. Daniels that what is making Jane late is that she is socializing in the locker room rather than concentrating on changing clothes and getting to class in a timely fashion. Ms. Daniels decides to use a self-management strategy with Jane.

Together, Jane and Ms. Daniels define the target behavior as follows: Jane will leave the locker room at 9:10 a.m. (in order to be on the gymnasium floor at 9:15) on 4 of 5 class days each week for 1 month. They design a self-recording worksheet that consists of a chart with boxes for 20 days (5 days for 4 weeks) and tape it to the inside of Jane's locker. Jane puts a checkmark in a box each day she is ready to leave the locker room and the clock says 9:10 a.m. If Jane is at her station in the gym by 9:15 a.m., Ms. Daniels also records a checkmark on a chart.

So that Jane does not have to wait until the end of the month for reinforcement, Jane and Ms. Daniels decide that if Jane meets her goal for a week, she will be allowed to pass out the equipment the following Monday. If Jane meets her goal for the month, she will be allowed to be the team leader for the activity of her choice during the next "free choice" Friday. Additionally, every time Jane is on time and ready for class by 9:15, Ms. Daniels gives her a thumbs-up.

Jane's on-time arrival to PE class increases significantly over the next few weeks. Eventually, Ms. Daniels is able to fade the self-monitoring sheet and Jane continues to arrive to class on time when she is reinforced, on a variable-interval schedule, with being allowed to pass out team equipment.

PROBLEM-SOLVING STRATEGIES

In addition to the components discussed previously, cognitive behavior management programs rely on students' use of problem-solving strategies. Problem solving is a "systematic process in which concerns are identified, defined, actions taken, and solutions evaluated" (Miller & Nunn, 2001, p. 472). Teachers need to provide problem-solving strategy instruction for those students who fail to use effective problem-solving strategies on their own (e.g., students with emotional/behavioral disabilities). Teachers should provide instruction in the area of problem solving just as they would provide instruction in an academic subject. Modeling appropriate problem-solving skills as part of daily classroom routines is also important (Robinson, 2007).

Teachers can use self-instruction as an approach to teaching problem-solving skills. Using a five-step process, students are first taught to define the problem. Next, students identify as many solutions as possible. Then, students evaluate the potential outcomes of the possible solutions identified in the previous step. Next, students choose and implement a solution. Finally, students evaluate the outcome and begin the process over if the solution was not successful (Robinson, 2007; Robinson, Smith, & Miller, 2002).

Social problem solving is the "process of solving all types of problems that may affect a person's ability to function in the natural environment, or 'real world'" (Isbell & Jolivette, 2011, p. 32). Using a strategy called "stop, think, proceed," students use steps with visual cues and questions to prompt them through the social problem-solving process. In the first phase, *stop*, students recognize the emotional clues, take a few breaths to calm down, and identify the problem. In the second phase, *think*, students come up with possible solutions, evaluate each solution, and decide which solution to try. In the final phase, *proceed*, students carry out the solution, verify the outcomes, and try another solution if the problem is unresolved (Isbell & Jolivette, 2011).

Social problem-solving strategies can be integrated into class meetings (Gartrell, 2006) or group discussions (Miller & Nunn, 2001) in which all students are allowed to become participants who work together to solve a problem. Class meetings should be regular activities in classrooms, especially at the preschool and primary levels. Holding class meetings on a consistent basis allows the group to address students' concerns before they become problems or conflicts. Teachers and students are likely to appreciate the full potential of class meetings when they are used to resolve problems and conflicts that affect the whole group. Teachers can be proactive leaders during classroom meetings by first setting guidelines for interactions. Teachers should make sure students understand that everyone will be given a chance to speak, that students should listen to one another, and that students should treat one another with respect. When solving problems during class meetings, teachers should follow a five-step procedure:

1. Calm everyone, including themselves if necessary, and orient the students to the process.

2. Define the problem cooperatively.

3. Brainstorm possible solutions together.

4. Decide together on a plan using the solutions suggested.

5. Take an active role in guiding the plan's implementation. (Gartrell, 2006, p. 55)

Problem-solving instruction can also take place within the framework of bibliotherapy. Bibliotherapy allows students to identify with characters from books that are similar to them, so that they can discuss their own behaviors and situations through the safe distance of fictional characters (Cook, Earles-Vollrath, & Ganz, 2006). Teachers can use children's literature to help students generate possible solutions to problems. This happens as students discuss the conflict that a character encounters and brainstorm and evaluate possible solutions using a problem-solving method (Konrad, Helf, & Itoi, 2007). Teachers can use bibliotherapy in their classrooms by engaging students in prereading, guided reading, postreading, and problem-solving/reinforcement activities (Forgan, 2002).

During prereading, materials are selected and the teacher activates students' background knowledge in order to help them link their past experiences to the content of the book they will read. During guided reading, the teacher reads the book aloud to the students. After finishing the book, the teacher may want to allow students to react to the book by writing in journals before discussion begins. During the postreading discussion, students can first retell the story. Then the teacher asks probing questions that help the students engage with the book's main character and the situation the character is facing. During the ensuing discussion, students come to understand that others experience the same problems they do and can gain insight into the problem as they come up with possible solutions. Throughout the discussion, the teacher should see students passing through the stages of identification, catharsis, and resolution as they learn to problem solve (Forgan, 2002).

During the final phase of teaching with bibliotherapy, students can apply the I SOLVE problem-solving strategy, which uses the following steps:

I   Identify the problem.

S   Solutions to the problem?

O   Obstacles to the solutions?

L   Look at the solutions again—choose one.

V   Very good! Try it!

E   Evaluate the outcome. (Forgan, 2002, p. 78)

Allen and colleagues (2012) have suggested four similar steps in the use of bibliotherapy:

1. Identify the problem.

2. Come up with possible solutions.

3. Consider the consequences of different actions.

4. Choose the best solution.

Finally, teachers should provide some type of reinforcement activity so that students can practice applying the solutions they have learned. A sample lesson plan that includes the four steps of bibliotherapy is presented in Figure 7.6.

Figure 7.6 Sample Bibliotherapy Lesson Plan

The Grouchies

Author: Debbie Wagenbach

Illustrator: Steve Mack

Copyright Date: 2009

Publisher: American Psychological Association

ISBN: 9781433805530

Topic: Bad moods

Age range: 4–8

Synopsis of the Book:

A 5-year-old boy wakes up with gray, grouchy clouds around him. They follow him all day as he fights with his sister, acts mean toward friends at the playground, and has an emotional meltdown at the end of the day. His parents are calm and understanding throughout and eventually give him advice on how to replace the grouchy clouds with yellow happy-face circles.

Lesson Goals

To help students understand their emotions and how to manage their emotions effectively.

Prereading Activities

Ask the students if they have ever been upset or mad and didn't know why. If they knew why they were upset, how did they handle it? Then the class can begin to hear other short stories of their peers about when they were upset. Is it okay to get angry sometimes? When? How do people act when they are angry?

Summarize by expressing that it is okay to feel angry and upset but what is important is how we handle our anger. Tell the students that you are going to read them a story about a young boy who wakes one morning with gray, grouchy clouds that follow him all day. These angry clouds represent the little boy being angry. Raise the book and show them the cover and title. Ask the students, By looking at the cover, what do you think the story is about?

During Reading

Read the story aloud. Once you are done with the story, you can allow the students to reflect on the story. You might ask students what they thought of the story.

Postreading

Have students further engage with the story by asking them what they learned from it. Asking higher-order thinking questions through a guided class discussion of the character's problem will help the students' comprehension of the story.

I SOLVE Strategy

I: Identify the problem.
  ○ The little boy woke up with "grouchy clouds" above him and they told him to be a grouch and grump at everyone he met throughout the day.

S: Solutions to the problem.
  ○ Book suggestion: The little boy's dad told him, "We all get grumpy, if the grouchies get their way."
  ○ Think of happy thoughts—that could shield him from grouchy cloud attacks.
  ○ The little boy's mom told him choosing to be nice stops grouchies in their tracks.
  ○ Draw pictures of things that make you happy.

O: Obstacles to the solutions.
  ○ The grouchy clouds may continue to come back.

L: Look at the solutions again—choose one.
  ○ Think of happy thoughts—that could shield him from grouchy cloud attacks.

V: Very good! Try it!
  ○ Use the reinforcement activity and try the role-play activity.

E: Evaluate the outcome.
  ○ Was the solution successful? If not, what other solution would you use?

Source: Adapted from Forgan (2002).

ANGER MANAGEMENT STRATEGIES

In Chapter 1, we discussed the distinction between classical conditioning, which accounts for respondent behaviors, and operant conditioning. The behavior management strategies examined so far in this chapter are effective in either increasing appropriate behaviors or decreasing inappropriate behaviors—that is, operant behaviors, or learned behaviors. Some respondent behaviors, particularly conditioned emotional responses, such as anger and anxiety, can also be addressed using management strategies, including relaxation techniques (Sarafino, 2012).

Before teaching anger management strategies to students, it is important for teachers to help students understand that anger is a human and sometimes common emotion. Everyone feels angry at one time or another. Some individuals get angry more frequently than others. Some students get angry over things like bad grades, while others get angry over things like parents fighting. Students need to understand that it is okay to feel angry, but it is not okay is for them to hurt themselves or others when they are angry. Students can be taught to recognize anger and practice positive responses to anger. These responses might include going for a walk, talking to someone, counting to 10, writing about the feeling, or distracting oneself.

Students who demonstrate disruptive behavior in the classroom often have problems expressing anger in acceptable ways. Some students learned when they were young that they could control circumstances and get what they wanted through anger. When people gave into their aggressive behavior, the connection between demonstrating inappropriate behavior when angry and control was strengthened. These students need to learn acceptable ways of showing frustration and anger. Teaching students to manage anger, and other emotions, should begin with young children in the preschool classroom.

Cognitive behavioral intervention (CBI) can provide students with the skills they need to control anger and handle disappointment. CBI strategies can help them to interact appropriately in school and other settings (Robinson, 2007).

In preschool and elementary settings, many incidents occur in which children bump into and knock over constructions made by others. Sometimes students interpret these accidents as purposeful and hostile acts. The "turtle technique" (Robin, Schneider, & Dolnick, 1976) is a CBI strategy that has been used successfully with preschool and kindergarten children. Through an illustrative story, children are told about a turtle that has problems at school because he does not stop and think:

Little Turtle was very upset about going to school. When he was there he got into trouble because he fought with his mates. Other turtles teased, bumped, or hit him. He then became angry and started fights. The teacher then punished him. One day he met the big old tortoise, who told him that his shell was the secret answer to many problems. The tortoise told Little Turtle to withdraw into his shell whenever he felt angry, and rest until he felt better. Little Turtle tried it the next day and it worked. He no longer became angry or started fights, his teacher now smiled at him, and he began to like school. (Robin et al., 1976, p. 450)

The turtle technique consists of four basic steps:

1. Recognizing that you feel angry

2. Thinking "stop"

3. Going into your "shell" and taking three deep breaths and thinking calming, coping thoughts ("It was an accident. I can calm down and think of good solutions. I am a good problem solver.")

4. Coming out of your "shell" when calm and thinking of some solutions to the problem (Joseph & Strain, 2010)

This technique can be adapted for use with both large and small groups. Research findings support the use of a metaphor, such as this technique's turtle, in teaching relaxation strategies. In one study, all children selected the "turtle game" as their favorite technique over others, such as literal instruction, for engaging in relaxation exercise (Heffner, Greco, & Eifert, 2003). In a recent study, Drogan and Kern (2014) studied the use of the turtle technique as a Tier 2 intervention with preschool children who engaged in problem behavior. At the end of the intervention, the researchers found a decrease in the level of problem behavior for all participants. The primary goal of strategies like the turtle technique and accompanying teaching supports is to offer children the cognitive and behavioral repertoire they need to be good managers of their feelings—particularly those occasioned by frustrating and anger-provoking circumstances (Joseph & Strain, 2010).

Anger management programs address a variety of skills, including coping, emotional awareness, self-control, problem solving, and relaxation (Candelaria, Fedewa, & Ahn, 2012). An example of one such program is In Control (Kellner, 2001), which is designed to teach coping skills to middle school students as a way of managing anger. The program can be used with an entire class, with small groups, or with individuals. It consists of step-by-step lessons with teaching guidelines, materials, scripts, and activities. The lessons and activities can be adapted to meet student needs, abilities, and interests.

Student Created Aggression Replacement Education (SCARE) is a school-based anger and aggression management program. The primary goals of the program are to "teach young people how to control impulsive, aggressive emotions, to encourage them to make better decisions in responding to provocative situations, and to provide alternatives to violent behavior" (Herrmann & McWhirter, 2001, p. xxii). The program has 15 sessions and is organized into three sections: recognizing anger and violence in our community, managing/reducing anger in yourself, and defusing anger and violence in others/prevention strategies. (SCARE, which is considered a model program by the U.S. Department of Justice's Office of Juvenile Justice and Delinquency Prevention and a promising program by the U.S. Department of Education, is available at http://www.arizonachildpsychology.com/The%20SCARE%20Program.pdf.)

The violence prevention curriculum Second Step (Committee for Children, 2002) is designed to help children, grades pre-K to 8, increase their social competency skills, thereby reducing impulsive and aggressive behavior. The elementary curriculum uses group discussion, modeling, coaching, and practices to "increase students' social competence, risk assessment, decision-making ability, self-regulation, and positive goal setting" (Office of Juvenile Justice and Delinquency Prevention, n.d.). It includes empathy training, impulse control, problem solving, and anger management. In addition to this content, middle school students learn how to deal with peer pressure and bullying, how to resist gang pressure, and how to defuse fights.

STRESS MANAGEMENT STRATEGIES

Students can use anxiety management/relaxation training (AM/RT) interventions to manage anxiety caused by stressors, both major and minor, in their lives. Individuals' responses to stressors have impacts on their anxiety levels. If they can learn more appropriate ways to respond to life's stressors, they can avoid the negative effects of anxiety, including depression (Lane, Cook, & Tankersley, 2013). Although AM/RT interventions vary in content, they tend to have several common components. One of these is their emphasis that "it is important for students to understand how their stress and anxiety are related to feelings of depression and how managing their reactions to stress can lessen depressive symptoms" (Lane et al., 2013, p. 65). Another commonality is the use of some form of progressive relaxation training, a technique first described by Jacobson (1938) and later adapted by Wolpe (1958).

Relaxation Procedures

Students' anger, stress, and anxiety can be tempered through the use of relaxation procedures that are easy to learn. Anger management interventions typically include relaxation exercises for stress and anxiety reduction, and these exercises often focus breathing (Gaines & Barry, 2008). Relaxation has been defined as "a state of calmness with low psychological and physiological tension or arousal" (Sarafino, 2012, p. 323). Relaxation therapy is an effective, self-regulatory intervention that allows students to develop direct self-control of their behaviors (Robinson, 2007). Progressive muscle relaxation (PMR) and yoga are two examples of relaxation technique approaches.

The goal of PMR is to improve daily performance by reducing factors such as arousal (increases in muscle tension, respiration, and heart rate), anxiety, tension, and stress, thus producing a relaxed and calm state that is inconsistent with aggressive behavior. PMR exercises consist of systematic tensing and releasing of different muscle groups. While performing these exercises, students gain increased awareness of the resulting sensations of tension and relaxation (Lopata, Nida, & Marable, 2006). PMR can be utilized in various settings, including the classroom, with all types of students. For instance, one study examined the effectiveness of PMR as an intervention for preventing aggression in elementary students with emotional/behavior disorders. Students who participated in PMR showed a significant decrease in physical aggression following the treatment phase, whereas students who did not participate in PMR showed no change in physical aggression (Lopata, 2003). Additional studies have demonstrated the positive psychological and physiological effects of PMR (Gaines & Barry, 2008; Lopata et al., 2006).

When using PMR in the general education or special education classroom, the teacher should use a calm and reassuring tone of voice to provide students with a sense of security and promote participation and relaxation. The PMR technique is very adaptable and can be integrated into different dynamics of the classroom routine and modified to accommodate student needs (Lopata, 2003; Lopata et al., 2006). Figure 7.7 details the PMR technique.

In addition to PMR, yoga is recommended as a relaxation technique in self-regulatory intervention treatment. The National Institute of Mental Health (2005) has suggested that mild exercise or yoga may have positive effects on various aspects of mental and physical health. Yoga therapy is one type of psychophysiological treatment, and yogic practices (including breathing, relaxation, and meditation techniques) have been found to influence the activity of the autonomic nervous system in studies of participants with and without externalizing and internalizing behaviors. The *yoga nidra* relaxation technique has been found to improve stability in amplitude and rate in

Figure 7.7 Progressive Muscle Relaxation

The following script is presented as a guide for teachers to use in leading their students through a session of progressive muscle relaxation (PMR). It is important that the teacher maintain a calm and soothing tone of voice while administering the PMR technique. It is recommended that the teacher use a timer to track the durations of the tension (squeeze) phases and the relaxation (letting go) phases. The tension phases should last 6–8 seconds, and the relaxation phases should last 15–20 seconds. The setting should be a quiet room.

1. Starting position: Sit comfortably in your chair, both feet flat on the ground and arms to your side. [Students can also lie down.]

2. Next you will close your eyes and listen to my voice. (Eyes closed and ears opened.)

3. First raise both arms up, now make two fists and squeeze as tight as you can. Squeeze [2 seconds] . . . squeeze [2 seconds] . . . squeeze [2 seconds]. Now release . . . feel your body letting go . . . relax. [15–20 seconds]

4. Now you are going to tighten your right forearm. You will tighten your forearm by making a fist. Ready, squeeze [2 seconds] . . . squeeze [2 seconds] . . . squeeze [2 seconds]. Now release . . . feel your body letting go . . . relax. [15–20 seconds]

5. Now you are going to tighten your left forearm. You will tighten your forearm by making a fist. Ready, squeeze [2 seconds] . . . squeeze [2 seconds] . . . squeeze [2 seconds]. Now release . . . feel your body letting go . . . relax. [15–20 seconds]

6. Next you are going to tighten your right upper arm, which is your bicep. Tighten that muscle by squeezing. Squeeze [2 seconds] . . . squeeze [2 seconds] . . . squeeze [2 seconds]. Now release . . . feel your body letting go . . . relax. [15–20 seconds]

7. Now you are going to tighten your left upper arm with the same movement you did with your right bicep. Ready, squeeze [2 seconds] . . . squeeze [2 seconds] . . . squeeze [2 seconds]. Now release . . . feel your body letting go . . . relax. [15–20 seconds]

8. Next you are going to lift your shoulders up toward your ears. Hold that position. Ready, squeeze [2 seconds] . . . squeeze [2 seconds] . . . squeeze [2 seconds]. Now release . . . feel your body letting go . . . relax. [15–20 seconds]

9. Now you are going to tuck your chin to your chest. Hold that position. Ready, squeeze [2 seconds] . . . squeeze [2 seconds] . . . squeeze [2 seconds]. Now release . . . feel your body letting go . . . relax. [15–20 seconds]

10. Now you are going to bend your head back as far as possible. Ready, squeeze [2 seconds] . . . squeeze [2 seconds] . . . squeeze [2 seconds]. Slowly bring your head back to starting position. Now release . . . feel your body letting go . . . relax. [15–20 seconds]

11. Next you are going to tighten your stomach muscles. Ready, squeeze [2 seconds] . . . squeeze [2 seconds] . . . squeeze [2 seconds]. Now release . . . feel your body letting go . . . relax. [15–20 seconds]

12. Now raise your legs and tighten your upper legs by pointing your toes up. Ready, squeeze [2 seconds] . . . squeeze [2 seconds] . . . squeeze [2 seconds]. Slowly bring your legs down. Now release . . . feel your body letting go . . . relax. [15–20 seconds]

13. Next you are going to tighten your calf muscles by pointing your toes down. Ready, squeeze [2 seconds] . . . squeeze [2 seconds] . . . squeeze [2 seconds]. Now release . . . feel your body letting go . . . relax. [15–20 seconds]

14. Now you are going to tighten all your muscles at once. Ready, squeeze [2 seconds] . . . squeeze [2 seconds] . . . squeeze [2 seconds]. Now release . . . feel your body letting go . . . relax. [15–20 seconds]

15. Your body has relaxed, and I want you take three deep breaths. [Guide with verbal cues such as inhale and exhale.] Now open your eyes and feel relaxed.

breathing patterns in boys between the ages of 10 and 15 with disruptive behavior. Teachers can be trained to use this technique in the classroom (Jensen, Stevens, & Kenny, 2012).

SUMMARY

Cognitive behavior management includes intervention strategies designed to teach students to control their own behaviors. It is considered a proactive strategy in the universal design for classroom management. Self-management techniques include goal setting, self-instruction, self-monitoring, self-evaluation, and self-reinforcement.

Cognitive behavior management programs use problem-solving strategies with students. Students who fail to use effective problem-solving strategies on their own will require problem-solving strategy instruction. The "stop, think, proceed" technique is an example of a problem-solving strategy that teachers might use. Additionally, bibliotherapy provides opportunities for students to solve problems through the reading and discussion of books. This procedure includes the steps of prereading, guided reading, postreading, and problem-solving/reinforcement activities.

Anger management strategies, such as the "turtle technique" for younger students and anger management programs such as In Control, SCARE, and Second Step, provide teachers with ways to help children and youth manage their anger and aggression. Finally, progressive muscle relaxation and yoga are two examples of relaxation procedures that can help students manage stress.

REVIEW ACTIVITIES

1. List and describe the steps a teacher should take in teaching a student to use self-instruction.

2. Create your own recording of an intermittent tone for use in student self-recording, or download a 3-, 5-, or 10-minute recording from the Utah Personnel Development Center's website (http://www.updc.org/beep).

3. Read this chapter's "What Would You Do?" and then answer the following questions:

   a. How would you help Belinda state a goal for herself? What would be an appropriate goal for Belinda?

   b. How would you define Belinda's target behavior in observable, measurable terms?

   c. What data collection system would be appropriate for collecting data on Belinda's behavior? Create a self-monitoring/recording worksheet for Belinda.

4. Bullying is a growing concern in U.S. schools. Locate a children's book that addresses bullying and could be used as bibliotherapy. Write a lesson plan for using the book, following the format in Figure 7.6.

5. With a classmate, try the progressive muscle relaxation technique outlined in Figure 7.7.

CHAPTER 8

FUNCTIONAL BEHAVIORAL ASSESSMENT

Trinity of Behavior Management

After reading this chapter, you should be able to do the following:

- Describe the differences among functional behavioral assessment, functional behavior analysis, and behavior intervention plans, and explain how they work together to modify student behavior.
- Name and describe the three characteristics of a target behavior.
- Describe the four attributes of behavior.
- Use an anecdotal observation form to define a target behavior.
- Use the appropriate recording methods for measuring frequency, duration, latency, and permanent products.
- Describe the similarities and differences among the most common types of graphs for displaying behavioral observations or student performance.

THE TRINITY OF BEHAVIOR MANAGEMENT

The primary purpose of a behavior and classroom management program is to maintain a safe and secure environment in which learning can take place. The majority of students in a classroom are intrinsically motivated to comply with well-defined rules and consequences; however, 5–10% of students do not follow classroom rules. These students display behaviors that are not conducive to the learning environment of the classroom, and it is the teacher's responsibility to manage these behaviors. The teacher needs to implement behavior modification strategies designed to replace or reduce inappropriate behaviors. Before the teacher can effectively manage the inappropriate behaviors of these students, she must define the behaviors and identify the causes, or the functions, of the behaviors. That is, the teacher needs to understand why the students behave in inappropriate ways before she can develop effective intervention strategies to change their behaviors. The three-step process that a teacher uses to define a student's inappropriate behavior, identify the function of the behavior, and develop intervention strategies is known as the trinity of behavior management. It consists of (a) conducting a functional behavioral assessment, (b) completing a functional behavior analysis, and (c) implementing a behavior intervention plan.

A **functional behavioral assessment** is a problem-solving process for addressing student behavior by identifying the characteristics of the behavior through observation. The teacher uses a functional behavioral assessment to create a detailed description of the behavior and consequences in observable and measurable terms. When conducting a functional behavioral assessment, the teacher gathers information regarding the student's behavior, identifies the environment and consequences that affect the behavior, and determines why the student behaves in a particular manner. This includes describing and recording the frequency, intensity, duration, and latency of the behavior. A **functional behavior analysis** completes the process started by the functional behavioral assessment. Through this analysis, the teacher develops a behavioral hypothesis that suggests ways to modify the behavior through the alteration of the antecedent or the consequences. Finally, the results of the functional behavioral assessment and functional behavior analysis are used to develop and implement a **behavior intervention plan**. The BIP implements strategies aimed at reducing or eliminating inappropriate behaviors.

Functional behavioral assessments, functional behavior analysis, and behavior intervention plans should also be used as active strategies to identify behaviors and develop alternative or replacement behaviors (see Table 8.1).

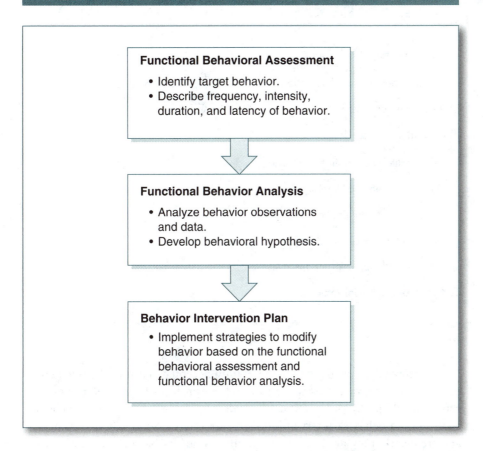

Figure 8.1 The Trinity of Behavior Management

Functional Behavioral Assessment
- Identify target behavior.
- Describe frequency, intensity, duration, and latency of behavior.

Functional Behavior Analysis
- Analyze behavior observations and data.
- Develop behavioral hypothesis.

Behavior Intervention Plan
- Implement strategies to modify behavior based on the functional behavioral assessment and functional behavior analysis.

This trinity of behavior management tools is an important part of a universal design for classroom management and should be incorporated at the third tier of a positive behavior support program. While functional behavioral assessments and behavior intervention plans are mandated for students with disabilities, many educational professionals are increasingly recognizing that these means of behavior management should be used as positive behavior supports in the general education classrooms for *all* students who are having behavior difficulties (Moreno & Bullock, 2011). At this level, functional behavioral assessments, functional behavior analysis, and behavior intervention plans can be used to help develop intensive supports for students who are still having behavior difficulties despite the strategies used in previous tiers.

Table 8.1 Trinity of Behavior Management: Functional Behavioral Assessment

1. Define the target behavior.

2. Conduct behavioral observation.

3. Chart the behavior.

4. Use single-subject design.

5. Identify the function of the behavior.

6. Develop a behavior hypothesis.

7. Develop alternative behavior.

8. Develop functional-based interventions.

9. Identify the function of the behavior.

10. Develop a behavior hypothesis.

Functional Behavioral Assessment

Unfortunately, not all schools have fully accepted the use of principles of proactive and preventive strategies to address problem behaviors in the classroom (Barnhill, 2005). Functional behavioral assessment, functional behavior analysis, and behavior intervention plans are often used as reactive strategies, and frequently they are not used until after students have been identified for special education services and after their behaviors have prompted changes in placement. With as many as one in five children at risk for mental, emotional, or behavioral problems (World Health Organization, 2004), schools should be using this trinity of behavior management as an active strategy and for *all* students experiencing behavior difficulties.

Culturally Responsive Functional Behavioral Assessments

When functional behavioral assessments are undertaken with diverse students, it is important for those conducting the assessments to determine whether the behaviors at issue are related to the students' cultural and linguistic backgrounds. Teachers, other education professionals, and others involved in functional behavioral assessments cannot adopt a "diversity-blind" ideology and ignore the impact that culture may have on behavior. Understanding the impact that culture has on behavior is especially pertinent given the fact that diverse students have higher rates of discipline referrals than do European American students and are more likely to be referred for special education services (Billingsley, Fall, & Williams, 2006; Drakeford, 2006; Dray & Wisneski, 2011; Imler, 2009; Linn, 2011).

The individuals conducting a functional behavioral assessment play a critical role in determining whether a student's behavior is a manifestation of the student's culture. These individuals must be culturally sensitive to the student's behavior by understanding their own cultures and how their cultural beliefs influence their perceptions of the student. Expanding the assessment team to include members of the student's family ensures that the team has some understanding of the cultural, experiential, and linguistic background of the student. The family members can provide the team with information about the sociocultural expectations of the student (Moreno & Gaytán, 2012). Through understanding the student's background, the team can determine whether the student's behavior has a cultural explanation.

CONDUCTING A FUNCTIONAL BEHAVIORAL ASSESSMENT

Requirements for functional behavioral assessments did not exist until the 1997 reauthorization of IDEA. A functional behavioral assessment is conducted when (a) a student with a disability is suspended or removed for school for more than 10 days, (b) a student's educational placement has been changed, and (c) when behavior goals and/or objectives have been added to a student's individualized education program (Allday, Nelson, & Russel, 2011). Since IDEA was reauthorized again in 2004, there has been increased interest in the use of functional behavioral assessments and behavior intervention plans in public schools, but these tools are still not widely employed except where required by IDEA. As we have noted, under a universal design for classroom management, schools should use functional behavioral assessments for all students displaying behavior difficulties.

A functional behavioral assessment is an essential precursor to a behavior intervention plan, and the assessment should be a comprehensive process supported by data (Killu, 2008). However, there are three barriers to using functional behavioral assessments, which pragmatically prevents the development and implementation of effective BIPs. First, IDEA does not provide any operational definition or standardized procedures for developing and implementing functional behavioral assessments. As a result, individual U.S. states have broad latitude to develop and implement functional behavioral assessments according to their own standards. Only 17 states have officially defined functional behavioral assessments, and many of these definitions are missing key components, including a clear connection to behavior intervention plans (Zirkel, 2011). Second, functional behavioral assessments are often used as a reactive practice rather than being integrated into positive behavior support programs in general education classrooms for students with and without disabilities. The third barrier is teachers' lack of training in conducting functional behavioral assessments (Couvillon, Bullock, & Gable, 2009; Scott, Anderson, & Spaulding, 2008; Stichter & Conroy, 2005), despite the fact that functional behavioral assessments are critical to the effectiveness of behavior intervention plans in reducing or eliminating social and behavior problems in schools.

Defining the Target Behavior

The first step in conducting a functional behavioral assessment is to define the target behavior in observable and measurable terms. Unfortunately, many teachers tend to define behaviors in general terms, and many functional behavioral assessments do not have adequate operational definitions of the target behaviors. "If the target behavior is not clearly specified and defined objectively, it becomes hard to collect the data necessary to identify the function of the behavior and to intervene effectively" (Van Acker, Boreson, Gable, & Potterton, 2005, p. 51). For example, a teacher may describe a student as "rude," but this description does not specify behaviors that constitute the student's rudeness. An imprecise definition of the target behavior can result in interventions that are ineffective or that could exacerbate the behavior (Borgmeier, Horner, & Koegel, 2006).

When the teacher identifies a student behavior to be assessed and modified, this behavior becomes the target behavior. Target behaviors must be *observable, measurable,* and *repeatable.* Observable behaviors are overt behaviors that students display and are easily perceived, such as speaking out without permission or throwing objects. Covert behaviors are generally internalized and cannot be easily observed; these are often inferred. For example, feeling sad, feeling depressed, and feeling lonely are covert behaviors. Behaviors are measurable when they can be quantified according to frequency, intensity, duration, and latency. Finally, repeatable behaviors are behaviors that occur frequently. The operational definition of the target behavior is based on the behavior's observability, measurability, and repeatability. The operational definition states the specific properties of the behavior in clear and explicit terms. This definition is the one that everyone involved in the behavioral functional assessment will use when observing and measuring the behavior.

For example, the teacher reports, "Clayton is rude." "Rude" is an inferred behavior, and it cannot be directly observed or measured. Since different behaviors can be "rude," it is also difficult to determine if it is repeatable. In contrast, if the teacher reports that Clayton frequently makes negative comments about peers' clothes, she is reporting behavior that is observable, measurable, and repeatable. Thus, Clayton's target behavior becomes "Clayton will refrain from making negative comments about peers' clothes." Rather than focusing on the inappropriate behaviors, statements of target behaviors are usually expressed in terms of action in a positive tone:

- Ricardo will raise his hand in class.
- Jane will ask for permission to leave her desk.
- Kale will complete assignments before the end of class.
- Timothy will say "thank you" when given items by peers.

The target behavior can also be stated as an alternative behavior. For example, instead of "Clayton will refrain from making negative comments about peers' clothes," Clayton's target behavior might be "Clayton will make positive statements about peers' clothes." Alternative or replacement behaviors are important factors in the development of behavior intervention plans.

CULTURAL IMPACT ON DEFINING BEHAVIOR

A clearly defined target behavior is necessary to the conduct of a functional behavioral assessment and a functional behavior analysis, which are the foundations for the creation of a behavior intervention plan. Without an accurately defined target behavior, a BIP is likely to be ineffective. Teachers must keep in mind that a student's culture may affect how he responds to a situation or event. For example, Mr. Salyer, a European American history teacher, notices that LeVar, an African American student, is not working on his U.S. history assignment during class time. Mr. Salyer instructs LeVar to work on his assignment. LeVar tells his teacher, "No," and does not comply with the request. Mr. Salyer has noted that LeVar's defiant behavior occurs frequently. As a result, LeVar's defiant behavior—which is observable, measurable, and repeatable—becomes his target behavior, the focus of a functional behavioral assessment and a functional behavior analysis. Using the results, a behavior intervention team develops a behavior intervention plan for LeVar with interventions designed to replace his defiant behavior with an alternative, appropriate behavior. Yet, despite all the time and effort spent on conducting assessments and implementing the BIP, LeVar's inappropriate behavior does not improve—in fact, it increases.

At least two mistakes were made in the development and implementation of LeVar's behavior intervention plan. First, Mr. Salyer's perception of LeVar's behavior was incorrect. He assumed that LeVar was exhibiting defiance and noncompliance; however, in some African American cultures, students learn to act assertively. Had Mr. Salyer understood LeVar's culture, he would have surmised that LeVar's response had an unspoken element. LeVar meant, but did not say, "No, I will not complete the assignment unless I see the importance of the assignment." LeVar's inappropriate behavior was one of communication, not defiance. Had Mr. Salyer understood the impetus of LeVar's behavior, the focus of the functional behavioral assessment and functional behavior analysis would have been different, and the resulting BIP would have prescribed different interventions that could have effectively modified LeVar's behavior. Indeed, had Mr. Salyer understood LeVar's behavior, he may have reacted differently to LeVar's response to his redirection, explaining to LeVar why the assignment was important. If he had done so, he might have saved himself and others the time and effort of conducting a functional behavioral assessment and functional behavior analysis and developing a behavior intervention plan. Because the target behavior and subsequent interventions were based on replacing defiant behavior and not on addressing inappropriate communication behavior, LeVar's BIP was ineffective.

Second, Mr. Salyer and the members of the behavior intervention team were not culturally sensitive, so they failed to assess LeVar's "defiant" behavior accurately, and they developed an ineffective BIP. It is important that the individuals conducting functional behavioral assessments and functional behavior analysis use culturally responsive methods of assessment.

BEHAVIORAL OBSERVATIONS

Behavioral observations are used to assess students' behaviors in natural settings. It is important that those who conduct behavioral observations collect information regarding the settings, antecedents, and consequences associated with the target behaviors. ABC analysis, or anecdotal observation, is a commonly used method; in such analysis, the observer notes the antecedent (A) that occurs before the behavior (B) and the consequence (C) that follows. Behavior is often affected by the events that occur prior to the behavior (antecedents) and reinforced by the consequences that follow the behavior. For example, Mario takes LeVar's favorite pen (antecedent), LeVar punches Mario (behavior), and Mario gives the pen back to LeVar (consequence). The purpose of the ABC analysis is to identify the target behavior through the antecedent that prompts the behavior and the reinforcing consequences that maintain the behavior (Erickson, Stage, & Nelson, 2006).

Antecedents include the time and place of the target behavior, the significant people involved prior to the behavior, and any events prior to the behavior, including the behavior of others. For example, the teacher observes that LeVar's inappropriate behavior generally occurs prior to the beginning of class, during unstructured time. It is possible that this unstructured time could be a factor in LeVar's behavior. Through additional observations, the teacher notes that LeVar is physically aggressive toward male peers who have offended him in some manner (e.g., taking his favorite pen, calling him names). LeVar's responses to these affronts are immediate. LeVar's relationships with peers and his reactions to their behaviors could be the result of poor social interaction skills. The teacher records this information on an ABC anecdotal observation form, which can be used later, with additional information, in the definition of a target behavior for LeVar (see Figure 8.2).

Consequences, or responses to stimulus, are positive or negative reinforcements that follow a behavior. Consequences include environmental events as well as the reactions of teachers, peers, and others present during the student's behavior. For example, when LeVar punches Mario, Mario returns the pilfered pen to LeVar. The consequence of LeVar's behavior is the successful return of his favorite pen. As a result, this positive reinforcement of LeVar's behavior may increase the probability of the behavior occurring again, and the teacher has noted this occurrence. Equally important is the teacher's reaction to LeVar's behavior. Does she verbally reprimand LeVar? Does she send him to the office? Does she reprimand the peers whose behaviors have triggered LeVar's behavior? The degree to which culture influences behavior is also an important consideration. LeVar is African American, and the teacher should take his cultural background into account: Is his behavior part of survival strategy? Does he want to avoid seeming weak in front of his friends? It is important for anyone conducting behavioral observation to consider and record all possible consequences of a student's target behavior.

Figure 8.2	ABC Anecdotal Observation Form

Student's Name: _LeVar_   Observer: _Mrs. Clarke_

Date of Observation: _March 19, 2016_

Antecedent	Behavior	Consequences
Time: _1:00 p.m._ Place: _Math class_ People: _Mario_ Events: _Students coming into class before class begins. Mario takes LeVar's pen._	_LeVar punches Mario._	_Mario gives pen back to LeVar._ _LeVar is sent to the office for punching Mario._
Possible Cultural Impact:	_LeVar may not want to appear weak before peers._	

Describing the Behavior

Once the operational definition of the target behavior has been determined, it is important to understand the characteristics of the behavior. Understanding the characteristics of a behavior makes it easier for the teacher to observe and measure the behavior. During behavioral observation, observers focus on measuring four characteristics of behavior: frequency, intensity, duration, and latency.

Frequency

The easiest characteristic of behavior to measure is **frequency**, or how often the behavior occurs in a specific period of time. Recording the frequency of a behavior includes recording the number of times the behavior occurs and the length of the observation. For example, when Mrs. Clarke asks questions during discussion, Natalie provides the answer without raising her hand four times in 30 minutes. This information alone is not useful unless it can be compared to the frequency of the behavior during another observation period. However, in order for the frequency of the behavior to be comparable to the frequency in another observation period, the duration of the two observation periods must be the same. For example, Natalie's target behavior (not raising her hand) is also observed in Mrs. Alvarado's class, where, during the same duration of 30 minutes, Natalie provides the answer without raising her hand nine times during a class discussion. Because it is difficult for teachers to have matched duration rates for different observations, the usefulness of just measuring the frequency of a behavior is limited. When the observation periods are different durations, the rate of the behavior is a more effective method for measuring the behavior's frequency.

The rate of a behavior can be calculated by dividing the number of times the behavior occurs (the frequency count) by the length of the observation:

Rate of the Behavior = Frequency of the Behavior/Observed Time

The rate of a behavior is often stated in times per minute. For example, when Mrs. Clarke asks questions during class, Natalie provides the answer without raising her hand four times in 30 minutes, so the rate of the behavior is 4/30, or 0.13 times per minute. The frequency rate is useful for comparing the frequency of a behavior across different settings where the lengths of the observation periods are different. For example, Natalie's target behavior (not raising her hand) is also observed in Mrs. Alvarado's class for 37 minutes. During that observation period, Natalie provides the answer without raising her hand nine times during a class discussion. The rate of the behavior in Mrs. Alvarado's class is 0.24 times per minute. Comparison of Natalie's rate of behavior in Mrs. Clarke's class (0.13 times per minute) with her rate of behavior in Mrs. Alvarado's class (0.24 times per minute) provides evidence that Natalie's behavior occurs at an increased rate in a class other than Mrs. Clarke's.

Intensity

Intensity refers to how much force is used when the student exhibits the behavior. Intensity is a useful measurement of overt behaviors such as aggression, verbal responses, and body movements. Measurement of the **intensity of a behavior** is extremely important in the identification of students with emotional and behavioral disorders. Under the current IDEA definition, one of the characteristics of a child with emotional and behavioral disorders is that the inappropriate behavior is exhibited to a marked degree. However, intensity is often a qualitative measure, because it is very difficult to measure and is often subjective. For example, Timothy comes into the classroom and begins calling a peer names. The intensity of this behavior may involve the loudness of the verbal barrage. Is it loud enough for only the peer to hear? Is it loud enough for the teacher to hear, or loud enough to be heard in the classroom next door? Intensity can often be measured as a level of strength (weak or strong), a level of volume (quiet or loud), or a level of speed (slow or fast), or it can be measured as mild to very severe. For example, Timothy's name-calling could be described as very loud, loud, quiet, or very quiet.

Duration

The **duration of a behavior** is the length of time the student displays that behavior. Having information about duration is useful when a teacher wants to increase or decrease the amount of time a student exhibits a behavior or performs a task. Teachers can measure two types of duration: duration per episode and total duration per observation.

Duration per episode is simply the amount of time a student engages in a behavior during one episode. For example, Kale is off task for 4 minutes. The duration per episode is 4 minutes. If Kale is off task again, the process is repeated. As a result, Kale may have an initial duration per episode of 4 minutes and a second duration per episode of 3 minutes during the same observation period. **Total duration per observation** measures the cumulative amount of time the student engages in a behavior. For instance, in a 30-minute period, Kale is off task four times, with episodes of 4 minutes, 3 minutes, 5 minutes, and 2 minutes in duration. Kale's total duration of the behavior during the 30-minute period is 14 minutes. Total duration may be reported as a percentage of the student's behavior during an observation. For example, the duration of Kale's off-task behavior was 14 minutes during a 30-minute period. Thus, Kale was off-task 47% of the 30-minute observation period.

$$14 \div 30 = 0.466 \times 100 = 47\%$$

For a teacher with 25 students in the classroom, measuring the duration of one student's particular behavior can be problematic. This method of measurement is time-intensive, because the teacher has to focus on and record the behavior when it begins and when it ends, which is difficult when the teacher has to be attentive to the other students in the classroom as well. Measuring the duration of behaviors is more practical if a classroom assistant or paraprofessional is available to collect the behavioral data.

Latency

The **latency of a behavior** is the amount of time between an environmental event (stimulus) and the behavior (response). Latency is an appropriate measurement if the teacher wants to know how long it takes a student to respond to an event. For example, the teacher instructs Ricardo to begin his assignment. Latency is a the measure of the time that elapses between the finish of the teacher's instruction to the beginning of the student's compliance with the instruction. In this case, the teacher finishes providing Ricardo with instruction to begin his assignment at 10:43 a.m., and Ricardo begins his assignment at 10:47 a.m. The latency response time is 4 minutes.

MEASURING BEHAVIOR

Teachers need to collect data on students' behaviors so that they can make informed decisions about which behavior intervention strategies to implement. The types of recording methods used depend on the specific characteristics the teachers are interested in measuring. Four general types of recording methods are described below: event-based recording, interval-based recording, time-based recording, and permanent products recording.

Event-Based Recording

Event-based recording methods are used to record the frequency of behaviors. These are among the easiest methods of recording behaviors, but they are best used with behaviors that are discrete, have well-defined beginnings and definite endings, and are repeatable. The teacher should have a concise and objective operational definition of the target behavior. Talking without permission, being out of one's seat, and being off task are examples of discrete behaviors. Event-based recording methods are used to record the frequency count or the rate of the behavior. The frequency count is the number of times the behavior occurs during an observation period. When the observation periods are constant in duration, a frequency count can be recorded for each observation; however, if the observation periods are different lengths, a rate of frequency should be reported. As noted above, the rate of the behavior can be calculated by dividing the number of times the behavior occurs by the length of the observation. For example, Jane is constantly talking without permission. The teacher observes that Jane talks seven times in a 30-minute period. The rate of the behavior is $7 \div 30 = 0.23$. Information on the rate of a behavior is useful when the teacher wants to compare the rates of the same behavior across periods of observation that differ in length. (For a sample of a form used for event-based recording, see Figure 8.3.)

Figure 8.3 Sample of Event-Based Recording

Student's Name: _Jane_   Observer: _Mrs. Clarke_

Place: _Math Class_   Date: _March 21-25, 2016_

Target Behavior: _Talking without permission_

Day	Observation period	Frequency of target behavior	Frequency count	Rate of behavior per minute
Monday	1:00-1:30 30 minutes	√√√√√√	7	0.23
Tuesday	1:00-1:15 15 minutes	√√√√	4	0.27
Wednesday	1:15-1:35 20 minutes	√√√√√	6	0.30
Thursday	1:00-1:30 30 minutes	√√√√√	5	0.17
Friday	1:10-1:25 15 minutes	√√√√√√	7	0.47

WHAT WOULD YOU DO? Dabir

You are a special education teacher and behavior specialist at O'Neill Middle School. The principal, Dr. Jackson, has asked you to observe Dabir, a seventh grader who has had a number of office referrals. A majority of the office referrals indicate that Dabir refuses to complete classroom assignments and does not comply with redirection.

Over the course of a week, you observe Dabir in his English, science, and math classes using an event-based recording method to record completion of assignments. The rates of behavior per minute for each class were as follows:

Day	English	Science	Math
Monday	0.57	0.10	0.00
Tuesday	0.43	0.03	0.03
Wednesday	0.46	0.07	0.03
Thursday	0.39	0.00	0.00
Friday	0.62	0.03	0.00

Based on the data you have collected, you examine Dabir's office referrals, and you find that many of the referrals came from his English teacher. What are some assumptions you could make regarding Dabir's behavior? What recommendations would you make to Dr. Jackson?

CASE STUDY   Timothy and Mrs. Miller

Timothy is a student in Mrs. Miller's fourth-grade class at McKay Elementary School. Whenever Mrs. Miller is not looking, Timothy takes items off the desks of other students in the classroom. Usually these items are small, such as pencils, erasers, and bottles of glue. The students complained to Mrs. Miller that Timothy takes their things. When Mrs. Miller confronted Timothy, he denied the allegation and adamantly insisted that his mother bought him those items for school.

Because of his behavior, Timothy's relationships with other students have deteriorated. The students avoid sitting with him at lunch and do not interact with him at recess.

Because Mrs. Miller's class is an inclusive one, a paraprofessional, Ms. Keller, is available to help students needing assistance with academic activities. Ms. Keller confirmed that she has seen Timothy take things from other students. Since Timothy's inappropriate behavior occurs

(Continued)

(Continued)

when Mrs. Miller is occupied with other students or writing on the board, Mrs. Miller asked Ms. Keller to conduct a behavioral observation of Timothy at various times throughout the week. The target behavior was *taking items from other students without permission*.

Using an event-based recording method, Ms. Keller provided the following information at the end of the week:

Day	Observation period	Frequency of target behavior	Frequency count	Rate of behavior per minute
Monday	10:00–10:30 30 minutes	√√√√	5	0.17
Tuesday	1:00–1:40 40 minutes	√√√√√	6	0.15
Wednesday	1:15–1:35 20 minutes	√√√	4	0.20
Thursday	9:00–9:40 40 minutes	√√√√	5	0.13
Friday	9:10–9:25 15 minutes	√√√√√	6	0.40

Since Timothy was taking items from the desks of other students, Mrs. Miller assumed that Timothy wanted those items. Using positive reinforcement, Mrs. Miller developed an intervention strategy in which Timothy would receive an item of his choice from her at the end of the day if he refrained from taking items from other students.

The following week, Ms. Keller conducted another behavioral observation with the intervention strategy in effect. The results of the intervention on Timothy's behavior were as follows:

Day	Observation period	Frequency of target behavior	Frequency count	Rate of behavior per minute
Monday	9:00–9:20 20 minutes	√√√√√√	7	0.35
Tuesday	10:00–10:30 30 minutes	√√√√√	6	0.20
Wednesday	1:00–1:35 35 minutes	√√√√√	6	0.17
Thursday	9:00–9:30 30 minutes	√√√√√√	7	0.23
Friday	2:00–2:25 25 minutes	√√√√√	6	0.24

The information obtained from the behavioral observations showed little difference between Timothy's initial behavior and his behavior with the intervention strategy. Mrs. Miller had to concede that the intervention strategy she had developed was not effective in modifying Timothy's behavior.

Interval-Based Recording

In interval-based recording, the observation period is divided into equal time intervals. For example, a 30-second observation period might be divided into six 5-second intervals. Interval-based recording does not use the frequency count of the behavior; rather, it measures the behavior as occurring (+) or not occurring (–) during specified time intervals. The intervals should not be too long, as this can lead to skewed data. Shorter intervals (of no more than 30 seconds) produce more accurate data. Interval-based recording provides a sample of the student's behavior during a classroom period; however, dividing the observation time into 30-second intervals is problematic for a teacher who is trying to manage 25 students in a classroom. If a teacher wants to use interval-based recording during a 20-minute observation period, she must divide the observation time into 40 intervals of 30 seconds each. Interval-based recording is more practical if a classroom assistant, paraprofessional, or some other education professional is available to conduct the recording. There are three basic types of interval-based recording methods: whole-interval recording, partial-interval recording, and point-time sampling.

During whole-interval recording, the student must display the target behavior during the entire interval for the event to be recorded. For example, if the student's behavior is talking without permission, the teacher records a plus sign (+) on the recording form only if the student talks during the entire 30-second interval. If the student does not talk at all during an entire interval or during part of an interval, the teacher records a minus sign (–). Unlike event-based recording, interval-based recording does not provide a measure of frequency. Interval-based recording is used to report the percentage of the intervals in which the observed behavior occurred. At the end of the observation period, the observer divides the number of plus signs recorded by the total number of intervals. The following formula is used to calculate the percentage:

Number of Behaviors (+) Recorded/Total Number
of Intervals × 100 = Percentage of Intervals

Whole-interval recording assesses the duration of the target behavior, but it often underestimates the actual duration of the target behavior. (For a sample of a form used for interval-based recording, see Figure 8.4.)

In **partial-interval recording**, the target behavior is recorded when it occurs at any time during the 30-second interval. For example, if the student talks during the first 5 seconds of the 30-second interval, the teacher records the event (+) as occurring during the interval. If the student talks several times during the 30-second interval, the behavior is recorded as having occurred once (+) during the interval. If the student does not talk at all during the 30-second interval, the teacher records the behavior as not occurring (−). Partial-interval recording measures the behavior only if it occurs during an interval. It does not measure the frequency or the duration of the behavior during the interval.

Point-time sampling is similar to interval recording in that the observation period is divided into equal time intervals; however, unlike in interval recording, in which the behavior is recorded if it occurs or does not occur at any time during an interval, in point-time sampling the status of the behavior at the end of the interval is recorded. For example, the teacher records a plus sign if the student talks at the end of an interval. If the student is not talking at the end of the interval, the teacher records a minus sign. Conversely, if the student is talking at the beginning of the interval but not at the end of the interval, the teacher records a minus sign. Point-time sampling is a good method for a teacher to use when he does not have enough time to observe a specific student's behavior.

Figure 8.4   Sample of Interval-Based Recording

Student's Name: _Jane_   Observer: _Mrs. Clarke_

Place: _Math Class_   Date: _March 21–25, 2016_

Target Behavior: _Talking without permission_

Observation Period: 10 minutes   Duration Interval: 30 seconds

1:00		1:01		1:02		1:03		1:04		1:05		1:06		1:07		1:08		1:09	
1	2	3	4	5	6	7	8	9	10	11	12	13	14	15	16	17	18	19	20
−	−	+	−	+	−	−	+	−	+	−	−	−	+	+	−	−	−	−	+

Total Behavior Occurring: 7   Percentage of Total Behavior Occurring: 35%

Total Behavior Not Occurring: 13   Percentage of Total Behavior Not Occurring: 65%

The teacher has to observe the behavior at a specific point in time rather than during an entire interval. However, point-time sampling will underestimate the frequency and duration of a behavior if the behavior is of short duration.

Time-Based Recording

Unlike event-based recording and interval-based recording, which measure the frequency of a behavior, time-based recording measures the duration or latency of a behavior. **Duration recording** is simply the recording of how long a student engages in the target behavior. Data collected through duration recording are important if the teacher wants to increase or decrease the duration of the target behavior. Duration recording can be used in conjunction with event-based recording to get a better description of the student's behavior. **Latency recording** methods measure how long it takes for a student to respond to an environmental event, such as instructions or redirection; this information is useful if the teacher is concerned with improving student compliance.

In duration recording, the teacher simply records the time at which the target behavior begins and the time when the behavior ends during the observation period. For example, if the student begins talking at 9:30 and stops talking at 9:40, the duration of the behavior is 10 minutes.

Duration can be reported as *total duration* or *average duration*. For example, if the student begins talking at 9:30 and stops talking at 9:40, the duration of the behavior is 10 minutes. However, if the student begins talking again at 9:55 and stops talking at 10:00, and again starts at 10:15 and stops at 10:25, the teacher has recorded three separate duration events of 10 minutes, 5 minutes, and 10 minutes in the same observation period. The total duration of the target behavior is 25 minutes (see Figure 8.5):

$$10 + 5 + 10 = 25$$

To calculate the average duration of the behavior, the teacher divides the total duration of the behavior (25 minutes) by the number of events (3 events). In this case the average duration is 8.33 minutes:

$$10 + 5 + 10 = 25 \div 3 = 8.33$$

In latency recording, the teacher records the time that elapses between a specific event and the start of the target behavior. For example, if the student is

Figure 8.5 Sample of Time-Based Recording

Student's Name: _Jane_   Observer: _Mrs. Clarke_

Place: _Math Class_   Date: _March 21-25, 2016_

Target Behavior: _Talking without permission_

Day	Observation period	Start time of target behavior	End time of target behavior	Duration
Monday	1:00-1:30 30 minutes	1:05 1:07 1:16	1:15 1:12 1:26	10 minutes 5 minutes 10 minutes
Tuesday				
Wednesday				
Thursday				
Friday				

Total Duration: 25 minutes

Average Duration: 8.33 minutes

asked to stop talking, the teacher records how long it takes for the student to comply with the request. Latency recording is useful when the teacher wants to reduce the latency time, especially with noncompliant behaviors.

Permanent Products Recording

Permanent products are the actual physical by-products of a behavior. These can sometimes be an important aspect of a functional behavioral assessment. For example, the number of permanent products of a behavior could be the number of assignments completed, the number of words spelled correctly on a written test, or the number of pencils the student has broken in frustration. Permanent products are actually the results of the behavior, and not an indication of the behavior itself, but they offer an easier form of measurement than event-based, interval-based, or time-based recording methods. For example, if a teacher wants to measure a student's academic progress in spelling, a spelling test would provide an appropriate assessment. It is also something that parents and other education professionals can readily comprehend.

RELIABILITY OF BEHAVIORAL OBSERVATIONS

Reliability is an important aspect of behavioral observations. *Reliability* refers to the accuracy of the data, which is maintained when similar results are obtained upon repeated measurement of the same thing. For behavioral observations, reliability can be obtained when two observers who view the same behavior during the same observation period come to a consensus regarding the rate of the behavior. This type of behavioral observation reliability is **interrater reliability (or interobserver reliability)**. For example, during a 30-minute observation period, Mrs. Martin reported that Jane talked without permission seven times, and Mr. Lewis reported that Jane talked without permission six times. Instead of trying to determine which observer was more accurate, interrater reliability determines whether there is a consensus between the two observers.

In the calculation of interrater reliability for event-based recording methods, the smaller frequency count is divided by the larger frequency count, and the result is multiplied by 100.

(Smaller Frequency Count ÷ Larger Frequency Count) × 100 = Agreement

For example, Mrs. Martin reported that Jane talked without permission seven times, and Mr. Lewis reported six incidents:

$$6 \div 7 = 0.85 \times 100 = 85\%$$

The percentage of consensus, or agreement, is 85%. Generally, interrater reliability levels greater than 80% are considered acceptable, but the closer to 100%, the better the reliability (Cooper, Heron, & Heward, 2007). Since the interrater reliability for Mrs. Martin and Mr. Lewis is 85%, the results of their observations are considered reliable.

For interval-based recording methods, the calculation of interrater reliability involves the comparison of corresponding intervals across the two observers. The number of agreements is divided by the number of agreements plus the number of disagreements on corresponding intervals. The result is multiplied by 100 to arrive at a percentage:

$$[\text{Number of Agreements}/(\text{Number of Agreements} + \text{Number of Disagreements})] \times 100 = \text{Reliability}$$

For example, during a 10-minute (20-interval) observation period, Mrs. Martin and Mr. Lewis agreed on 17 intervals and disagreed on 3 intervals:

$$17 \div (17 + 3) = 0.85 \times 100 = 85\%$$

The interrater reliability for the 10-minute observation period between Mrs. Martin and Mr. Lewis was 85%. Again, this is an acceptable consensus, and the results of their observations are considered reliable.

In time-based recording methods, the calculation of interrater reliability uses a similar formula for the duration or latency of the target behavior:

$$(\text{Shorter Time} \div \text{Longer Time}) \times 100 = \text{Reliability}$$

For example, in a 30-minute observation period, Mrs. Martin recorded a total duration rate of 25 minutes for Jane's talking without permission. Mr. Lewis recorded a total duration rate of 19 minutes for the same 30-minute observation period. Using the time-based recording formula for determining reliability, a 75% consensus is calculated:

$$19 \div 25 = 0.76 \times 100 = 75\%$$

While this is still within the acceptable range for reliability, it is further from 100% and the reliability is not as compelling.

Interrater reliability for latency is calculated in the same manner. For example, Mrs. Martin recorded that it took Jane 5 minutes to stop talking after the teacher instructed her to be quiet the first time. The second time it took Jane 4 minutes, the third time it took 7 minutes, and the fourth time it took 5 minutes. The total latency time was 21 minutes. During the same observation period, Mr. Lewis recorded a total latency time of 17 minutes. Using the time-based formula for determining interrater reliability, an 80% consensus is calculated:

$$17 \div 21 = 0.80 \times 100 = 80\%$$

In the use of behavioral observations, there are several important reasons for determining reliability. When assessing a student, it is important for the teacher to try to obtain a score within the range of the student's true score. A student's true score can be obtained only if there are no errors in measurement. Unfortunately, many measurements have errors, and behavioral observations are often subjective. As a result, a student's true score is never obtained, which is why it is important that the observed scores are reliable. A second reason for determining reliability is to reduce observer bias, which may include unintentional cultural biases. Finally, interrater consensus within the acceptable range indicates that the target behavior is well defined.

Behavioral observations are generally cost-efficient and easy to implement. However, such observations can be time-intensive, requiring the teacher to focus on one student for a significant amount of time. Multiple observations require the teacher to invest even more time in one student (Riley-Tillman, Christ, Chafouleas, Boice-Mallach, & Briesch, 2011). Additionally, as with all assessment methods, proper training is crucial; teachers and others who conduct behavioral observations must receive enough training to achieve proficiency in the methods being used.

CHARTING THE BEHAVIOR

Data from behavioral observations can be displayed visually using graphs. Well-designed and well-organized graphs can reveal behavior patterns that are easily understood by teachers, students, parents, and administrators, and can provide visual representation of a student's progress. By graphing and analyzing a student's progress on a consistent basis, the teacher can determine whether interventions are effective and can make adjustments to strategies when interventions are not effective.

With today's technology, teachers can use software programs like Microsoft Excel to convert data into graphs. Such programs are increasingly easy to use and can save teachers a great deal of time. Instead of plotting points on graph paper, a teacher only needs to input the raw data into a spreadsheet, and the software creates a clear and concise graph that is readily printable.

Teachers can use various types of graphs to display data on behavioral observations or student performance in organized visual formats. Many graphs are simple to create, while some are a bit more complex. The most common types of graphs are simple line graphs, cumulative graphs, and bar graphs.

Simple Line Graphs

A simple line graph is the most common visual format for displaying behavioral observations or student performance over a period of time. Data obtained from event-based, interval-based, time-based, and permanent products recording methods can easily be depicted in graph form. The simple line graph has two main parts: the abscissa, or x-axis, and the ordinate, or y-axis. The abscissa is the horizontal line on the bottom of the graph that generally indicates the passage of time (independent variable). It may be labeled in equal intervals as observation periods, days, dates, or weeks. The ordinate is the vertical line on the left-hand side of the graph that generally indicates the behavioral dimensions (dependent variable), which could include the frequency, behavioral rate, duration, latency, or permanent products of the target behavior. The scale of the ordinate always begins at zero, which is usually where the abscissa and the ordinate intersect, and goes as high as necessary to display the largest number obtained from the behavioral observation.

For example, data were collected for Jane's target behavior (talking without permission) over 10 days. On the first day, Jane was observed talking without permission seven times. On the graph, the frequency count is indicated by a **data point**, which can be denoted by a circle, triangle, or square. This data point is placed at the intersection of 1 on the x-axis (day 1) and 7 of the y-axis (number of observed behaviors). During the second day, Jane's target behavior was observed six times, so the data point is placed at the intersection of 2 on the abscissa and 6 on the ordinate. A solid line called the data path connects these two points. The data path is the focus of the analysis of the behavior because it represents the continuity of the behavior. The rest of the data are plotted in a similar fashion (see Figure 8.6).

Cumulative Graphs

As the name implies, in a cumulative graph the frequency count of the target behavior for each session is added to the data plotted from the previous session. The cumulative graph includes all the frequency counts plotted for all previous sessions in subsequent data points. In effect, a cumulative graph displays a total view of the target behavior. For example, Jane was observed talking without permission seven times on the first day. The data point for the first session is placed at the intersection of 1 on the x-axis and 7 on the y-axis. On the second day, the target behavior was observed six times. This frequency count is added to the frequency count obtained on the first day (7 + 6 = 13), and the data point is placed at the intersection of 2 on the x-axis and 13 on the y-axis. On the third day, Jane talked five times without permission. This count of the target behavior is added to the previous

Figure 8.6 Simple Line Graph: Jane

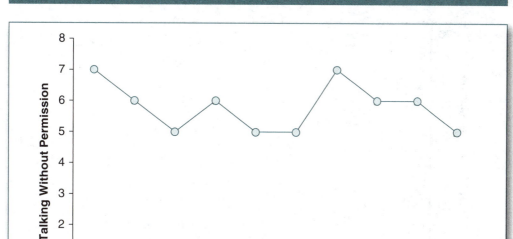

data point of 13 from the second day to create a data point of 18 for the third day (13 + 5 = 18). Each new data point includes the number of behaviors observed for that day plus the number of behaviors observed on previous days (see Figure 8.7).

Bar Graphs

A bar graph, or histogram, is similar to a simple line graph in that it uses the abscissa and the ordinate; however, a bar graph does not use data points or data paths. Instead, it uses vertical bars to depict the data. Each vertical bar represents one observation period (see Figure 8.8).

While bar graphs can display the raw data given in simple line graphs, bar graphs are better suited for comparing discrete sets of unrelated data and for providing a visual summary of the behaviors or academic performance of an individual or group. For example, a bar graph is useful for comparing similar target behaviors of a group of students.

Figure 8.7   Cumulative Graph: Jane

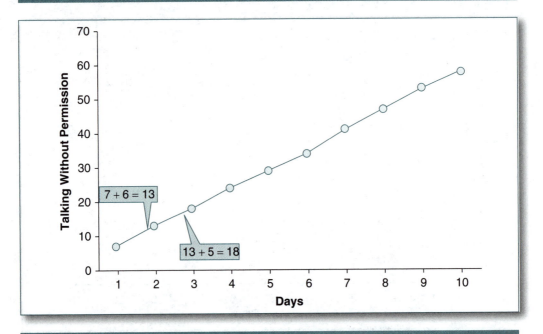

Figure 8.8   Bar Graph: Jane

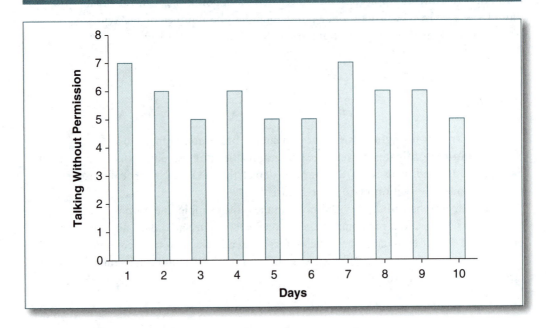

SUMMARY

The majority of students in the classroom are intrinsically motivated to comply with well-defined rules and consequences; however, 5–10% of students will not follow classroom rules. Teachers need to implement behavior modifications designed to replace or reduce inappropriate behaviors for these students. Before teachers can begin modifying student behaviors, however, they need to understand the attributes of those behaviors. One method of defining a student's inappropriate behavior is through the implementation of a functional behavioral assessment.

A functional behavioral assessment is used to provide a detailed description of the behavior and consequences. The first step in conducting a functional behavioral assessment is to define the target behavior, which must be observable, measurable, and repeatable. Target behaviors can be quantified according to their frequency, intensity, duration, and latency, which can be measured through behavioral observations. A common method for observing behavior is the ABC analysis, the purpose of which is to identify the target behavior through the antecedent that prompts the behavior and the reinforcing consequences that maintain the behavior. An understanding of the frequency, intensity, duration, and latency of a behavior is important for the development of alternative or replacement behaviors. Event-based recording, interval-based recording, time-based recording, and permanent products recording can be used to measure these characteristics of behavior. Data from behavioral observations can be displayed visually on simple line graphs, cumulative graphs, or bar graphs. These data and data on the effectiveness of intervention strategies can be evaluated through the use of single-subject designs (see Chapter 11).

Measuring and recording the target behavior and intervention strategies are crucial parts of the development and implementation of functional behavioral assessments, functional behavior analysis, and behavior intervention plans. These methods of modifying behaviors of students who do not comply with the traditional classroom rules and hierarchy of consequences are important because they allow teachers to meet the behavior needs of all students within the classroom and to implement an effective universal design for classroom management.

REVIEW ACTIVITIES

1. What are the three characteristics that a teacher must consider when determining the operational definition of a target behavior?

2. A teacher with whom you are consulting says that Amanda is off task. Write an operational definition of the target behavior "off task."

3. Name and describe the four characteristics of a target behavior that a teacher should consider when conducting an anecdotal observation of the behavior.

4. After being given an assignment to complete at his desk, Alexander does not begin working on it for about 5 minutes. If you were his teacher, what characteristic would you attribute to Alexander's behavior? Based on your decision, which recording method(s) would you use to evaluate the effectiveness of any possible intervention?

5. Kirk's target behavior is leaving his seat without permission. Using the results of behavioral observations conducted by Kirk's teacher (below), calculate the rate of this behavior per minute for each day. Create a visual representation of the observation data using a simple line graph, cumulative graph, or bar graph.

Day	Observation period	Frequency of target behavior	Frequency count	Rate of behavior per minute
Monday	9:00-9:30 30 minutes	√√√√	5	
Tuesday	9:00-9:20 20 minutes	√√√	4	
Wednesday	9:15-9:35 20 minutes	√√√√√	6	
Thursday	9:00-9:10 10 minutes	√√√	4	
Friday	9:10-9:25 15 minutes	√√√√√	6	

CHAPTER 9
FUNCTIONAL BEHAVIOR ANALYSIS

Trinity of Behavior Management

After reading this chapter, you should be able to do the following:

- Explain the purposes of a functional behavior analysis.
- Define and explain the relationship between behavior and the function of behavior.
- Explain how a behavioral hypothesis is developed.
- Describe the possible functions of behavior.
- Explain how culture can influence the functions of behavior.
- Describe the attributes of the two functional categories of behavior.
- Write a behavioral hypothesis.
- Explain the differences among the various kinds of functional-based interventions.

Many teachers use reactive strategies to manage inappropriate student behaviors in the classroom. These default strategies are easy to implement and often result in the reduction of the inappropriate behaviors in the short term, but they result in the removal of students from the classroom and the cessation of the learning process (Clunies-Ross, Little, & Kienhuis, 2008). Unfortunately, unless they address the causes, or functions, of students' inappropriate behaviors, teachers are unable to make effective behavior modifications that could result in long-term alterations of these behaviors. A functional behavior analysis is the only method that allows identification of the function of an inappropriate behavior (Pence, Roscoe, Bourret, & Ahearn, 2009). Once the function of the behavior has been identified, a function-based intervention can be implemented to reduce the behavior. The purposes of a functional behavior analysis are to determine the function of the inappropriate behavior and to determine the causal factors for the behavior (LaRue et al., 2011).

The functional behavior analysis completes the process started by the functional behavioral assessment through the development of a behavioral hypothesis that serves as the basis for a strategy to modify the behavior by altering the antecedent or the consequences (see Table 9.1). A functional behavior analysis consists of five basic steps:

1. Clearly define the target behavior.

2. Collect observable data related to the target behavior.

3. Identify the function of the behavior.

4. Develop a behavioral hypothesis.

5. Develop an alternative behavior.

If a functional behavioral assessment has been conducted, the first two steps of the functional behavior analysis have already been completed. The functional behavioral assessment uses behavioral observation to gain information about the student's behavior (Ducharme & Shecter, 2011). In the third step, the function of the inappropriate behavior is identified. The fourth step of the functional behavior analysis is the development of a behavioral hypothesis. The behavioral hypothesis is generated based on the function of the behavior and the information obtained from the data collected during the functional behavioral assessment (Allday, Nelson, & Russel, 2011). Once a behavioral hypothesis has been formulated, an appropriate alternative behavior that serves the same function as the inappropriate behavior is developed and introduced to the student (Scott, Anderson, & Spaulding, 2008). The functional behavior analysis

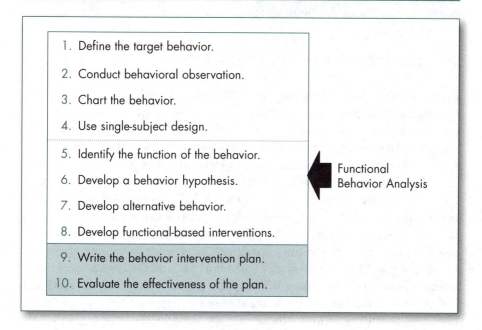

Table 9.1 Trinity of Behavior Management: Functional Behavior Analysis

1. Define the target behavior.

2. Conduct behavioral observation.

3. Chart the behavior.

4. Use single-subject design.

5. Identify the function of the behavior.

6. Develop a behavior hypothesis.

7. Develop alternative behavior.

8. Develop functional-based interventions.

9. Write the behavior intervention plan.

10. Evaluate the effectiveness of the plan.

Functional Behavior Analysis

concludes with "the development of an alternative behavior based on the identified functional reinforcement to replace aberrant responding" (LaRue et al., 2011, p. 2450). Once the functional behavior analysis is completed and alternative behaviors have been determined, a behavior intervention plan can be developed and implemented.

The Individuals with Disabilities Education Improvement Act (IDEA, 2004) mandates that students with disabilities receive functional behavioral assessments under specific circumstances, and most functional behavior analyses are conducted with students with identified disabilities. In the limited research that has examined the use of functional behavior analysis with students without disabilities who display aberrant behaviors, functional behavior analyses have been found to be successful in identifying the functions of these behaviors, which resulted in appropriate interventions that reduced the behaviors (Shumate & Wills, 2010).

Identifying the function of a student's inappropriate behavior can help the teacher to develop alternative behaviors and interventions designed to reduce the inappropriate behavior and provide the student with the opportunity to be successful in school. Incorporating a functional behavior analysis in a universal design for classroom management increases the effectiveness of a behavior and classroom management program and provides students the interventions they need to be successful in school.

IDENTIFYING THE FUNCTION OF A BEHAVIOR

Every behavior has a function, or a dependent variable for the behavior. Identifying the purpose that a behavior serves is the first step in understanding the behavior. Behavior is an individual's observable and measurable interaction with the environment, which is constantly changing and determined by a functional relationship to events (Cooper, Heron, & Heward, 2007). The function of a behavior is the purpose it serves for the individual; the functions of our behaviors are "why we do the things we do." A person behaves in a particular way in order to obtain something (positive reinforcement) or avoid something (negative reinforcement). For example, Mayra goes to school every day (behavior) because she likes being with her friends (obtaining attention). Or Mayra goes to school every day (behavior) because the law requires her to attend school (avoiding truant officers). Or Mayra goes to school every day because her stepfather, who is home during the day, emotionally abuses her (avoiding abusive situation). Notice that the same behavior (going to school every day) has three possible functions. This is why it is important for teachers to determine the function of a behavior before trying to modify the behavior. An intervention based on the wrong function will not be effective in changing the behavior.

Behavior is also constantly changing. For example, Mayra is now missing school (alternative behavior) because she broke up with her boyfriend (avoiding boyfriend at school). The function of the behavior is different, and the behavior is different; however, a change in function does not always necessitate a change in behavior. For example, Mayra's mother and stepfather are divorced, and the stepfather, who was emotionally abusive toward Mayra, is no longer a variable in Mayra's behavior. Yet Mayra still goes to school every day (behavior) to please her mother (obtaining attention from mother).

The function, or purpose, of a behavior is generally not inappropriate; it is the behavior that is appropriate or inappropriate. For example, one student may work very hard to complete her assignments in a timely manner; another student may refuse to do his assignments. Both students are seeking the teacher's attention. One behavior is deemed appropriate while the other is deemed inappropriate; however, gaining the teacher's attention is not considered inappropriate. It is the behavior that needs to be modified, not the function of the behavior. School personnel need to replace the inappropriate behavior with an alternative behavior that has the same function.

There are numerous reasons for students' behaviors, but compiling lists of these reasons would be difficult and impractical, and the results would be incomplete. However, the reasons for behaviors can be simplified into two functional categories: *attainment* and *avoidance/escape of a situation*. Each category includes functional motivations (see Table 9.2).

Attainment

Many individuals behave in certain ways in order to obtain things they desire. People go to work to earn money; in turn, they use their pay to purchase things they need or want. Students study for tests so they can earn good grades. Children behave appropriately because they desire their parents' attention. Attainment is a functionally motivated behavior in which an individual acquires something he or she wants. The functional motivations of attainment include attention, rewards and privileges, and power or control.

Table 9.2 Functional Motivations

Function of behavior	Functional motivation	Brief description
Attainment	Attention	Gain recognition from peers or adults
	Rewards and privileges	Gain tangible and nontangible reinforcements
	Power or control	Gain control over a situation or event
Avoidance/escape of a situation	Social isolation	Avoid recognition from peers or adults
	Nonpreferred activities	Avoid unpleasant activities such as difficult assignments
	Adverse interactions	Avoid unpleasant interactions with peers or adults in certain settings

Attention

Attention is a common functional motivation for students (Mueller, Nkosi, & Hine, 2011; Shumate & Wills, 2010). Attention can include verbal and non-verbal praise from peers and adults (see Chapter 6). Most students want to be liked and accepted by their peers and by adults. They are not likely to seek negative attention. These students are likely to comply with expected classroom rules and work hard on academic assignments. They often respond positively to attention from teachers, which may take the form of verbal and nonverbal praise (e.g., "I like the way that Tim is working on his assignment," a pat on the back, a smile). As a positive reinforcement, praise is often an effective method of providing students with attention. For teacher praise to be effective in managing behavior, it needs to be sincere and must be given to the student immediately after the student displays the appropriate behavior. Students can differentiate between sincere praise and praise that is forced or insincere, and the latter type of praise is ineffective in modifying students' behaviors.

Attention can also reinforce and maintain inappropriate behaviors. Inappropriate behaviors include talking without permission, refusing to complete assignments, and noncompliance with directions. Again, it is important to understand that it is not the function of the behavior that is inappropriate, but the actual behavior. The key to modifying behavior is to find an alternative behavior for the same function served by the inappropriate behavior. For example, Roberto constantly talked in class. No matter what consequences he received from Mr. Martin, his third-grade teacher, Roberto's behavior did not improve. When a functional behavior analysis was finally conducted, it was determined that the function of Roberto's behavior was attainment and the functional motivation was attention. Roberto, who did not have a father at home, wanted attention from Mr. Martin, who had become a surrogate father figure. Roberto was taught appropriate ways of gaining attention from Mr. Martin, and his inappropriate behaviors decreased.

WHAT WOULD YOU DO?   Mayra

Mayra is a fourth-grade student in Mrs. Peeples's science class. She comes from a single-parent home. Her father is a Mexican immigrant who works as a truck driver for the city's sanitation facility. Mayra's mother passed away 5 years ago in an automobile accident.

Mayra has always been a quiet student and has done well in science class. However, recently, Mayra has not been completing classroom assignments. Mrs. Peeples has discussed this with Mayra's father, but he assures her that Mayra completes all her homework. It is only her classroom assignments in science that Mayra does not complete. When Mrs. Peeples hands out a science assignment, Mayra initially begins to work on the assignment but then starts looking around the classroom. Mrs. Peeples has been keeping Mayra in the classroom during the lunch period to complete the assignments, but this has not helped. In fact, her behavior has gotten worse; Mayra no longer tries to complete the science assignments.

What would you do to determine the reason for Mayra's behavior? What are the possible functions of her behavior? What intervention would be effective in helping Mayra complete her science assignments?

Rewards and Privileges

Rewards and privileges constitute another functional motivation of attainment. A common and effective reward in elementary schools, especially with younger students, is giving students gold or silver stars on exemplary work. A token system in which students receive points toward purchasing items (candy bars, inexpensive toys, and the like) from the classroom store is another example of rewards. Older students may prefer earning computer time for appropriate behaviors. Not only do activities reward students for appropriate behaviors, but they can also be used as part of a behavior modification strategy. For example, students with emotional and behavioral disorders may earn time to play a board game when they display appropriate behaviors. The teacher could also use this activity to develop social skills (e.g., getting along, taking turns, being a good loser).

Conversely, rewards and privileges can serve to increase inappropriate behavior. For example, a mother and her 3-year-old daughter go to a retail store to buy some clothes. The daughter sees a small toy she wants and begins to throw a tantrum when her mother refuses to buy it for her. Even though the mother tells the daughter several times that she cannot have the toy, the mother finally relents and gives the toy to the daughter so she will stop her tantrum. Thus, the daughter learns that she can get certain rewards by exhibiting inappropriate behaviors.

Power or Control

The final functional motivation of attention is power or control over a situation or event. One of the most common examples is the "power struggle" between the teacher and a student. Gaining power is a basic human need, and when that need is not met, the result can be conflict. In the teacher–student relationship, the student is often trying to maintain some type of control in his life, especially if he feels that he has little control or power in other areas of his life.

Although preservice teachers are often advised to avoid power struggles with students, the dominant culture encourages a win-at-all-costs mind-set that contradicts this lesson. Winners are respected and idolized; losers are insignificant. Teachers need to fight the inclination to try to "win" in power struggles with students. If a teacher wins such a power struggle, the result is likely to be damage to the relationship between the teacher and the student, and teacher–student rapport is a crucial element of effective behavior and classroom management. Additionally, the student will probably view the classroom as a threatening place, and this contradicts the teacher's duty to provide a safe and secure environment in which learning can take place—another integral component of an effective behavior and classroom management plan. When a teacher wins a power struggle, forcing the student to comply with the teacher's demands, the student may be left feeling insignificant and powerless.

Avoidance/Escape of a Situation

Sometimes individuals behave in certain ways to avoid or escape nonpreferred activities. For example, a person may avoid going to a social gathering with colleagues because he has had negative interactions with the individual hosting the event. Instead, the person informs the host that he has already made other plans and cannot attend. Avoidance/escape of a situation is a functionally motivated behavior. Self-injury, aggression, disruption, and inappropriate vocalizations are common behaviors associated with avoidance/escape of a situation (Ingvarsson, Hanley, & Welter, 2009). The functional motivations of avoidance and escape include social isolation, nonpreferred activities, adverse interactions, and changes.

Social Isolation

Sometimes a student will behave in a certain manner in order to avoid attention from others. For example, a student may try to make himself invisible by taking a seat distant from the teacher's desk, sitting low in his chair, and keeping his eyes lowered to avoid being noticed by the teacher. Students who behave this way often do so because they lack confidence in their ability to answer questions posed by the teacher. A low sense of self-efficacy can affect students' beliefs in their abilities and their behavior (Bandura, 1986, 1997; Briones, Tabernero, & Arenas, 2007).

Students who have been abused will also often avoid attention from others. They may feel detached from others and feel like they do not belong at school. Even though they may not want the teacher to call on them, and they may disengage from social interaction, abused children are likely to perceive that others are distancing themselves from them (Elliott, Cunningham, Linder, Colangelo, & Gross, 2005).

Nonpreferred Activities

Students often behave in certain ways when they want to avoid unpleasant activities. Some students display inappropriate behaviors when avoiding boring and difficult academic tasks that are especially frustrating and do not meet their academic needs. Again, the behaviors displayed by such students vary, even though the function of the behaviors remains the same. For example, Michael may defiantly refuse to complete an assignment on double-digit multiplication by failing to comply with the teacher's redirection to work on the assignment or by tearing up the assignment worksheet. Conversely, Marta may covertly refuse to complete the same assignment by sitting quietly at her desk and not drawing attention to herself. While the two behaviors are completely different, the function of the behaviors is the same.

Adverse Interactions

Students sometimes display inappropriate behaviors when trying to avoid certain interactions with peers or adults in certain settings. For example, because Frank is a student with emotional and behavioral disorders, his teacher, Mr. Poteet, is less tolerant of Frank than he is of other students. As a result of the poor rapport between Frank and Mr. Poteet, Frank displays inappropriate behaviors in order to be sent back to the resource room. Students may also avoid interactions with peers in certain settings because they are likely to be teased or bullied. For example, peers constantly tease Mary at recess. In Mrs. Clarke's history class, which meets prior to recess, Mary always refuses to finish her assignment. As a result of her behavior, Mrs. Clarke keeps her in at recess to complete her assignment, and Mary avoids an unpleasant interaction with her peers.

Sometimes, adverse interactions in school can lead to school refusal, or the student's attempt to miss school. School refusal is generally the result of cultural factors, family factors, peer factors, and/or neuropsychiatric factors (Casoli-Reardon, Rappaport, Kulick, & Reinfield, 2012; Wimmer, 2008). Diverse students may have difficulty "fitting in" at school because of language and cultural differences. Students with language differences may have problems communicating with peers and making friends, leading to social isolation. Students with cultural differences may have difficulty connecting with a European American curriculum. If lessons have little meaning to students' lives, they are more likely to demonstrate off-task behaviors. As a result, language and cultural differences could lead to a sense of isolation, which in turn could lead to school refusal.

Family factors can also lead to school refusal. Families from socioeconomically disadvantaged backgrounds may put education second to family financial needs. Some adolescents remain at home to help take care of younger siblings. Abusive families may keep children home from school when the children show evidence of abuse (Casoli-Reardon et al., 2012). Children from low socioeconomic backgrounds may not feel welcome in school because teachers perceive their families as dysfunctional and often blame them for the children's behaviors (Hyland & Heuschkel, 2010). Teachers often do not know enough about these families to help these students, which is why it is important for teachers to establish relationships with their students' families (see Chapter 3).

Relationships with peers are often a crucial factor influencing the academic and behavioral performance of students. Students who are belittled, teased, or bullied often do not do well in school, and these students will avoid such interactions through their behaviors (Pina, Zerr, Gonzales, & Ortiz, 2009). Students who are harassed by their peers seldom seek help from adults, which is why it is so important for teachers to determine the functions of the students' behaviors in order to provide effective interventions for peer factors.

Neuropsychiatric factors that may lead to school refusal include generalized anxiety disorders, separation anxiety disorders, and depression (Casoli-Reardon et al., 2012; Wimmer, 2008). For example, Jimmy is a second grader who is afraid that something will happen to his mother while he is at school. Because of this fear, he goes to the nurse's office nearly every day complaining of feeling ill in an attempt to be sent home. School refusal may also be triggered by fear of the school environment because of test taking (an increasing problem due to the proliferation of standardized testing mandated by states and the federal government) or the possibility of violence in the school (such as the school shootings at Columbine High School and Sandy Hook Elementary School). It may also result from students' desire to escape aversive social situations such as negative interactions with peers (bullying, gang activities) and teachers (lack of support, poor student–teacher relationships).

Cultural Impact on Behavioral Functions

Societal and cultural norms often influence the functional motivations of behaviors. Individual accomplishment is stressed in European American cultures, which is why many students are motivated to do well in school (attention, rewards), but this is not always true for other cultures. Teachers need to understand that cultural influences affect the functions of behaviors. Many Native Americans, Asian Americans, and Hispanics value group identity and the needs of the group. For example, Soon-Tek is a first-generation Korean American. Korean family values dictate that the actions of one family member reflect on the entire family. As a result, Soon-Tek is doing well in school to avoid bringing shame to his family, not to gain attention for his accomplishments.

African American students sometimes engage in power struggles with teachers; however, this behavior may not be malicious or have anything to do with a student's relationship with the teacher. African American culture may dictate that males not show indications of weakness in front of friends or family (Milner & Tenore, 2010). It is important that teachers understand the cultural and linguistic backgrounds of their students when trying to identify the functions of students' behaviors. Once the function of a student's inappropriate behavior has been identified, a behavioral hypothesis can be developed to modify the student's behavior.

DEVELOPING A BEHAVIORAL HYPOTHESIS

The behavioral hypothesis proposes an explanation of the factors that elicit the inappropriate behavior. It is based on data obtained from behavioral observations and determines the function of the behavior. The identified function of the behavior is used to develop a behavioral hypothesis, an important step toward the development of a behavior intervention plan.

A multidisciplinary/multicultural team should determine the most plausible and testable explanation for the occurrence of the behavior. The team should ask the following questions regarding the behavior:

1. Why is the student displaying the target behavior?

2. What is the function of the target behavior?

For example, Jane continually talks in class without permission. From behavioral observations and analysis of the data, team members can see that there are several plausible explanations for Jane's behavior. Since Jane's behavior generally occurs during class discussion, however, they decide that seeking the teacher's attention is the most obvious function of the behavior.

The behavioral hypothesis can be written in a format similar to the ABC analysis, using the components of antecedent, behavior, and consequence. For example, a behavioral hypothesis for Jane's behavior could be stated in the following format:

During class discussions   /   Jane talks without permission   /   to gain the teacher's attention
       (antecedent)   (behavior)   (consequence)

However, the most obvious possible reason for a behavior is sometimes not the actual reason, and other explanations need to be examined. LeVar has displayed aggressive tendencies toward male peers who have offended him in some manner. He has punched Mario for taking his pen. His aggressive behavior generally occurs during unstructured time at the beginning of class. It would appear that the function of LeVar's behavior is attainment; however, the functional motivation is not that obvious. Is the functional motivation of LeVar's behavior attention from peers or adults? Is LeVar's behavior reinforced by his reclaiming his pen from Mario (tangible reward)? Or is LeVar trying to gain control over a situation? Since LeVar is African American, the multidisciplinary team needs to consider any cultural factors that might affect the determination of the function of the behavior. Is LeVar trying to display strength in front of his peers (recognition)? LeVar's behavioral hypothesis could be as follows:

During unstructured class time, / LeVar is aggressive toward peers / to gain positive peer attention.
       (antecedent)   (behavior)   (consequence)

It is important to remember that the function of a behavior is generally not inappropriate; it is the behavior that is appropriate or inappropriate. For example, one student may work very hard to complete her assignments in a timely manner; another student may refuse to do his assignments. Both students are seeking the teacher's attention.

CASE STUDY **Timothy and Mrs. Miller (Part 2)**

Timothy continued to take items from other students, and his relationships with peers deteriorated even more. Other students were now threatening to hit him if he took their things again.

Mrs. Miller had to determine why Timothy takes items from other students. She had developed an intervention strategy that provided Timothy with an item of his choice if he did not take any items from other students without permission, but that proved to be ineffective. Considering the two types of behavioral functions, she was fairly confident that Timothy was not trying to avoid or escape a situation.

Function of behavior	Functional motivation	Timothy's behavior
Avoidance/escape of a situation	Social isolation	Timothy did not seem to be trying to avoid recognition from peers or adults. If anything, he was receiving more recognition due to his inappropriate behavior.
	Nonpreferred activities	Timothy was not trying to avoid any nonpreferred activities. He was doing well academically, so it did not seem that he was trying to avoid academic activities.
	Adverse interactions	Timothy did not seem to be trying to avoid interaction with peers, although his peers were trying to avoid interacting with him.

Mrs. Miller considered whether the function of Timothy's behavior might be attainment.

Function of behavior	Functional motivation	Timothy's behavior
Attainment	Attention	Timothy was getting attention from peers and Mrs. Miller.
	Rewards and privileges	Since the first intervention strategy was not effective, it did not seem that Timothy wanted to receive items for appropriate behavior.
	Power or control	There did not seem to be any evidence that Timothy wanted power or control over other students.

(Continued)

(Continued)

Mrs. Miller concluded that the function of Timothy's behavior was attainment, with a functional motivation of peer attention. Based on her analysis of Timothy's behavior, Timothy's behavioral hypothesis could be as follows:

When the teacher is not looking, / Timothy takes items from peers / to gain peers' attention.

    (antecedent)   (behavior)   (consequence)

Mrs. Miller needed to develop an alternative behavior for Timothy that would serve the same function as his inappropriate behavior. She felt the best option would be to use differential reinforcement of alternative behavior. Timothy needed to be reinforced when he displayed the alternative behavior. Once Mrs. Miller had developed the alternative behavior, an intervention strategy could be implemented to modify Timothy's behavior. Mrs. Miller felt that a behavior intervention plan needed to be implemented to help Timothy modify his behavior.

DEVELOPING ALTERNATIVE BEHAVIORS

One of the most difficult aspects of developing a behavior intervention plan is creating an alternative behavior that serves the same function as the target behavior. Unfortunately, many classroom interventions are ineffective because they are not based on the functions of the students' inappropriate behaviors (Shumate & Wills, 2010). An intervention that is selected without consideration of the function of the behavior can actually increase the frequency of inappropriate behavior through incorrect reinforcements. When the function of the behavior has been determined, effective alternative behaviors can be selected.

The purpose of an alternative behavior is to replace the target behavior with an appropriate behavior that has the same function (Ducharme & Shecter, 2011). A teacher can choose, teach, and reinforce an alternative behavior once the function of a student's inappropriate behavior has been accurately identified (Blood & Neel, 2007; Crone, Hawkens, & Bergstrom, 2007).

For example, when Kale is given an assignment during math class, she sometimes tears up the assignment and begins pounding on her desk. After completing a functional behavior analysis, the multidisciplinary team determined that the function of Kale's behavior was avoidance/escape of a situation, and the functional motivation was nonpreferred activities:

When working on math assignments, / Kale sometimes bangs on her desk / to avoid completing the assignments.
        (antecedent)   (behavior)   (consequence)

Simply stated, Kale's inappropriate behavior was caused by the frustration she sometimes felt when trying to complete a math assignment.

Functional-Based Interventions

Once the function of the student's behavior has been identified, an alternative behavior needs to be developed. Functional-based interventions, which take the function of the behavior into account, can be used to implement alternative behaviors. Five different kinds of interventions can be used to develop alternative behaviors: functional communication training, antecedent-based interventions, instructional accommodations, extinction, and differential reinforcement.

Functional Communication Training

Functional communication training is a systematic technique for replacing an inappropriate behavior with an appropriate communication response as a means

Table 9.3 Functional-Based Interventions

Intervention	Description
Functional communication training	A systematic strategy designed to replace inappropriate behaviors with appropriate behaviors through effective communication
Antecedent-based interventions	Environmental modifications that prevent or reduce the occurrence of inappropriate behaviors and increase the probability of appropriate behaviors
Instructional accommodations	Strategies that change the method and manner in which academic materials are presented
Extinction	A strategy that reduces or eliminates inappropriate behaviors by removing the reinforcements that maintain the behaviors
Differential reinforcement	A strategy used to increase the frequency of an appropriate behavior while simultaneously reducing the inappropriate behavior

to obtain reinforcement (Schieltz et al., 2010). The basic premise of functional communication training is the association between communication difficulties and the inappropriate behavior (Ducharme & Shecter, 2011; Neitzel, 2010). Once the function of a student's inappropriate behavior is identified, the student is taught a functionally relevant response to replace the inappropriate behavior (Winborn-Kemmerer et al., 2010). For example, Kale tears up her assignment and bangs on the desk when trying to complete math problems that are difficult for her. Using functional communication training, the teacher would teach Kale to ask for assistance when she becomes frustrated with a math assignment. However, it is important that the response the student is taught matches the function of the behavior. For Kale, "I don't understand this problem" is a functionally relevant response. Kale is asking for assistance from the teacher because she is frustrated with her math assignment. In contrast, asking the teacher, "Is this okay?" is not a relevant response for Kale because it does not match the function of her target behavior. With such a response Kale would be gaining the teacher's attention, but not assistance with the math assignment (Dwyer, Rozewski, & Simonsen, 2012). Teaching students to request assistance as an alternative behavior to escaping instructional tasks that are frustrating has been found to result in decreased inappropriate behaviors (Kamps, Wendland, & Culpepper, 2006).

Antecedent-Based Interventions

Antecedent-based interventions are modifications of the environment that prevent or decrease the occurrence of the inappropriate behavior and increase the probability of appropriate behavior. Environmental modifications may include rearranging the physical layout of the classroom, managing transition times, and altering the routes students take to and from the bathroom, playground, or cafeteria (Maag & Katsiyannis, 2006). Such modifications have been found to decrease or prevent behavior problems and provide a learning environment without disruptions (Guardino & Fullerton, 2010). For example, Emily is a student with attention deficit disorder. Thinking that the front of the classroom would have the least number of distractions, the teacher seated Emily at the front of the room. However, the door to the hallway was at the front of the room, and because the classroom was near the principal's office, there was a lot of activity in the hallway. As a result, Emily was constantly distracted and had difficulty maintaining focus on academic activities. The teacher's environmental modification for Emily was not effective. The teacher could either close the door when Emily was in the classroom or find Emily another spot in the classroom with fewer distractions.

The arrangement of the classroom can be an effective element in a proactive approach to classroom and behavior management (see Chapter 5). If the teacher is aware that a student has had a history of behavior difficulties, she may place the student near the teacher's desk. This allows the teacher to monitor the student's behavior and respond with strategies designed to reduce inappropriate behaviors but also provide positive feedback when the student displays appropriate behaviors.

In addition to physical aspects, environmental variables can include personnel and the school setting. Teachers may need to consider the effects of environmental variables in school settings when conducting functional behavior analyses. Academic demands (academic instruction, assignments) may compete with other potential reinforcers (teacher attention, peer attention, preferred activities) (Sarno et al., 2011). For example, Kale's behavior to escape from academic demands (tearing up her math assignment and banging on the table) could have received reinforcement (teacher attention).

Instructional Accommodations

Instructional accommodations are alterations to the delivery of instruction, method of student performance, or method of assessment. Such accommodations do not significantly change the content or the difficulty level of the curriculum. Some students do not respond to traditional teaching methods, and so they find academic tasks to be aversive. Among such students, inappropriate behaviors and poor academic performance are often attempts to avoid completing academic assignments.

Extinction

Extinction is the reduction or elimination of inappropriate behavior through the withdrawal of the positive reinforcement that maintains the behavior (see Chapter 6). The most common example of extinction is that of ignoring a small child who is throwing a tantrum because she has been denied something she wants. Ignoring the behavior, or not reinforcing the behavior, results in the reduction and eventual elimination of the behavior. The child learns that she does not get what she wants if she throws a tantrum. Extinction is sometimes impossible to implement. For example, if a student is banging his head on his desk, the teacher cannot ignore it. Also, if two students are starting to fight each other, an immediate intervention is necessary to protect the students.

Differential Reinforcement

Differential reinforcement is an operant procedure that is used to increase the frequency of an appropriate behavior while decreasing the inappropriate behavior (Vladescu & Kodak, 2010). It includes differential reinforcement of other behavior, differential reinforcement of alternative behavior, differential reinforcement of incompatible behavior, and differential reinforcement of lower rates.

With **differential reinforcement of other behavior (DRO)**, the teacher reinforces any appropriate behavior when the problem behavior has not been displayed for a period of time. For example, Kale is working well with peers on an assignment in a cooperative learning activity. Since Kale has not torn up any assignments or banged on her desk for several hours, the teacher reinforces Kale's work with the group by commenting positively on her contributions to the group. The teacher is actually reinforcing the absence of the target behavior.

Differential reinforcement of alternative behavior (DRA) is one of the most frequently used of the differential reinforcements. Differential reinforcement of alternative behavior involves providing reinforcements when the student displays a specific alternative behavior in lieu of the inappropriate behavior. In other words, the teacher and the student come up with an appropriate alternative behavior to replace the inappropriate behavior. When the student exhibits the alternative behavior, the behavior is reinforced. For example, if Kale were trying to escape from an academic task (nonpreferred activities), asking for a 1-minute break would be a functionally appropriate behavior to replace the inappropriate behavior (tearing up the assignment/banging on the desk). The reduction and elimination of the target behavior is more likely if the student is allowed to choose among alternative responses (Dwyer et al., 2012).

DRA and extinction are often implemented together (Athens & Vollmer, 2010; Ingvarsson et al., 2009). This is especially true when the modeling and physical prompting of extinction are ineffective. However, studies have also shown that DRA is not as effective at modifying inappropriate behaviors when implemented without extinction (Volkert, Lerman, Call, & Trosclair-Lasserre, 2009).

Differential reinforcement of incompatible behavior (DRI) involves reinforcing an appropriate behavior that is incompatible with the problem behavior and therefore cannot occur at the same time (Wheatley et al., 2009). For example, Emily is looking out the classroom window and not paying attention to the lesson. If Emily is watching the teacher, she cannot also be looking out the window—these two behaviors cannot physically occur at the same time. When Emily watches the teacher, the teacher touches her finger to the side of her nose. This signal acknowledges Emily's alternative behavior and provides her with teacher attention.

Differential reinforcement of lower rates (DRL) reduces an inappropriate behavior when reinforcement is provided after the frequency of the behavior in a specific period of time is less than a set limit. For example, Ricardo talks seven times without permission during the 45-minute social studies class. The set limit is established at five times during the 45 minutes. If Ricardo keeps the target behavior to five or fewer times, he will earn 5 minutes on the computer at the end of class. As Ricardo makes progress, the teacher can reduce the frequency criteria to three occurrences of the behavior or reduce the length of time to 30 minutes. It is important to remember that DRL can reduce inappropriate behaviors, but it cannot eliminate them.

Implementing Alternative Behaviors

The implementation of alternative behaviors generally involves the following steps, which are similar to the procedures for implementing the functional behavior analysis:

1. Define the target behavior.
2. Gather observable and measurable data on the behavior.
3. Determine the function of the behavior.
4. Develop an alternative behavior that has the same function as the target behavior.
5. Teach the student a functional response to replace the target behavior.
6. Provide the student with opportunities to engage in the alternative behavior.
7. Provide the student with reinforcement for the alternative behavior.

After accurately identifying the function of the inappropriate behavior and developing an alternative behavior to replace that behavior, the teacher can teach and reinforce the alternative behavior, which will effectively reduce or eliminate the inappropriate behavior.

ASSUMPTIONS OF FUNCTIONAL BEHAVIOR ANALYSIS

Teachers need to be aware of several assumptions of functional behavior analysis and how these affect the development of alternative behaviors. First, it is possible for multiple behaviors to have the same function. When that is the case, one or two alternative behaviors could have the potential for modifying multiple behavior difficulties (Ducharme & Shecter, 2011).

Further, functional behavior analysis conducted in one setting is often used to develop interventions in other settings. Teachers often erroneously assume that the variables that affect the behavior in one setting are the same as the variables in another setting. Teachers need to consider the possibility that the results of a functional behavior analysis may not generalize to another setting where the function of the behavior is different. For example, Benjamin talks without permission in both his math and science classes. In math class, the function of the behavior may be seeking attention from the teacher. In science class, Benjamin may be frustrated with the assignments, and the function of his talking without permission may be to escape nonpreferred activities. In this case, the behavior is the same for both classes, but the function is different. When an alternative behavior is successful in one setting but not in another, the teacher needs to consider the possibility that the functions are not the same and develop different functional-based interventions for the two settings.

GENERATING A BEHAVIOR INTERVENTION PLAN

Once the functional behavior analysis has been completed and the multidisciplinary team has developed alternative behaviors to replace the target behavior, the team needs to generate a behavior intervention plan. The BIP should include information obtained from the functional behavioral assessment, the functional behavior analysis, behavioral hypotheses, specific behavioral goals, intervention strategies, and a method to assess the effectiveness of the plan. Unfortunately, many behavior intervention plans are not based on functional behavioral assessments or functional behavior analysis, and many do not include hypothesis statements or alternative behaviors (Blood & Neel, 2007). Without conducting a functional behavior analysis, a teacher will find it difficult to identify the function of a student's inappropriate behavior or to develop a behavioral hypothesis, both of which are essential to the generation of an effective behavior intervention plan.

SUMMARY

Teachers need to identify the functions of students' inappropriate behaviors in order to make effective behavior modifications that can reduce or eliminate those behaviors. A functional behavior analysis will help a teacher determine the function of a student's behavior and develop alternative behaviors to replace the aberrant behavior.

The functions of behaviors are the purposes they serve, or "why we do the things we do." It is important to remember that the function of a behavior is not likely to be inappropriate; rather, it is the behavior itself that is either appropriate or inappropriate. As a result, it is the behavior that needs to be modified, not the function of the behavior.

The two functional categories of behavior are *attainment* and *avoidance/ escape of a situation*. Each functional category includes functional motivations. For attainment, the functional motivations are attention, rewards and privileges, and power or control. The functional motivations for avoidance/escape of a situation are social isolation, nonpreferred activities, and adverse interactions.

Societal and cultural norms also influence the functional motivations of behaviors. Teachers need to understand the cultural and linguistic backgrounds of their students when trying to identify the functions of students' behavior.

Once the function of an inappropriate behavior has been identified, a behavioral hypothesis can be developed. The behavioral hypothesis proposes an explanation of the factors that cause the behavior. A multidisciplinary/multicultural team should determine the function of the behavior. When a behavioral hypothesis has been established, an effective alternative behavior can be developed to reduce or eliminate the target behavior. Five kinds of functional-based interventions are used to implement alternative behaviors: functional communication training, antecedent-based interventions, instructional accommodations, extinction, and differential reinforcement.

It is important that teachers accurately identify the functions of students' inappropriate behaviors. This is an important step in generating and implementing effective behavior intervention plans.

REVIEW ACTIVITIES

1. What is the purpose of a functional behavior analysis?

2. What is a behavioral hypothesis?

3. Michael is constantly asking Mr. Thompson for help on his English assignment. List at least two possible functional motivations for Michael's behavior.

4. During class discussions, Patricia puts her head on her desk and does not participate. Write a behavioral hypothesis for Patricia's behavior.

5. Describe the differences among the various kinds of functional-based interventions and give one example for each.

Visit the Student Study Site at www.sagepub.com/shepherd to access additional study tools including mobile-friendly eFlashcards and web quizzes as well as links to SAGE journal articles and web resources.

CHAPTER 10
BEHAVIOR INTERVENTION PLAN

Trinity of Behavior Management

After reading this chapter, you should be able to do the following:

- Identify the eight components of a behavior intervention plan.
- Understand the importance of having culturally proficient members on the behavior intervention team.
- Explain the difference between behavior goals and behavior objectives.
- Write behavior goals and behavior objectives.
- Understand the barriers that prevent teachers from developing and implementing effective behavior intervention plans.

COMPONENTS OF A BEHAVIOR INTERVENTION PLAN

The final step in modifying student behavior is the development and implementation of a behavior intervention plan, a written plan that describes the interventions, strategies, and supports that will be implemented to address the social, emotional, and behavioral needs of a student. The purpose of a BIP is to implement strategies that will reduce or eliminate the target behavior. As part of a universal design for classroom management, a behavior intervention plan should (a) be developed for any student whose behavior is interfering with the student's learning or the learning of other students in the classroom; (b) be based on the data obtained from the functional behavioral assessment; (c) include a behavioral hypothesis developed from the functional behavior analysis; (d) be individualized and based on the student's social, emotional, and behavioral needs; (e) include positive behavioral strategies; and (f) be implemented and monitored.

Behavior intervention plans contain many of the same steps as functional behavioral assessments and functional behavior analysis, and are a logical extension of the two assessment procedures (Shippen, Simpson, & Crites, 2003; see Table 10.1). While there are no federal guidelines or standardized procedures for developing and implementing BIPs, nine components of such plans have been identified that correspond to the trinity of behavior management:

1. Definition of target behavior

2. Attempted interventions

3. Summary of functional behavioral assessment

4. Behavioral hypothesis

5. Alternative behavior 1

6. Intervention strategies (alternative behavior 1)

7. Alternative behavior 2

8. Intervention strategies (alternative behavior 2)

9. Evaluation of the effectiveness of the plan (Curtiss, Mathur, & Rutherford, 2002)

The best practice for developing and implementing a behavior intervention plan is a team-based approach. Such an approach has many advantages.

Table 10.1 Trinity of Behavior Management: Behavior Intervention Plan

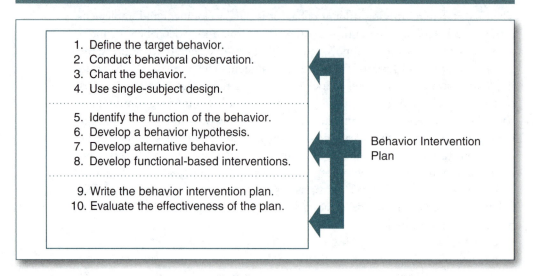

1. Define the target behavior.
2. Conduct behavioral observation.
3. Chart the behavior.
4. Use single-subject design.

5. Identify the function of the behavior.
6. Develop a behavior hypothesis.
7. Develop alternative behavior.
8. Develop functional-based interventions.

9. Write the behavior intervention plan.
10. Evaluate the effectiveness of the plan.

Behavior Intervention Plan

For instance, the members of a behavior intervention team can share the work, consider multiple perspectives, and generate a variety of suggestions. The involvement of a number of individuals increases the likelihood that an appropriate and effective BIP will be developed.

The composition of the behavior intervention team is important. The team should include general education teachers and other professionals who are familiar with the student, special education teachers who are familiar with developing and implementing behavior intervention plans, administrators, school counselors, and parents. Additionally, the team plays a critical role in determining the impact that culture may have on a student's behavior. The team needs to be culturally proficient, which means that the members must understand the differences between their own values and the cultural values of students, parents, and the community (Nuri-Robins, Lindsey, Terrell, & Lindsey, 2007). The inclusion of culturally sensitive professionals enables the team to understand the cultural, experiential, and linguistic background of the student. If a behavior intervention team is composed primarily of European Americans who are not culturally proficient and they are developing a BIP for an African American student, it is unlikely that the plan will be effective in modifying the target behavior, especially if the student's culture affects the behavior. In such a case, the behavior intervention team should be expanded to include community professionals who are sensitive to the student's culture.

The members of the behavior intervention team have a number of responsibilities. They need to evaluate the target behavior, collect and analyze data on the behavior, develop a behavioral hypothesis and alternative behaviors, design intervention strategies, and implement and evaluate the effectiveness of the behavior intervention plan (Maag & Katsiyannis, 2006). The team should use the information obtained from the functional behavioral assessment and functional behavior analysis to develop intervention strategies that will modify the target behavior. The behavior intervention plan should be developed to meet the individual behavior needs of the student and should include positive behavior strategies (Etscheidt, 2006).

Unfortunately, many schools use BIPs as a reactive strategy to deal with problem behaviors or as a perfunctory requirement of the Individuals with Disabilities Education Improvement Act (Killu, Weber, Derby, & Barretto, 2006). Additionally, BIPs are often implemented for students receiving special education services, but seldom for students in general education programs, despite the fact that well-developed intervention plans have been found to improve learner outcomes and ameliorate the behavior problems of all kinds of students. Behavior intervention plans constitute an essential aspect of a universal design for classroom management, and they should be an integral part of a school-wide positive behavior support system.

Behavior intervention plans are a logical extension of functional behavioral assessments and functional behavior analysis (see Table 10.2). As a result, many of the components of a BIP are completed prior to the development and implementation of the plan. Unfortunately, many of the BIPs currently being used do not incorporate data collected during functional behavioral assessments and functional behavior analyses, and a large majority use adverse consequences for inappropriate behaviors, a strategy that is unlikely to be effective in modifying the behaviors (Van Acker, Boreson, Gable, & Potterton, 2005). A well-developed BIP incorporates the information obtained from the functional behavioral assessment and the functional behavior analysis.

Implementation of a Behavior Intervention Plan

The development and implementation of a behavior intervention plan involves a number of steps (see Figure 10.1). The fidelity of the plan's implementation is essential to the plan's integrity (Killu, 2008). The steps are all woven together to create a tapestry of information that creates an effective BIP. If one step is not done well, the strength of the plan is diminished. The individuals involved in the development and implementation of a behavior intervention plan must ensure that each step leads to an effective plan.

Table 10.2 Procedures for Developing and Implementing a Behavior Intervention Plan

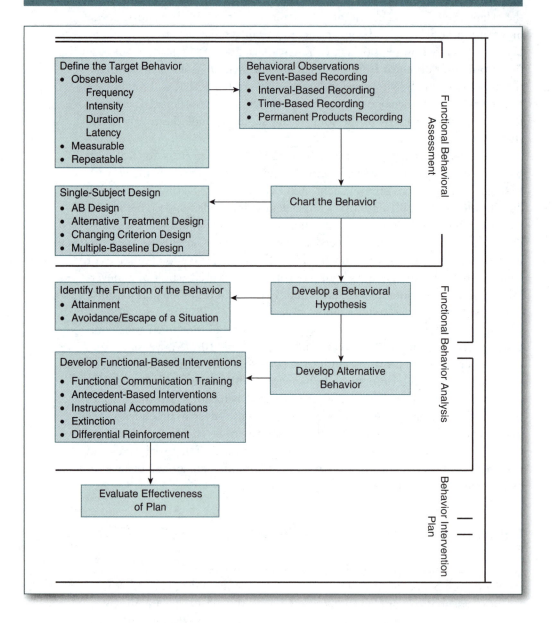

Target Behavior

The first task in developing a behavior intervention plan is that of defining the target behavior. It cannot be overemphasized that defining the target behavior is the most important step. Without a clearly defined target behavior, it is

Figure 10.1 Behavior Intervention Plan

Behavior Intervention Plan

Student _____   Age _____

School _____   Grade _____

Start Date _____   Review Date _____

Target Behavior: Observable, measurable, and repeatable.

Previously Attempted Interventions and Effectiveness:

Summary of Functional Behavioral Assessment:

Anecdotal Observation	Setting	
	Antecedents	
	Consequences	
Frequency, Intensity, Duration, Latency, Permanent Products		
Possible Cultural Impact on Behavior		

Behavioral Hypothesis:

Avoidance	
Attention Seeking	
Reinforcement of Behavior	
Other Functions	

Alternative Behavior 1: List appropriate and attainable alternative behavior.

Intervention Plan for Alternative Behavior 1:

Identify Intervention Strategy	
Designate Person to Implement Strategy	
Method to Evaluate Effectiveness of Intervention Strategy	

Alternative Behavior 2: List appropriate and attainable alternative behavior.

Intervention Plan for Alternative Behavior 2:

Identify Intervention Strategy	
Designate Person to Implement Strategy	
Method to Evaluate Effectiveness of Intervention Strategy	

Monitoring the Effectiveness of Interventions:

difficult to collect the data necessary to develop and implement appropriate interventions to address the behavior (Van Acker et al., 2005). The operational definition should describe the target behavior as observable, measurable, and repeatable. For example, Jane's target behavior is "During class discussions, Jane will receive permission from the teacher by raising her hand when she needs to talk 9 out of 10 times in five consecutive sessions on a daily basis." The behavior is observable, measurable, and repeatable.

The target behavior is initially defined during the functional behavioral assessment; however, many functional behavioral assessments do not adequately define target behaviors. To ensure that the target behavior is well defined, the operational definition of the target behavior should be reviewed and refined during the functional behavior analysis and the actual development of the behavior intervention plan.

It is also important to remember that students' cultures may affect their behaviors, and culturally and linguistically diverse students may not respond to situations or events in anticipated ways. Teachers' perceptions of students whose cultural and linguistic backgrounds are different from their own are often based on misperceptions and stereotypes (Cartledge, Gardner, & Ford, 2009). While a student's behavior may seem atypical to the teacher, the behavior may be the norm for someone with the student's cultural expectations. When defining a student's target behavior, the teacher needs to consider whether the behavior may be influenced by the student's culture. By taking the time to learn about the students in their classrooms and establish positive relationships with students' families, teachers improve their ability to determine the nature of their students' behavior difficulties.

Attempted Interventions

It is important that any previously attempted interventions be noted on the BIP, along with information on the effectiveness of those interventions. This provides all behavior intervention team members with information regarding any ineffective interventions attempted and helps them develop different interventions that may be more effective. For example, on Jane's BIP, it was noted that a previous intervention, writing sentences every time she talked without raising her hand, was not effective.

This step is also aligned with a positive behavior support program, which establishes three tiers of support with increasing levels of intensity. The summary of attempted interventions could list strategies that were attempted at the secondary and third tiers of a positive behavior support program. This step could also indicate that previous interventions were not attempted or that a student was immediately placed at the third tier, which provides the student with intensive interventions that might not have been necessary. For example, instead of attempting intervention strategies at Tier 2 for Jane's target behavior of talking without permission, the teacher referred Jane for assistance at Tier 3, which includes the development and implementation of a behavior intervention plan. It is possible that Tier 2 interventions could have been successful at ameliorating Jane's behavior, and the development and implementation of a behavior intervention plan was not necessary.

Summary of the Functional Behavioral Assessment

The summary of the functional behavioral assessment further describes the target behavior. The description of the behavior should include its frequency, intensity, duration, and/or latency. The information regarding the setting, antecedents, and consequences associated with the target behavior obtained from anecdotal observations, or the ABC analysis, should also be reported on the behavior intervention plan. Baseline data and any intervention data should be included in the summary. These descriptions of the target behavior could also help explain the reasons for the behavior. For example, on Jane's BIP, it was noted that, according to data collected using an event-based recording method, Jane had an average rate of behavior per minute of 0.29. An interval-based recording method indicated that the total rate of behavior was 35%.

The behavior intervention plan should also report any possible cultural impact on the student's behavior. The BIP should include culturally appropriate behavior management strategies and should note any strategies that may be in conflict with the cultural background of the student. Culturally diverse students may challenge behavior and classroom management strategies that dismiss their cultures, values, and beliefs. Culturally responsive behavior strategies provide a learning environment in which culturally diverse students can be successful in school.

Behavioral Hypothesis

A functional behavior analysis completes the process started by the functional behavioral assessment through the development of a behavioral hypothesis. Using data collected on the student's target behavior, the behavior intervention team determines if the function of the behavior is attainment or avoidance/escape of a situation (see Chapter 9). For example, Jane's behavior intervention team has identified attainment as the function for Jane talking without permission. The functional motivation for Jane's behavior was seeking the teacher's attention. Identifying the function of the behavior is an important step in developing alternative behaviors. Unfortunately, many of the behavior intervention plans currently in use do not indicate behavioral hypotheses, and if they do, the alternative behaviors the plans suggest are not based on the behavioral hypotheses. In many instances, alternative behaviors are developed without any understanding of the causes of the target behaviors, which creates an arbitrary approach toward modifying student behavior.

Alternative Behaviors

Once the behavior intervention team has arrived at a behavioral hypothesis based on the functional behavior analysis, the team develops alternative behaviors. Alternative behaviors should serve the same function as the target behavior and should be defined in a specific manner "that focus[es] on what to do, when to do it, when it will not be appropriate, and why" (Scott, Anderson, & Spaulding, 2008, p. 45). For example, Jane's target behavior was *talking without permission.* The team has identified the function of Jane's behavior as attainment; thus, the function of the alternative behavior should also be attainment. The team has identified *raising her hand for permission to talk* as Jane's alternative behavior. Once the function of the target behavior has been identified, the team can develop alternative behaviors using environmental modifications, instructional strategies, consequence interventions, and future alternative/replacement behavior strategies (see Chapter 8). For example, Jane's behavior intervention team used consequence interventions to develop an alternative behavior. When Jane raises her hand for permission to talk, she will eat lunch with the teacher. The function of the alternative behavior is the same as the function of the target behavior.

The Intervention Plan

The intervention plan for alternative behaviors should include specific information on the intervention strategy to be used, the person designated to implement the strategy, and the method that will be used to evaluate the effectiveness of the strategy. The choice of an intervention strategy often depends on the function of the target behavior. As described previously, possible functions of a behavior are attainment and avoidance/escape of a situation. Intervention strategies for avoidance of an activity might include some type of reinforcement or manipulation of the antecedent variables. Strategies for attention seeking might include some type of reinforcement or development of new behavior through imitation. Reinforcement of the target behavior might include some type of reinforcement, modification of antecedent variables, or development of new behaviors through shaping or chaining. Finally, since behaviors sometimes do not fit neatly into prescribed parameters, some target behaviors have other functions that can be difficult to identify. In such cases, teachers need to be creative in developing and implementing intervention strategies.

When developing intervention strategies, the behavior intervention team must clearly outline the interventions to be implemented. For example, the behavior intervention plan should state if the teacher should modify lessons and how they should be modified, or it should state exactly what the teacher should do, such as provide more verbal praise (Killu, 2008). As with defining the target behavior, intervention strategies that are vague are most likely to be ineffective.

The behavior intervention team should also take note of any previously attempted interventions and the effectiveness of those interventions. This information, particularly regarding ineffective interventions attempted, should help the team develop new interventions that may be effective. Unfortunately, teams often implement strategies that have already been found to be ineffective, and they often develop intervention plans that are not based on the functions of students' target behaviors. Many BIPs also include adverse consequences for target behaviors, a strategy that has been found to be unlikely to be effective in modifying the behaviors (Van Acker et al., 2005). Behavior intervention strategies should be chosen based on their likelihood of effectively modifying the target behavior.

The BIP should designate the person responsible for implementing the strategy. The designated person is usually the general education teacher or the special education teacher, but, depending on the strategy implemented, this individual could also be the school counselor or even an administrator. Additionally, two or more persons could share the responsibility of implementing the intervention strategy.

Finally, the intervention plan should specify the method that will be used to evaluate the effectiveness of the strategy. The behavior intervention team could decide to use anecdotal observation (ABC analysis), various recording methods, or single-subject designs. For example, Jane's team determined that a reversal design, or ABAB design, would be the most appropriate method for evaluating the effectiveness of the intervention strategy developed for Jane.

Evaluating the Effectiveness of BIPs

Once implemented, the BIP needs to be evaluated for effectiveness on a continuous basis (Etscheidt, 2006; Maag & Katsiyannis, 2006). The behavior intervention team is responsible for monitoring the student's behavior, determining whether the plan is modifying the target behavior, and deciding whether the plan needs to be revised. Unfortunately, many teams fail to monitor the effectiveness of behavior intervention plans and the maintenance of the students' behavior over time (Van Acker et al., 2005).

The effectiveness of a behavior intervention plan can be monitored through the use of direct observations (anecdotal observations), behavioral assessments, recording methods, and single-subject designs. For example, Jane's behavior intervention team decided to use an event-based recording method and an AB single-subject design to evaluate the effectiveness of the intervention. The information obtained from the evaluation of the BIP provides members of the behavior intervention team the tools they need to work through any problems involved with the implementation of the plan (Codding, Feinberg, Dunn, & Pace, 2005; Hagermoser Sanetti, Luiselli, & Handler, 2007). If the team determines that the target behavior has not been reduced or eliminated—or, as happens in some instances, has been exacerbated—new alternative behaviors and intervention strategies need to be developed and implemented. The use of controlled procedures is essential for effective behavior intervention plans (Killu et al., 2006).

In addition to evaluating the effectiveness of the behavior intervention plan, the members of the behavior intervention team need to evaluate their own performance in the implementation of the plan. Evaluating the effectiveness of the BIP ensures treatment integrity, or the degree to which the BIP is implemented (Killu, 2008). One way to maintain treatment integrity is for the behavior intervention team to meet on a regular basis to evaluate the effectiveness of the plan. Arranging a regularly scheduled time for the team to meet is essential given teachers' numerous responsibilities and the unpredictable schedules of other team members. Members of the team need to give and receive verbal and graphic feedback about their level of treatment integrity, which may include the numbers of observations team members make during the intervention period and whether all components of the plan are implemented in a consistent manner. Evaluation of treatment integrity is critical for the effectiveness of behavior intervention plans (Hagermoser Sanetti et al., 2007). Treatment integrity is consistent with reflective practices that teachers should use to evaluate behavior and classroom management plans and a universal design for classroom management.

DEVELOPING BEHAVIOR GOALS

Without well-written behavior goals and objectives, behavior intervention plans will not be effective. However, writing clear and useful behavior goals and objectives remains an elusive skill for many teachers, despite the training they receive at universities and colleges. As with all skills, learning to write effective behavior goals and objectives takes practice. A behavior goal is a broad statement about a student outcome within a specific period of time, generally from 3 months to a year, depending on the behavior needs of the student. For example, Jane's behavior goal is "Jane will participate appropriately in class discussions." Behavior objectives are created from behavior goals and are based on behaviors that can be completed in 1 to 3 months.

Behavior objectives are specific statements about student performance that include the condition, the target behavior, and the criterion of the performance (Lignugaris/Kraft, Marchand-Martella, & Martella, 2001). The *condition* is the circumstance in which the target behavior is observed or will be observed. For Jane's target behavior, *talking without permission,* the condition might be "During class discussions . . ."

The target behavior for the behavior objective is usually the alternative behavior. The behavior must be clearly defined, observable, and measurable. The behavior should also indicate what the student is expected to do. For example, Jane's behavior is "Jane will receive permission from the teacher by raising her hand when she needs to talk."

Finally, the behavior objective should include the *criterion,* or the standard level of acceptable performance. The criterion should include the performance level, the number of times the student demonstrates the behavior, and the evaluation schedule (Lignugaris/Kraft et al., 2001). The criterion level is the level the student must achieve to demonstrate mastery. For example, Jane will raise her hand when she needs to talk "90% of the time" or "9 out of 10 times." The number of times Jane demonstrates the behavior is how often she demonstrates the criterion level before she has met the behavior objective. For example, Jane will raise her hand when she needs to talk 9 out of 10 times in "five consecutive sessions." Finally, the evaluation schedule is how often the teacher is going to evaluate the behavior objective. In this case, the teacher will evaluate Jane's behavior objective on a daily basis. Thus, Jane's behavior goal is stated as follows:

Jane will participate appropriately in class discussions.

And the behavior objective based on this goal is stated this way:

During class discussions, Jane will receive permission from the teacher by raising her hand when she needs to talk 9 out of 10 times in five consecutive sessions on a daily basis.

Jane's behavior objective contains the condition, a clearly defined target behavior, and the criterion.

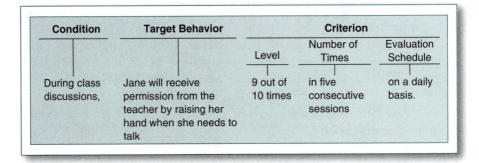

Figure 10.2 Anatomy of a Behavior Objective

Condition	Target Behavior	Criterion		
		Level	Number of Times	Evaluation Schedule
During class discussions,	Jane will receive permission from the teacher by raising her hand when she needs to talk	9 out of 10 times	in five consecutive sessions	on a daily basis.

In another example, Timothy has been fighting with peers after school. This is Timothy's behavior goal:

Timothy will demonstrate appropriate behavior on the school grounds after school.

The behavior goal is used to develop Timothy's behavior objective, which is stated as follows:

When interacting with peers after school, Timothy will refrain from fighting with peers 9 out of 10 times in 1 month.

Timothy's behavior objective contains the condition, the target behavior, and the criterion. It is important to remember that in conjunction with behavior goals and objectives, intervention strategies and consequences are also included in the behavior intervention plan. In the event that Timothy does fight with peers after school, he will be subject to some type of reinforcement or consequence because of his behavior. As discussed previously, reinforcements or consequences should be natural outcomes of the behavior and implemented as soon as possible after the behavior has been displayed.

It is important to remember that a well-written—that is, clear and concise—behavior objective is based on the behavior goal and includes the condition, the target behavior, and the criterion. Problems usually occur when a behavior objective is missing one or more of the components necessary to enable all members of the behavior intervention team to understand the student and the

Figure 10.3 Jane's Behavior Intervention Plan

Behavior Intervention Plan

Student _Jane_   Age _11 years old_

School _Franklin Pierce Elementary_   Grade _Fifth grade_

Start Date _April 4, 2016_   Review Date _May 27, 2016_

Target Behavior: Observable, measurable, and repeatable.

During class discussions, Jane will receive permission from the teacher by raising her hand when she needs to talk 9 out of 10 times in five consecutive sessions on a daily basis.

Previously Attempted Interventions and Effectiveness:

Jane was given lines every time she talked without raising her hand. According to a single-subject AB design, this intervention was not effective.

Summary of Functional Behavioral Assessment:

Anecdotal Observation	Setting	_Math class, class discussion_
	Antecedents	
	Consequences	_Verbal redirection_
Frequency, Intensity, Duration, Latency, Permanent Products	_Event-Based Recording: Jane had an average rate of behavior per minute of 0.29. Interval-based recording indicated the total rate of behavior occurring at 35%._	
Possible Cultural Impact on Behavior	_No foreseeable cultural impact on behavior._	

Behavioral Hypothesis:

Attainment	_Jane is seeking the teacher's attention._
Avoidance/Escape	
Reinforcement of Behavior	_Jane does not respond to reinforcements._
Other Functions	

Alternative Behavior 1: List appropriate and attainable alternative behavior.

During class discussions, Jane will receive permission from the teacher by raising her hand when she needs to talk 9 out of 10 times in five consecutive sessions on a daily basis.

Intervention Plan for Alternative Behavior 1:

Identify Intervention Strategy	_Lunch with Mrs. Clark_
Designate Person to Implement Strategy	_Mrs. Clark_
Method to Evaluate Effectiveness of Intervention Strategy	_AB single-subject design_

Alternative Behavior 2: List appropriate and attainable alternative behavior.

Intervention Plan for Alternative Behavior 2:

Identify Intervention Strategy	
Designate Person to Implement Strategy	
Method to Evaluate Effectiveness of Intervention Strategy	

Monitoring the Effectiveness of Interventions:

Event-based recording and AB single-subject design.

student's target behavior. For example, "Morgan will respect the rights of others" is a poorly written behavior objective. It does not contain the condition or a criterion. Additionally, the target behavior is not clearly defined, observable, and measurable. The objective does not state what Morgan will do. A better objective would be as follows:

> When moving from one workstation to another, Morgan will refrain from taking items from other students' desks four out of five times per week on a daily basis.

The revised behavior objective includes the condition, the target behavior, and the criterion. Notice that the behavior objective does not require the student to admit guilt; rather, it focuses on the behavior.

The intervention should be directly related to the target behavior. A number of interventions are available for Morgan. The teacher could reinforce Morgan when he demonstrates appropriate behavior by giving him tangible rewards (e.g., free time, first in line for lunch) or intangible rewards (e.g., praise, pat on the back), remove him from workstations, create a behavior contract with him, provide him with social skills training, and so on.

The writing of behavior goals and behavior objectives and the development and implementation of behavior intervention plans together constitute one piece of the puzzle that creates a universal design for classroom management. Teachers who put all the pieces together will have highly effective behavior and classroom management programs that consider the needs of all students in their classrooms.

CASE STUDY   Timothy and Mrs. Miller (Part 3)

In Mrs. Miller's fourth-grade class, Timothy had been taking pencils, erasers, glue, and other objects from other students. An earlier intervention strategy had been ineffective, and Timothy's relationships with his peers had deteriorated. Based on behavioral observations, Mrs. Miller had concluded that Timothy was trying to get attention from his peers.

The behavioral hypothesis for Timothy's behavior was as follows:

When the teacher is not looking / Timothy takes items from peers / to gain peers' attention.

(the antecedent)   (the behavior)   (the consequence)

Based on the behavioral hypothesis, the following target behavior was developed for Timothy:

When the teacher is not looking, Timothy will refrain from taking items from peers 95% of the time on a daily basis.

This target behavior was observable, measurable, and repeatable.

With the help of a behavior intervention team that included Timothy's mother, a behavior intervention plan was developed. Since attention from peers was the functional motivation, it was determined that Timothy would have time with peers at the end of the day at one of the activity tables. Activities would include putting together puzzles, playing board games, and playing card games. Taking part in these activities would also help Timothy develop social skills.

Behavior Intervention Plan

Student	Timothy	Age	10 years old
School	McKay Elementary	Grade	Fourth grade
Start Date	September 19, 2016	Review Date	May 31, 2016

Target Behavior: Observable, measurable, and repeatable.

When the teacher is not looking, Timothy will refrain from taking items from peers 95% of the time on a daily basis.

Previously Attempted Interventions and Effectiveness:

Timothy was provided with an item of his choice if he did not take any items from other students without permission. This intervention was not effective.

Summary of Functional Behavioral Assessment:

Anecdotal Observation	Setting	Mrs. Miller's classroom
	Antecedents	When Mrs. Miller was occupied
	Consequences	Angry peers. Peers avoiding Timothy at lunch and recess.
Frequency, Intensity, Duration, Latency, Permanent Products	Event-Based Recording: Timothy had an average rate of behavior per minute of 0.23.	
Possible Cultural Impact on Behavior	No foreseeable cultural impact on behavior.	

Behavioral Hypothesis:

Attainment	Timothy is seeking attention from peers.
Avoidance/Escape	
Reinforcement of Behavior	Timothy did not respond to receiving items from the teacher if he did not take items from peers.
Other Functions	

Alternative Behavior 1: List appropriate and attainable alternative behavior.

When the teacher is not looking, Timothy will refrain from taking items from peers 95% of the time on a daily basis.

(Continued)

(Continued)

Intervention Plan for Alternative Behavior 1:	
Identify Intervention Strategy	*Time with peers at the activity table*
Designate Person to Implement Strategy	*Mrs. Miller*
Method to Evaluate Effectiveness of Intervention Strategy	*Event-based recording method*
Alternative Behavior 2: List appropriate and attainable alternative behavior.	
Intervention Plan for Alternative Behavior 2:	
Identify Intervention Strategy	
Designate Person to Implement Strategy	
Method to Evaluate Effectiveness of Intervention Strategy	
Monitoring the Effectiveness of Interventions:	
Event-based recording method.	

A couple of weeks after Timothy's behavior intervention plan was implemented, Ms. Keller, the paraprofessional in Mrs. Miller's classroom, did a behavioral observation of Timothy using an event-based recording method, as shown in the following table:

Day	Observation period	Frequency of target behavior	Frequency count	Rate of behavior per minute
Monday	9:00–9:40 40 minutes	√	1	0.03
Tuesday	10:00–10:30 30 minutes		0	0
Wednesday	9:00–9:25 25 minutes		0	0
Thursday	9:00–9:30 30 minutes		0	0
Friday	2:00–2:30 30 minutes	√	1	0.03

Based on the information obtained from the observation of Timothy's behavior, it appeared that the behavior intervention plan was effective.

IMPLICATIONS OF BEHAVIOR INTERVENTION PLANS

The implementation of functional behavioral assessments and behavior intervention plans is mandated for any student receiving special education services when the school is considering a change of placement due to the student's behavior. However, this is a reactive strategy that applies only to students with disabilities and almost exclusively involves students with emotional and behavior disorders. As part of a universal design for classroom management and positive behavior supports, schools should use behavior intervention plans as an active strategy for *all* students displaying behavior difficulties. Developing and implementing a behavior intervention plan when a student begins displaying challenging behaviors is often effective in reducing and eliminating the behaviors. Additionally, early interventions that include alternative behaviors are more effective if implemented when the challenging behaviors are first presented (Moreno, 2010).

However, a number of barriers have hindered the development and implementation of behavior intervention plans in schools. One of these barriers stems from the perceptions that many education professionals have of behavior and classroom management. Many teachers and administrators still follow the traditional hierarchy of rules and consequences as the main emphasis of their behavior and classroom management plans. These types of plans do not meet the behavior needs of all students in the classroom. Additionally, many behavior and classroom management plans tend to be punishment based, including punitive measures such as suspension, expulsion, and zero-tolerance policies (Couvillon, Bullock, & Gable, 2009). Schools need to adopt a universal design for classroom management that incorporates a number of strategies designed to meet the behavior needs of all students. Teachers, administrators, and other education professionals need to embrace proactive, active, and reactive strategies for addressing behavior problems in the classroom.

Another barrier is the lack of training most teachers receive in developing and implementing behavior intervention plans in the general education setting. Few general education teachers have had any training in the development of BIPs, and, as a result, many do not have sufficient knowledge about the collection and interpretation of behavioral data, nor do they understand teachers' responsibilities regarding the development and implementation of BIPs. Many general education teachers do not know how to write an operational definition of a target behavior, which is an essential element of an effective behavior intervention plan (Van Acker et al., 2005). Without an understanding of the function of a student's inappropriate behavior, it is difficult to maintain the integrity of a behavior intervention plan for the student.

When the members of a behavior intervention team do not have training in the development and implementation of behavior intervention plans, they often ignore the results of the student's functional behavioral assessment and functional behavior analysis when developing intervention strategies. Often, they will use intervention strategies that have already proved unsuccessful, and frequently BIPs developed by untrained teams include strategies that are ineffective in modifying inappropriate behaviors or may even exacerbate them.

In addition to a lack of training, many teachers do not have the time to conduct functional behavioral assessments and functional behavior analysis, followed by the development of behavior intervention plans. The increasing demands placed on teachers by administrators, parents, and state and federal legislation prevent teachers from having the time necessary to implement assessment procedures and develop BIPs (Killu et al., 2006). Increased emphasis on academic accountability and preparing students for state-mandated examinations means that planning for behavior and classroom management is often a low priority. However, unless teachers can implement effective behavior and classroom management plans that include behavior intervention plans for students with challenging behaviors, many students will not make academic progress. Teachers need to be given the time, training, practice, and support they need to develop and implement effective behavior intervention plans.

IMPACT OF CULTURE ON BIPS

When teachers are developing behavior intervention plans for students with problematic behaviors, it is important that they understand how culture affects behavior. If a teacher fails to consider the cultural and linguistic background of a student, the behavior intervention plan is likely to be ineffective in modifying the student's behavior. For example, when talking to a student who is a Native American, the teacher might consider the child rude and disrespectful because the student will not look at her. This becomes a target behavior, and a functional behavioral assessment and functional behavior analysis are conducted. The function of the behavior is identified, and alternative behaviors are determined. Finally, a behavior intervention plan is developed and implemented to modify the inappropriate behavior. However, if the teacher had used culturally responsive practices in behavior and classroom management and had taken the time to understand the cultural backgrounds of the students in her classroom, she would have understood that in some Native American cultures it is considered disrespectful for a child to make eye contact with an adult. The student's behavior was not inappropriate, and the process leading to the behavior intervention plan did not need to be initiated. Teachers need to be aware that their reactions to some behaviors of culturally and linguistically diverse students are often based on misperceptions (Cartledge et al., 2009).

Unfortunately, while researchers and educators agree that understanding how culture may affect behavior is crucial in today's diverse schools, few culturally sensitive strategies are available for collecting data leading to the development of a behavior intervention plan. First, teachers should not make assumptions about cultures they do not understand. Teachers should also remember that there are considerable variations within cultural typologies. For example, the culture and traditions of Hispanics in south Texas are different from the culture and traditions of Hispanics in Florida. Second, the behavior intervention team should make an effort to obtain information from the families of culturally and linguistically diverse students by using culturally sensitive data collection strategies such as the following:

1. Learn about the families' cultural perspectives and language backgrounds prior to collecting data.

2. Involve family members in planning the data collection.

3. Adapt the procedures for collecting data based on the families' interaction styles.

4. Examine the appropriateness of the items on the assessment.

When involving students' families in the data collection process leading to the development and implementation of behavior intervention plans, teachers need to demonstrate respect toward the families and use culturally responsive strategies, such as listening to family members' responses and considering alternatives based on those responses.

WHAT WOULD YOU DO? Jake

Jake is a seventh grader at Washington Middle School. He comes from a single-parent setting. Jake's mother and father are divorced. Before they separated, the father was extremely abusive toward Jake, his sister, and his mother. Jake has reported to Child Protective Services that his father slammed him against a wall several times. One incident was so severe that Jake was taken to the hospital with a concussion. The father also perpetrated incidents of severe emotional abuse. As a result of the abuse, the father is not allowed any contact with the family. Jake's mother works two jobs, barely making enough money to meet the family's financial needs, and is seldom home when Jake and his sister are home.

(Continued)

(Continued)

Jake has no history of truancy; however, he has been suspended from school many times for aggressive behavior. These incidents have all taken place within the first hour of the school day. For example, he has threatened to "beat up" peers, he has taken a full trash can and dumped it on the teacher's desk, and last week, he activated the fire alarm. As a result, he is seldom in school for more than a single day each week.

Jake has not been identified as having a disability, and he is not receiving special education services. Additionally, the traditional hierarchy of rules and consequences has been ineffective in modifying Jake's behavior.

If you were Jake's teacher, what would you do about his behavior?

SUMMARY

The purpose of the behavior intervention plan is to use the information obtained through functional behavioral assessment and functional behavior analysis in the development and implementation of strategies that will reduce or eliminate a student's inappropriate behavior. A BIP should be an individualized plan that includes positive behavioral strategies (Etscheidt, 2006). Once a behavior intervention plan has been implemented, the members of the student's behavior intervention team need to monitor and evaluate the student's behavior to determine whether the strategies of the BIP are effective in reducing or eliminating the inappropriate behavior (Etscheidt, 2006; Maag & Katsiyannis, 2006).

Unfortunately, a number of barriers prevent the implementation and development of effective BIPs for all students. Teachers need to change their perceptions of behavior and classroom management plans; rather than one-size-fits-all, traditional hierarchies of rules and consequences, these plans need to incorporate proactive, active, and reactive strategies of a universal design for classroom management that meets the needs of all students.

REVIEW ACTIVITIES

1. Benjamin is having difficulty following directions in the classroom. When would be the best time to develop a behavior intervention plan for him?

2. Mario, who is Hispanic and an English language learner, refuses to complete his assignments. Who should be on his behavior intervention team, and why?

3. What components are missing from the following behavior objectives? Rewrite each objective so that it includes the appropriate components.

   - Kale demonstrates inappropriate behaviors in a small-group setting.
   - Timothy will not fight during five out of seven conflict situations.
   - When given instructions for worksheets by the teacher, LeVar will follow instructions.
   - Kim will not cheat.

Visit the Student Study Site at www.sagepub.com/shepherd to access additional study tools including mobile-friendly eFlashcards and web quizzes as well as links to SAGE journal articles and web resources.

CHAPTER 11
SINGLE-SUBJECT DESIGN

After reading this chapter, you should be able to do the following:

- Explain the purpose of single-subject designs.
- Define baseline data and intervention data.
- Describe the level, trend, and variability of behavior data and their importance for the analysis of data from a single-subject design.
- Analyze the level, trend, and variability of baseline and intervention data.
- Describe the different types of single-subject designs and discuss the advantages and disadvantages of each.

PURPOSE OF SINGLE-SUBJECT DESIGN

Once implemented, intervention strategies need to be evaluated for their effectiveness in modifying the target behavior. The strategies included in behavior intervention plans, in particular, should be evaluated on a continuous basis (Etscheidt, 2006; Maag & Katsiyannis, 2006). A number of different methods may be used to evaluate the effectiveness of intervention strategies, but only a few enable an assessment of the functional relationship between the behavior and the intervention. If a functional relationship does not exist between the behavior and the intervention, the intervention will most likely be ineffective, or it may actually exacerbate the behavior through ineffective reinforcement.

Single-subject designs allow teachers to measure the effectiveness of intervention strategies for the specific behavior of one student or a group of students treated as one entity. For example, each data point on a single-subject design graph represents the behavior of a single student or the behavior of a group of students. The teacher can measure the effectiveness of the intervention by comparing the data points of the behavior prior to intervention with the data points of the behavior during intervention. Single-subject designs require repeated measures of the target behavior (dependent variable) and repeated measures of the behavior during the intervention strategy (independent variable) designed to modify the behavior.

Single-subject designs have been used successfully to demonstrate the effectiveness of intervention strategies for students with behavioral, social, emotional, and academic difficulties. For example, Katz and Girolametto (2013) used a single-subject design to demonstrate the effectiveness of an intervention designed to increase interactions between students with autism spectrum disorders and their peers. Another study using a single-subject design demonstrated a functional relationship between academic choice and academic performance among students with emotional and behavioral disorders (Skerbetz & Kostewicz, 2013). Yet another study used a single-subject design to demonstrate the effectiveness of listening to music as a reinforcer for the verbal and physical behaviors of a student with severe ADHD (Nolan & Filter, 2012). Single-subject designs have been used extensively in education to compare the effects of interventions on behavior (Shabani & Lam, 2013), but most studies involving such designs have been conducted in the field of special education. However, if teachers are to develop an effective universal design for classroom management, many strategies currently used primarily in special education need to be implemented in general education classrooms. One such strategy is the use of single-subject designs to determine the effectiveness of interventions developed for students without disabilities.

BASELINE DATA AND INTERVENTION DATA

The first step in implementing a single-subject design is to collect and record baseline data. Baseline data, or data on Condition A, consist of information collected on the student's target behavior, usually during the functional behavioral assessment. Baseline data establish a benchmark against which the student's behavior can be compared when subsequent interventions are introduced, enabling evaluation of the interventions' effectiveness (Byiers, Reichle, & Symons, 2012). For example, the data obtained during Jane's functional behavioral assessment (see Chapter 8) are baseline data. Baseline data describe the student's existing behavior prior to any intervention.

The baseline data also let the teacher know whether the target behavior is appropriate for intervention (see Figure 11.1). For example, on a systematic visual representation, or graph, of Jane's baseline data, if the line representing her behavior is descending, this would indicate that the frequency of the target behavior is decreasing. If the inappropriate behavior is decreasing, intervention for the behavior is not necessary. Conversely, if the line representing her behavior is ascending, this means that the frequency of the behavior is increasing. However, the ascending data path also indicates that the behavior is changing, and the teacher needs to determine why the behavior is changing. Is the behavior getting worse, or are the data inaccurate because of a poor operational definition of the target behavior? Additionally, if the target behavior is changing, this may make it difficult for the teacher to determine the effectiveness of any interventions implemented to change the behavior, given that it would not be clear whether the changes are related to the intervention or to other variables. However, if the target behavior is worsening, the teacher may need to implement an intervention strategy immediately, especially if the behavior is severely disruptive or dangerous. Such a case often calls for a reactive strategy that results in time-out or an office referral. It is important for teachers to remember that while proactive intervention strategies are desirable, reactive strategies are sometimes necessary to maintain a safe and secure learning environment.

Finally, a variable baseline indicates highly unstable data. The data points do not fall within a narrow range of values, which means that observed incidents of the target behavior does not occur consistently. For example, Jane exhibits her target behavior seven times during one observation period, two times during another period, and five times during a third. When a variable baseline is found, the teacher should not introduce an intervention strategy. Generally, an unstable baseline indicates that environmental variables are affecting the student's behavior, and those variables need to be identified before an intervention can be developed.

Figure 11.1 Types of Baseline Data

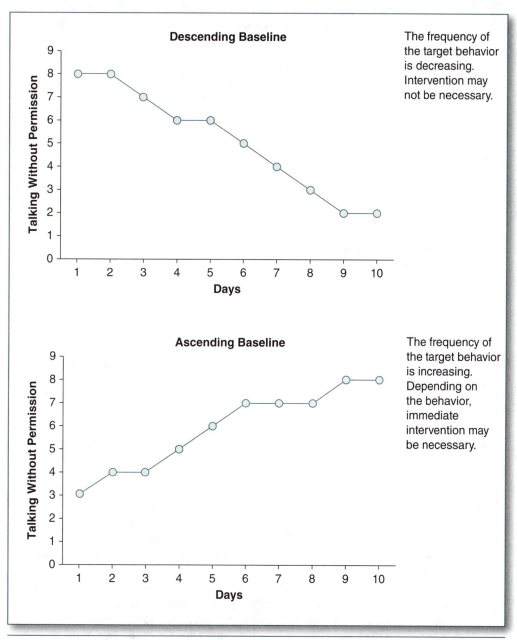

The frequency of the target behavior is decreasing. Intervention may not be necessary.

The frequency of the target behavior is increasing. Depending on the behavior, immediate intervention may be necessary.

(Continued)

Figure 11.1 (Continued)

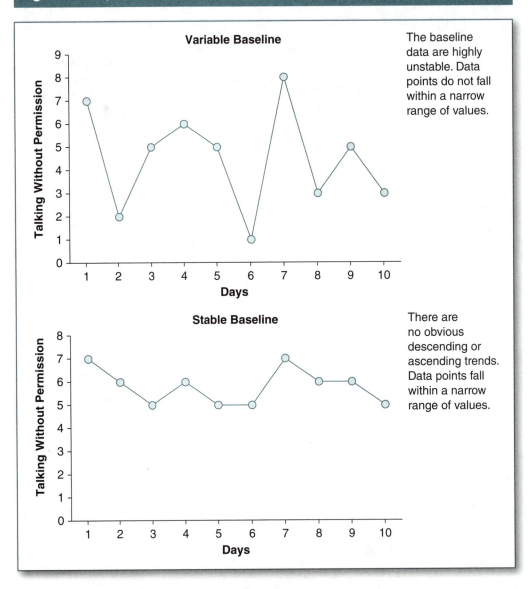

The baseline data are highly unstable. Data points do not fall within a narrow range of values.

There are no obvious descending or ascending trends. Data points fall within a narrow range of values.

A **stable baseline** shows no descending or ascending trend, and the data points fall within a small range of values. A stable baseline provides the best context for determining if an intervention strategy is effective. Measurement of the target behavior should continue until a consistent pattern occurs. Usually, a minimum of five baseline data points are needed to establish stability of the target behavior (Horner, Swaminathan, Sugai, & Smolkowski, 2012). For example, Jane's data path indicates minor descending and ascending data points, and the behavior is relatively stable between five and seven incidents per observation. A stable baseline indicates that the target behavior is neither decreasing nor increasing prior to intervention and provides confidence that any change in the target behavior during and after intervention is a result of the effects of the intervention strategy.

Once a stable baseline has been established, the next step is to implement the prescribed intervention strategy, often as part of a behavior intervention plan. The teacher observes, measures, and records the target behavior under the intervention strategy. The data collected during this period are the intervention data, or Condition B data. These data are plotted on a graph in the same manner as the baseline data. A single-subject design compares the baseline data and the intervention data to reveal any changes in the target behavior. Visual analysis of the baseline and intervention data usually involves examination of the level, trend, and variability of observed behaviors.

LEVEL, TREND, AND VARIABILITY

Once the baseline and intervention data have been collected and charted on a graph, the teacher can examine changes in the target behavior along one or more of three parameters: level, trend, and variability (Byiers et al., 2012). Level is the average rate of the behavior during a condition. For example, in the top graph in Figure 11.2, Jane's level during the baseline is higher than that found during the intervention. Trend is a consistent one-direction change (increasing or decreasing) in the rate of the behavior during a condition. The middle graph in Figure 11.2 shows a consistent decrease in Jane's inappropriate behavior during the intervention. Variability is fluctuation in the rate of the behavior during a condition. In the bottom graph in Figure 11.2, an obvious degree of variability can be seen in the baseline condition. The variability of the baseline has a minimum of three observed incidents per observation to a maximum of eight observed incidents per observation. This is a difference, or range, of five observed incidents ($8 - 3 = 5$). The intervention has a minimum of two observed incidents per observation to a maximum of three incidents per observation. This is a range of one observed incident ($3 - 2 = 1$).

The teacher also needs to examine three other factors of level, trend, and variability of behavior to determine if there is a functional relationship between the behavior and the intervention: (a) the immediacy of the change of behaviors following a condition, (b) any overlap of data points between conditions, and (c) the degree of changes in the behaviors (Horner, Carr, Halle, Odom, & Wolery, 2005). For example, the level (top) graph in Figure 11.2 shows that the change between the baseline and the intervention occurred immediately. Also, the difference between the baseline condition and the intervention condition is especially evident since the two conditions do not overlap; the lowest baseline data point (5) is higher than the highest intervention data point (2). However, the trend (middle) graph in Figure 11.2 shows overlapping data points, and the change in behaviors between the baseline and intervention was not immediate. Yet there is an obvious descending trend and a degree of change in the behaviors. In the variability (bottom) graph in Figure 11.2, there is obvious evidence of change. Despite overlapping data points, the baseline condition is unstable, while the intervention condition is stable. The level in this graph also indicates evidence of change.

Teachers can choose among several types of single-subject designs to measure the effectiveness of interventions. The type a teacher should select depends on the number, sequence, and various baseline and intervention conditions. The various types of single-subject designs are the AB design, the withdrawal design, the alternating treatment design, the changing criterion design, and the multiple-baseline design.

TYPES OF SINGLE-SUBJECT DESIGNS

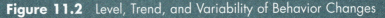

The AB Design

The basic single-subject design is known as the **AB design** because it uses one set of baseline data (Condition A) and one set of intervention data (Condition B). The

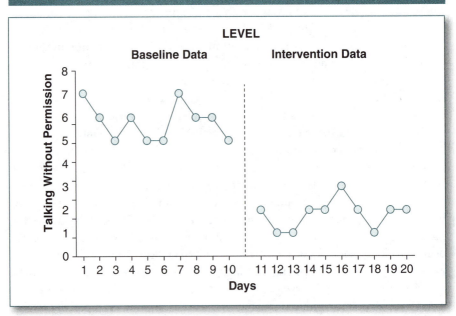

Figure 11.2 Level, Trend, and Variability of Behavior Changes

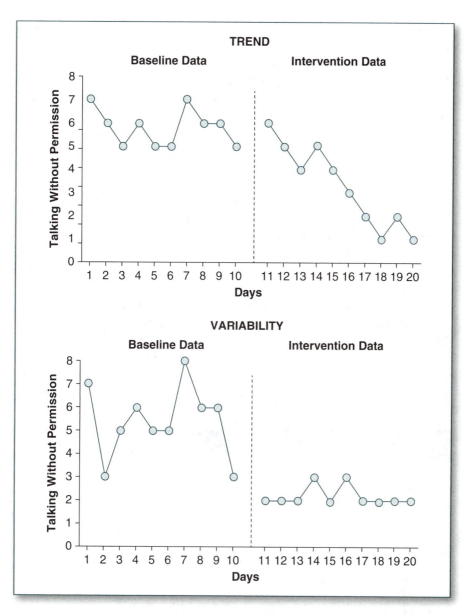

first step is to collect baseline data on the existing target behavior. Once the teacher has established a stable baseline, the intervention strategy is implemented and data are collected on the behavior under the intervention. The baseline data and the intervention data are charted and compared for any changes in the behavior. For example, baseline data have been collected on Jane's target behavior (talking without permission). As a consequence of her behavior, each time Jane talks without permission, she has to write five times "I will not talk without permission."

The teacher implements the intervention strategy and measures and records the data points of the behavior under the intervention on a graph as depicted in Figure 11.3. The baseline data and the intervention data are separated by the condition change line, which is the vertical dotted line drawn upward from the abscissa (horizontal axis). Additionally, condition labels are printed at the top of the graph to identify the baseline data and the intervention data.

Visual inspection of the graph reveals that the intervention strategy (writing five lines) did not affect Jane's behavior. There was no change in level, trend, or variability. There was no immediate change of behavior under the condition, data points overlapped between baseline and intervention, and there was no degree of change in behavior. However, one should be cautious when making assumptions based on the AB design. While the AB design is the easiest kind of single-subject design for teachers to implement, it cannot accurately determine the effectiveness of an intervention because it does not provide for replication of the procedure. Because of this lack of replication, the teacher cannot be sure if any observed changes in the behavior are reliable. It is possible that any behavior changes were due to any number of external factors (Byiers et al., 2012), such as interaction with peers, the student's relationship with the teacher, conditions at the student's home, and other environmental factors. For example, if the AB design had indicated an improvement in Jane's behavior under the intervention condition, the teacher could not be sure if the change of behavior was due to "writing lines" or because Jane's peers were encouraging her to raise her hand before talking.

Figure 11.3 AB Design: Jane

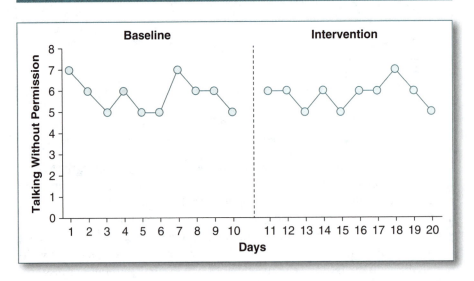

Replication is the repeating of the intervention strategy, or independent variable, to determine the likelihood that the change in the behavior was not due to external variables. Additionally, if the replication of the intervention strategy produces results similar to the first implementation of the strategy, it may be reasonably assumed that the data are reliable. One method of replication is to repeat the baseline and intervention conditions. A simple single-subject design that replicates the conditions is the withdrawal design.

CASE STUDY   Kale

Kale is a fifth grader at Franklin Pierce Middle School. She and her family are *Kanaka Maoli* (Native Hawaiians) who moved to Kentucky a year ago. Kale has been a quiet and respectful student, but weeks after the fall semester began, her teacher, Mrs. Daily, began noticing that Kale's grades were not reflecting her ability. Kale's records from her previous school showed that Kale made above-average to excellent grades in all classes there. However, now, instead of earning above-average grades, Kale was earning average to below-average grades, and sometimes failing grades.

Mrs. Daily began monitoring Kale's behavior in class. She noted that when Kale was given a seat assignment in class, she did not remain on task. Mrs. Daily had her classroom assistant conduct an anecdotal observation and used a duration recording method to measure the duration of Kale's off-task behavior. The results of the behavioral observation were as follows:

Day	Observation period	Start time of target behavior	End time of target behavior	Duration
Monday	10:00–10:30 30 minutes	10:05 10:07 10:16	10:15 10:12 10:26	10 minutes 5 minutes 10 minutes
Tuesday	10:15–10:30 15 minutes	10:17 10:27	10:23 10:30	6 minutes 3 minutes
Wednesday	10:05–10:25 20 minutes	10:08 10:17	10:14 10:22	6 minutes 5 minutes
Thursday	10:00–10:15 15 minutes	10:01 10:11	10:09 10:15	8 minutes 4 minutes
Friday	10:10–10:20 10 minutes	10:12	10:19	7 minutes
	Total Duration: Average Duration:			64 minutes 6.4 minutes

(Continued)

(Continued)

The classroom assistant also noted that when Kale worked in a cooperative group she was an active participant and seemed knowledgeable about the group's assignment. Since Mrs. Daily understood that Hawaiian culture emphasizes the cooperation of individuals and the needs of the whole, she wondered if Kale's behavior was influenced by her culture. As an intervention strategy, Mrs. Daily assigned a peer buddy to work on seat assignments with Kale. She evaluated the effect of the intervention on Kale's behavior by using an AB single-subject design.

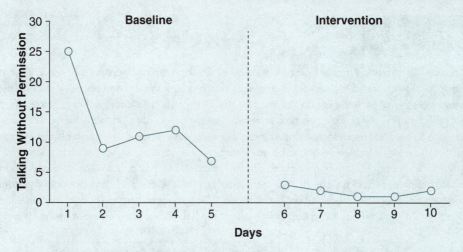

Based on the results, Mrs. Daily concluded that the intervention strategy was effective in modifying Kale's behavior. Do you agree with Mrs. Daily's conclusion?

The Withdrawal Design

The withdrawal design (or ABAB design) is simply an extension of the AB design. The withdrawal design adds a second baseline after the intervention strategy, and then reintroduces the intervention strategy after the second baseline. The teacher first measures and records the baseline data (Condition A1). Once a stable baseline has been established, the teacher implements the intervention strategy (Condition B1). After an equal number of sessions, the teacher withdraws the intervention strategy. The target behavior without intervention is measured and recorded for a second time (Condition A2). Finally, after a set number of observation sessions, the intervention strategy is reintroduced (Condition B2). This provides the teacher with an additional opportunity to evaluate whether the behavior is actually affected by the intervention.

For example, the teacher implements the withdrawal design, or ABAB design, for Jane's target behavior, as shown in Figure 11.4. Visual inspection of the graph once again indicates that the intervention strategy (writing five sentences) did not affect the target behavior. There was no change in level, trend, or variability. There was no immediate change of behavior under the condition, data points overlapped between baseline and intervention, and there was no degree of change in behaviors. Since the data points were consistent across multiple conditions, the data obtained are considered to be more reliable than data in an AB design. However, Jane's behaviors across the conditions were basically at the same level. As a result, a functional relationship between the target behavior and the intervention strategy cannot be demonstrated.

The withdrawal design is fairly simple to implement, and it provides replication of the intervention strategy. However, the teacher should not assume that after the first intervention phase the behavior would return to the same level as that prior to the first intervention. Some residual effects may remain from the first AB experience that could affect the second baseline condition.

Figure 11.4 Withdrawal Design (ABAB): Jane

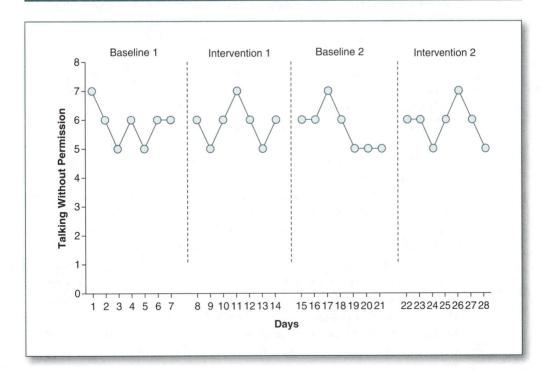

Additionally, the teacher needs to consider the ethical issue of withdrawing an effective intervention to return to a baseline condition. For example, LeVar has been hitting other students. The first intervention that was implemented was effective in reducing LeVar's behavior. The teacher may not want to withdraw this intervention in order to conduct a second baseline condition and a second intervention condition.

The Alternating Treatment Design

The alternating treatment design (ABAC) is similar to the withdrawal design, but instead of reintroducing the same intervention, the teacher adds a second, different intervention (Condition C). For example, in Jane's case, the teacher first measures and records the baseline data (Condition A1) on Jane's target behavior (talking without permission). The teacher then implements and records the data from the first intervention (writing sentences), which is Condition B. The teacher withdraws the intervention strategy and measures and records the target behavior without intervention for a second time (Condition A2). Then, instead of reintroducing the same intervention strategy (Condition B), as in a withdrawal design, the teacher implements a different intervention. In this case, each time Jane raises her hand before speaking, the teacher gives her a token worth 2 minutes of computer time at the end of day. This second intervention is known as Condition C. The resulting graph (Figure 11.5) seems to indicate that the first intervention (Condition B) did not affect Jane's target behavior, but the second intervention (Condition C) had a significant effect on the behavior. The graph shows an obvious descending trend in Condition C, and the data points for Condition C do not overlap with any of the previous conditions, which would seem to indicate that Condition C affected the target behavior. However, it is not known if Condition C would be consistent across multiple conditions, which would increase the reliability of the data.

Baselines and interventions can be repeated often in alternating treatment designs across multiple conditions, but each intervention should be implemented an equal number of times. For example, the teacher could implement an alternative design for Jane that uses the following sequence: ABACABAC. In this instance, both the first intervention (Condition B) and the second intervention (Condition C) would be repeated twice. Another variation of the alternating treatment design is a rotating design involving the following sequence: ABCBCBC. In this design, both Condition B and Condition C are repeated three times. Both variations of the alternating treatment design provide replication of the intervention strategies and increase reliability.

Figure 11.5 Alternating Treatment Design: Jane

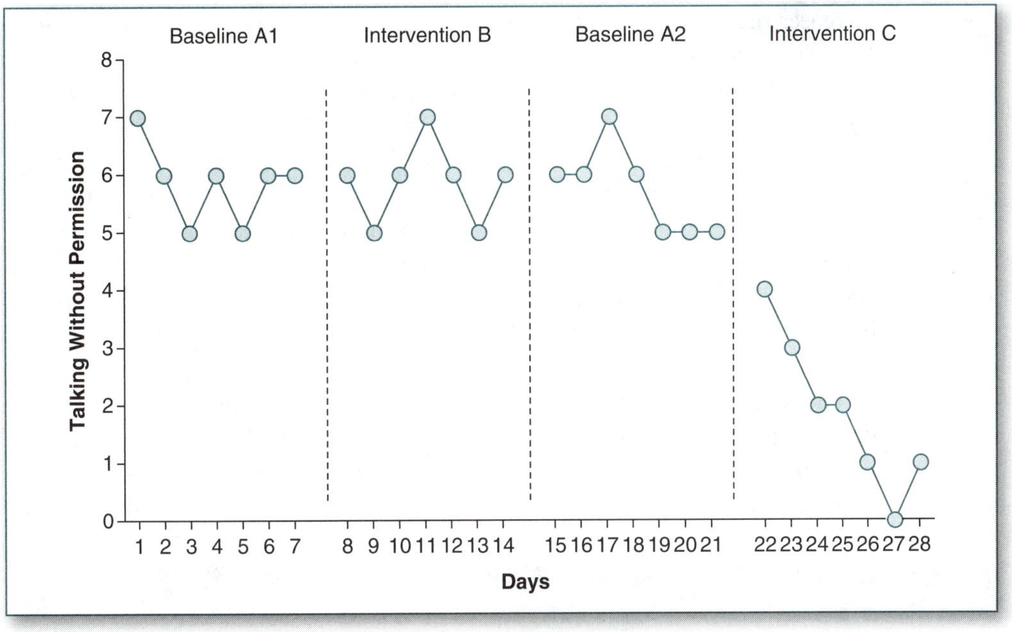

The alternating treatment design allows the teacher to compare the results of two or more intervention strategies and determine which intervention has been most effective in modifying the student's target behavior. However, the teacher needs to remember that the alternating treatment design does not establish the cause of the behavior, and it does not determine whether the results are due to the cumulative effects of both interventions.

The Changing Criterion Design

When using the **changing criterion design**, the teacher evaluates the effectiveness of an intervention strategy by progressively increasing or decreasing the behavior in stepwise changes by manipulating the conditions of the intervention. The changing criterion design starts with an initial baseline condition, which is followed by a series of intervention conditions based on distinctive, or stepwise, levels of the criterion for the behavior. This series of intervention conditions serves as a baseline for subsequent intervention conditions (McDougall, Hawkins, Brady, & Jenkins, 2006). For example, Jane's teacher wants to decrease the frequency of Jane's target behavior (talking without permission) while also decreasing Jane's reliance on the intervention strategy (token for computer time). Using the changing criterion design, the teacher increases the criterion for receiving a token. In the initial intervention strategy, Jane receives a token every time she raises her hand to ask for permission to talk (alternative behavior). In the second, subsequent intervention strategy, the criterion is increased to two occurrences of raising her hand before she receives a token. The criterion is increased by one occurrence at a time until the frequency is four occurrences of the alternative behavior per token. From the data in the resulting graph (Figure 11.6), it appears that the teacher was successful in reducing Jane's target behavior while simultaneously increasing the criterion across the intervention strategies. There are few overlapping data points between the different criterion conditions, and, generally, the criterion conditions resulted in decreases in Jane's behavior.

The teacher should consider three factors when using the changing criterion design. The first is the length of the intervention stages. Each subsequent intervention stage should be long enough to establish stable intervention data so that the effectiveness of the intervention strategy can be determined. Usually, a

Figure 11.6 Changing Criterion Design: Jane

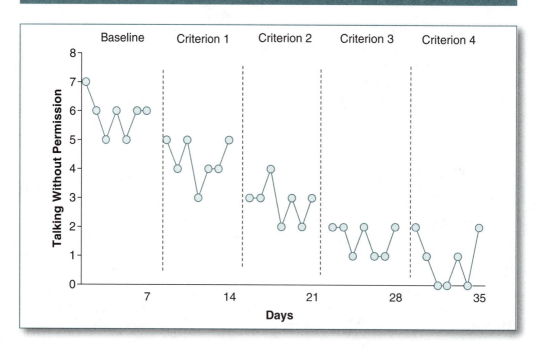

minimum of five baseline data points are needed to establish stability of the behavior. The second factor is the size of the criterion change. The change should be reasonable in size, because a large increase in the criterion may negate the effectiveness of the intervention strategy. For example, if Jane's teacher were to increase the criterion dramatically all at once, from one token for every incident of the alternative behavior to one token per four incidents of the alternative behavior, Jane may not respond favorably, but she may respond well to gradual increases in the criterion. Finally, the number of criterion changes can determine the effectiveness of the intervention strategy. The more changes, the more confidence the teacher can have in the effectiveness of the intervention strategy, but the number of criterion changes should be relevant to the length of the intervention stages and the size of the criterion for each intervention stage. The longer the intervention stage, the longer it takes to complete the observation of the target behavior. Shorter intervention stages allow the teacher to implement more criterion changes in a shorter amount of time.

Unlike the withdrawal design, the changing criterion design does not require withdrawal of the intervention, and so does not delay the intervention or present any of the ethical issues related to withdrawing an effective intervention (Byiers et al., 2012). Given the time constraints many teachers face in today's classrooms, the crucial factors they must consider when using the changing criterion design are the length of the intervention stages and the size and number of criterion changes.

The Multiple-Baseline Design

The multiple-baseline design is an extension of the AB design that allows teachers to examine intervention strategies across students, behaviors, and settings (dependent variables). The three different types of multiple-baseline design utilize multiple baselines across behaviors, across individuals, and across settings. Using the *multiple-baseline across-behaviors design*, a teacher can analyze the effectiveness of an intervention strategy on two or more behaviors of one student in a single observation period. For example, Jane's teacher could analyze the effectiveness of an intervention strategy for Jane's talking-without-permission and out-of-seat behaviors. Using the *multiple-baseline across-individuals design*, a teacher could analyze the effectiveness of an intervention strategy for two or more students with the same target behavior. For example, the teacher could analyze the effectiveness of an intervention strategy for both Jane's and Timothy's talking-without-permission behaviors (see Figure 11.7). Finally, using the *multiple-baseline across-settings design* allows the teacher to

Figure 11.7   Multiple-Baseline Design: Jane and Timothy

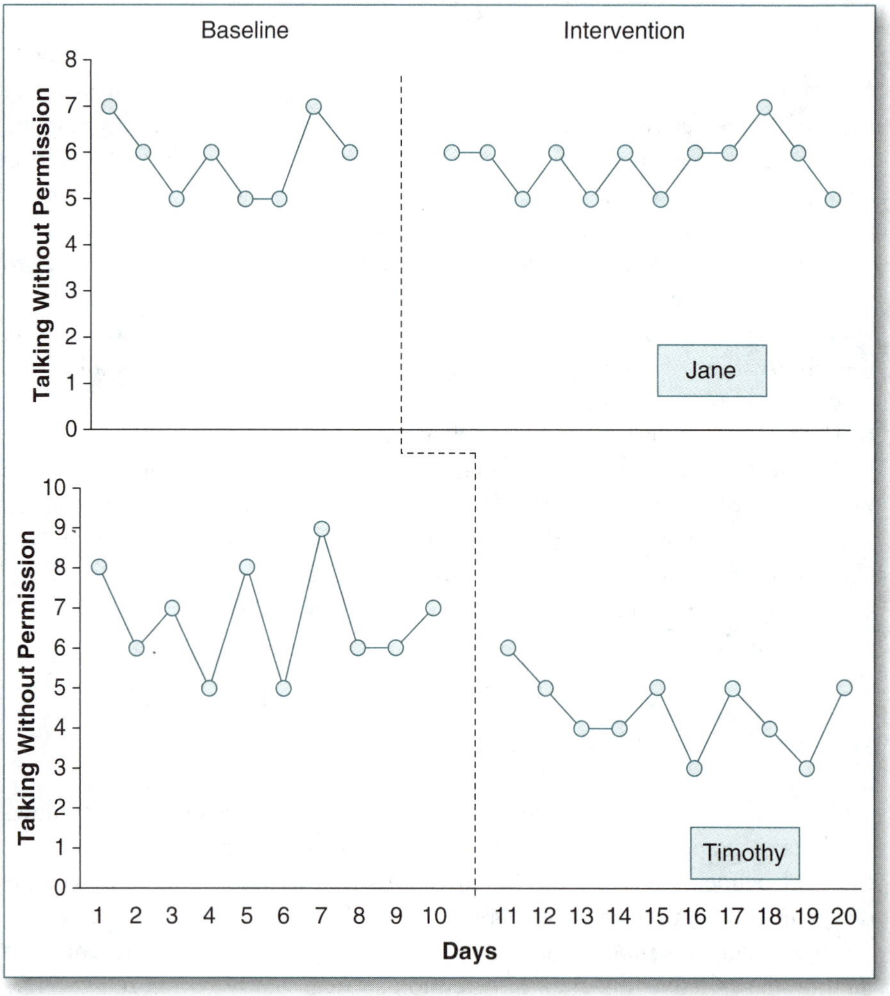

analyze the effectiveness of the intervention strategy for one student in two or more settings. The teacher could analyze the effectiveness of the intervention strategy for Jane's target behavior in both her English class and her math class.

The multiple-baseline design provides replication of the intervention strategy, and the data obtained are considered more reliable. Additionally, such a design may provide information on causality between the behavior and the intervention when there is a change in the target behavior. The multiple-baseline design may not be practical for some teachers, as it can be challenging for teachers to find the time it takes to observe two or more behaviors of a single student or to observe the behaviors of a single student in multiple settings. However, the multiple-baseline design is appropriate for observation of the effectiveness of a single intervention strategy on the same target behavior of two or more students in a single observation period.

Table 11.1   Summary of Single-Subject Designs

Design	Conditions samples	Purpose	Considerations
AB design	AB	Does intervention change behavior?	Easy to implement. Does not provide for replication. Data may not be reliable. Changes could be due to external factors.
Withdrawal design	ABAB	Does behavior change with the introduction and withdrawal of an intervention?	Provides for replication of conditions. More reliable than AB design. Not all behaviors return to the level where they were prior to first intervention. It may not be ethical to withdraw a working intervention.
Alternating treatment design	ABAC ABACABAC ABCBCBC ABACAD (adding a third intervention)	Does behavior change with the introduction of Condition B or Condition C?	Compares the results of two or more interventions. Does not establish cause of behavior. Does not determine if results are due to cumulative effects of interventions.
Changing criterion design	Baseline, Criterion 1, Criterion 2, Criterion 3, and so on	Does behavior change with stepwise manipulation of the conditions of the intervention?	Does not require withdrawal of the intervention. Does not require the intervention to be delayed.
Multiple-baseline design	AB	Does behavior change with intervention across students, behaviors, or setting?	Allows teachers to examine intervention strategies across students, behaviors, and settings. Does not require withdrawal of the intervention. Provides replication of the intervention strategy.

WHAT WOULD YOU DO?   Joseph

Joseph is a seventh-grade student in your state history class. When he becomes annoyed with other students, he punches them in their arms. The perceived offenses committed by other students include being in Joseph's way, making seemingly negative comments about him, and appearing to stare at him. You have completed a functional behavioral assessment and a functional behavior analysis and have concluded that the function of Joseph's behavior is peer attention. Based on this information, you develop an intervention strategy in which Joseph has 10 minutes of time-out at the isolation table in the back of the classroom. The following are the results of a single-subject design:

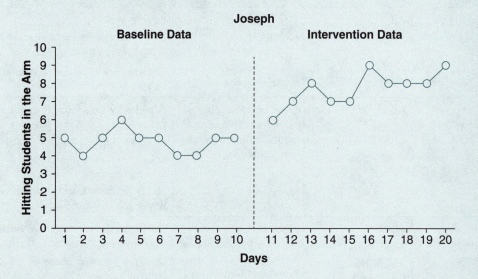

Is there a functional relationship between Joseph's behavior and the intervention? Does the intervention seem to be effective? Based on your analysis of the results of the single-subject design, what would you do about Joseph's behavior?

SUMMARY

Single-subject designs are methods of evaluating the effectiveness of intervention strategies. Single-subject designs require repeated measures of the target behavior and repeated measures of the behavior during an intervention strategy that has been implemented to modify the behavior. The first step of a single-subject design is to collect and record baseline data on the student's target behavior. The next step is to measure the effectiveness of an intervention strategy in modifying the target behavior. The data collected on the observed behavior under the intervention strategy are the intervention data. Single-subject designs determine the functional relationship between the baseline data and the intervention data. Once the baseline and intervention data have been collected and charted on a graph, changes in the target behavior are examined along one or more of three parameters: level, trend, and variability. Level is the average rate of the behavior during a condition. Trend is a consistent one-direction change (increasing or decreasing) in the rate of the behavior during a condition. Variability is fluctuation of the behavior during a condition.

Several types of single-subject designs can be used to measure the effectiveness of interventions. The basic single-subject design is the AB design, which uses one baseline condition and one intervention condition. However, the AB design may not accurately evaluate the functional relationship between the behavior and the intervention. The withdrawal design (ABAB) is simply an extension of the AB design that adds a second baseline after the intervention strategy and then reintroduces the intervention strategy after the second baseline. The withdrawal design is fairly simple to implement and provides replication of the intervention strategies. The alternating treatment design (ABAC) is similar to a withdrawal design, but instead of the same intervention being reintroduced, a second, different intervention (Condition C) is added. The alternating treatment design compares the results of two or more intervention strategies and determines which intervention has been most effective in modifying the student's target behavior. The changing criterion design enables evaluation of the effectiveness of an intervention strategy by progressively increasing or decreasing the behavior in stepwise changes through manipulation of the conditions of the intervention. The changing criterion design starts with an initial baseline condition, which is followed by a series of intervention conditions based on "stepwise" changes in the criterion for the behavior. Finally, the multiple-baseline design examines intervention strategies across students, behaviors, or settings. The multiple-baseline design may provide information on causality between the behavior and the intervention when there is a change in the target behavior.

REVIEW ACTIVITIES

1. For each of the following examples, explain why you would or would not implement an intervention strategy based on the baseline data.

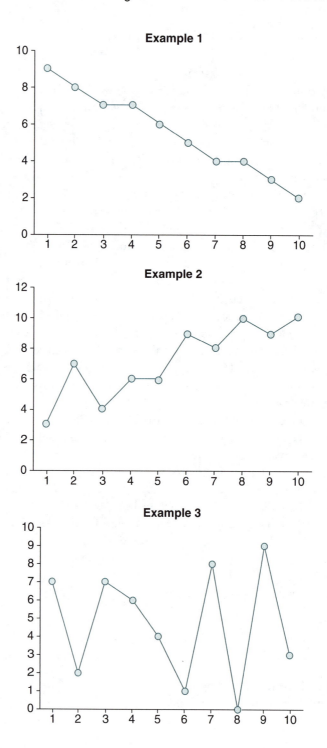

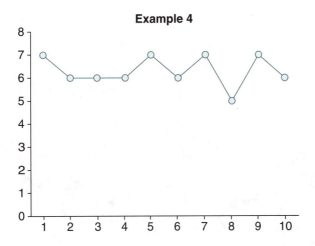

Example 4

2. Why is a withdrawal design better than an AB design for evaluating the effectiveness of an intervention strategy?

3. Erika and Marty are first-grade students. Both have difficulty remaining in their seats. You have developed an intervention strategy utilizing a token system. Using the data below, create a single-subject design to visually display the functional relationship between the behavior and the intervention. Then use visual analysis to make a statement about the level, trend, and variability of the data. Was the intervention more effective for Erika or for Marty? Justify your answer.

	Erika		Marty	
	Baseline data	**Intervention data**	**Baseline data**	**Intervention data**
Day 1	7	6	8	3
Day 2	6	6	6	2
Day 3	7	5	7	2
Day 4	5	7	6	3
Day 5	6	5	7	1

Visit the Student Study Site at www.sagepub.com/shepherd to access additional study tools including mobile-friendly eFlashcards and web quizzes as well as links to SAGE journal articles and web resources.

CHAPTER 12
RESPONSE-TO-INTERVENTION

After reading this chapter, you should be able to do the following:

- Describe the advantages and disadvantages of the discrepancy model.
- Identify the key components of the different tiers of response-to-intervention.
- Explain the impact of culture and language on the effectiveness of response-to-intervention.
- List the advantages and disadvantages of a response-to-intervention program.

THE EVOLUTION OF RESPONSE-TO-INTERVENTION

With the passage of the Education for All Handicapped Children Act in 1975, schools began identifying children with learning disabilities through the use of a **discrepancy model**. Under such a model, a child is identified as having a specific learning disability if there is a severe difference between the child's potential (measured by IQ) and the child's achievement. For example, if a student has an average IQ score (around 100) and an average score on achievement tests (again, around 100), then the student is performing as expected. If a student has an IQ score of 100 and an average score of 65 on achievement tests, then a severe discrepancy exists between the student's potential and achievement. The discrepancy model is objective and uses statistical, quantitative procedures to identify learning disabilities.

Despite the advantages of this method, many educators became concerned that the use of the discrepancy model requires students to fail before they can be identified as having learning disabilities. Additionally, the discrepancy model is not practical for use with young students. As a result, response-to-intervention was developed as an alternative to the discrepancy model.

Response-to-intervention (RTI) has been conceptualized as a multitiered approach to the provision of interventions and services at increasing levels of intensity for students with academic and behavior problems. RTI became an important intervention strategy after the passage of the No Child Left Behind Act of 2001, which mandated that educational professionals use scientifically based research methods in instruction and interventions. Mirroring No Child Left Behind, the Individuals with Disabilities Education Improvement Act (IDEA, 2004) states that schools are no longer required to use the discrepancy model when determining whether a child has a learning disability, but "may use a process that determines if the child responds to scientific, research-based intervention as part of the evaluation procedures" (Section 1414[b][6]). While response-to-intervention is not mentioned in IDEA, the law emphasizes scientifically based interventions as means to identify students with learning disabilities (Sugai & Horner, 2009).

Response-to-intervention is not a new concept. It is an outgrowth of earlier prereferral intervention strategies in which interventions were made in the general education classroom before students were referred for special education services. However, while accommodations were developed for students with academic difficulties, these interventions were not carried out to the degree needed to meet the needs of the students. RTI provides interventions through an inclusive service delivery model by integrating general education and special education (Sanger, Friedli, Brunken, Snow, & Ritzman, 2012).

Although response-to-intervention was initially developed as an alternative to the discrepancy model for identifying students with learning disabilities, it is increasingly being used to identify and provide interventions for students with emotional and behavioral disorders (Fairbanks, Sugai, Guardino, & Lathrop, 2007; Gresham, Hunter, Corwin, & Fischer, 2013), autism spectrum disorders (Hammond, Campbell, & Ruble, 2013), anxiety disorders (Sulkowski, Joyce, & Storch, 2012), blindness and visual impairments (Kamei-Hannan, Holbrook, & Ricci, 2012), and attention-deficit/hyperactivity disorder (Vujnovic & Fabiano, 2011). As part of a universal design for classroom management, RTI can be used as a universal screening strategy and to provide interventions for all students with academic, behavioral, and emotional difficulties.

COMPONENTS OF RTI

The major components of response-to-intervention include universal screening, early intervention, problem solving with emphasis on continuous progress monitoring, and increasingly intensive interventions at different levels (National Association of State Directors of Special Education, 2008). The basic premise of RTI requires school personnel to develop effective instruction and interventions using scientifically based methods appropriate to the needs of the students. The three different levels or tiers of RTI provide interventions and services at progressive levels of intensity for students with academic and behavioral problems. If a student shows adequate response to an intervention at the first level, then he remains at that level and continues to receive the intervention. However, if the student does not meet benchmarks after he has received appropriate intervention, he is provided services at the next level, which involves more intensive instruction or interventions. If the student does not show adequate response to the interventions at this stage, he proceeds to the final level. The three levels of the standard treatment RTI model are known as the primary, secondary, and tertiary tiers.

Primary Tier

The primary tier is the "point of entry into subsequent tiers" of response-to-intervention (Johnson, Melard, Fuchs, & McKnight, 2006). This tier involves all students and has three functions. First, culturally responsive teachers provide high-quality instruction (Klingner & Edwards, 2006) and effective classroom management within the general education classroom. Teachers need to provide opportunities for differentiated instruction with accommodations that allow all students access to the high-quality instructional and behavior programs of the primary tier (Fuchs, Fuchs, & Compton, 2012).

A number of strategies for universal design for classroom management can be implemented at the primary tier. These include development and implementation of a hierarchical behavior management plan, development and implementation of culturally responsive strategies, management of content, management of conduct, teaching of routines and expectations, equitable treatment, and universal interventions (see Chapters 2 and 5). Schools need to teach school-wide expectations to students, consistently provide consequences for inappropriate behaviors and acknowledgments of appropriate behaviors, and review their progress toward meeting school-wide goals (Fairbanks et al., 2007; Sanger et al., 2012).

Second, the primary tier provides for universal screening to identify students who are at risk for academic, behavioral, and social difficulties (Ferri, 2012). This universal screening generally includes routine assessments of all students, including group intelligence tests, achievement tests (such as state-mandated examinations), and vision and hearing tests. For example, Alexander, a second-grade student, is having difficulty paying attention when his teacher presents lessons in class. A vision examination reveals that Alexander is nearsighted and unable to see the front of the classroom from his seat at the back of the room. He is provided with eyeglasses and the teacher moves him to the front of the classroom. As a result of these interventions, Alexander now can focus on the lessons.

Universal screening may also include school data about students, such as numbers of days absent or tardy, and behavioral observations. Information on the frequency of and reasons for a student's time-outs or office referrals can shed valuable light on the student's academic and behavior difficulties.

During the screening process, teachers should use the problem-solving model of response-to-intervention when determining interventions for students with academic, behavioral, and social difficulties. Teachers should develop interventions based on individual students' needs, working in consultation with the students' other teachers and the students' parents. At the primary tier, many of the interventions for students displaying inappropriate behaviors in the classroom are basic classroom management strategies, such as positive and negative reinforcement, token economies, and time-outs (see Chapter 6).

The final function of the primary tier is continuous progress monitoring (Klingner & Edwards, 2006; Sanger et al., 2012). **Continuous progress monitoring** is a procedure in which a teacher gathers information on a student's behaviors to determine whether interventions are effective in modifying the behaviors

(Gresham et al., 2013). By implementing continuous progress monitoring, teachers can determine whether students are responding to the interventions that are provided and making adequate progress or need to be referred to the next tier.

WHAT WOULD YOU DO?   Luis

Luis is a first-generation Hispanic student in the third grade. His parents emigrated from Mexico, and the primary language the family speaks at home is Spanish. Luis has had difficulty complying with requests made by Mrs. Clarke, his general education teacher; Ms. Vermilyer, his music teacher; and Mrs. Daily, his art teacher. He has not had any difficulty in his class with Mr. Salyer, his teacher for physical education. As a teacher, how would you develop a primary tier of a response-to-intervention program for Luis?

Secondary Tier

When a student does not show adequate progress after receiving appropriate interventions at the primary tier, she is provided more intensive intervention at the secondary tier. The main focus of the secondary tier is to provide specific services for students with academic, behavioral, and social difficulties in instructional groups that are smaller and more homogeneous than those of the general education classroom (Sugai, O'Keeffe, & Fallon, 2012). Along with smaller instructional groups, four additional strategies increase the intensity of interventions for students at the secondary tier:

1. More teacher-centered instruction

2. More frequent instruction

3. Increased duration of instruction

4. Inclusion of educational personnel with greater expertise in specific areas. (Fuchs & Fuchs, 2006, p. 94)

Behavior and classroom management strategies appropriate for the secondary tier include contingency contracts (see Chapter 6), self-management techniques (see Chapter 7), functional communication training, differential reinforcements (see Chapter 9), and social skills training (see Chapter 14). Teachers also need to determine whether students' inappropriate behaviors stem from skill deficits or performance deficits when trying to decide on interventions. A student who has a skill deficit does not have the ability to perform the appropriate behavior or skill. For example, Benjamin punches peers in the arm because he does not know any other way to initiate a conversation with a peer. Knowing that this is a skill deficit, the teacher provides social skills training to address the deficiency. Conversely, a student who has a performance deficit has the ability to perform the appropriate behavior or skill but chooses not to do so. For example, Natalie is always tardy to math class because she does not like math class. Since this is a motivational issue, the teacher may try to modify the behavior through differential reinforcements. For example, if Natalie is on time for class, she gets to pass out the math worksheets to other students (a preferred activity). As with the primary tier, teachers should continue to monitor students' progress at the secondary tier to determine whether they have made adequate progress or need to be referred to the next tier.

Tertiary Tier

At the final level of response-to-intervention, the tertiary tier, students are provided intensive, individualized interventions (Bradley, Danielson, & Doolittle, 2005; Sanger et al., 2012). Interventions at the tertiary level often include functional assessments of the unacceptable behaviors and behavior intervention plans (Gresham et al., 2013).

Again, continuous progress monitoring should be incorporated at the tertiary level. Teachers can use progress monitoring data to evaluate the adequacy of student progress, determine when instructional changes are necessary, and determine when modifications to interventions are necessary. Additionally, teachers can use these data to develop goals for students' individualized education programs if they need special education services (Stecker, 2007).

CASE STUDY   **Timothy**

Timothy is a fifth-grade student at Washington Elementary School, a school that has adopted a response-to-intervention program to identify at-risk students and provide interventions designed to meet their academic, behavioral, and social needs. Timothy's teachers have noted that he is not completing his assignments and is failing or close to failing nearly all of his classes. Additionally, Timothy does not interact with peers, often choosing to keep to himself. School records indicate that he had some academic and social difficulties last year, but not to the extent he is having difficulties this year.

(Continued)

(Continued)

During the primary tier of response-to-intervention, Timothy was provided differential instruction with accommodations in many of his classes. He was allowed more time to complete assignments, was provided with peer tutors, and had the numbers of questions on examinations reduced. A review of Timothy's performance on a state-mandated standardized test revealed that while he scored poorly on the test because of a number of unanswered questions, the answers he did provide were generally correct. Unfortunately, continuous progress monitoring showed that the interventions Timothy received were not effective, even though universal screening seemed to indicate that Timothy had the ability to do his academic assignments. The at-risk team determined that Timothy needed to move to the next tier for more intensive interventions.

At the secondary tier, Timothy received instruction with a small of group of students also experiencing academic difficulties. Believing that Timothy's difficulties stemmed from a performance deficit, the at-risk team implemented various types of differential reinforcement as a primary intervention, but it was difficult finding an alternative behavior that was effective with Timothy. Additionally, Timothy was provided social skills training in an effort to improve his peer interactions. However, continuous progress monitoring indicated that the interventions at the secondary tier were ineffective; in fact, Timothy's academic and social difficulties had increased. He was no longer attempting to complete assignments or making any effort to interact with peers.

Timothy was moved to the tertiary tier, where he was provided intensive, individualized instruction and interventions. A voluntary classroom assistant was assigned to Timothy to help him with his assignments. Differential instruction and differential reinforcements were continued. Additionally, a clinical mental health counselor from the community was asked to evaluate Timothy. She determined that Timothy was suffering from depression. Timothy's parents were never married, and his father was increasingly absent from Timothy's life. The pain of his father's absence became more acute for Timothy as he grew older. The at-risk team determined that Timothy should remain on the tertiary tier with weekly counseling sessions to treat the depression. However, if Timothy did not show any improvement in a reasonable amount of time, the team would refer him for a nondiscriminatory evaluation to determine whether he might qualify for classification as a student with emotional and behavioral disorders.

While response-to-intervention was initially conceived as an alternative method for identifying students with learning disabilities, it has evolved into a strategy for addressing the academic, behavioral, and social difficulties of all students. As a result, disagreements have arisen regarding whether special education should have a role in RTI (Fuchs et al., 2012). Since special education teachers often have expertise that many general education teachers do not have, their involvement in the development of intensive, individualized interventions at the tertiary tier can be helpful. However, the tertiary tier should not be considered the "special education level"; rather, it is the level at which experts provide intensive interventions in the general education setting.

Under a universal design for classroom management, response-to-intervention should be embedded in the second level of a school-wide positive behavior support program (see Chapter 13). If a student does not make adequate progress at this level, she should move to the third level, or comprehensive level, of the school-wide positive behavior support program. At this level, the student should receive a nondiscriminatory evaluation. The Individuals with Disabilities Education Improvement Act requires a nondiscriminatory evaluation to determine if a student has a disability and whether the child needs special education and related services. A culturally sensitive, multidisciplinary team should conduct the nondiscriminatory evaluation and compile student data based on a variety of assessments. These assessments must be free of cultural and linguistic biases.

RTI AND CULTURALLY AND LINGUISTICALLY DIVERSE STUDENTS

Response-to-intervention can improve educational opportunities for culturally and linguistically diverse students by providing supports and interventions to meet these students' academic, behavioral, and social needs (McKinney, Bartholomew, & Gray, 2010; Xu & Drame, 2008). Additionally, RTI has the potential to address long-standing issues of equity in the representation of culturally and linguistically diverse learners among students with learning disabilities and emotional and behavioral disorders (Artiles, Bal, & King Thorius, 2010). However, some education professionals have raised concerns that, owing to the rapid acceptance of response-to-intervention, little empirical evidence exists to support the efficacy of RTI for culturally and linguistically diverse students (Artiles et al., 2010; Reynolds & Shaywitz, 2009). Response-to-intervention is predicated on the belief that students receive high-quality instruction and effective behavior and classroom management strategies. However, teachers cannot assume that instructional and behavior strategies that work for European American students will also work for culturally and linguistically diverse students. Teachers need to determine whether students with academic and behavioral difficulties, particularly culturally and linguistically

Figure 12.1   Tiers of Response-to-Intervention

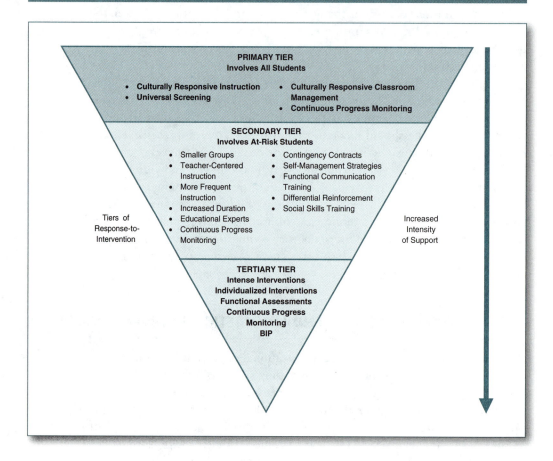

diverse students, are receiving adequate instruction in the general education classroom (Klingner & Edwards, 2006). A strong foundation of high-quality instruction and effective behavior management strategies is necessary at the primary level if RTI is to be successful.

RTI can also give teachers false confidence that assessments and instructional practices are aligned with the educational needs of culturally and linguistically diverse students (Orosco & Klingner, 2010). In other words, teachers might believe that since assessments and instructional practices are scientifically based, they are effective for all students. However, culturally and linguistically diverse students are often not included when benchmarks for assessments and instructional practices are normed (Linan-Thompson, Cirino, & Vaughn, 2007). Thus, diverse students are often provided interventions and more restrictive services based on invalid assessment data. Many teachers assume that the implementation of response-to-intervention removes cultural bias from their decisions to move students from one tier to another or to refer students for special education services. As a result, they employ the same deficit-based assumptions as the discrepancy model—that is, they assume that students who exhibit academic or behavioral difficulties do not have the ability to perform well academically or behave appropriately (Ferri, 2012; Klingner & Edwards, 2006).

As part of a universal design for classroom management, teachers must consider the needs of culturally and linguistically diverse students when developing and implementing the response-to-intervention model in schools. Teachers need to reflect on whether their behavior and classroom management strategies are effective with culturally and linguistically diverse students and whether these strategies are in conflict with the cultural backgrounds of students. For example, research has shown that structured cooperative methods and small-group instruction are effective with culturally and linguistically diverse students (Calderón, Slavin, & Sánchez, 2011). These are especially important strategies for the primary level, where cooperative learning can be effective for diverse students who put the needs of the group first.

Teachers should also incorporate local norms, or local achievement levels, that include culturally and linguistically diverse students in continuous progress monitoring procedures (Linan-Thompson et al., 2007). Since it should be used in all three tiers, continuous progress monitoring that accurately evaluates the progress of diverse students is crucial for providing culturally responsive instruction and behavior management for students. The need to use reliable norms that include diverse students applies also to assessments used for nondiscriminatory evaluations at the tertiary tier. To put it simply, the use of strategies and assessments that do not consider the characteristics of culturally and linguistically diverse students is unacceptable in behavior and classroom management programs.

CONCERNS OF RTI

Although RTI has gained national acceptance, some education professionals have voiced concerns regarding its implementation and effectiveness. RTI is aligned with the premise of inclusion and a universal design for classroom management, but little empirical research has been conducted on the efficacy of the approach (Ferri, 2012). This lack of research is most problematic for the implementation of the primary tier (Hill, King, Lemons, & Partanen, 2012; Xu & Drame, 2008), which is where all students should be provided high-quality, evidence-based instruction and behavior management strategies. The primary tier is the gateway to the succeeding levels and the foundation on which interventions and strategies for the secondary and tertiary tiers are based. High-quality instruction, effective behavior management strategies, universal screening, and continuous progress monitoring are essential elements of an effective RTI program. If the primary tier is not fully implemented, a number of students will be moved inappropriately to the secondary tier.

Further, teachers may assume that students who do not respond to instruction or interventions are deficient and need more intensive interventions. Such assumptions are often supported by the belief that instruction and interventions embedded in RTI programs are evidenced based. However, this does not consider the fact that what may be effective for a majority of students is not effective for all students (Ferri, 2012). This belief is the complete antithesis of inclusion, differential instruction, and a universal design for classroom management, and it reduces response-to-intervention to a deficit-based model similar to the discrepancy model. It is assumed that the student is deficient rather than the instructional strategies or interventions. Teachers and administrators need to determine whether students with academic, behavioral, and social difficulties are receiving adequate instruction and interventions in the general education classroom before making decisions regarding response-to-intervention.

Finally, RTI does not include a formal process for evaluating the cognitive ability of students; such a process could lead to identifying slow learners as having specific learning disabilities (Lindstrom & Sayeski, 2013). Additionally, response-to-intervention cannot differentiate specific learning disabilities from emotional and behavioral disorders, intellectual disabilities, attention-deficit/hyperactivity disorder, or other disabilities (Mastropieri & Scruggs, 2005).

For response-to-intervention to be effective in providing preventive and intervention strategies for all students with academic, behavioral, and social difficulties, administrators and teachers must be fully committed to making it work. The essential elements of a successful RTI program are as follows:

1. A scientifically based method of screening a large number of students who are at risk for academic, behavioral, and social difficulties

2. Teachers who have the knowledge and pedagogy to provide high-quality core academic instruction and effective behavior and classroom management strategies

3. Evidence-based continuous progress monitoring

4. Well-defined benchmarks to determine whether students are responding to academic and behavior interventions

5. Resources to implement supplemental strategies and programs for students who are at risk for academic, behavioral, and social difficulties (Vaughn & Fuchs, 2003)

If teachers and school administrators are not committed to implementing an effective program, response-to-intervention becomes another deficit-based method in which teachers feel justified in moving students from one tier to another until they are referred for special education services or more restrictive settings. Response-to-intervention is not simply noticing that students are having difficulties, providing them with interventions, and checking their progress (Barnes & Harlacher, 2008). It is a carefully developed and

Table 12.1   Advantages and Disadvantages of the Discrepancy Model and Response-to-Intervention

Discrepancy model		Response-to-intervention	
Advantages	Disadvantages	Advantages	Disadvantages
Provides statistical, quantitative procedures to identify learning disabilities	Requires students to fail before they receive interventions	Provides early identification and instruction	Little empirical evidence exists to support efficacy
Is objective and easy to understand	Does not accurately identify young students	Does not require students to fail before they receive interventions	Has no process for evaluating cognitive abilities
Evaluates learning style and processing skills during formal testing	Degree of discrepancy not uniform across schools, districts, or states	Focuses on student outcomes	Creates false confidence that assessments and instructions are effective
Can differentiate among students with learning disabilities, students with other disabilities, and slow learners		Aligns with inclusive practices and universal design for classroom management	Cannot differentiate among students with various disabilities and slow learners

implemented program that addresses the academic, behavioral, and social needs of all students by providing evidence-based instruction, interventions, strategies, and evaluation at all levels.

SUMMARY

Response-to-intervention has fundamentally changed general education into a multilevel system of early intervention (e.g., National Association of State Directors of Special Education & Council of Administrators of Special Education, 2006). While RTI was initially developed as an alternative to the discrepancy model for identifying students with learning disabilities, it is increasingly being used to identify and provide interventions for all students with academic, behavioral, and social difficulties.

Response-to-intervention has three levels or tiers of progressive intensity for providing interventions and services for students with academic and behavior problems. The primary tier provides all students with high-quality instruction and effective classroom management, universal screening, and continuous progress monitoring. The secondary tier provides specific services for students in smaller and more homogeneous instructional groups. The tertiary tier provides students with intensive, individualized interventions.

Response-to-intervention has the potential to improve educational opportunities for culturally and linguistically diverse students by providing them with appropriate supports and interventions. Additionally, RTI may provide a means of addressing the issue of overrepresentation of culturally and linguistically diverse students in special education (Artiles et al., 2010). Teachers need to consider the needs of culturally and linguistically diverse students when developing and implementing a response-to-intervention model. Teachers should also incorporate local norms that include culturally and linguistically diverse students in continuous progress monitoring procedures.

Some education professionals have voiced concerns regarding the implementation and effectiveness of response-to-intervention, and little empirical research has examined the efficacy of RTI. Essential elements of an effective RTI program include high-quality instruction, appropriate interventions and behavior management strategies, universal screening, and continuous progress monitoring. An effective response-to-intervention program should be part of a systemic school-wide positive behavior support program (Hernández Finch, 2012).

REVIEW ACTIVITIES

1. Explain how response-to-intervention can be an effective strategy for improving the academic, behavioral, and social needs of all students.

2. What are the differences among the three tiers of response-to-intervention?

3. In your opinion, which tier of response-to-intervention is the most crucial? Support your conclusion.

4. Tommy has a history of noncompliance. He refuses to complete assignments, to comply with school and classroom rules, and to follow redirections. He has had numerous office referrals, time-outs, and suspensions. The traditional hierarchy of classroom management has been ineffective in addressing his behavior. On state-mandated standardized examinations, Tommy performs in the average to above-average range. The at-risk team has determined that Tommy needs instruction and interventions at the secondary tier of RTI. As his teacher, what components would you include in a secondary tier program for Tommy?

5. Review this chapter's case study on Timothy. Evaluate the interventions and decisions made at each tier for effectiveness.

6. What are some of the advantages and disadvantages of response-to-intervention?

Visit the Student Study Site at www.sagepub.com/shepherd to access additional study tools including mobile-friendly eFlashcards and web quizzes as well as links to SAGE journal articles and web resources.

CHAPTER 13
SCHOOL-WIDE
POSITIVE BEHAVIOR SUPPORT

After reading this chapter, you should be able to do the following:

- Discuss the purpose of school-wide positive behavior support.
- Explain the three factors that affect the sustainability of school-wide positive behavior support.
- Describe the basic premise of each tier of school-wide positive behavior support.
- Explain the different strategies for identifying students at risk for behavior difficulties.
- List the five steps to implementing Tier 1 of school-wide positive behavior support.
- Explain the procedures of the Behavior Education Program.
- Describe the four phases of the wraparound process.
- Explain how school-wide positive behavior support can affect teacher self-efficacy.

COMPONENTS OF SCHOOL-WIDE POSITIVE BEHAVIOR SUPPORT

Most of the behavior and classroom management plans used in American schools today are reactionary and based on the traditional hierarchy of rules and consequences. For example, Ricardo shoves Timothy and threatens to "beat him up" after school. As a result of his inappropriate behavior, Ricardo receives in-school suspension. The premise of this strategy is that the consequence will prevent the behavior from occurring again. However, reactive and punitive strategies are not effective in modifying student behaviors (Scheuerman & Hall, 2012; Shields & Gredler, 2003) and may actually exacerbate some situations and increase inappropriate behaviors (Safran, 2006). For example, Ricardo may grow increasingly frustrated during in-school suspension, especially if there is no subsequent intervention, which is typical of reactive behavior strategies. Ricardo may direct his anger toward Timothy, whom he blames for his current predicament, and he may be more determined to follow through on his previous threat to harm Timothy after school.

An alternative to traditional reactive behavior strategies is school-wide positive behavior support (SWPBS), a proactive, positive strategy designed to promote acceptable behavioral expectations for all students within the school and establish a safe school environment in which learning can take place (Chitiyo, May, & Chitiyo, 2012; Feuerborn & Chinn, 2012; Horner, Sugai, Todd, & Lewis-Palmer, 2005). Through SWPBS, students are taught socially acceptable behavior and the school environment is restructured to provide increased intensive levels of support to meet the academic, behavioral, and social needs of all students. If implemented with fidelity, SWPBS can reduce behavioral difficulties in the classroom and improve students' academic outcomes (Algozzine & Algozzine, 2007; Bradshaw, Mitchell, & Leaf, 2010; Lassen, Steele, & Sailor, 2006). The six core components of an SWPBS program are as follows:

1. A brief statement of purpose

2. Clear expectations of student behaviors

3. Procedures for teaching expected behaviors

4. A continuum of procedures for reinforcing expected behaviors using tangible and intangible incentives

5. A continuum of procedures for discouraging inappropriate behavior using appropriate consequences

6. Procedures for using data to assess the effectiveness of the program (Lewis & Sugai, 1999)

SWPBS involves three tiers of support. Tier 1 provides universal support for all students. This includes defining and teaching behavior expectations, developing and implementing appropriate consequences, and identifying and implementing evidence-based instruction and interventions. Tier 2 provides small-group instruction for students who have been unresponsive to the instruction and interventions provided in Tier 1. Tier 3 provides intensive, individualized supports, which may include functional behavior analysis, wraparound services, and behavior intervention plans (Feuerborn & Chinn, 2012; Lynass, Tsai, Richman, & Cheney, 2012; Walker, Cheney, Stage, Blum, & Horner, 2005). Together, these three tiers provide a continuum of support to meet the diverse needs of all students.

IMPLEMENTATION OF SWPBS

In order for SWPBS to be effective and sustainable, careful planning and implementation must take place. It is essential that teachers, administrators, and support staff be involved in the development and implementation of SWPBS, which requires the investment of significant time and resources. All school personnel must be committed to the development of SWPBS with fidelity. Once implemented, SWPBS can be sustained only if school personnel remain committed to the program. Sustaining SWPBS can be difficult because schools are dynamic. New administrators, new teachers, shifting student characteristics, and changing mandates imposed on schools by state and federal legislation contribute to the variability of the school context. Shared vision, administrative support, and continuous regeneration are factors that promote the sustainability of SWPBS.

Shared Vision

For any innovation to be implemented successfully in schools and classrooms, teachers must feel a sense of ownership of the innovation. Such ownership deepens teachers' commitment to a program, which supports both the fidelity of the program's implementation and the program's sustainability. At least 80% of the teachers in a school must "buy into," or support, a program for it to be successfully implemented and sustained (Slavin, 2004). For teachers to support a program, a shared vision, or widespread agreement, must exist among administrators, teachers, and support staff regarding the core components of the innovation, the implementation of the core components, and the desired outcomes of the innovation (Coffey & Horner, 2012). This shared vision should be described clearly in a mission statement that identifies the purpose of the program; explains the program's vision, actions, and operations in straightforward language so all participants can understand the program; and promotes the program as a common experience that defines the school's culture.

Examining School Culture

Before SWPBS is implemented, the school culture should be examined. School culture—that is, the beliefs, values, traditions, attitudes, and behaviors that characterize a school—is a crucial component in the successful implementation of SWPBS, but it is often disregarded because it is an elusive entity. Additionally, school culture is dynamic; it is constantly changing as interactions take place among students, parents, teachers, support staff, and administrators. Yet, without an understanding of their school's culture, the members of a school community cannot develop a shared vision.

School culture is part of the mesosystem of the larger community (see Chapter 1). Teachers, students, parents, and the community interact and influence one another. If a school's culture promotes a shared belief in collegiality, innovation, improvement, and hard work, SWPBS is likely to be effective and sustainable in the school.

Attitudes toward student behavior are part of school culture. As noted previously, many teachers have preconceptions regarding students with behavior difficulties and treat these students differently than other students. For example, when Michael throws a crumpled piece of paper at another student, his teacher reprimands him verbally. When Ricardo, a student identified as having emotional and behavioral disorders, throws a crumpled piece of paper at another student, the same teacher sends him to the office for disrupting her class. SWPBS determines strategies and interventions that provide equitable treatment for all students with similar behavior digressions while also implementing intense interventions for students who have more problematic behavior difficulties.

Since school cultures are reflections of the mesosystems in which they are found, they vary from school to school and from district to district. For example, students refusing to follow redirections may be the most problematic behavior at a rural school in northern Indiana, while gang-related fighting is the most pressing behavior problem in an urban school in Chicago. Schools with increasing numbers of culturally and linguistically diverse students should solicit input from their communities as they develop the behavior expectations and culturally responsive practices of SWPBS programs (Jones, Caravaca, Cizek, Horner, & Vincent, 2006). Once an analysis of school culture has been completed, teachers, administrators, and other school personnel can select and implement research-based interventions, instructions, and behavior strategies that are applicable to the school (McIntosh, Filter, Bennett, Ryan, & Sugai, 2010).

Administrative Support

Administrative support is critical to the successful implementation and sustainability of any program in school (McIntosh et al., 2013). Such support ensures that teachers have the resources and the time to implement SWPBS. The school principal is usually the key administrator involved in the development, implementation, and sustainability of SWPBS. The principal needs to provide teachers the time to plan and create an environment in which teachers are encouraged to develop creative and innovative strategies and interventions. The principal must also make sure that teachers have the resources they need to maintain an effective SWPBS program, including training that enables them to review previously learned skills and learn new skills. Consistent administrative support is a key factor in the sustainability of SWPBS (Handler et al., 2007).

Continuous Regeneration

A system must be in place for teachers to evaluate the effectiveness of the procedures and strategies of SWPBS. Since school culture is dynamic, teachers need to compare their current practices with the changing needs of the students on a continuous basis and constantly adjust, or regenerate, those practices. Teachers need to collect program data and make changes based on the data. SWPBS programs can be sustained only if their fidelity is maintained through these cultural changes over time (McIntosh et al., 2013). Without continuous regeneration, programs become stale, and stale programs are often cursorily acknowledged and halfheartedly implemented. Even though time, resources, and effort went into their development, such programs end up gathering dust on some bookshelf from lack of use.

TIERS OF SWPBS

School-wide positive behavior support has been envisioned as an approach providing multiple tiers of behavior support. While the numbers of tiers may vary, most SWPBS programs have three (see Figure 13.1). Tier 1 encompasses

Figure 13.1 School-Wide Positive Behavior Support

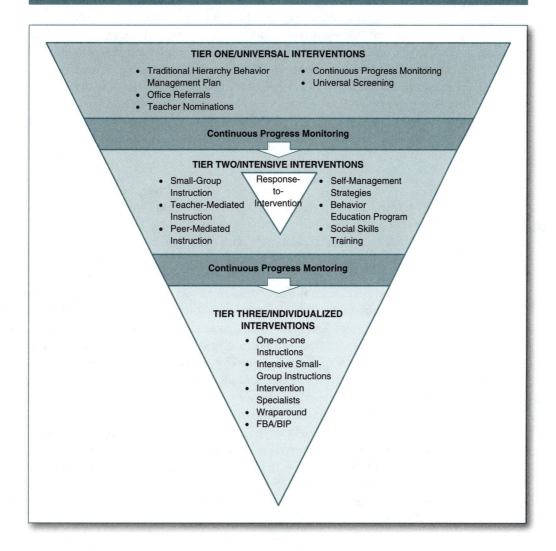

universal interventions, which provide support for all students within the school and are generally effective with 80% of the student population. Tier 2 provides targeted interventions to support the 10–15% of students who do not respond to Tier 1 supports. Finally, Tier 3 provides individualized interventions for the 5–10% of students who are not responsive to either Tier 1 or Tier 2 supports (Sugai & Horner, 2006; Sugai et al., 2010).

Tier 1: Universal Interventions

Universal interventions constitute the most important tier of SWPBS. The development and implementation of SWPBS is a proactive strategy of a universal design for classroom management, and the implementation of universal supports that promote a positive school environment is an active strategy. Students are taught behavioral expectations, and appropriate behavior is reinforced. Students who are not successful at Tier 1 are referred to Tier 2 for more targeted support. However, if Tier 1 is not effectively developed and implemented, a number of students will be moved to Tier 2 inappropriately.

Five Steps to Implementing Tier 1

As a first step, prior to the beginning of the academic year, teachers within the school need to agree on five classroom rules, keeping in mind the culturally and linguistically diverse students they may have in their classrooms. School-wide behavior management plans are more effective than individual classroom plans because they generalize from classroom to classroom. Second, teachers need to agree on positive reinforcement strategies that will be used school-wide to increase the probability that students will follow the behavioral expectations laid out in the five rules. Third, teachers also need to agree on consequences for students who do not comply with school-wide rules and expectations. The development of such a traditional hierarchy of rules and consequences is the foundation of any behavior management plan and a foundational strategy of a universal design for classroom management. As stated previously, teachers should develop their traditional hierarchy behavior management plans before the start of the academic year, keeping in mind the diversity among the students they may have in their classrooms. The fourth step in implementing Tier 1 is to teach students the rules, positive reinforcements, and consequences once these have been developed. The final step is to collect and use data from universal screening and continuous progress monitoring to make decisions regarding students' progress (Burke et al., 2012).

Identifying At-Risk Students

One component of Tier 1 is the identification of students who are at risk for behavior difficulties. At-risk students who may need more intensive interventions at subsequent tiers can be identified through office referrals, teacher nomination, continuous progress monitoring, and universal screening (Carter, Carter, Johnson, & Pool, 2013).

Office referrals. The easiest method of identifying students who are having behavior difficulties is through office referrals. Teachers or at-risk teams should look for patterns of student behaviors and examine the times and places where the behaviors occur (see Table 13.1). For example, it is obvious

Table 13.1 Office Referrals

		Franklin Pierce Middle School Office Referrals Week: October 2–October 6		
Student	**Reason for referral**	**Location of incident**	**Date**	**Time**
Ricardo	Shoving students in hallway	Math hallway between classes	October 2	9:30 a.m.
Ricardo	Tripped student in hallway	English hallway between classes	October 2	10:20 a.m.
Jane	Disrespectful to teacher	Mrs. Clarke's math class	October 2	1:15 p.m.
Ricardo	Threatening to hit another student	Mr. Poteet's PE class/ locker room	October 2	2:20 p.m.
Timothy	Refusing to follow directions	Mrs. Clarke's math class	October 3	9:20 a.m.
Andrea	Sleeping in class	Mrs. Clarke's math class	October 3	10:30 a.m.
Ricardo	Throwing food at students	Cafeteria	October 3	12:15 p.m.
LeVar	Throwing spit wads	Mrs. Cox's English class	October 3	1:30 p.m.
Ricardo	Knocked books out of students' hands	Science hallway between classes	October 3	2:00 p.m.
David	Refusing to complete assignment	Mrs. Clarke's math class	October 3	2:40 p.m.
Ricardo	Prevented student from getting into his locker	Math hallway between classes	October 4	8:30 a.m.
Michael	Called teacher "stupid"	Mrs. Clarke's math class	October 4	9:10 a.m.
Zoe	Third tardy	Mr. Thompson's English class	October 4	10:15 a.m.

from a review of office referrals that Ricardo has behavior difficulties during unstructured times. He displays aggressive behavior between classes and during lunch. The universal supports embedded in Tier 1 may not be effective for Ricardo, and he may benefit from the targeted supports of Tier 2. However, teachers and at-risk teams need to be cognizant that various factors can affect student behaviors, and these might skew the numbers of office referrals. For example, Mrs. Clarke has referred a high number of students to the office over the course of a semester. Mrs. Clarke could be a novice teacher who has unintentionally created a learning environment that fosters misbehavior. The principal or an SWPBS team member may want to observe Mrs. Clarke's class to determine whether sufficient supports are in place to encourage appropriate student behaviors and that Mrs. Clarke's classroom management plan is aligned with SWPBS. If additional support is needed, a mentor could be assigned to Mrs. Clarke to assist her with lesson plans, pedagogy, and classroom management.

Teacher nomination. Another method of identifying students who are at risk for behavior difficulties is teacher nomination. Teachers use their professional judgment to refer students for intensive, targeted interventions at the Tier 2 level. Teacher nomination is based on the teacher's perception that the student's needs cannot be met through the use of universal classroom strategies. Usually, teachers refer students to Tier 2 because of behavioral difficulties. The school's at-risk team, consisting of a number of teachers and other education professionals, could also refer students for interventions at successive tiers. Additionally, the at-risk team should identify academic and behavior strategies to be implemented with these students. Such strategies, which might include small-group instruction targeting specific skills or goals, should be implemented by the teacher (Debnam, Pas, & Bradshaw, 2012).

Teacher nomination should not be the school's sole avenue for identifying students who are at risk for behavior difficulties, because teacher nomination is naturally subjective. For example, male students displaying externalizing behaviors are more likely than other students to be referred because externalizing behaviors are difficult to manage in the classroom (Dowdy, Doane, Eklund, & Dever, 2011). Students displaying internalizing behaviors tend to be underreported, and many female students tend to exhibit internalizing behaviors. These students are often ignored, and their needs are not met.

WHAT WOULD YOU DO?   Ana

Franklin Pierce High School has been using school-wide positive behavior support for the past 2 years. Since the SWPBS program's inception, school personnel have noted a moderate decline in office referrals and suspensions and a slight increase in the academic performance of students. However, these results do not seem to apply to Ana, a student in your math class.

Ana is Hispanic, and while Spanish is the primary language spoken in her home, she seems to have appropriate English skills. Ana has not had any behavior difficulties. She tends to sit quietly in the back of the room and keeps to herself. She seldom engages in any class discussions, despite your prompts. You have also noticed that Ana seldom interacts with her peers.

During times when the students are working individually on assignments in class, Ana tends to stare at her paper. When you have asked her if she needs help, Ana has responded that she does not understand the problem. Even when you have tried to explain problems to Ana, she does not seem to understand the concepts.

Ana's other teachers have confirmed that she does not complete assignments in their classes either, and, as a result, she is failing many of her courses. However, since Ana does not have behavior difficulties, her internalizing behaviors are often overlooked.

Within the context of school-wide positive behavior support, what could you do to help Ana be successful in school?

Continuous progress monitoring. As described in Chapter 12, continuous progress monitoring is a procedure in which teachers gather information concerning student behaviors to determine whether interventions are effective in modifying the behaviors (Gresham, Hunter, Corwin, & Fischer, 2013). Teachers can use data on office referrals, time-outs, expulsions, absences, and tardies to determine whether behavior interventions are effective. For example, despite interventions implemented at Tier 1, Ricardo has received office referrals resulting in two in-school suspensions and one 3-day out-of-school suspension over a period of 4 weeks. Continuous progress monitoring can help teachers determine whether students are responding to the interventions provided and making adequate progress or need to be referred to the next tier.

Universal screening. While office referrals, teacher nomination, and continuous progress monitoring may be effective means of identifying students with externalizing behaviors, they may overlook students with internalizing behaviors. Universal screening may be a useful strategy for confirming behavior difficulties for students with both externalizing and internalizing behaviors. A number of different assessment tools may be used to evaluate student behavior. These include the Systematic Screening for Behavior Disorders, the Student Risk Screening Scale, and the BASC-2 (Behavior Assessment System for Children, second edition) Behavioral and Emotional Screening System.

The Systematic Screening for Behavior Disorders (SSBD; Walker & Severson, 1992) is a three-stage, multigated procedure for identifying children who are at risk for behavior difficulties. The SSBD uses a combination of teacher nomination, teacher rating scales, and direct observation of the child's behavior. At the first gate of the SSBD, teachers are given descriptions of externalizing behaviors (aggressive, disruptive, and undercontrolled behaviors) and internalizing behaviors (anxiety, withdrawal, depression, and overcontrolled behaviors). Teachers rank students in the externalizing or internalizing domains using a Likert scale of 1 (*most like*) to 10 (*least like*). Students with a rank of 1, 2, or 3 in either domain are moved to the second gate. At the second gate, teachers use two normed rating scales, the Critical Events Index and the Combined Frequency Index, to rate the top three students displaying externalizing behaviors and the top three students displaying internalizing behaviors. The Critical Events Index rates high-intensity, low-frequency student behaviors according to 33 items that reflect the expectations of the teacher. The Combined Frequency Index measures low-intensity, high-frequency student behaviors. Students exceeding the normative cutoff points for adaptive and maladaptive behaviors are moved to the third gate. At the third gate, teachers observe the children in structured settings (such as the general education classroom) and nonstructured settings (such as the playground or lunchroom) using direct observation strategies. Students who exceed the normative cutoff points are moved to Tier 2 for more intensive interventions (Kalberg, Lane, & Menzies, 2010).

The Student Risk Screening Scale (SRSS; Drummond, 1994) is a behavior rating scale designed to identify students with behavior difficulties. The SRSS is easy to use, and a teacher can rate all students in a class in about 10 to 15 minutes. Using a 4-point Likert scale, the teacher rates students across seven behavior benchmarks: (a) steals; (b) lies, cheats, sneaks; (c) behavior problems; (d) peer rejection; (e) low academic achievement; (f) negative attitude; and (g) aggressive behavior. The scores of the seven items are summed to create total scores that are used to classify students as low risk, moderate risk, or high risk (Carter et al., 2013; Kalberg et al., 2010). Those classified as moderate risk or high risk are moved to Tier 2. Recent research on the SRSS indicates that additional behavior benchmarks may improve the instrument's effectiveness in identifying students with externalizing and internalizing behaviors (Lane et al., 2012).

The BASC-2 Behavioral and Emotional Screening System (BESS; Kamphaus & Reynolds, 2007) is designed to identify students who currently have emotional and behavior difficulties as well as students with the potential to develop such difficulties. The BESS measures externalizing behavior problems, internalizing behavior problems, adaptive behavior, and attention. Students' parents and teachers complete behavior rating scales on the students, and the students record their perceptions of their own behaviors on a self-report form (Dowdy, Chin, Twyford, & Dever, 2011; Dowdy, Twyford, et al., 2011). The forms take about 5 to 10 minutes to complete. The teacher and parent forms require reading ability at a sixth-grade level to complete, and the student self-report form requires reading ability at a second-grade level.

Universal screening practices such as those described above are generally easy to administer, but they still require teachers to respond subjectively to lists of questions about their students. Additionally, males are more likely than females to be identified as exhibiting problem behaviors due to externalizing behaviors. However, screening instruments provide structured questions that help reduce teacher bias and enable increased identification of students who are at risk for behavior difficulties (Dowdy, Doane, et al., 2011). A number of assessment strategies should be used to identify students who are at risk for behavior difficulties, with universal screening instruments employed in conjunction with office referrals, teacher nomination, and continuous progress monitoring to arrive at evaluations of student behaviors that are as accurate as possible.

Tier 2: Targeted Interventions

Tier 1 interventions are ineffective for approximately 5–15% of students with behavior difficulties (Hawken, O'Neill, & MacLeod, 2011; Sugai & Horner, 2006, Sugai et al., 2010). These students are moved to Tier 2 for additional supports. The targeted interventions at Tier 2 include small-group instruction, teacher-mediated instruction, peer-mediated instruction, and self-management strategies. Additional Tier 2 interventions that build on SWPBS include the Behavior Education Program and social skills training.

The Behavior Education Program

The Behavior Education Program (BEP; Crone, Hawken, & Horner, 2010) is a Tier 2 intervention that has received empirical support. The BEP provides frequent feedback on social behaviors and rewards students for demonstrating appropriate behavior (Hawken et al., 2011). The elements of the program include (a) daily check-in, (b) feedback from classroom teachers throughout the day, (c) daily check-out, (d) data collection with progress monitoring, and (e) parent feedback (Hawken & Horner, 2003; Hawken et al., 2011; Todd, Campbell, Meyer, & Horner, 2008). For example, Jane checks in with Mrs. Garcia, a classroom assistant and the BEP coordinator, prior to going to her first class. Mrs. Garcia makes sure that Jane has her pencils, homework, and supplies. She also gives Jane a progress report form, which lists Jane's behavioral expectations and provides a visual reminder of her goals. Jane gives the form to each of her teachers throughout the day; each one ranks how well Jane has followed her expectations and then returns the form to her. At the end of the day, Jane checks out with Mrs. Garcia and turns in her progress report form. Mrs. Garcia tabulates the points Jane has earned for the day and provides her with appropriate reinforcements. A copy of the progress report form is sent to Jane's parents for their signatures and comments. At the end of 2 weeks, the at-risk team reviews the data from the progress reports to determine if Jane's BEP needs to be maintained, if expectations need to be modified, or if Jane is ready to monitor her own behavior.

The BEP is an easy strategy to implement, and it can be used on a number of students simultaneously (Carter et al., 2013). It can also be integrated into an SWPBS program. Additionally, research has shown the BEP to be effective with students with behavior difficulties, although it may be more effective for students whose functional behavior is adult attention and not as effective with students whose functional behavior is escape/avoidance or peer attention (Hawken et al., 2011; McIntosh, Campbell, Carter, & Dickey, 2009; Mitchell, Stormont, & Gage, 2011).

Social Skills Training

The major goals of SWPBS are to improve students' academic performance and increase appropriate behaviors, but SWPBS should also focus on building students' social competencies (Coffey & Horner, 2012). Many students with behavior difficulties exhibit poor social skills. These students have difficulty interacting with others, which often leads to teacher and peer rejection, school failure, and limited social involvement.

While a number of social skills training programs are available for teachers to use in their classrooms (see Chapter 14), many teachers do not feel that it is their responsibility to provide students with social and emotional supports (Feuerborn & Chinn, 2012). Teachers should be aware, however, that for many students, without improvement in their social competencies, academic and behavioral improvement may not be possible. Additionally, students who lack social competencies may not be successful in their post-educational lives. The remonstration that schools cannot be all things to all students rings hollow when students lack the skills they need to be successful in life. Part of an effective universal design for classroom management is meeting the needs of all students, including social and emotional needs.

Response-to-Intervention

An effective response-to-intervention program should be integrated into SWPBS as part of Tier 2. In effect, the three tiers of RTI become a subset of Tier 2 (see Figure 13.1). When students enter Tier 2, they begin with the first tier of response-to-intervention and are moved to subsequent tiers of RTI if they do not respond to the interventions of the previous tier (see Chapter 12). If response-to-intervention is not integrated into Tier 2, many of the interventions associated with RTI will need to be incorporated at different levels of SWPBS. Functional assessments and behavior intervention plans will especially need to be included in Tier 3 of SWPBS.

Tier 3: Individualized Interventions

When the behavior intervention team determines, through continuous progress monitoring, that a student is not responding to Tier 2 supports, the student is moved to Tier 3, which provides individualized interventions. Students who reach Tier 3 have multifaceted behavioral and emotional difficulties and may be at risk for emotional and behavioral disabilities (Eber, Hyde, & Suter, 2011). Interventions at this level are individualized and based on the needs of the student. Tier 3 supports may include one-on-one instruction or counseling, intensive small-group interventions, and interventions provided by specialists (e.g., behavior specialists, mental health counselors).

One strategy for addressing the needs of students with severe behavior difficulties is the provision of wraparound services, an approach based on a system-of-care philosophy. School-based system-of-care programs improve access to mental health services and have shown promise for promoting increased communication and collaboration among school districts, families, and community services in meeting the needs of students with severe behavior difficulties (Anderson, Wright, Smith, & Kooreman, 2007).

Wraparound Services

Wraparound services are the components of a team-based intervention that provides the necessary planning and implementation of care services for students with emotional and behavioral difficulties and their families. Consistent with the ecological systems model (Bronfenbrenner, 1979), the provision of wraparound services recognizes the influence of environment on behavior. The individualized needs of students are matched to effective services and supports (Bruns, Walrath, & Sheehan, 2007; Eber, Breen, Rose, Unizycki, & London, 2008), and these services are "wrapped around" the students and their families (Painter, 2012; Stambaugh et al., 2007). A student's wraparound team includes community-based "experts" such as teachers, clinical mental health counselors, and caseworkers, as well as natural support individuals such as friends, family, mentors, and other persons important to the student and the family. A care manager, or designated individual, works with the family members to involve them in the process, assess their needs, and arrange for the delivery of any necessary mental health and other services.

Wraparound services focus on (a) reducing the problem behavior of the student *and* improving the quality of life of the student and family; (b) continuous progress monitoring, which includes input from the student, family, and teachers; and (c) frequent meetings to develop intervention strategies based on the strength and perspectives of the student, family, and teacher (Eber et al., 2008). Wraparound services might include respite care, parent partners, child care, individual and group therapy, assistance in transportation, and assistance with programming and compliance issues in the school.

During the first step of the wraparound process, the care manager meets with the family to explain the wraparound process, determine the needs of the family, and help the family decide who they want on the wraparound team. During the second step, the family and the wraparound team develop a plan that includes the desired quality-of-life outcomes based on the needs and strengths of the student and the family. The plan is implemented in the third step. Natural activities and traditional interventions are combined to meet the student's needs. Support is also provided for the parents and for teachers who are having difficulty meeting the academic and behavior needs of the student. Finally, if the student shows progress, he and the family are transitioned from wraparound services to continuous progress monitoring through parent–teacher conferences (Eber et al., 2011; Fries, Carney, Blackman-Urteaga, & Savas, 2012).

Mental health facilities and child welfare agencies offer community-based wraparound services, but using the school as the entry point for wraparound services has at least two advantages. First, because children and adolescents spend significant portions of their lives in school, the school offers an appropriate access point for wraparound services. Second, schools have well-trained staff, access to support services, and mandated service delivery procedures in place (Epstein et al., 2005). In fact, research has suggested that schools are a key factor in the success of wraparound services (Painter, 2012).

CASE STUDY **Ricardo: Wraparound Plan**

Ricardo has a history of failing grades and getting into fights with other students. His attendance has been sporadic, and he has been assigned a truant officer by the juvenile court system. Ricardo has not been successful in Tier 1 or Tier 2 of school-wide positive behavior support, and he is currently at Tier 3. The at-risk team at Franklin Pierce High School has recommended the development and implementation of a wraparound plan for Ricardo and his family. Mr. Jackson, the care manager assigned to Ricardo, meets with Ricardo's mother to discuss the wraparound process. Mr. Jackson and Ricardo's mother develop a list of Ricardo's strengths and needs. They also discuss who should be part of Ricardo's wraparound team. The mother suggests that Coach O'Neill should be on the team because Ricardo and the coach have developed a positive relationship and Ricardo likes basketball. Mr. Jackson understands that the inclusion of Coach O'Neill is extremely pertinent because Ricardo's father is absent from Ricardo's life. Mr. Jackson suggests including Dr. Carter, a community counselor who could help Ricardo deal with abandonment issues. Ricardo's mother also suggests that Mr. Judge, the school's assistant principal, should be involved. The mother feels that Mr. Judge likes Ricardo and could help Ricardo in school.

At the first meeting of the wraparound team, the members develop an intervention plan for Ricardo based on his strengths and needs. For example, Ricardo needs to feel accepted by his peers and needs to feel successful at school. Since Ricardo has a strong relationship with Coach O'Neill, a team member suggests that Ricardo join the school's basketball team. Some members of the wraparound team are concerned that attempting to implement this plan may exacerbate Ricardo's inappropriate behaviors, since he would not be able to play in any basketball games until he has passing grades. Others argue that giving Ricardo the opportunity to work with other students as a team could improve his peer relationships, and also that his desire to play basketball could be an incentive for him to complete assignments. Mr. Judge volunteers to continue the Behavior Education Program with Ricardo and to follow up with teachers regarding his attendance, behavior, and grades. Dr. Carter agrees to meet with Ricardo twice a week at the school to work with him on emotional issues and social skills.

After Ricardo's wraparound plan is implemented, the wraparound team conducts continuous progress monitoring and adjusts the plan as needed on a regular basis. The team also

(Continued)

(Continued)

addresses additional needs that were not identified in the initial development of the plan. For example, Ricardo is still frequently truant because he does not want to ride the bus to school. He feels that the school bus is for "little kids." So the wraparound team arranges for the truant officer to pick Ricardo up every morning and bring him to school. To help with Ricardo's academic needs, peers from the basketball team are assigned to be his peer partners in a couple of classes. Any successes that Ricardo experiences are reinforced.

The wraparound team continues to monitor Ricardo's progress, using the data collected to develop a transition plan for Ricardo that will decrease the use of individualized interventions and increase the use of natural activities and more traditional interventions.

The Trinity of Behavior Management

Functional behavioral assessment, functional behavior analysis, and behavior intervention plans should be used to help develop intensive supports for students receiving interventions and strategies at Tier 3. As explained in previous chapters, functional behavioral assessment is used to define the target behavior and assess the frequency, intensity, duration, and latency of the behavior (see Chapter 8). Functional behavior analysis determines the function, or cause, of the behavior (see Chapter 9). Finally, an individualized behavior intervention plan is developed based on the function of the behavior (see Chapter 10).

The trinity of behavior management is often used after a student has been identified as needing special education services, and then only when school personnel are considering changing the current placement of the student. Often, this results in an alternative placement outside the home school setting. Thus, functional behavioral assessment, functional behavior analysis, and behavior intervention plans are often used as reactive strategies, which is inconsistent with SWPBS and a universal design for classroom management. Functional behavioral assessment, functional behavior analysis, and behavior intervention plans should be incorporated into Tier 3 as proactive and active strategies.

Special Education Referral

Some models of SWPBS include special education services as Tier 3 support (Burns & Coolong-Chaffin, 2006); however, special education services should be reserved for students who do not respond to Tier 3 interventions and support. IDEA emphasizes early intervention for students with behavior difficulties and the reduction of referrals for special education services (Lynass et al., 2012). As with response-to-intervention, SWPBS can be used as part of a comprehensive evaluation of special education services, which can include a functional behavioral assessment and functional behavior analysis.

BENEFITS OF SWPBS

A number of positive outcomes have been associated with SWPBS. The reduction of behavior problems in the classroom is the most notable of these (Bradshaw et al., 2010; Feuerborn & Chinn, 2012; Muscott, Mann, & LeBrun, 2008). Reduced behavior problems directly affect numbers of office referrals, detentions, and suspensions. Additionally, the reduction of behavior problems allows teachers more time to engage in academic instruction, which promotes the academic achievement of students (Algozzine & Algozzine, 2007).

A positive classroom environment created by the implementation of SWPBS can also improve student–teacher relationships. When students feel that teachers support them by caring about them, respecting them, and praising them, they are more likely to be motivated to do well in school. Teacher support encourages students' sense of self-efficacy. In turn, students tend to like school and engage in activities that promote friendships, respect, and cooperative behaviors (Hallinan, 2008; Montalvo, Mansfield, & Miller, 2007).

However, despite the positive outcomes associated with SWPBS, many schools continue to employ reactive discipline systems. Additionally, teachers tend to express confidence about solving academic difficulties rather than behavior difficulties. Whether this is due to the belief that social, emotional, and behavior issues are beyond the purview of general education teachers or to lack of training (Feuerborn & Chinn, 2012), this perception has implications for the success of SWPBS.

CULTURAL IMPACT ON SWPBS

SWPBS has the potential to reduce the disproportionate discipline outcomes of culturally and linguistically diverse students. Within the SWPBS framework, academic and behavior outcomes are developed based on a shared vision and the analysis of the school culture, which should involve administrators, teachers, students, parents, and community leaders. Additionally, many of the practices recommended for reducing the numbers of office referrals for diverse students are embedded in SWPBS. These include the use of data-driven decision making regarding the academic and behavior needs of students, the use of evidence-based behavior support practices, and support for positive academic and behavior outcomes from all school stakeholders (Vincent, Randall, Cartledge, Tobin, & Swain-Bradway, 2011).

Again, it is important for teachers to remember that strategies and interventions that are effective for European American students may not necessarily be effective for culturally and linguistically diverse students. However, two components of Tier 1, used to identify students at risk for behavior difficulties, are teacher nomination and office referrals. These are subjective measures and are often based on the behavior expectations of individual teachers. Teacher subjectivity can lead to a higher rate of discipline referrals for culturally and linguistically diverse students than for European American students, with the result that a disproportionate number of diverse students are moved to Tier 2. Additionally, many culturally and linguistically diverse students are referred for special education services, and despite the overrepresentation of diverse students in special education, only half of U.S. teacher education programs provide training on cultural competence (Debnam et al., 2012). To employ culturally responsive behavior intervention strategies, teachers need to understand their own cultures as well as the cultures of their students (Vincent et al., 2011). School districts may need to cultivate teachers' cultural knowledge and cultural self-awareness through training and in-service programs.

TEACHER SELF-EFFICACY

A well-developed and well-implemented SWPBS program can have positive effects on teachers' sense of self-efficacy. As defined by Bandura (1986, 1997), self-efficacy is an individual's belief in his or her ability to perform specific tasks despite difficulties, obstacles, and initial failures. Teacher self-efficacy can be defined as a teacher's belief in his or her ability to affect student learning even with the most difficult students (Shepherd, 2013). School environments that promote high levels of teacher self-efficacy have been linked to teacher effectiveness, teacher resilience, student achievement, and the implementation of innovative teaching strategies (Lee, Patterson, & Vega, 2011). Conversely, low teacher self-efficacy is associated with less effective teaching practices (Skaalvik & Skaalvik, 2007), which may create a vicious academic and behavior management cycle within the classroom: Less effective teaching practices affect students' academic and behavioral performance, poor student performance reinforces the teacher's low self-efficacy, and the teacher continues to use less effective teaching strategies and interventions. Effective SWPBS programs have been shown to improve students' academic and behavioral performance and to encourage students to be actively involved in learning (Kelm & McIntosh, 2012). As a result, teacher self-efficacy is high, and teachers feel that they can meet the needs of all students.

SUMMARY

School-wide positive behavior support has been accepted by many educators and researchers as a promising approach for creating a positive school environment in which learning can take place (Handler et al., 2007; Kelm & McIntosh, 2012). Through SWPBS, the school environment is restructured to provide increasingly intensive levels of support to meet the academic, behavioral, and social needs of all students. For SWPBS to be effective and sustainable, careful planning and implementation must take place, the program must be implemented with fidelity, and all stakeholders must have a vested interest in the outcomes of the program.

For teachers to support SWPBS, a shared vision must exist among all stakeholders regarding the program's core components, implementation, and desired outcomes. The school principal needs to provide teachers with the time, resources, and training they need to develop innovative strategies and interventions. Finally, a system must be in place for teachers to evaluate the effectiveness of the SWPBS procedures and strategies.

SWPBS generally involves three tiers of support. Tier 1 provides universal interventions, or universal support for all students. Tier 1 includes defining and teaching behavior expectations, developing and implementing appropriate consequences, and identifying and implementing evidence-based instruction and interventions. An important component of Tier 1 is identifying students who are at risk for behavior difficulties. Tier 2 provides targeted interventions, such as small-group instruction, for students who are unresponsive to instructions and interventions provided at Tier 1. One promising Tier 2 intervention is the Behavior Education Program, which provides frequent feedback on social behaviors and rewards students for demonstrating appropriate behavior. Tier 3 provides individualized interventions, intensive supports such as functional behavior analysis, wraparound services, and behavior intervention plans.

SWPBS has been shown to reduce behavior problems in the classroom, resulting in increased student academic achievement, and it has the potential to reduce the disproportionate discipline outcomes of culturally and linguistically diverse students. SWPBS can also contribute to high levels of teacher self-efficacy, which has been linked to teacher effectiveness, teacher resilience, student achievement, and the implementation of innovative teaching strategies.

REVIEW ACTIVITIES

1. You and several other teachers would like to implement a school-wide positive behavior support program at your school. How would you convince your principal of the importance of SWPBS? How would you convince your fellow teachers of the importance of SWPBS?

2. Due to ongoing neighborhood rejuvenation, the population of the community in which your school is located has changed from mostly working-class to more affluent. Do you think the SWPBS your school developed before the community changed is still appropriate? What procedures would you implement to determine whether the current SWPBS needs to be regenerated?

3. Develop an SWPBS plan for your school. Include procedures and interventions for each of the tiers. Make sure you consider the culture of your school and the diversity of your students.

Visit the Student Study Site at www.sagepub.com/shepherd to access additional study tools including mobile-friendly eFlashcards and web quizzes as well as links to SAGE journal articles and web resources.

CHAPTER 14
SOCIAL SKILLS TRAINING

After reading this chapter, you should be able to do the following:

- Define and describe the features of social skills.
- Use different methods to assess the social skills deficits of students.
- Describe the components of direct teaching of social skills to students.
- List the different evidence-based social skills programs and classroom strategies that can be used to teach social skills.
- Explain how social skills instruction can be incorporated into school-wide positive behavior support programs.
- Use culturally responsive social skills instruction with culturally and linguistically diverse students.

FEATURES OF SOCIAL SKILLS TRAINING

Social skills training programs are often overlooked components of behavior and classroom management plans. Teachers generally feel that it is not within their purview to teach social skills, or they feel that they do not have the skills or knowledge to provide social skills training. Additionally, most of the research conducted in social skills training has been in the field of emotional and behavioral disorders, even though many students who have not been identified as having such disorders have poor social skills. Students who have poor social skills and inadequate social competencies are at risk for peer rejection, failure to maintain satisfactory relationships with others, victimization, loneliness, poor academic performance, dropping out of school, and difficulties maintaining employment (Cook et al., 2008; Gresham, Van, & Cook, 2006; Maag, 2006). Students who receive social skills interventions increase their social skills and social competencies and decrease their problematic behaviors (Hemmeter, Fox, Jack, & Broyles, 2007). Additionally, when social skills are taught in school, students' problem-solving skills, interaction skills, and cooperation skills improve (Pinar & Sucuoglu, 2013).

Social skills training is an intervention used to increase the social skills and social competencies of students with behavior difficulties (Van Vugt, Dekovic, Prinzie, Stams, & Asscher, 2013). Social skills are specific behaviors related to the competent performance of social tasks (e.g., listening to others, asking for help, compromising). Social competency is the degree to which an individual performs a social task competently (Cook et al., 2008). For example, Kale has difficulty initiating conversations with peers and teachers (social skill). After providing Kale with social skills training in initiating conversations, her teachers monitor the number of times she initiates conversations throughout the day. If Kale initiates conversations four times per day, she has met the criteria for competence in this skill established by her teachers (social competency).

Another important concept related to social skills training is the difference between social skills deficits and performance deficits (Gresham et al., 2006). As explained in Chapter 12, a student who has a social skill deficit may not have the ability to perform a certain social skill, and may not even know which social skill is appropriate for a situation. Conversely, a student who has a social skill performance deficit has the ability to perform the social skill but chooses not to do so. The teacher needs to understand which kind of deficit a student has in order to be able to develop interventions and strategies that can be effective in modifying the student's social skills.

Many social skills training programs are based on developmental theories that explain behavior and provide practical applications to improve student behavior (see Chapter 1). Social skills training based on the principles of operant conditioning (Skinner, 1953) is grounded in the premise that reinforcers increase the probability that the desired behavior will occur again and with increased frequency. Social skills training based on social cognitive theory (Bandura, 1997) is centered on the principle of observational learning—that is, the idea that students learn behavior by observing and imitating the behavior modeled by others. Social learning theory emphasizes coaching and modeling, and can easily lend itself to the use of video vignettes on social skills. Video modeling has been shown to be effective for teaching complex social skills to individuals with autism spectrum disorder (Plavnick, Sam, Hume, & Odom, 2013).

Social skills training based on the ecological systems model (Bronfenbrenner, 2005) focuses on the relationship between the student and the environment, which is the foundation of a school-wide positive behavior support program. Finally, social skills training programs that rely on cognitive approaches use problem-solving scripts to teach students coping skills they can use in social situations. The social skills training program Skillstreaming teaches social competencies through the use of scripted instruction (Goldstein, 1999). Many social skills training programs use behavioral and cognitive techniques independently and jointly (Maag, 2006).

Regardless of the theoretical approaches on which they are based, most social skills training programs have the following objectives:

1. To promote skill acquisition

2. To enhance skill performance

3. To reduce or eliminate competing problem behaviors

4. To facilitate generalization and maintenance of social skills (Cook et al., 2008)

Before initiating strategies for students with social skills acquisition/performance deficits, teachers need to assess the social skills that students need to be successful in school. Identifying these skills is essential to the development of effective social skills instruction.

ASSESSING SOCIAL SKILLS

Teachers need to determine what social skills students are deficient in before they can design specific interventions to teach or increase those skills. Unfortunately, teachers rarely assess the social skill deficiencies of their students, often because they perceive this task as too difficult and time-consuming (Maag, 2006). Without such assessment, teachers cannot determine which social skills training programs or strategies are likely to be effective.

Teachers can use several methods to assess students' social skills. One is to conduct functional behavioral assessments, using behavioral observations to determine the frequency, intensity, duration, and latency of social behaviors (see Chapter 8). Teachers can also conduct functional behavior analysis to determine whether students' inappropriate behaviors are due to social skills deficits (see Chapter 9). Behavior rating scales offer another method of assessing social skills deficits. Such scales have been used to assess behavior, social skills, depression, anxiety, and attention-deficit/hyperactivity disorder.

The Social Skills Rating System (SSRS; Gresham & Elliott, 1990) has been one of the most widely used tools for measuring social behaviors in schools (Gresham, Elliott, Vance, & Cook, 2011). It has been revised as the Social Skills Improvement System (SSIS-RS; Gresham & Elliott, 2008), which can easily be incorporated into a school-wide positive behavior support program. The SSIS-RS Performance Screening Guide can be used as a universal screening instrument for all students. Teachers complete a social skills rubric with five levels of social behavior. Students who are ranked at the first level usually need social skills instruction. The SSIS-RS Classwide Intervention Program can also be used at Tier 1 of an SWPBS program. The Classwide Intervention Program provides teachers with a structured method of teaching 10 of the most important social skills as rated by teachers and parents (Gresham et al., 2011).

The SSIS-RS also includes a series of rating scales completed by teachers, parents, and students. These scales assess social skills, problem behaviors, and academic competence, providing a context for the development of interventions for students with social skills deficits. Communication, cooperation, assertion, responsibility, empathy, engagement, and self-control are assessed in the social skills domain. The problem behavior scale assesses externalizing behaviors, bullying, hyperactivity/inattention, internalizing behaviors, and autism spectrum. The academic competence scale, which is completed by the teacher, assesses student performance in reading, math, motivation, parental support, and general cognitive functioning (Gresham, Elliott, & Kettler, 2010). The Intervention Guide can help teachers plan and implement social skills strategies identified by the rating scales. It provides 20 instructional units in communication, cooperation, assertion, responsibility, empathy, engagement, and self-control. Both the rating scales and the Intervention Guide can be used at the Tier 2 level of SWPBS.

Once teachers have identified students' deficits in social skills, they can provide effective programs and strategies to improve students' skills. Many social skills programs use direct teaching of social skills, but some strategies seek to replace inappropriate behaviors with prosocial behaviors or provide students with information about social situations.

COMPONENTS OF SOCIAL SKILLS PROGRAMS

Best practice for social skills training is direct teaching of skills, because this method provides clear behavior expectations and modification of environmental variables (Riney & Bullock, 2012). Direct teaching of a social skill includes direct instruction of the skill, modeling, rehearsal, performance feedback and reinforcement, and generalization of the desired social behavior (Gresham et al., 2006; Miller, Lane, & Wehby, 2005).

Direct Instruction of Social Skills

In direct instruction of a specific social skill, the teacher introduces the skill to students and explains the benefits of the skill to their lives. If students do not see the relevance of using the targeted skill in everyday life, it is unlikely that they will learn the skill and use it in different settings.

Once the teacher has introduced and explained the relevance of the social skill, she teaches the steps to performing the skill. For example, teaching students to ask a question when they need help involves the following five-step process:

1. What question do you want to ask?

2. Who do you ask?

3. How do you ask your question?

4. When do you ask your question?

5. Ask your question.

The teacher goes through the steps one by one and provides examples for each step. For example, Ricardo did not hear the instructions for the homework assignment near the end of class. He needs to ask for the instructions for the homework assignment (Step 1). Since Mrs. Daily is the teacher assigning the homework, Ricardo needs to ask her the question (Step 2). He can tell Mrs. Daily that he did not understand the instructions for the assignment and ask her to repeat them (Step 3). Ricardo can ask her the question before the bell rings or after class, or he can send her an e-mail later through the school e-mail service (Step 4). If he asks his question before the class ends, he fears that he might look "stupid" to his classmates. If he asks his question after class, he might be late to his next class. If he waits to e-mail Mrs. Daily later, she may not respond quickly enough to answer his question, and he may not get his homework completed. Ricardo decides to ask his question immediately after class (Step 5).

Modeling

Once students fully understand the steps for exhibiting a specific social skill, the teacher reinforces the skill through guided practice. Modeling is one of the best methods of providing guided practice for social skills. In this technique, the social skill to be taught is demonstrated or performed, giving students visual instruction in the skill. This may be accomplished through participation modeling, video modeling, or peer-mediated modeling.

In participation modeling, students observe the teacher and other students in the group as they demonstrate the specific social skill in different situations (Van Vugt et al., 2013). All students in the group take turns modeling the behavior. Video modeling as an intervention strategy is gaining interest, especially for students with autism. Video modeling is based on the principles of social learning theory, which posits that students learn behaviors by watching the behaviors of others. In video modeling, students are shown a video recording of someone performing the desired social skill (Green et al., 2013; Walton & Ingersoll, 2013). Prompts, direct statements of behavioral expectations, and reinforcements often accompany video modeling to facilitate learning (Wilson, 2013). In peer-mediated modeling of social skills, peers serve as models of appropriate behavior by directly interacting with the students learning the skills. Peer-mediated social skills instruction fosters inclusion, enhances student engagement, and builds relationships with peers (Chan et al., 2009; Spencer, 2006). Additionally, social skills taught through peer-mediated instruction may generalize to other settings (Walton & Ingersoll, 2013).

In a typical modeling strategy, the teacher models the specific social skill by verbalizing each step as she performs the skill. By observing this demonstration of the skill, students learn the desired behavior; however, in order to maintain the social skill and generalize it to different settings, students need further instruction and practice.

Rehearsal

Once students have learned the steps of a specific social skill, they need to practice the skill. They can do this by rehearsing the skill in a safe environment (i.e., their own classroom) after the teacher models the skill. Rehearsal of social skills has been shown to lead to increased effectiveness and efficiency in behavioral performance (Gresham et al., 2006). After the teacher has modeled the social skill, she asks a student to demonstrate the skill while interacting with the teacher, also verbalizing each step. Once the teacher and student actors complete their performance, pairs of students take turns demonstrating the social skill and verbalizing each step. Each student in the class should have the opportunity to play the main actor once. For example, Roberto and Kale are demonstrating *how to ask a question*. Roberto demonstrates the social skill while also verbalizing each step, as Kale responds naturally to Roberto's performance. Once Roberto has finished performing the skill, Kale takes the lead as the main actor and demonstrates the skill while Roberto responds to her performance. When the teacher is confident that the students understand the steps to the social skill, she has the group practice the skill again without verbalizing the steps. Rehearsal continues until the teacher is confident that the students have acquired the skill.

Performance Feedback and Reinforcement

Positive feedback and reinforcement, such as praise, approval, and constructive criticism, are used to improve students' performance of social skills (Gresham et al., 2006). Performance feedback and reinforcement should occur immediately after a student has demonstrated a specific social skill, and everyone in the group should take turns offering feedback. For example, after Roberto finishes performing *how to ask a question,* his coactor, Kale, should be the first person to provide feedback. After Kale has offered her feedback, other students in the group should provide feedback one at a time. The teacher should be the last person to provide feedback and reinforcement. Positive reinforcement increases the possibility that the desired behavior will occur again by presenting a preferred consequence and facilitates the performance of social skills. Once everyone else has commented on a student's performance, the student should evaluate his or her own performance. Performance feedback and reinforcement help students maintain and improve acquired behaviors.

Generalization

One of the most difficult components of any behavior intervention strategy is the generalization of acquired behaviors to different settings and situations. Providing students with opportunities to practice acquired social skills in different settings and situations is instrumental in maintaining and generalizing these skills. One strategy for enhancing generalization of social skills is to assign students "homework" in practicing the skills. Initially, the teacher might assign students to practice newly learned skills in different classrooms. This involves collaboration with other teachers, who need to know that students will be attempting to practice certain social skills in their classrooms. The collaborative teachers need to buy into this strategy because they need to support the students attempting the skills, observe and report the desired behaviors to the primary social skills teacher, and even provide situations in which students can practice the behaviors. Social skills homework can easily be incorporated into a school-wide positive behavior support program.

Another strategy for enhancing generalization of social skills is to encourage self-monitoring. At the end of each day, students record in journals the number of times they used the acquired social skills, the ways in which they used the skills, and the results of their using the skills. One advantage of a self-monitoring strategy is that it encourages students to practice the acquired social skills outside the school in natural settings. If social skills training does not include practice of the skills in the child's natural settings, generalization of the skills will be limited (Maag, 2006).

SOCIAL SKILLS PROGRAMS AND STRATEGIES

A number of social skills programs and strategies are available for teachers (see Table 14.1). Many have been found to increase students' social skills and social competencies and decrease problematic behaviors. The social skills programs described below are recognized by the National Association of School Psychologists as examples of evidence-based strategies that teachers can implement in their classrooms.

Skillstreaming

Based on social learning theory, which is based on observational learning, the Skillstreaming program is designed to meet the needs of children at three

Table 14.1 Social Skills Programs and Strategies

Program	Developmental level	Methodology	Website
ACCEPTS	Kindergarten through sixth grade	Direct instruction	http://www.proedinc.com
ACCESS	Middle school and high school	Direct instruction	http://www.proedinc.com
Replacement behavior training	All grade levels	Differential reinforcement of alternative behaviors	
Skillstreaming in Early Childhood	Early childhood	Direct instruction	https://www.researchpress.com
Skillstreaming the Elementary School Child	Elementary school	Direct instruction	https://www.researchpress.com
Skillstreaming the Adolescent	Middle school and high school	Direct instruction	https://www.researchpress.com
Social stories	All grade levels	Affective teaching	
Stop & Think	Prekindergarten through eighth grade	Direct instruction	http://www.projectachieve.info
Videotherapy	All grade levels	Affective teaching	

instructional/developmental levels: early childhood, elementary school age, and adolescence. Skillstreaming uses direct instruction of social skills, modeling, rehearsal, performance feedback, and generalization to teach social skills. At each level, Skillstreaming encompasses a range of observable social skills in teachable units (Sheridan et al., 2011). Skillstreaming in Early Childhood (McGinnis & Goldstein, 2003) includes instruction for teaching 40 prosocial skills that are organized into six skill areas: beginning social skills, school-related skills, friendship-making skills, dealing with feelings, alternatives to aggression, and dealing with stress. Skillstreaming the Elementary School Child (McGinnis & Goldstein, 1997) includes instruction for teaching 60 prosocial skills that are organized into five skill areas: classroom survival skills, friendship-making skills, skills for dealing with feelings, skill alternatives to aggression, and skills for dealing with stress. Finally, Skillstreaming the Adolescent (Goldstein & McGinnis, 1997) includes instruction for teaching 50 prosocial skills that are organized into five skill areas: classroom survival skills, friendship-making skills, skills for dealing with feelings, skill alternatives to aggression, and skills for dealing with stress.

Skillstreaming emphasizes collaboration, targeting of specific developmental levels, flexibility across settings and population, generalization, and evaluation of the effectiveness of behavior modification of students. Research suggests that students in Skillstreaming programs show improvement in social skills (Sheridan et al., 2011).

Walker Social Skills Curricula

A Curriculum for Children's Effective Peer and Teacher Skills (ACCEPTS; Walker et al., 1983) is designed to teach social competencies essential for inclusive school settings. Originally developed for use with students with mild and moderate disabilities, ACCEPTS can be used effectively with students who are at risk for behavior difficulties at the elementary school level. The curriculum groups 28 skills into five content areas: classroom skills (teacher expectations, following rules, and completing assignments), basic interaction skills (eye contact, listening, and taking turns), getting along (using polite words, sharing, and assisting others), making friends (grooming, smiling, complimenting, and expressing anger), and coping skills (when someone says no, when someone teases, and when things do not go right). The nine-step instructional procedure includes the basic components of social skills training: identification of a skill, modeling, rehearsal, performance feedback, and generalization. ACCEPTS can be used in one-on-one, small-group, or large-group instructional formats.

The Adolescent Curriculum for Communication and Effective Social Skills (ACCESS; Walker & Holmes, 1983) is designed for students in middle school and high school. ACCESS groups 30 social skills into three content areas: relating to peers (listening, making and keeping friends, and handling peer pressure), relating to adults (getting attention, following rules, and responding to requests), and relating to yourself (taking pride in your appearance, self-control, accepting consequences, and feeling good about yourself). ACCESS also uses direct instruction of social skills to teach students appropriate, prosocial behavior.

Stop & Think Social Skills Program

The Stop & Think Social Skills Program (Knoff, 2001) is based on the developmental theories of Bronfenbrenner (ecological systems approach), Meichenbaum (cognitive behavior), and Bandura (social learning theory). Divided into four developmental levels (prekindergarten to first grade, second to third grade, fourth to fifth grade, and sixth to eighth grade), the program uses the five components of social skills training: direct instruction of social skills, modeling, rehearsal, performance feedback, and generalization. At each developmental level, the program focuses on 10 core skills (e.g., listening, following directions, reacting to teasing, apologizing) and 10 advanced skills (e.g., asking for permission, avoiding trouble, dealing with anger). The Stop & Think program has five sequential steps, which students first verbalize and then learn to internalize:

1. Think about the situation.

2. Decide to choose an appropriate plan of action.

3. Develop a plan of action to address the situation.

4. Implement the plan.

5. Self-reinforce appropriate behavior.

Used as a multicomponent or a stand-alone intervention strategy, the Stop & Think program increases the social skills of students (Hall, Jones, & Claxton, 2008). It is also easily adaptable to a school-wide positive behavior support program and can be used as a school-wide intervention or for targeted intervention.

Replacement Behavior Training

Based on functional behavior analysis, **replacement behavior training (RBT)** is a social skills strategy in which competing problem behaviors are replaced by prosocial behaviors that serve the same functions. Competing problem behaviors interfere with, or block, the acquisition of appropriate social skills (Gresham et al., 2006, 2011).

RBT is similar to differential reinforcement of alternative behavior (see Chapter 9). The first step in implementing RBT is to identify the function, or purpose, of the inappropriate social skill. Generally, a student behaves in a particular way in order to obtain something (attention, rewards and privileges, or power or control) or to avoid a situation (social isolation, nonpreferred activities, or adverse interactions). RBT cannot be effective unless the function of the student's inappropriate behavior is correctly identified.

Once the teacher has identified the function of the inappropriate behavior, the teacher and student work together to determine an alternative prosocial behavior that serves the same function. For example, Timothy insults Kale on a daily basis, which causes her to become upset. The teacher discovers that the function of Timothy's inappropriate behavior is to get Kale's attention. With input from Timothy, the teacher provides him with social skills training that addresses interacting appropriately with peers, behavior that serves the same function as the competing problem behavior. Through social skills training, Timothy learns how to initiate and maintain a conversation. When used with social skills training, RBT enhances generalization because the alternative prosocial behavior has the same function as the competing behavior, so the student is more likely to use the preferred social skill outside the training setting (Maag, 2006).

Social Stories

Social stories are short scenarios written for students to teach them appropriate behaviors in specific situations. Social stories may include photographs or illustrations that provide visual support to the contents of the text. The stories may be read to students by the teacher, or students with appropriate reading skills may read the stories themselves. Many social stories address skills similar to those taught through social skills training programs (e.g., following directions, problem solving). The use of social stories in social skills training is based on the premise that students will improve their social skills if they have better understanding of specific social situations (Kokina & Kern, 2010).

Some of the key criteria for the use of social stories are as follows:

- Accurate and individualized information regarding the social needs of the student
- A nurturing approach to presenting and discussing social situations
- Language that is age appropriate and meaningful to the student
- Careful consideration of the technical aspects of the stories (e.g., length, font style/size, organization of text and illustrations)
- Use of stories that describe social information rather than address behavior
- Evaluation of the effectiveness of the stories (Hutchins, 2012)

For example, a teacher obviously would not present the story of Tony the Turtle, who has problems sharing with the other animals in the forest, to a young adolescent who is having difficulty learning to take turns. Such a story's plot, illustrations, and length would be more appropriate for and meaningful to an early elementary student than to a young adolescent, who might even be insulted or humiliated by being presented with the story.

Social stories generally contain animal characters that illustrate particular social situations (Kam, Greenberg, & Kusche, 2004), and the skills are taught through role-playing. Social stories are often presented in the following format:

1. The main character (an animal) is introduced.

2. The problem is identified.

3. The skill steps are outlined.

4. The problem is solved through the use of a particular skill.

For example, the animals in the woods do not like Jarrod the Javelina because he always interrupts their games and conversations (typical impulse difficulties for someone with attention-deficit/hyperactivity disorder). The students at Jarrod's school do not want to play with him, eat lunch with him, or have him in their academic groups. The teacher, Mrs. Doe, helps Jarrod identify which of his behaviors have isolated him from his peers and teaches him the skills of engaging in conversation at appropriate times and asking to be included in games. Using the skills that he has learned, Jarrod is successful in improving his relationships with the other animals.

Teachers may use computers, CDs, DVDs, or robot-assisted technology to present social stories to students with social skills deficits. For example, in a study using a social robot named Probo, Vanderborght et al. (2012) found that the social abilities of students with autism spectrum disorders improved when the students heard social stories told by Probo.

Teachers can easily make social stories more relevant for culturally and linguistically diverse students by interweaving culturally familiar elements and language into the stories. However, research has indicated that the longer these students participate in European American, English-language-dominated classrooms, the less effective culturally based stories are for improving the students' social skills (Hsu, Hammond, & Ingalls, 2012). Nevertheless, the inclusion of culturally based stories in the classroom is best practice for providing all students with culturally sensitive experiences.

Research has shown that the use of social stories is an effective behavior intervention strategy (Crozier & Tincani, 2007; Sansosti & Powell-Smith, 2006; Scattone, Tingstrom, & Wilczynski, 2006). Social stories can be used alone, as a single intervention strategy, or in combination with other interventions and strategies. However, it is important for teachers to remember that the aim of using social stories is not to change the behavior of the audience (students), but to provide information regarding social situations in a safe and nurturing environment.

Videotherapy

Similar to bibliotherapy, videotherapy uses movies and television episodes to allow students to identify with characters similar to themselves and discuss their own behaviors and situations through the safe distance of the characters (Cook, Earles-Vollrath, & Ganz, 2006). Videotherapy involves sharing movies or television episodes with students in the therapeutic attempt to assist them in dealing with difficulties in their lives (Dole & McMahan, 2005). Through discussions, questions, and activities, videotherapy can help students learn the appropriate social behaviors for specific situations. The use of videotherapy has six potential goals:

1. To provide information about social skills in a nonthreatening format

2. To provide insight into specific experiences or situations

3. To provide alternative solutions to the problems faced by characters in the movies or television shows and by students with social skills deficits

4. To stimulate discussion of problems faced by characters and students

5. To communicate new values and attitudes

6. To help students understand that they are not the only ones who have experienced the problems depicted (Cook et al., 2006)

Videotherapy involves the guided viewing of a specific movie or television show. Before guiding students through this viewing, the teacher becomes thoroughly familiar with the movie or television show and how it presents specific social skills issues. While previewing the movie or show, the teacher prepares a list of questions to facilitate discussion with students (Shepherd, 2007). If students identify with a character and feel they have similar difficulties, they feel an emotional attachment to the character, and catharsis takes place (Dole & McMahan, 2005). After viewing the movie or show with students, the teacher leads a discussion of the difficulties faced by the characters, using the questions generated previously, starting with introductory questions and then following up with more specific questions.

Once the class has concluded the discussion of the difficulties faced by the characters and how these are similar to difficulties the students may have experienced, the teacher introduces a related student-preferred activity, such as artistic expression, role-playing, creative writing, or music (Hebert & Sergent, 2005). For example, students might be asked to draw or paint the main character, write a sequel that continues the story of the character, or role-play a mock interview with the character.

Like social stories, videotherapy is not intended to change students' behavior; rather, it provides students with information about social situations and helps them understand that others may experience the same difficulties they do. Additionally, videotherapy may be appropriate for adolescents who have reading difficulties and do not like to read. Videotherapy is a strategy that has the potential to help students with social difficulties and can be expanded to meet the affective needs of students.

WHAT WOULD YOU DO? Sherry

Sherry is a student in your fourth-grade language arts class at Franklin Pierce Elementary School. Although she is considered a slow learner, she loves to read. However, every time you take your class to the library, Sherry puts a couple of books in her backpack and then takes the books out of the library without checking them out. The first time you notice this, you explain to Sherry that she has to check out the books before taking them out of the library. You then walk her back to the library and help her check the books out. The second time she takes books without checking them out, you send her back to the library to apologize to the librarian for not checking the books out. The third time your class goes to the library, you do not allow Sherry to bring her backpack with her, yet she walks out of the library with books under her arm without checking them out. Again you try explaining that taking books in this way is wrong, and could even be considered stealing. The fourth time she takes books without checking them out, you send Sherry to the principal's office and she has to stay in at recess. However, you are beginning to consider that Sherry may have a social skills deficit, which means she may not have the ability or knowledge to perform the appropriate behavior. What would you do to help Sherry?

SOCIAL SKILLS AND SWPBS

Social skills programs are natural interventions and strategies for a school-wide positive behavior support program (see Chapter 13). Social skills training might be used at Tier 2 of SWPBS for students who have poor social skills and social competencies. It is also conceivable that schools could use social skills training as an intervention for *all* students at Tier 1. In one study, a school surveyed teachers to identify the specific skills students need to be successful in school—often known as survival skills (interpersonal skills, school expectations, and so on). Using the results of the survey, the school developed an SWPBS intervention in which one of the identified skills was taught to all students each month (Lane, Wehby, & Cooley, 2006). With the advent of social media, texting, sexting, and cyberbullying, and given the decreased amount of time students spend interacting with peers face-to-face, social skills training is particularly pertinent for today's students.

CULTURALLY RESPONSIVE SOCIAL SKILLS INSTRUCTION

Culturally responsive social skills instruction (CRSSI) may help reduce the disruptive behaviors of culturally and linguistically diverse students, especially African American males, who receive disproportionate numbers of office referrals, suspensions, and referrals for special education services. Relevant and proactive CRSSI is essential for culturally and linguistically diverse students whose cultural experiences clash with the cultures of their schools, resulting in disparate punitive and ineffective consequences (Cartledge, Singh, & Gibson, 2008). When teaching critical social skills to culturally and linguistically diverse students, teachers must consider the cultural experiences and real-life challenges of these students (Lo, Mustian, Brophy, & White, 2011). Additionally, teachers must understand the cultural backgrounds of their students and how culture affects behavior, social interaction, and responses to academic content. Universal design for classroom management also stresses that *all* students must be treated equitably—that is, teachers must provide all students with what they need to succeed in school.

For example, LeVar was texting on his cell phone during a class discussion. Mr. Edgar, his history teacher, confiscated the phone and told LeVar he could pick it up after class. LeVar pounded his fists on his desk and threw his books to the floor. Mr. Edgar immediately sent him to the office. Through direct CRSSI, LeVar could learn aggression-resolution and classroom-related social skills that take into account his cultural experiences (Lo et al., 2011). When teaching aggression-resolution social skills, the teacher needs to acknowledge the student's cultural experiences but point out the necessity for the student to learn alternative skills in order to be successful in school (Cartledge et al., 2008).

Since a disparity between students' cultural experiences and the culture of the school often results in disruptive behavior in the classroom (Cartledge et al., 2008), CRSSI should include the teaching of classroom survival skills.

Classroom survival skills are nonacademic behaviors that meet the daily classroom expectations, such as arriving to class on time, completing assignments, communicating with teachers and peers appropriately, and following directions. The ability to meet these expectations is critical for a student's school success. Many culturally and linguistically diverse students may not fully understand classroom expectations, and this acquisition deficit could inadvertently lead to unwarranted consequences such as office referrals and even suspensions. It is crucial that during the first weeks of school, teachers explain classroom expectations and state clearly that these expectations are generally immutable. For example, all students are expected to arrive to class on time. Barring extenuating circumstances, this expectation holds true for all classes and does not change. For students who have difficulty arriving to class on time, social skills instruction could help them master this classroom survival skill.

SUMMARY

Although social skills training programs are often overlooked, they are important components of behavior and classroom management plans. Based on developmental theories, social skills interventions increase the social skills and social competencies of students with behavior difficulties. Social skills are specific behaviors related to the competent performance of social tasks. Social competency is the degree to which an individual performs a social task competently.

Social skills interventions include direct instruction, modeling, rehearsal, feedback and reinforcement, and generalization of desired social behaviors. First, the teacher provides direct instruction by introducing the relevance of the specific social skill and listing the steps to performing the skill. Once students fully understand the steps for the skill, the teacher reinforces the skill through modeling, or demonstrating, the skill for the students. After the teacher has modeled the skill, students rehearse, or practice, the skill in a safe environment. The teacher and peers provide positive and constructive performance feedback and reinforcement immediately after a student has performed the social skill. Once the teacher is confident that students have mastered the social skill, she provides them with opportunities to practice the skill in different settings and situations to promote generalization.

A number of social skills programs and strategies are available for teachers to use. Many commercial social skills programs use direct instruction of social skills and have been shown to increase students' social skills and social competencies and decrease problematic behaviors. Replacement behavior training is a social skills strategy in which the competing problem behavior is replaced by a prosocial behavior that serves the same function. Social stories can be used to teach students appropriate behaviors in specific situations, and videotherapy, which involves guided viewing of movies and television episodes, allows students to identify with characters and discuss their own behaviors and situations through the safe distance of those characters.

Culturally responsive social skills instruction may help reduce the disruptive behaviors of culturally and linguistically diverse students. When teaching social skills, teachers must consider the cultural experiences and real-life challenges of their culturally and linguistically diverse students.

REVIEW ACTIVITIES

1. Develop a social skills training program to use in your school. Consider the different strategies and components discussed in this chapter, and keep in mind the possible cultural impact of each strategy you choose.

2. Should teachers be responsible for teaching social skills in their classrooms? Support your answer.

3. Your principal has asked you to review social skills programs and make a recommendation concerning the best program for your school. What factors should you take into consideration in determining which program to recommend?

4. Read some of the examples of social stories on the Region 2 Digital Lending Library website (http://www.region2library.org/SocialStories .htm). Write a social story for Sherry, whose situation is described in this chapter's "What Would You Do?" feature.

Visit the Student Study Site at **www.sagepub.com/shepherd** to access additional study tools including mobile-friendly eFlashcards and web quizzes as well as links to SAGE journal articles and web resources.

GLOSSARY

ABC analysis: A behavioral observation method that focuses on the antecedent to a behavior (A), the behavior (B), and the consequence of the behavior (C).

AB design: A basic single-subject design that uses one set of baseline data (Condition A) and one set of intervention data (Condition B).

Academic optimism: A teacher's belief that he or she can make a difference in the academic performance of students, academic emphasis, and trust between the teacher and students' families.

Acculturation: The process through which an individual adapts to and adopts the values, beliefs, and traditions of another culture.

Activity reinforcers: Any preferred activities presented to a student after a behavior occurs, resulting in an increase of the behavior.

Alternating treatment design (ABAC): A single-subject design in which the AB design is extended through the addition of a second, different intervention (Condition C).

Antecedent-based interventions: Modifications of the environment that prevent or decrease the occurrence of inappropriate behaviors and increase the probability of appropriate behaviors.

Baseline data: Information collected on a student's target behavior prior to any intervention.

Behavioral hypothesis: A proposed explanation of the factors that elicit inappropriate behaviors based on data obtained from behavioral observations.

Behavior intervention plan: A written plan that describes the interventions, strategies, and supports that will be implemented to address the social, emotional, and behavior needs of a student.

Behaviorism: A developmental theory based on the measurement of observable behaviors and reactions and the exclusion of the emotional and mental states of individuals.

Changing criterion design: A single-subject design in which a behavior is progressively increased or decreased in stepwise changes through manipulation of the conditions of the intervention; used to evaluate the effectiveness of an intervention strategy.

Classical conditioning: The repeated pairing of a neutral stimulus with an unconditioned stimulus to produce a conditioned response.

Cognitive behavior management: The use of intervention strategies designed to teach students to control their own behaviors.

Condition change line: The line in a graph that separates baseline data from intervention data.

Condition labels: Labels on a graph that identify the baseline data and the intervention data.

Contingency contract: A formal, written agreement between the student and teacher that addresses the behavioral, academic, and social goals of the student and the reinforcers the student is to receive after achieving these goals.

Contingent praise: An affirmative statement that immediately follows the completion of appropriate academic or social behaviors.

Continuous progress monitoring: A procedure in which teachers gather information on students' behaviors following behavior management interventions to determine whether the interventions have been effective in modifying inappropriate behaviors.

Continuous reinforcement: A reinforcement schedule in which each instance of the desired behavior is reinforced.

Data point: An indicator of a frequency count on a graph or single-subject design; may be denoted by a circle, triangle, or square.

Depersonalization: A detached attitude that teachers feel toward their job, students, and other teachers due to stress and burnout.

Differential reinforcement: An operant procedure that is used to increase the frequency of an appropriate behavior while decreasing an inappropriate behavior.

Differential reinforcement of alternative behavior (DRA): Reinforcement of a specific alternative behavior in lieu of an inappropriate behavior.

Differential reinforcement of incompatible behavior (DRI): Reinforcement of an appropriate behavior that is incompatible with a problem behavior and therefore cannot occur at the same time.

Differential reinforcement of lower rates (DRL): Reinforcement that reduces an inappropriate behavior through the provision of reinforcers after the frequency of the behavior in a specific period of time is less than a set limit.

Differential reinforcement of other behavior (DRO): Reinforcement of any appropriate behavior when a problem behavior has not been displayed for a period of time.

Discrepancy model: A model used in the identification of students with specific learning disabilities, in which a student's potential (measured by IQ) is compared with his or her achievement (measured by average score on standardized achievement tests).

Duration of a behavior: The length of time a student displays a specified behavior.

Duration per episode: The length of time a student engages in a behavior during one episode.

Duration recording: The measurement of the length of time a student engages in a behavior.

Ecological systems theory: A developmental theory that explains how interrelated environments affect the development of a child.

Enculturation: The process of acquiring and maintaining cultural norms and values.

Event-based recording: A behavioral observation recording method used to measure the frequency of behaviors.

Exclusion time-out: Time-out in which the student is removed from a reinforcing activity or setting for a specified period of time.

Extinction: The reduction of a target behavior through the withholding of the reinforcer that maintains the behavior.

Family cohesion: The emotional bonding or closeness that family members have toward each other.

Family communication: The talking, listening, and understanding skills that family members use in facilitating levels of family cohesion and flexibility.

Family engagement: Reciprocal communication between teachers and students' families that actively encourages parents' input into their children's academic and behavior needs.

Family flexibility: The amount or degree of change that takes place in family leadership, role relationships, and relationship rules.

Family functions: The routines, tasks, and activities individual family members perform to meet the members' diverse needs as well as those of the family as a unit.

Family involvement: Mostly one-sided communication from teachers to students' parents, informing them how they can contribute to fulfilling their children's academic and behavior needs.

Family life cycle: The set of developmental stages that families pass through, from childhood to retirement.

Family systems model: A model that views the family as an interrelated and interactive social system in which the events and experiences of each member of the family unit affect other members of the family.

Fixed-ratio schedule: A reinforcement schedule in which reinforcers are delivered after certain fixed numbers of responses.

Frequency: How often a behavior occurs in a specific period of time.

Frequency count: The number of times a behavior occurs during an observation period.

Functional behavioral assessment: A problem-solving process for addressing a student's inappropriate behavior by identifying the characteristics of the behavior through behavioral observation.

Functional behavior analysis: A method of analysis used to identify the function, or purpose, of an inappropriate behavior.

Functional communication training: A systematic technique for replacing an inappropriate behavior with an appropriate communication response as a means to obtain reinforcement.

Goal setting: The establishment of objectives for academic or behavioral performance.

Inclusion time-out: Time-out in which the student remains in his or her seat and observes classroom instruction but does not have the opportunity to participate or receive reinforcements.

Individualized interventions: Interventions that constitute Tier 3 of school-wide positive behavior support, providing strategies for the 5–10% of students who do not respond to either Tier 1 or Tier 2 supports.

Intensity of a behavior: The amount of force with which a student exhibits a behavior.

Intermittent reinforcement: A reinforcement schedule in which only some incidents of the behavior are reinforced.

Interrater reliability (or interobserver reliability): The level of reliability obtained when two observers who view the same behavior during the same observation period come to a consensus regarding the rate of the behavior.

Interval-based recording: A behavioral observation recording method in which the observation period is divided into equal time intervals.

Interval schedules: Reinforcement schedules based on the passage of time since the last reinforcer was delivered.

Intervention data: Data collected on an observed behavior under an intervention strategy.

Latency of a behavior: The amount of time between an environmental event and the behavior.

Latency recording: A method of measuring how long it takes for a student to respond to an environmental event, such as instructions or redirection.

Level: The average rate of a behavior during a condition phase of a single-subject design.

Moral development theory: A child development theory concerned with systems of beliefs, values, and fundamental judgments about human behavior and how it relates to societal expectations.

Multiple-baseline design: An extension of the AB design that enables examination of the effectiveness of intervention strategies across students, behaviors, and settings.

Negative punishment: The withdrawal of a desired reinforcement after an inappropriate behavior is displayed, resulting in decreased probability that the behavior will be repeated.

Negative reinforcement: The removal of an adverse stimulus after a desired behavior has been exhibited, resulting in increased probability that the behavior will be repeated.

Observational learning: Learning that occurs through an individual's observation of the behavior of another person and how the consequences of the behavior are reinforced.

Operant conditioning: A method of learning in which the probability that an individual's behavior will increase or decrease is manipulated through the use of reinforcements that are pleasurable or not pleasurable.

Overcorrection: A negative punishment that uses repetitive behavior as a consequence for exhibiting inappropriate behaviors.

Partial-interval recording: An interval-based behavioral observation recording method in which the target behavior is recorded when it occurs at any time during an interval.

Performance deficit: The failure to perform appropriate behaviors or skills despite having the ability to do so.

Planned ignoring: A procedure designed to decrease or eliminate an inappropriate behavior by abruptly withdrawing the reinforcer that is maintaining the behavior.

Point-time sampling: An interval-based behavioral observation recording method in which a behavior is recorded if it occurs at the end of an interval.

Positive-practice overcorrection: A negative punishment in which the student displaying an inappropriate behavior must repeatedly perform an appropriate behavior.

Positive punishment: The provision of an aversive consequence immediately following a behavior, resulting in decreased probability that the behavior will be repeated.

Positive reinforcement: The provision of a preferred consequence following a behavior, resulting in increased probability that the behavior will be repeated.

Preventive discipline: Strategies and interventions implemented before problems arise to prevent or minimize misbehavior.

Primary reinforcers: Reinforcers that are of biological importance to a person, including food, water, sleep, and sex.

Professional self-esteem: An individual's belief in his or her worth and acceptance in a work-related position.

Proximity control: A nonverbal strategy that alters behavioral responses through the physical presence of an authority figure.

Punishment: A consequence following a behavior that decreases the probability that the behavior will be repeated; may be either positive or negative.

Rate of a behavior: The number of times a behavior occurs divided by the amount of time over which the behavior was observed.

Ratio schedules: Reinforcement schedules that are based on numbers of correct responses; may be fixed or variable.

Reduced personal accomplishments: A state experienced by teachers who feel they cannot accomplish anything, believe they cannot make a difference in the lives of their students, and feel incompetent.

Reinforcement: The attainment or avoidance of a consequence following a behavior, resulting in increased probability that the behavior will occur in the future.

Relaxation: A quiet, calm state of being with low psychological and physiological tension.

Replacement behavior training (RBT): A social skills strategy in which competing problem behaviors are replaced by prosocial behaviors that serve the same functions.

Replication: The repeating of an intervention strategy, or independent variable, to determine the likelihood that a change in the behavior was not due to external variables.

Response cost: A negative punishment in which the positive reinforcer is removed contingent on an inappropriate behavior.

Response-to-intervention (RTI): A multitiered approach to providing interventions and services at increasing levels of intensity for students with academic and behavior problems.

Restitutional overcorrection: Overcorrection in which the student displaying an inappropriate behavior must restore and improve the environment, leaving it in a better state than it was in before the inappropriate behavior.

Routines: Well-defined procedures that help to create an orderly environment in the classroom.

Rules: Prescribed modes of conduct that serve as guidelines for student behavior.

School culture: The beliefs, values, traditions, attitudes, and behaviors that characterize a school.

School-wide positive behavior support (SWPBS): A proactive strategy designed to promote acceptable behavioral expectations for all students within a school and establish a safe school environment in which learning can take place.

Seclusion time-out: Time-out in which the student is removed from the classroom to a designated place, a secluded area or a time-out room, for a specified period of time.

Secondary reinforcers: Reinforcers whose value is learned or conditioned.

Self-efficacy: An individual's belief in his or her abilities to perform specific tasks despite difficulties, obstacles, and initial failures.

Self-evaluation: A self-management strategy in which students compare their own performance to a set criterion.

Self-instruction: A self-management strategy in which self-talk is used to help regulate behaviors.

Self-management: Individuals' control of their own behaviors.

Self-monitoring: A self-management technique in which students observe their own behaviors and record whether they are exhibiting particular behaviors.

Self-reinforcement: A self-management technique in which students manage their own behaviors by rewarding themselves when they successfully complete self-prescribed activities.

Shared vision: Agreement among many parties—such as administrators, teachers, and school support staff—regarding the core components of an innovation, the implementation of those components, and the desired outcomes for the innovation.

Skill deficit: The inability to perform appropriate behaviors or skills.

Social cognitive theory: A social learning theory that states that behavior is learned through the process of observational learning.

Social competency: The degree to which an individual performs a social task competently.

Social skills: Specific behaviors related to the competent performance of social tasks.

Social skills training: An intervention used to increase the social skills and social competencies of students with behavior difficulties.

Social stories: Short scenarios written for students to teach them appropriate behaviors in specific social situations.

Stable baseline: A baseline that shows no descending or ascending trend, with data points that fall within a small range of values.

Stimulus: An external event that affects an individual's behavior or response.

Supportive discipline: Strategies that help students use self-control to stay on task.

Tangible reinforcers: Preferred items presented after a behavior occurs, resulting in an increase of the behavior.

Target behavior: A student behavior identified to be assessed and modified; must be observable, measurable, and repeatable.

Targeted interventions: Interventions that make up Tier 2 of school-wide positive behavior support, providing support for the 10–15% of students who do not respond to Tier 1 supports.

Time-out: A behavior modification strategy in which a student displaying inappropriate behaviors is removed from a reinforcing environment to an austere environment for a specified period of time.

Token economy: A contingency management system that allows students to earn tokens that can be exchanged for predetermined reinforcers.

Total duration per observation: The cumulative amount of time a student engages in a behavior during an observation period.

Transitions: Intervals of time during which students move from one lesson or activity to another.

Trend: A consistent one-direction change (increasing or decreasing) in the rate of a behavior during a condition phase of a single-subject design.

Unconditioned response: A naturally occurring reaction to a stimulus.

Unconditioned stimulus: A stimulus that triggers an unconditioned response.

Universal design for classroom management (UDCM): A proactive approach to developing behavior and classroom management plans that meet the academic, behavioral, emotional, and social needs of students with disabilities, culturally and linguistically diverse students, struggling learners, and students of all ability levels.

Universal interventions: Interventions that fall within Tier 1 of school-wide positive behavior support, providing support for all students within the school and generally effective with 80% of the student population.

Variability: Fluctuation in the rate of a behavior during a condition phase of a single-subject design.

Variable-interval schedule: A reinforcement schedule that involves unspecified and changing amounts of time.

Variable-ratio schedule: A reinforcement schedule in which behavior is reinforced after an average number of instances of the target behavior.

Whole-interval recording: An interval-based behavioral observation recording method in which a behavior is recorded only if it is displayed during an entire interval.

Withdrawal design (or ABAB design): An extension of the AB design in which a second baseline is added after the intervention strategy and the intervention strategy is reintroduced after the second baseline.

Wraparound services: The components of a team-based intervention that provides the necessary planning and implementation of care services for students with emotional and behavioral difficulties and their families.

REFERENCES

Chapter 1 References

Achilles, G. M., McLaughlin, M. J., & Croninger, R. B. (2007). Sociocultural correlates of disciplinary exclusion among students with emotional, behavioral, and learning difficulties in the SEELS national dataset. *Journal of Emotional and Behavioral Disorders, 15*(1), 33–45.

Apter, S. J. (1977). Applications of ecological theory: Toward a community special education model for troubled children. *Exceptional Children, 43*(6), 366–373.

Apter, S. J., & Conoley, J. C. (1984). *Childhood behavior disorders and emotional disturbance: An introduction to teaching troubled children.* Englewood Cliffs, NJ: Prentice-Hall.

Bandura, A. (1986). *Social foundations of thought and action: A social cognitive theory.* Englewood Cliffs, NJ: Prentice-Hall.

Bandura, A. (1993). Perceived self-efficacy in cognitive development and functioning. *Educational Psychologist, 28*(2), 117–148.

Bandura, A. (1997). *Self-efficacy: The exercise of control.* New York: W. H. Freeman.

Bandura, A., Caprara, G. V., Barbaranelli, C., Gerbino, M., & Pastorelli, C. (2003). Role of affective self-regulatory efficacy in diverse spheres of psychosocial functioning. *Child Development, 74*(3), 769–782.

Beck, H. P., Levinson, S., & Irons, G. (2009). Finding little Albert: A journey to John B. Watson's infant laboratory. *American Psychologist, 64*(7), 605–614. doi:10.1037/a0017234

Billingsley, B. S., Fall, A., & Williams, T. O., Jr. (2006). Who is teaching students with emotional and behavioral disorders? A profile and comparison to other special educators. *Behavioral Disorders, 31*(3), 252–264.

Blanco-Vega, C. O., Castro-Olivo, S. M., & Merrell, K. W. (2008). Social-emotional needs of Latino immigrant adolescents: A sociocultural model for development and implementation of culturally specific interventions. *Journal of Latinos and Education, 7*(1), 43–61.

Briones, E., Tabernero, C., & Arenas, A. (2007). Effects of disposition and self-regulation of self-defeating behavior. *Journal of Social Psychology, 147*(6), 657–679.

Bronfenbrenner, U. (1979). *The ecology of human development: Experiments by nature and design.* Cambridge, MA: Harvard University Press.

Bronfenbrenner, U. (1995). The bioecological model from a life course perspective: Reflections of a participant observer. In P. Moen, G. H. Elder, Jr., & K. Luscher (Eds.), *Examining lives in context* (pp. 599–618). Washington, DC: American Psychological Association.

Bronfenbrenner, U. (2005). Interacting systems of human development. Research paradigms: Present and future. In U. Bronfenbrenner (Ed.), *Making human beings human: Bioecological perspectives on human development* (pp. 67–93). Thousand Oaks, CA: Sage.

Calzada, E. J., Brotman, L. M., Huang, K. Y., Bat-Chava, Y., & Kingston, S. (2009). Parent cultural adaptation and child functioning in culturally diverse, urban families of preschoolers. *Journal of Applied Developmental Psychology, 30*(4), 515–524.

Cartledge, G., Gardner, R., III, & Ford, D. Y. (2009). *Diverse learners with exceptionalities: Culturally responsive teaching in the classroom.* Upper Saddle River, NJ: Pearson Education.

Cartledge, G., & Kourea, L. (2008). Culturally responsive classrooms for culturally diverse students with and at risk for disabilities. *Exceptional Children, 74*(3), 351–371.

Cartledge, G., Singh, A., & Gibson, L. (2008). Practical behavior-management techniques to close the accessibility gap for students who are culturally and linguistically diverse. *Preventing School Failure, 52*(3), 29–38.

Castillo, L. G., López-Arenas, A., & Saldivar, I. M. (2010). The influence of acculturation and enculturation on Mexican American high school students' decision to apply to college. *Journal of Multicultural Counseling and Development, 38*(2), 88–98.

Cole, M., & Packer, M. (2011). Culture in development. In M. H. Bornstein & M. E. Lamb (Eds.), *Developmental science. An advanced textbook* (6th ed., pp. 51–107). New York: Psychology Press.

Colker, L. (2008). Twelve characteristics of effective early childhood teachers. *Young Children, 63*(2), 68–73.

Drakeford, W. (2006). *Racial disproportionality in school disciplinary practices.* National Center for Culturally Responsive Education Systems. Retrieved from http://www.nccrest.org/publications/briefs.html

Dray, B. J., & Wisneski, D. B. (2011). Mindful reflection as a process for developing culturally responsive practices. *Teaching Exceptional Children, 44*(1), 28–36.

Driver, J. (2005). Consequentialism and feminist ethics. *Hypatia, 20*(4), 183–239.

Dumka, L. E., Gonzales, N. A., Bonds, D. D., & Millsap, R. E. (2009). Academic success of Mexican origin adolescent boys and girls: The role of mothers' and fathers' parenting and cultural orientation. *Sex Roles, 60*(7/8), 588–599. doi:10.1007/s11199–008–9518-z

Garcia, S. B., & Guerra, P. L. (2004). Deconstructing deficit thinking: Working with educators to create more equitable learning environments. *Education and Urban Society, 36*(2), 150–167. doi:10.1177/0013124503261322

Gibbs, J. C., Basinger, K. S., Grime, R. L., & Snarey, J. R. (2007). Moral judgment development across cultures: Revisiting Kohlberg's universality claims. *Developmental Review, 27*(4), 443–500.

Gilligan, C. (1979). Woman's place in man's life cycle. *Harvard Educational Review, 49*(4), 431–446.

Gilligan, C. (1982). *In a different voice: Psychological theory and women's development.* Cambridge, MA: Harvard University Press.

Gollnick, D. M., & Chinn, P. C. (2013). *Multicultural education in a pluralistic society* (9th ed.). Upper Saddle River, NJ: Pearson.

Holt, C., Hargrove, P., & Harris, S. (2011). An investigation into the life experiences and beliefs of teachers exhibiting highly effective classroom management behaviors. *Teacher Education and Practice, 24*(1), 96–113.

Hong, J. S., Cho, H., Allen-Meares, P., & Espelage, D. L. (2011). The social ecology of the Columbine High School shootings. *Children and Youth Services Review, 33*, 861–868. doi:10.1016/j.childyouth.2010.12.005

Imler, S. J. (2009). Becoming culturally responsive: A need for preservice teacher candidates. *Teacher Education and Practice, 22*(3), 351–367.

Kim, B. S. K. (2007). Acculturation and enculturation. In F. T. L. Leong, A. G. Inman, A. Ebreo, L. Yang, L. Kinoshita, & Y. M. Fu (Eds.), *Handbook of Asian American psychology* (2nd ed., pp. 141–158). Thousand Oaks, CA: Sage.

Klassen, R. M. (2004). Optimism and realism: A review of self-efficacy from a cross-cultural perspective. *International Journal of Psychology, 39*(3), 205–230. doi:10.1080/00207590344000330

Koenig, A. L., Cicchetti, D., & Rogosch, F. A. (2004). Moral development: The association between maltreatment and young children's prosocial behaviors and moral transgressions. *Social Development, 13*(1), 87–106.

Kohlberg, L. (1975). Moral education for a society in moral transition. *Educational Leadership, 33*(1), 46–54.

Kohlberg, L., & Hersh, R. H. (1977). Moral development: A review of the theory. *Theory into Practice, 16*(2), 53–59.

Kraft, M. A. (2010). From ringmaster to conductor: 10 simple techniques can turn an unruly class into a productive one. *Phi Delta Kappan, 91*(7), 44–47.

Krezmien, M. P., Leone, P. E., & Achilles, G. M. (2006). Suspension, race, and disability: Analysis of statewide practices and reporting. *Journal of Emotional and Behavioral Disorders, 14*(4), 217–226.

Laursen, E. K. (2003). Principle-centered discipline. *Reclaiming Children and Youth, 12*(2), 78–82.

Lee, C. (2011). An ecological systems approach to bullying behaviors among middle school students in the United States. *Journal of Interpersonal Violence, 26*(8), 1664–1693. doi:10.1177/0886260510370591

Lindsey, R. B., Robins, K. N., Lindsey, D. B., & Terrell, R. D. (2009). Cultural proficiency: Changing the conversation. *Leadership, 38*(4), 12–15.

Liu, C. H., & Matthews, R. (2005). Vygotsky's philosophy: Constructivism and its criticisms examined. *International Education Journal, 6*(3), 386–399.

Miller, N. E., & Dollard, J. (1941). *Social learning and imitation.* New Haven, CT: Yale University Press.

Milner, H. R., III, & Tenore, F. B. (2010). Classroom management in diverse classrooms. *Urban Education, 45*(5), 560–603. doi:10.1177/0042085910377290

Murray, C., & Greenberg, M. T. (2006). Examining the importance of social relationships and social contexts in the lives of children with high-incidence disabilities. *Journal of Special Education, 39*(4), 220–233.

Partington, G. (1996–1997). Cultural invariance and the denial of moral regression: A critique of Piaget and Kohlberg. *International Journal of Social Education, 11*(2), 105–119.

Piaget, J. (1997). *The moral judgment of the child* (M. Gabain, Trans.). New York: Free Press. (Original work published 1932)

Prat-Sala, M., & Redford, P. (2010). The interplay between motivation, self-efficacy and approaches to studying. *British Journal of Educational Psychology, 80,* 283–305.

Rivera, L. M., Chen, E. C., Flores, L. Y., Blumberg, F., & Ponterotto, J. G. (2007). The effects of perceived barriers, role models, and acculturation on the career self-efficacy and career consideration of Hispanic women. *Career Development Quarterly, 56*(1), 47–61.

Sam, D. L., & Berry, J. W. (2010). Acculturation: When individuals and groups of different cultural backgrounds meet. *Perspectives on Psychological Science, 5*(4), 472–481. doi:10.1177/1745691610370375

Sayeski, K. L., & Brown, M. R. (2011). Developing a classroom management plan using a tiered approach. *Teaching Exceptional Children, 44*(1), 8–17.

Skiba, R. J., Horner, R. H., Chung, C., Rausch, M. K., May, S. L., & Tobin, T. (2011). Race is not neutral: A national investigation of African American and Latino disproportionality in school discipline. *School Psychology Review, 40*(1), 85–107.

Skinner, B. F. (1953). *Science and human behavior.* New York: Free Press.

Skinner, B. F. (1969). *Contingencies of reinforcement: A theoretical analysis.* New York: Appleton-Century-Crofts.

Spilt, J. L., Koomen, H. M. Y., & Thijs, J. T. (2011). Teacher wellbeing: The importance of teacher–student relationships. *Educational Psychology Review, 23*(4), 457–477. doi:10.1007/s10648-011-9170-y

Strayhorn, T. L. (2010). The role of schools, families, and psychological variables on math achievement of Black high school students. *High School Journal, 93*(4), 177–194.

Thelen, E. (2005). Dynamic systems theory and the complexity of change. *Psychoanalytic Dialogues, 15*(2), 255–283.

Thorndike, E. L. (1905). *The elements of psychology*. New York: Seiler.

Tulviste, T., & Koor, M. (2005). "Hands off the car, it's mine!" and "The teacher will be angry if we don't play nicely": Gender-related preferences in the use of moral rules and social conventions in preschoolers' dyadic play. *Sex Roles, 53*(1/2), 57–66.

Vikan, A., Camino, C., & Biaggio, A. (2005). Note on a cross-cultural test of Gilligan's ethic of care. *Journal of Moral Education, 34*(1), 107–111.

Walker, R. J. (2008). Twelve characteristics of an effective teacher: A longitudinal, qualitative, quasi-research study of in-service and pre-service teachers' opinions. *Educational Horizon, 87*(1), 61–68.

Wang, Y., Kim, S. Y., Anderson, E. R., Chen, A. C., & Yan, N. (2012). Parent-child acculturation discrepancy, perceived parental knowledge, peer deviance, and adolescent delinquency in Chinese immigrant families. *Journal of Youth and Adolescence, 41*(7), 907–919. doi:10.1007/s10964–011–9705-z

Watson, J. B. (1914). *Behavior: An introduction to comparative psychology*. New York: Holt, Rinehart and Winston.

Watson, J. B. (1925). *Behaviorism*. New York: W. W. Norton.

Watson, J. B., & Rayner, R. (1920). Conditioned emotional reactions. *Journal of Experimental Psychology, 3*(1), 1–14.

Weinstein, C. S., Tomlinson-Clarke, S., & Curran, M. (2004). Toward a conception of culturally responsive classroom management. *Journal of Teacher Education, 55*(1), 25–38. doi:10.1177/0022487103259812

Weinstock, M., Assor, A., & Broide, G. (2009). Schools as promoters of moral judgment: The essential role of teachers' encouragement of critical thinking. *Social Psychology of Education, 12*(1), 137–151. doi:10.1007/s11218–008–9068–9

Zewelanji, S., Hayling, C. C., Stevenson, H., & Kem, L. (2013). Cultural considerations in the development of school-based interventions for African American adolescent boys

with emotional and behavioral disorders. *Journal of Negro Education, 78*(3), 321–332.

Zimbardo, P. G., & Gerrig, R. J. (2004). *Psychology and life* (17th ed.). Boston: Allyn & Bacon.

Chapter 2 References

Achilles, G. M., McLaughlin, M. J., & Croninger, R. G. (2007). Sociocultural correlates of disciplinary exclusion among students with emotional, behavioral, and learning disabilities in the SEELS national dataset. *Journal of Emotional and Behavioral Disorders, 15*(1), 33–45.

Americans with Disabilities Act of 1990, 42 U.S.C.A. § 12131 *et seq.* (1990).

Americans with Disabilities Act Amendments of 2008, Pub. L. No. 110–325, 42 U.S.C.A § 12101 *et seq.* (2008).

Arnberger, K., & Shoop, R. (2006). A principal's guide to manifestation determination. *Principal Leadership, 6*(9), 16–21.

Board of Education of Independent School District No. 92 of Pottawatomie County v. Earls, 536 U.S. 822 (2002).

Bowman, L. (2011). Americans with Disabilities Act as amended: Principles and practice. *New Directions for Adult and Continuing Education, 132*, 85–95. doi:100.1002/ace.434

Couvillon, M. A., Bullock, L. M., & Gable, R. A. (2009). Tracking behavior assessment methodology and support strategies: A national survey of how schools utilize functional behavioral assessments and behavior intervention plans. *Emotional and Behavioural Difficulties, 14*(3), 215–228. doi:10.1080/13632750903073459

Dray, B. J., & Wisneski, D. B. (2011). Mindful reflection as a process for developing culturally responsive practices. *Teaching Exceptional Children, 44*(1), 28–36.

Education for All Handicapped Children Act of 1975, Pub. L. No. 94–142, 89 Stat. 773 (1975).

Erickson, M. J., Stage, S. C., & Nelson, J. R. (2006). Naturalistic study of the behavior of students with EBD referred for functional behavioral assessment. *Journal of Emotional and Behavioral Disorders, 14*(1), 31–40.

Espelage, D. L., & Swearer, S. M. (Eds.). (2010). *Bullying in North American schools: A social-ecological perspective on prevention and intervention* (2nd ed.). New York: Routledge.

Etscheidt, S. (2006). Behavioral intervention plans: Pedagogical and legal analysis of issues. *Behavioral Disorders, 31*(2), 223–243.

Fowler, D. (2011a). School discipline feeds the "pipeline to prison." *Phi Delta Kappan, 93*(2), 14–19.

Fowler, D. (2011b). *Texas' school to prison pipeline: Ticketing, arrest, and use of force in schools.* Austin: Texas Appleseed.

Goss v. Lopez, 419 U.S. 565 (1975).

Gottlieb v. Laurel Highlands School District, 272 F.3d 168, 172 (3rd Cir. 2001).

Hemet California Unified School District, 54 IDELR 328 (OCRIX, San Francisco [CA] 2009).

Honig v. Doe, 484 U.S. 305 (1988).

Horner, R. H., Sugai, G., Smolkowski, K., Eber, L., Nakasato, J., Todd, A. W., & Esperanza, J. (2009). A randomized, wait-list controlled effectiveness trial assessing school-wide positive behavior support in elementary schools. *Journal of Positive Behavior Interventions, 11*(3), 133–144. doi:10.1177/1098300709332067

Imler, S. J. (2009). Becoming culturally responsive: A need for preservice teacher candidates. *Teacher Education and Practice, 22*(3), 351–367.

Individuals with Disabilities Education Improvement Act of 2004, Pub. L. No. 108–446, 20 U.S.C. § 300 *et seq.* (2004).

Ingraham v. Wright, 430 U.S. 651 (1977).

Jackson v. Northwest Local School District, 55 IDELR 71 (S.D. Ohio 2010).

JGS by Sterner v. Titusville Area School District, 737 F. Supp. 2d 449 (W.D. PA 2010).

Kaplan, S. G., & Cornell, D. G. (2005). Threats of violence by students in special education. *Behavioral Disorders, 31*(1), 107–119.

Katsiyannis, A., Losinski, M., & Prince, A. M. T. (2012). Litigation and students with disabilities: A persistent concern. *NASSP Bulletin, 96*(1), 23–43. doi:10.1177/0192636511431008

Killu, K., Weber, K. P., Derby, K. M., & Barretto, A. (2006). Behavior intervention planning and implementation of positive behavioral support plans: An examination of states' adherence to standards for practice. *Journal of Positive Behavior Interventions, 8*(4), 195–199.

Maag, J. W., & Katsiyannis, A. (2006). Behavioral intervention plans: Legal and practical considerations for students with emotional and behavioral disorders. *Behavioral Disorders, 31*(4), 348–362.

McAfee, J. K., Schwilk, C., & Mitruski, M. (2006). Public policy on physical restraint of children with disabilities in public schools. *Education and Treatment of Children, 29*(4), 711–728.

Melissa S. v. School District of Pittsburgh, 183 Fed. Appx. 184 (3d Cir. 2006).

Mohr, W. K., LeBel, J., O'Halloran, R., & Preustch, C. (2010). Tied up and isolated in the schoolhouse. *Journal of School Nursing, 26*(2), 91–101.

Moreno, G. (2010). No need to count to ten: Advocating for the early implementation of the functional behavioural assessment in addressing challenging behaviors. *Emotional and Behavioural Difficulties, 15*(1), 15–22. doi:10.1080/13632750903512373

New Jersey v. T.L.O., 469 U.S. 325 (1980).

Niesyn, M. (2009). Strategies for success: Evidence-based instructional practices for students with emotional and behavioral disorders. *Preventing School Failure, 53*(4), 227–233.

Peterson, R., Albrecht, S., & Johns, B. (2009). CCBD's position summary on the use of physical restraint procedures in school settings. *Behavioral Disorders, 34*(4), 223–234.

Rehabilitation Act of 1973, Section 504, 29 U.S.C. § 794 *et seq.* (1973).

Reinke, W. M., Herman, K. C., & Stormont, M. (2013). Classroom-level positive behavior supports in schools implementing SW-PBIS: Identifying areas for enhancement. *Journal of Positive Behavior Interventions, 15*(1), 39–50. doi:10.11771098300712459079

Ryan, J., & Peterson, R. (2004). Physical restraint in school. *Behavioral Disorders, 29*(2), 154–168.

Shah, N. (2011). Policy fight brews over discipline. *Education Week, 31*(7), 1–2.

Shepherd, T. L. (2010). *Working with students with emotional and behavior disorders: Characteristics and teaching strategies.* Upper Saddle River, NJ: Merrill.

Sindelar, P. T., Shearer, D. K., Yendol-Hoppey, D., & Liebert, T. W. (2006). The sustainability of inclusive school reform. *Exceptional Children, 72*(3), 317–331.

Stormont, M., & Reinke, W. (2009). The importance of precorrective statements and behavior-specific praise and strategies to increase their use. *Beyond Behavior, 18*(3), 26–32.

Stormont, M., Reinke, W., & Herman, K. (2011). Teachers' knowledge of evidence-based interventions and available school resources for children with emotional and behavioral problems. *Journal of Behavioral Education, 20*(2), 138–147.

Sugai, G., & Horner, R. H. (2009). Responsiveness-to-intervention and school-wide positive behavior supports: Integration of multi-tiered system approaches. *Exceptionality, 17*(4), 223–237. doi:10.1080/09362830903235375

Sutton v. United Air Lines, Inc., 527 U.S. 471 (1999).

Thompson, H. A. (2011). Criminalizing kids: The overlooked reason for failing schools. *Dissent, 58*(4), 23–27.

Tinker v. Des Moines Independent School District, 393 U.S. 503 (1969).

Toyota Motor Manufacturing v. Williams, 534 U.S. 184 (2002).

Turner, R. K., & Goodner, M. (2010). *Passing the paddle: Nondisclosure of children's criminal cases.* Austin: State Bar of Texas.

U.S. Department of Education, Office for Civil Rights. (1988). Letter of finding. EHLR 307.06.

U.S. Department of Education, Office for Civil Rights. (2010, October 26). *Dear colleague letter: Harassment and bullying.* Retrieved from http://www2.ed.gov/about/offices/list/ocr/letters/colleague-201010.pdf

U.S. Department of Education, Office of Special Education Programs. (1995). Memorandum 95–16, 22 IDELR 531.

Van Acker, R., Boreson, L., Gable, R. A., & Potterton, T. (2005). Are we on the right course? Lessons learned about current FBA/BIP practices in schools. *Journal of Behavioral Education, 14*(1), 35–56.

Van Haren, B. A., & Fiedler, C. (2004). Physical restraint and seclusion of students with disabilities. *Beyond Behavior, 13*(3), 17–19.

Vernonia School District v. Acton, 515 U.S. 646 (1995).

Weber, M. C. (2010). A new look at Section 504 and the ADA in special education cases. *Texas Journal on Civil Liberties and Civil Rights, 16*(1), 1–27.

Zirkel, P. A. (2009). What does the law say? *Teaching Exceptional Children, 41*(5), 73–75.

Chapter 3 References

Amatea, E. S., Cholewa, B., & Mixon, K. A. (2012). Influencing preservice teachers' attitudes about working with low-income and/or ethnic minority families. *Urban Education, 47*(4), 801–834. doi:10.1177 10042085912436846

Beard, K. S., Hoy, W. K., & Woolfolk Hoy, A. (2010). Academic optimism of individual teachers: Confirming a new construct. *Teaching and Teacher Education, 26*(5), 1136–1144.

Bower, H. A., Bowen, N. K., & Powers, J. D. (2011). Family-faculty trust as measured with the Elementary School Success Profile. *Children & Schools, 33*(3), 158–167. doi:10.1093/cs/33.3.158

Bronfenbrenner, U. (1979). *The ecology of human development: Experiments by nature and design.* Cambridge, MA: Harvard University Press.

Bronfenbrenner, U. (2005). Interacting systems of human development. Research paradigms: Present and future. In U. Bronfenbrenner (Ed.), *Making human beings human: Bioecological perspectives on human development* (pp. 67–93). Thousand Oaks, CA: Sage.

Carter, B., & McGoldrick, M. (1999). *The expanded family life cycle: Individual, family, and social perspectives* (3rd ed.). Boston: Allyn & Bacon.

Children's Defense Fund. (2012). *The state of America's children: 2012.* Washington, DC: Author.

Children's Defense Fund. (2013). *Factsheet: Children in the United States.* Retrieved from http://www.childrensdefense.org/child-research-data-publications/data/state-data-repository/cits/2013/2013-united-states-children-in-the-states.pdf

Christian, L. G. (2006). Understanding families: Applying family systems theory to early childhood practice. *Young Children, 61*(1), 12–20.

Council for Exceptional Children. (2008). *What every special educator must know: Ethics, standards, and guidelines* (6th ed.). Arlington, VA: Author.

Dardig, J. C. (2005). The *McClurg Monthly Magazine* and 14 more practical ways to involve parents. *Teaching Exceptional Children, 38*(2), 46–51.

Ferlazzo, L. (2011). Involvement or engagement? *Educational Leadership, 68*(8), 10–14.

Hoy, W. K., Tarter, C. J., & Woolfolk Hoy, A. (2006). Academic optimism of schools: A force for student achievement. *American Educational Research Journal, 43*(3), 425–446.

Hyland, N., & Heuschkel, K. (2010). Fostering understanding of institutional oppression among U.S. preservice teachers. *Teaching and Teacher Education, 26*(4), 821–829.

Ide, B., Dingmann, C., Cuevas, E., & Meehan, M. (2010). Psychometric testing of the FACES III with rural adolescents. *Journal of Family Social Work, 13*(5), 410–419. doi:10.1080/10522150903513993

Khaleque, A. (2013). Perceived parental warmth, and children's psychological adjustment, and personality dispositions: A meta-analysis. *Journal of Child and Family Studies, 22*(2), 297–306. doi:10.1007/s10826–012–9579-z

Leflot, G., Onghena, P., & Colpin, H. (2010). Teacher–child interactions: Relations with children's self-concept in second grade. *Infant and Child Development, 19*(4), 385–405. doi:10.1002/icd.672

McGoldrick, M., Carter, B., & Garcia-Preto, N. (2011). *The expanded family life cycle: Individual, family, and social perspectives* (4th ed.). Upper Saddle River, NJ: Pearson.

Michael-Tsabari, N., & Lavee, Y. (2012). Too close and too rigid: Applying the circumplex model of family systems to first-generation family firms. *Journal of Marital & Family Therapy, 38*(1), 105–116. doi:10.1111/j.1752–0606.2012.00302.x

National Center for Education Statistics. (2010). *2010 condition of education.* Washington, DC: U.S. Department of Education.

National Center for Education Statistics. (2013). *The condition of education 2013: English language learners.* Washington, DC: U.S. Department of Education.

Olson, D. (2011). FACES IV and the circumplex model: Validation study. *Journal of Marital & Family Therapy, 37*(1), 64–80. doi:10.1111/j.1752–0606.2009.00175.x

Turnbull, A., Turnbull, R., Erwin, E. J., Soodak, L. C., & Shogren, K. A. (2011). *Families, professionals, and exceptionality: Positive outcomes through partnerships and trust* (6th ed.). Upper Saddle River, NJ: Pearson.

Uludag, A. (2008). Elementary pre-service teachers' opinions about parental involvement in elementary children's education. *Teaching and Teacher Education, 24*(3), 807–817.

U.S. Department of Agriculture, Food and Nutrition Service. (2013). Program data. Retrieved from http://www.fns.usda.gov/pd/cnpmain.htm

Van Campen, K. S., & Russell, S. T. (2010). *Cultural differences in parenting practices: What Asian American families can teach us* (Frances McClelland Institute for Children, Youth, and Families ResearchLink, Vol. 2, No. 1). Tucson: University of Arizona.

Vine, K. (2011, December). The breakfast taco. *Texas Monthly*. Retrieved from http://www.texasmonthly.com/story/breakfast-taco

Wiley, A. L., Brigham, F. J., Kauffman, J. M., & Bogan, J. E. (2013). Disproportionate poverty, conservatism, and the disproportionate identification of minority students with emotional and behavioral disorders. *Education and Treatment of Children, 36*(4), 29–50.

Woolfolk Hoy, A., Hoy, W. K., & Kurz, N. M. (2008). Teacher's academic optimism: The development and test of a new construct. *Teaching and Teacher Education, 24*(4), 821–835.

Yoshikawa, H., Aber, J. L., & Beardslee, W. R. (2012). The effects of poverty on the mental, emotional, and behavioral health of children and youth: Implications for prevention. *American Psychologist, 67*(4), 272–284.

Chapter 4 References

Association of American Educators. (2013). Code of ethics for educators. Retrieved from http://www.aaeteachers.org/index.php/about-us/aae-code-of-ethics

Barrett, D. E., Casey, J. E., Visser, R. D., & Headley, K. N. (2012). How do teachers make judgments about ethical and unethical behaviors? Toward the development of a code of conduct for teachers. *Teaching and Teacher Education, 28*(6), 890–898.

Bullough, R. V., Jr. (2011). Ethical and moral matters in teaching and teacher education. *Teaching and Teacher Education, 27*(1), 21–28.

Clunies-Ross, P., Little, E., & Kienhuis, M. (2008). Self-reported and actual use of proactive and reactive classroom management strategies and their relationship with teacher stress and student behaviour. *Educational Psychology, 28*(6), 693–710.

Council for Exceptional Children. (2008). *What every special educator must know: Ethics, standards, and guidelines* (6th ed.). Arlington, VA: Author.

Fernet, C., Guay, F., Senécal, C., & Austin, S. (2012). Predicting intraindividual changes in teacher burnout: The role of perceived school environment and motivational factors. *Teaching and Teacher Education, 28*(4), 514–525. doi:10.1016/j.tate.2011.11.013

Foulger, T. S., Ewbank, A. D., Kay, A., Popp, S. O., & Carter, H. L. (2009). Moral spaces in MySpace: Preservice teachers' perspectives about ethical issues in social networking. *Journal of Research on Technology in Education, 42*(1), 1–28.

Harmer, J. (2007). *The practice of English language teaching* (4th ed.). London: Person Longman ELT.

Leiter, M. P., & Maslach, C. (2005). *Banishing burnout: Six strategies for improving your relationship with work*. New York: Jossey-Bass.

Löfström, E., & Poom-Valickis, K. (2013). Beliefs about teaching: Persistent or malleable? A longitudinal study of prospective student teachers' beliefs. *Teaching and Teacher Education, 35*, 104–113.

Mehta, S. B., Cornell, D., Fan, X., & Gregory, A. (2013). Bullying climate and school engagement in ninth-grade students. *Journal of School Health, 83*(1), 45–52. doi:10.1111/j.1746-1561.2012.00746.x

Morones, A. (2013). Paddling persists in U.S. schools. *Education Week, 33*(9), 1–11.

National Education Association. (2013). Code of ethics. Retrieved from http://www .nea.org/home/30442.htm

Olson, J., Clough, M., & Penning, K. (2009). Prospective elementary teachers gone wild? An analysis of Facebook self-portrayals and expected dispositions of preservice elementary teachers. *Contemporary Issues in Technology and Teacher Education, 9*(4), 443–475.

Olweus, D. (1993). *Bullying at school: What we know and what we can do.* Cambridge, MA: Blackwell.

Preston, J. (2011, December 17). Rules to stop pupil and teacher from getting too social online. *New York Times.* Retrieved from http://www.nytimes.com/2011/12/18/business/media/rules-to-limit-how-teachers-and-students-interact-online.html?_r=0

Read, B. (2007, April 27). A MySpace photo costs a student a teaching certificate. *Chronicle of Higher Education.* Retrieved from https://chronicle.com/blogs/wired campus/a-myspace-photo-costs-a-student-a-teaching-certificate/2994

Smith, P. K., Mahdavi, J., Carvalho, M., Fisher, S., Russell, S., & Tippett, N. (2008). Cyberbullying: Its nature and impact in secondary school pupils. *Journal of Child Psychology and Psychiatry, 49,* 376–385.

Tabassum, F., & Ali, M. A. (2012). Professional self-esteem of secondary school teachers. *Asian Social Science, 8*(2), 206–210. doi:10.5539/ass.v8n2p206

Thomas, L., & Beauchamp, C. (2011). Understanding new teachers' professional identities through metaphor. *Teaching and Teacher Education, 27*(4), 762–769.

U.S. Department of Health and Human Services. (n.d.). StopBullying.gov website, http://www.stopbullying.gov.

Whitted, K. S., & Dupper, D. R. (2005). Best practices for preventing or reducing bullying in schools. *Children & Schools, 27*(3), 167–175.

Chapter 5 References

Bennett, N., & Blundell, D. (1983). Quantity and quality of work in rows and classroom groups. *Educational Psychology, 3*(2), 93–105.

Betoret, F., & Artiga, A. (2004). Trainee teachers' conceptions of teaching and learning, classroom layout and exam design. *Educational Studies, 30*(4), 354–372.

Bicard, D. F., Ervin, A., Bicard, S. C., Baylot-Casey, L. (2012). Differential effects of seating arrangements on disruptive behavior of fifth grade students during independent seatwork. *Journal of Applied Behavior Analysis, 45*(2), 407–411.

Bonus, M., & Riordan, L. (1998). *Increasing student on-task behavior though the use of specific seating arrangements.* ERIC Document Reproduction Service No. ED422129.

Burden, P. R. (2003). *Classroom management: Creating a successful learning community* (2nd ed.). New York: John Wiley.

Cangelosi, J. S. (2000). *Classroom management strategies: Gaining and maintaining students' cooperation* (4th ed.). New York: John Wiley.

Canter, L., & Canter, M. (1992). *Assertive discipline: Positive management for today's classroom* (2nd ed.). Santa Monica, CA: Canter and Associates.

Canter, L., & Canter, M. (2001). *Assertive discipline: Positive management for today's classroom* (3rd ed.). Seal Beach, CA: Canter and Associates.

Charles, C. M. (2011). *Building classroom discipline* (10th ed.). Boston: Pearson.

Colker, L. J. (2008). Twelve characteristics of effective early childhood teachers. *Young Children, 63*(2), 86–73.

Cotton, K. (1995). *Effective schooling practices: A research synthesis 1995 update.* Retrieved from http://www.nwrel.org/scpd/esp/esp95 .html

Cotton, K. (2000). *The schooling practices that matter most.* Alexandria, VA: Association for Supervision and Curriculum Development.

Downing, J. E., & Peckham-Hardin, K. D. (2001). Daily schedules: A helpful learning tool. *Teaching Exceptional Children, 33*(3), 62–68.

Doyle, W. (2006). Ecological approaches to classroom management. In C. Evertson & C. Weinstein (Eds.), *Handbook of classroom management: Research, practice, and contemporary issues* (pp. 97–125). New York: Lawrence Erlbaum.

Epstein, M., Atkins, M., Cullinan, D., Kutash, K., & Weaver, R. (2008). *Reducing behavior problems in the elementary school classroom: A practice guide* (NCEE No. 2008–012). Washington, DC: National Center for Education Evaluation and Regional Assistance, Institute of Education Sciences, U.S. Department of Education. Retrieved from http://ies.ed.gov/ncee/wwc/publications/practiceguides

Fernandes, A. C., Huang, J., & Rinaldo, V. (2011). Does where a student sits really matter? The impact of seating locations on student classroom learning. *International Journal of Applied Environmental Studies, 10*(1), 66–77.

Ginott, H. (1965). *Between parent and child: New solutions to old problems.* New York: Macmillan.

Ginott, H. (1969). *Between parent and teenager.* New York: Macmillan.

Ginott, H. (1972). *Teacher and child: A book for parents and teachers.* New York: Macmillan.

Ginott, H. (2009/2010). They said it first, . . . *Phi Delta Kappan, 9*(4), 7.

Ingersoll, R. M., & Smith, T. M. (2003). The wrong solution to the teacher shortage. *Educational Leadership, 60*(8), 30–33.

Jones, F. (1987). *Positive classroom discipline.* New York: McGraw-Hill.

Kamps, D. M. (2002). Preventing problems by improving behavior. In B. Algozzine & P. Kay (Eds.), *Preventing problem behaviors: A handbook of successful prevention strategies* (pp. 11–36). Thousand Oaks, CA: Corwin.

Kaya, N., & Burgess, B. (2007). Territoriality: Seat preferences in different types of classroom arrangements. *Environment & Behavior, 39*(6), 859–876.

Kounin, J. S. (1970). *Discipline and group management in classrooms.* New York: Holt, Rinehart and Winston.

Little, S. G., & Akin-Little, K. A. (2003). Classroom management. In W. O'Donohue, J. Fisher, & S. Hayes (Eds.), *Cognitive behavior therapy: Applying empirically supported techniques in your practice* (pp. 65–70). Hoboken, NJ: John Wiley.

Little, S. G., & Akin-Little, A. (2008). Psychology's contribution to classroom management. *Psychology in the Schools, 45*(3), 227–234. doi:10.1002/pits.20293

Malmgren, K. W., Trezek, B. J., & Paul, P. V. (2005). Models of classroom management as applied to the secondary classroom. *The Clearing House, 79*(1), 36–39.

Martella, R. C., Nelson, J. R., Marchand-Martella, N. E., & O'Reilly, M. (2012). *Comprehensive behavior management: Individualized, classroom, and schoolwide approaches* (2nd ed.). Thousand Oaks, CA: Sage.

Marx, A., Fuhrer, U., & Hartig, T. (2000). Effects of classroom seating arrangements on children's question-asking. *Learning Environments Research, 2*(3), 249–263.

McIntosh, K., Herman, K., Sanford A., McGraw K., & Kira, F. (2004). Teaching transitions: Techniques for promoting success between lessons. *Teaching Exceptional Children, 37*(1), 32–38.

Meadan, H., Ostrosky, M. M., Triplett, B., Micha, A., & Fettig, A. (2011). Using visual supports with young children with autism spectrum disorders. *Teaching Exceptional Children, 43*(2), 28–35.

Meese, R. L. (2001). *Teaching learners with mild disabilities: Integrating research and practice* (2nd ed.). Belmont, CA: Wadsworth/Thomson Learning.

Ratcliff, N. J., Jones, C. R., Costner, R. H., Savage-Davis, E., Sheehan, H., & Hunt, G. H.

(2010). Teacher classroom management behaviors and student time-on-task: Implications for teacher education. *Action in Teacher Education, 32*(4), 38–51. doi:10.1080/01626620.2010.549714

Reutzel, D. R., & Clark, S. (2011). Organizing literacy classrooms for effective instruction: A survival guide. *Reading Teacher, 65*(2), 96–109.

Rosenfield, P., Lambert, N. M., & Black, A. (1985). Desk arrangement effects on pupil classroom behavior. *Journal of Educational Psychology, 77*(1), 101–108.

Shook, A. C. (2012). A study of preservice educators' dispositions to change behavior management strategies. *Preventing School Failure, 56*(2), 129–136. doi:10.1080/1045 988X.2011.606440

Short, P. M., Short, R. J., & Blanton, C. (1994). *Rethinking student discipline: Alternatives that work.* Thousand Oaks, CA: Corwin.

Stronge, J. H. (2007). *Qualities of effective teachers* (2nd ed.). Alexandria, VA: Association for Supervision and Curriculum Development.

Trussell, R. P. (2008). Classroom universals to prevent problem behaviors. *Intervention in School and Clinic, 43*(3), 179–185. doi:10.1177/1053451207311678

Walker, R. J. (2008). Twelve characteristics of an effective teacher: A longitudinal, qualitative, quasi-research study of in-service and pre-service teachers' opinions. *Educational Horizons, 87*(1), 61–68.

Wannarka, R., & Ruhl, K. (2008). Seating arrangements that promote positive academic and behavioural outcomes: A review of empirical research. *Support for Learning, 23*(2), 89–93.

Winterman, K. G., & Sapina, R. H. (2002). Everyone's included: Supporting young children with autism spectrum disorders in a responsive classroom learning environment. *Teaching Exceptional Children, 35*(1), 30–35.

Chapter 6 References

Allday, R. A. (2011). Responsive management: Practical strategies for avoiding overreaction to minor misbehavior. *Intervention in School and Clinic, 46*(5), 292–298. doi:10.1177/1053451210395383

Berk, R. (updated by Baird, D., & Nozik, B.). (2008). *What everyone should know about humor and laughter.* Association for Applied and Therapeutic Humor. Retrieved from http://www.laffingoutloud.com/pdf/aath.pdf

Borrego, J., Jr., Ibanez, E. S., Spendlove, S. J., & Pemberton, J. R. (2007). Treatment acceptability among Mexican American parents. *Behavior Therapy, 38*(3), 218–227.

Donaldson, J. M., & Vollmer, T. R. (2011). An evaluation and comparison of time-out procedures with and without release contingencies. *Journal of Applied Behavior Analysis, 44*(4), 693–705.

Gable, R. A., Hester, P. H., Rock, M. L., & Hughes, K. G. (2009). Back to basics: Rules, praise, ignoring, and reprimands revisited. *Intervention in School and Clinic, 44*(4), 195–205. doi:10.1177/10534 51208328831

Garrick Duhaney, L. M. (2003). A practical approach to managing the behaviors of students with ADD. *Intervention in School and Clinic, 38*(5), 267–279.

Hammond, H., Dupoux, E., & Ingalls, L. (2004). Culturally relevant classroom management strategies for American Indian students. *Rural and Special Education Quarterly, 23*(4), 3–9.

Hester, P. P., Hendrickson, J. M., & Gable, R. A. (2009). Forty years later: The value of praise, ignoring, and rules for preschoolers at risk for behavior disorders. *Education and Treatment of Children, 32*(4), 513–535.

Holt, C., Hargrove, P., & Harris, S. (2011). An investigation into the life experiences and beliefs of teachers exhibiting highly effective classroom management behaviors. *Teacher Education and Practice, 24*(1), 96–113.

Kalis, T. M., Vannest, K., & Parker, R. (2007). Praise counts: Using self-monitoring to increase effective teaching practices. *Preventing School Failure, 51*(3), 20–27. doi:10.3200/PSFL.51.3.20–27

Kazdin, A. E. (1977). *The token economy: A review and evaluation.* New York: Plenum Press.

Kodak, T., Northup, J., & Kelley, M. (2007). An evaluation of the types of attention that maintain problem behavior. *Journal of Applied Behavior Analysis, 40*(1), 167–171. doi:10.1901/jaba.2007.43–06

Kostewicz, D. E. (2010). A review of timeout ribbons. *Behavior Analyst Today, 11*(2), 95–104.

Little, S. G., & Akin-Little, A. (2008). Psychology's contributions to classroom management. *Psychology in the Schools, 45*(3), 227–234. doi:10.1002/pits.20293

Maggin, D. M., Chafouleas, S. M., Goddard, K. M., & Johnson, A. H. (2011). A systematic evaluation of token economies as a classroom management tool for students with challenging behavior. *Journal of School Psychology, 49*(5), 529–554. doi:10.1016/j.jsp.2011.05.001

Moore Partin, T. C., Robertson, R. E., Maggin, D. M., Oliver, R. M., & Wehby, J. H. (2010). Using teacher praise and opportunities to respond to promote appropriate student behavior. *Preventing School Failure, 54*(3), 172–178. doi:10.1080/10459880903493179

Mruzek, D. W., Cohen, C., & Smith, T. (2007). Contingency contracting with students with autism spectrum disorders in a public school setting. *Journal of Developmental and Physical Disabilities, 19*(2), 103–114.

Murray, C., & Greenberg, M. T. (2006). Examining the importance of social relationships and social contexts in the lives of children with high-incidence disabilities. *Journal of Special Education, 39*(4), 220–233.

Musti-Rao, S., & Haydon, T. (2011). Strategies to increase behavior-specific teacher praise in an inclusive environment. *Intervention in School and Clinic, 47*(2), 91–97. doi:10.1177/1053451211414187

Navarro, J. I., Aguilar, M., Aguilar, C., Alcalde, C., & Marchena, E. (2007). Positive behavioral intervention in children who were wards of the court attending a mainstream school. *Psychological Reports, 101*(3), 1067–1078. doi:10.2466/pr0.101.4.1067–1078

Niesyn, M. (2009). Strategies for success: Evidence-based instructional practices for students with emotional and behavioral disorders. *Preventing School Failure, 53*(4), 227–233.

Obenchain, K. M., & Taylor, S. S. (2005). Behavior management: Making it work in middle and secondary schools. *The Clearing House, 79*(1), 7–11.

Payne, L. D., Mancil, G. R., & Landers, E. (2005). Consequence-based behavioral interventions for classroom teachers. *Beyond Behavior, 15*(1), 13–20.

Pierangelo, R., & Giuliani, G. (2008). *Classroom management for students with emotional and behavioral disorders: A step-by-step guide for educators.* Thousand Oaks, CA: Corwin.

Premack, D. C. (1965). Reinforcement theory. In D. Levine (Ed.), *Nebraska Symposium on Motivation* (pp. 123–180). Lincoln: University of Nebraska Press.

Ryan, J. B., Sanders, S., Katsiyannis, A., & Yell, M. L. (2007). Using time-out effectively in the classroom. *Teaching Exceptional Children, 39*(4), 60–67.

Sarafino, E. P. (2012). *Applied behavior analysis: Principles and procedures for modifying behavior.* Hoboken, NJ: John Wiley.

Sidman, M. (2006). The distinction between positive and negative reinforcement: Some additional considerations. *Behavior Analyst, 29*(1), 135–139.

Skinner, B. F. (1953). *Science and human behavior.* New York: Free Press.

Skinner, B. F. (1994). Selection by consequences. In A. C. Catania & S. Harnad (Eds.), *The selection of behavior: The operant behaviorism of*

B. F. Skinner. Comments and consequences (pp. 11–76). Cambridge: Cambridge University Press.

Skinner, M. E. (2010). All joking aside: Five reasons to use humor in the classroom. *Education Digest, 76*(2),19–21.

Stormont, M., & Reinke, W. (2009). The importance of precorrective statements and behavior-specific praise and strategies to increase their use. *Beyond Behavior, 18*(3), 26–32.

Trussell, R. P. (2008). Classroom universals to prevent problem behaviors. *Intervention in School and Clinic, 43*(3), 179–185. doi:10.1177/1053451207311678

Walker, H. M., Ramsey, E., & Gresham, F. M. (2004). *Antisocial behavior in school: Strategies and best practices* (2nd ed.). Pacific Grove, CA: Brooks/Cole.

Weinstein, C. S., Tomlinson-Clarke, S., & Curran, M. (2004). Toward a conception of culturally responsive classroom management. *Journal of Teacher Education, 55*(1), 25–38. doi:10.1177/0022487103259812

Chapter 7 References

Allen, J. R., Allen, S. F., Latrobe, K. H., Brand, M., Pfefferbaum, B., Elledge, B., . . . Guffey, M. (2012). The power of story: The role of bibliotherapy for the library. *Children and Libraries, 10*(1), 44–49.

Bandura, A. (1976). Self-reinforcement: Theoretical and methodological considerations. *Behaviorism, 4*(2), 135–155.

Briesch, A. M., & Chafouleas, S. M. (2009). Review and analysis of literature on self-management interventions to promote appropriate classroom behaviors (1988–2008). *School Psychology Quarterly, 24*(2), 106–118. doi:10.1037/a0016159.

Candelaria, A. M., Fedewa, A. L., & Ahn, S. (2012). The effects of anger management on children's social and emotional outcomes: A meta-analysis. *School Psychology International, 33*(6), 596–614. doi:10.1177/0143034312454360

Chafouleas, S. M., Hagermoser Sanetti, L. M., Jaffery, R., & Fallon, L. M. (2012). An evaluation of a classwide intervention package involving self-management and a group contingency on classroom behavior of middle school students. *Journal of Behavioral Education, 21*(1), 34–57. doi:10.1007/s10864–011–9135–8

Committee for Children. (2002). *Second Step: A violence prevention curriculum*. Seattle: Author. Retrieved from http://www.cfchildren.org

Cook, K. E., Earles-Vollrath, T., & Ganz, J. B. (2006). Bibliotherapy. *Intervention in School and Clinic, 42*(2), 91–100.

Drogan, R. R., & Kern, L. (2014). Examination of the mechanisms underlying effectiveness of the turtle technique. *Topics in Early Childhood Special Education, 33*(4), 237–248.

Forgan, J. W. (2002). Using bibliotherapy to teach problem solving. *Intervention in School and Clinic, 38*(2), 75–82.

Gaines, T., & Barry, L. M. (2008). The effect of a self-monitored relaxation breathing exercise on male adolescent aggressive behavior. *Adolescence, 43*(170), 291–302.

Gartrell, D. (2006). The beauty of class meetings. *YC: Young Children, 61*(6), 54–55.

Heffner, M., Greco, L., & Eifert, G. (2003). Pretend you are a turtle: Children's responses to metaphorical versus literal relation instruction. *Child & Family Behavior Therapy, 25*(1), 19–33.

Herrmann, D. S., & McWhirter, J. J. (2001). *SCARE: Student Created Aggression Replacement Education: Anger reduction for students*. Dubuque, IA: Kendall/Hunt. Retrieved from http://www.arizonachildpsychology.com/The%20SCARE%20Program.pdf

Isbell, J. S., & Jolivette, K. (2011). Stop, think, proceed: Solving problems in the real world. *Intervention in School and Clinic, 47*(1), 31–38.

Jacobson, E. (1938). *Progressive relaxation*. Chicago: University of Chicago Press.

Jensen, P. P., Stevens, P. P., & Kenny, D. D. (2012). Respiratory patterns in students enrolled in schools for disruptive behaviour before, during, and after yoga nidra relaxation. *Journal of Child and Family Studies, 21*(4), 667–681.

Joseph, G. E., & Strain, P. S. (2010). *Helping young children control anger and handle disappointment.* Center on the Social and Emotional Foundations for Early Learning, Vanderbilt University. Retrieved from http://csefel.vanderbilt.edu/modules/module2/handout7.pdf

Kellner, M. H. (2001). *In control: A skill-building program for teaching young adolescents to manage anger.* Champaign, IL: Research Press.

King-Sears, M. E. (2008). Using teacher and researcher data to evaluate the effects of self-management in an inclusive classroom. *Preventing School Failure, 52*(4), 25–34.

Konrad, M., Helf, S., & Itoi, M. (2007). More bang for the book: Using children's literature to promote self-determination and literacy skills. *Teaching Exceptional Children, 40*(1), 64–71.

Lane, K. L., Cook, B. G., & Tankersley, M. (2013). *Research-based strategies for improving outcomes in behavior.* Boston: Pearson Education.

Lopata, C. (2003). Progressive muscle relaxation and aggression among elementary students with emotional or behavioral disorders. *Behavioral Disorders, 28*(2), 162–172.

Lopata, C., Nida, R. E., & Marable, M. A. (2006). Progressive muscle relaxation: Preventing aggression in students with EBD. *Teaching Exceptional Children, 38*(4), 20–25.

Meichenbaum, D. H., & Goodman, J. (1971). Training impulsive children to talk to themselves: A means of developing self-control. *Journal of Abnormal Psychology, 77*(2), 115–126. doi:10.1037/h0030773

Menzies, H. M., Lane, K. L., & Lee, J. M. (2009). Self-monitoring strategies for use in the classroom: A promising practice to support productive behavior for students with emotional or behavioral disorders. *Beyond Behavior, 18*(2), 27–35.

Miller, M., & Nunn, G. D. (2001). Using group discussions to improve social problem-solving and learning. *Education, 121*(3), 470–475.

Mooney, P., Ryan, J. B., Uhing, B. M., Reid, R., & Epstein, M. H. (2005). A review of self-management interventions targeting academic outcomes for students with emotional and behavioral disorders. *Journal of Behavioral Education, 14*(3), 203–221. doi:10.1007/s10864–005–6298–1

Moore, D. W., Anderson, A., Glassenbury, M., Lang, R., & Didden, R. (2013). Increasing on-task behavior in students in a regular classroom: Effectiveness of a self-management procedure using a tactile prompt. *Journal of Behavioral Education, 22*(4), 302–311. doi:10.1007/s10864–013–9180–6

National Institute of Mental Health. (2005). *Depression: What every woman should know.* Retrieved from http://www.nimh.nih.gov/publicat/depwomenknows.cfm

Oakes, W., Lane, K., Cox, M., Magrane, A., Jenkins, A., & Hankins, K. (2012). Tier 2 supports to improve motivation and performance of elementary students with behavioral challenges and poor work completion. *Education and Treatment of Children, 35*(4), 547–584.

Office of Juvenile Justice and Delinquency Prevention. (n.d.). *Second Step: A violence prevention curriculum.* Retrieved from http://www.ojjdp.gov/mpg/mpgprogramdetails.aspx?ID=422

Patton, B., Jolivette, K., & Ramsey, M. (2006). Students with emotional and behavioral disorders can manage their own behaviors. *Teaching Exceptional Children, 39*(2), 14–21.

Rafferty, L. A. (2010). Step-by-step: Teaching students to self-monitor. *Teaching Exceptional Children, 43*(2), 50–58.

Robin, A., Schneider, M., & Dolnick, M. (1976). The turtle technique: An extended case study of self-control in the classroom. *Psychology in the Schools, 13*(4), 449–453.

Robinson, T. (2007). Cognitive behavioral interventions: Strategies to help students make wise behavioral choices. *Beyond Behavior, 17*(1), 7–13.

Robinson, T., Smith, S. W., & Miller, M. (2002). Effect of a cognitive-behavioral intervention on responses to anger by middle school students with chronic behavior problems. *Behavioral Disorders, 27*(3), 256–271.

Sarafino, E. P. (2012). *Applied behavior analysis: Principles and procedures for modifying behavior.* Hoboken, NJ: John Wiley.

Wolpe, J. (1958). *Psychotherapy by reciprocal inhibition.* Stanford, CA: Stanford University Press.

Chapter 8 References

Allday, R. A., Nelson, J. R., & Russel, C. S. (2011). Classroom-based functional behavioral assessment: Does the literature support high fidelity implementation? *Journal of Disability Policy Studies, 22*(3), 140–149. doi:10.1177/1044207311399380

Barnhill, G. P. (2005). Functional behavioral assessment in schools. *Intervention in School and Clinic, 40*(3), 131–143.

Billingsley, B. S., Fall, A., & Williams, T. O., Jr. (2006). Who is teaching students with emotional and behavioral disorders? A profile and comparison to other special educators. *Behavioral Disorders, 31*(3), 252–264.

Borgmeier, C., Horner, R. H., & Koegel, R. L. (2006). An evaluation of the predictive validity of confidence ratings in identifying functional behavioral assessment hypothesis statements. *Journal of Positive Behavior Interventions, 8*(2), 100–105.

Cooper, J. O., Heron, T. E., & Heward, W. L. (2007). *Applied behavior analysis* (2nd ed.). Upper Saddle River, NJ: Pearson.

Couvillon, M. A., Bullock, L. M., & Gable, R. A. (2009). Tracking behavior assessment methodology and support strategies: A national survey of how schools utilize functional behavioral assessments and behavior intervention plans. *Emotional and Behavioural Difficulties, 14*(3), 215–228. doi:10.1080/13632750903073459

Drakeford, W. (2006). *Racial disproportionality in school disciplinary practices.* National Center for Culturally Responsive Education Systems. Retrieved from http://www.nccrest.org/publications/briefs.html

Dray, B. J., & Wisneski, D. B. (2011). Mindful reflection as a process for developing culturally responsive practices. *Teaching Exceptional Children, 44*(1), 28–36.

Erickson, M. J., Stage, S. C., & Nelson, J. R. (2006). Naturalistic study of the behavior of students with EBD referred for functional behavioral assessment. *Journal of Emotional and Behavioral Disorders, 14*(1), 31–40.

Imler, S. J. (2009). Becoming culturally responsive: A need for preservice teacher candidates. *Teacher Education and Practice, 22*(3), 351–367.

Killu, K. (2008). Developing effective behavior intervention plans: Suggestions for school personnel. *Intervention in School and Clinic, 43*(3), 140–149. doi:10.1177/1053451207311610

Linn, D. (2011) Representation of English language learners in special education programs in Texas. *National Teacher Education Journal, 4*(2), 35–40.

Moreno, G., & Bullock, L. M. (2011). Principles of positive behaviour supports: Using the FBA as a problem-solving approach to address challenging behaviours beyond special populations. *Emotional and Behavioural Difficulties, 16*(2), 117–127.

Moreno, G., & Gaytán, F. X. (2012). Reducing subjectivity in special education referrals by educators working with Latino students: Using functional behavioral assessment as a pre-referral practice in student support teams. *Emotional and Behavioural Difficulties, 18*(1), 1–14. doi:10.1080/1363 2752.2012.675132

Riley-Tillman, T. C., Christ, T. J., Chafouleas, S. M., Boice-Mallach, C. H., & Briesch, A. (2011). The impact of observation duration on the accuracy of data obtained from direct behavior rating (DBR). *Journal of Positive Behavior Interventions, 13*(2), 119–128. doi:10.1177/1098300710361954

Scott, T. M., Anderson, C. M., & Spaulding, S. A. (2008). Strategies for developing and carrying out functional assessment and behavior intervention planning. *Preventing School Failure, 52*(3), 39–49.

Stichter, J. P., & Conroy, M. A. (2005). Using structural analysis in natural settings: A responsive functional assessment strategy. *Journal of Behavioral Education, 14*(1), 19–34.

Van Acker, R., Boreson, L., Gable, R. A., & Potterton, T. (2005). Are we on the right course? Lessons learned about current FBA/BIP practices in schools. *Journal of Behavioral Education, 14*(1), 35–56.

World Health Organization. (2004). *Prevention of mental disorders: Effective interventions and policy options.* Geneva: Author.

Zirkel, P. A. (2011). State special education laws for functional behavioral assessment and behavior intervention plans. *Behavioral Disorders, 36*(4), 262–278.

Chapter 9 References

Allday, R. A., Nelson, J. R., & Russel, C. S. (2011). Classroom-based functional behavioral assessment: Does the literature support high fidelity implementation? *Journal of Disability Policy Studies, 22*(3), 140–149. doi:10.11 n/1044207311399380

Athens, E. S., & Vollmer, T. R. (2010). An investigation of differential reinforcement of alternative behavior without extinction. *Journal of Applied Behavior Analysis, 43*(4), 569–589.

Bandura, A. (1986). *Social foundations of thought and action: A social cognitive theory.* Englewood Cliffs, NJ: Prentice-Hall.

Bandura, A. (1997). *Self-efficacy: The exercise of control.* New York: W. H. Freeman.

Blood, E., & Neel, R. S. (2007). From FBA to implementation: A look at what is actually being delivered. *Education and Treatment of Children, 30*(4), 67–80.

Briones, E., Tabernero, C., & Arenas, A. (2007). Effects of disposition and self-regulation of self-defeating behavior. *Journal of Social Psychology, 147*(6), 657–679.

Casoli-Reardon, M., Rappaport, N., Kulick, D., & Reinfield, S. (2012). Ending school avoidance. *Educational Leadership, 70*(2), 50–55.

Clunies-Ross, P., Little, E., & Kienhuis, M. (2008). Self-reported and actual use of proactive and reactive classroom management strategies and their relationship with teacher stress and student behavior. *Educational Psychology, 28*(6), 693–710.

Cooper, J. O., Heron, T. E., & Heward, W. L. (2007). *Applied behavior analysis* (2nd ed.). Upper Saddle, NJ: Pearson.

Crone, D. A., Hawkens, L. S., & Bergstrom, M. K. (2007). A demonstration of training, implementing, and using functional behavioral assessment in 10 elementary and middle school settings. *Journal of Positive Behavior Interventions, 9*(1), 15–29. doi:10.1177 /10983007070090010301

Ducharme, J. M., & Shecter, C. (2011). Bridging the gap between clinical and classroom intervention: Keystone approaches for students with challenging behavior. *School Psychology Review, 40*(2), 257–274.

Dwyer, K., Rozewski, D., & Simonsen, B. (2012). A comparison of function-based replacement behaviors for escape-motivated students. *Journal of Emotional and Behavioral Disorders, 20*(2), 115–125. doi:10.1177/1063426610387432

Elliott, G. C., Cunningham, S. M., Linder, M., Colangelo, M., & Gross, M. (2005). Child physical abuse and self-perceived social isolation among adolescents. *Journal of Interpersonal Violence, 20*(12), 1663–1684. doi:10.1177/0886260505281439

Guardino, C. A., & Fullerton, E. (2010). Changing behaviors by changing the classroom environment. *Teaching Exceptional Children, 42*(6), 8–13.

Hyland, N., & Heuschkel, K. (2010) Fostering understanding of institutional oppression among U.S. preservice teachers. *Teaching and Teacher Education, 26*(4), 821–829.

Individuals with Disabilities Education Improvement Act of 2004, Pub. L. No. 108–446, 20 U.S.C. § 300 *et seq.* (2004).

Ingvarsson, E. T., Hanley, G. P., & Welter, K. M. (2009). Treatment of escape-maintained behavior with positive reinforcement: The role of reinforcement contingency and density. *Education and Treatment of Children, 32*(3), 371–401.

Kamps, D., Wendland, M., & Culpepper, M. (2006). Active teacher participation in functional behavior assessment for students with emotional and behavior disorder risks in general education classrooms. *Behavioral Disorders, 31*(2), 128–146.

LaRue, R. H., Sloman, K. N., Weiss, M. J., Delmolino, L., Hansford, A., Szalony, J., Madigan, R., & Lambright, N. M. (2011). Correspondence between traditional models of functional analysis and a functional analysis of manding behavior. *Research in Developmental Disabilities, 32*(6), 2449–2457.

Maag, J. W., & Katsiyannis, A. (2006). Behavioral intervention plans: Legal and practical considerations for students with emotional and behavioral disorders. *Behavioral Disorders, 31*(4), 348–362.

Milner, H. R., III, & Tenore, F. B. (2010). Classroom management in diverse classrooms. *Urban Education, 45*(5), 560–603. doi:10.1177/0042085910377290

Mueller, M. M., Nkosi, A., & Hine, J. F. (2011). Functional analysis in public schools: A summary of 90 functional analyses. *Journal of Applied Behavior Analysis, 44*(4), 807–818. doi:10.1901/jaba.2011.44–807

Neitzel, J. (2010). Positive behavior supports for children and youth with autism spectrum disorders. *Preventing School Failure, 54*(4), 247–255. doi:10.1080/10459881003745229

Pence, S. T., Roscoe, E. M., Bourret, J. C., & Ahearn, W. H. (2009). Relative contributions of three descriptive methods: Implications for behavioral assessment. *Journal of Applied Behavior Analysis, 42*(2), 425–446. doi:10.1901/jaba.2009.42–425

Pina, A. A., Zerr, A. A., Gonzales, N. A., & Ortiz, C. D. (2009). Psychosocial interventions for school refusal behavior in children and adolescents. *Child Development Perspectives, 3*(1), 11–20. doi:10.1111/j.1750–8606.2008.00070.x

Sarno, J. M., Sterling, H. E., Mueller, M. M., Dufrene, B., Tingstrom, D. H., & Olmi, D. J. (2011). Escape-to-attention as a potential variable for maintaining problem behavior in the school setting. *School Psychology Review, 40*(1), 57–71.

Schieltz, K., Wacker, D., Harding, J., Berg, W., Lee, J., & Padilla Dalmau, Y. (2010). An evaluation of manding across functions prior to functional communication training. *Journal of Development and Physical Disabilities, 22*(2), 131–147. doi:10.1007/s10882–009–9181–5

Scott, T. M., Anderson, C. M., & Spaulding, S. A. (2008). Strategies for developing and carrying out functional assessment and behavior intervention planning. *Preventing School Failure, 52*(3), 39–50. doi:10.3200/PSFL.52.3.39–50

Shumate, E. D., & Wills, H. P. (2010). Classroom-based functional analysis and intervention for disruptive and off-task behaviors. *Education and Treatment of Children, 33*(1), 23–48.

Vladescu, J. C., & Kodak, T. (2010). A review of recent studies on differential reinforcement during skill acquisition in early intervention. *Journal of Applied Behavior Analysis, 43*(2), 351–355.

Volkert, V. M., Lerman, D. C., Call, N. A., & Trosclair-Lasserre, N. (2009). An evaluation of resurgence during treatment with functional communication training. *Journal of Applied Behavior Analysis, 42*(1), 145–160.

Wheatley, R. K., West, R. P., Charlton, C. T., Sanders, R. B., Smith, T. G., & Taylor, M. J. (2009). Improving behavior through differential reinforcement: A praise note system for elementary school students. *Education and Treatment of Children, 32*(4), 551–571.

Wimmer, M. (2008). School refusal. *Principal Leadership, 8*(8), 10–14.

Winborn-Kemmerer, L., Wacker, D. P., Harding, J., Boelter, E., Berg, W., & Lee, J. (2010). Analysis of mand selection across different stimulus conditions. *Education and Treatment of Children, 33*(1), 49–64.

Chapter 10 References

Cartledge, G., Gardner, R., III, & Ford, D. Y. (2009). *Diverse learners with exceptionalities: Culturally responsive teaching in the classroom.* Upper Saddle River, NJ: Pearson Education.

Codding, R. S., Feinberg, A. B., Dunn, E. K., & Pace, G. M. (2005). Effects of immediate performance feedback on the implementation of behavior support plans. *Journal of Applied Behavior Analysis, 38*(20), 205–219.

Couvillon, M. A., Bullock, L. M., & Gable, R. A. (2009). Tracking behavior assessment methodology and support strategies: A national survey of how schools utilize functional behavioral assessments and behavior intervention plans. *Emotional and Behavioural Difficulties, 14*(3), 215–228. doi:10.1080/13632750903073459

Curtis, V. S., Mathur, S. R., & Rutherford, R. B., Jr. (2002). Developing behavioral intervention plans: A step-by-step approach. *Beyond Behavior, 11*(2), 28–31.

Etscheidt, S. (2006). Behavioral intervention plans: Pedagogical and legal analysis of issues. *Behavioral Disorders, 31*(2), 223–243.

Hagermoser Sanetti, L. M., Luiselli, J. K., & Handler, M. W. (2007). Effects of verbal and graphic performance feedback on behavior support plan implementation in a public elementary school. *Behavior Modification, 31*(4), 454–465.

Killu, K. (2008). Developing effective behavior intervention plans: Suggestions for school personnel. *Intervention in School and Clinic, 43*(3), 140–149. doi:10.1177/105345120 7311610

Killu, K., Weber, K. P., Derby, K. M., & Barretto, A. (2006). Behavior intervention planning and implementation of positive behavioral support plans: An examination of states' adherence to standards for practice. *Journal of Positive Behavior Interventions, 8*(4), 195–199.

Lignugaris/Kraft, B., Marchand-Martella, N. E., & Martella, R. C. (2001). Strategies for writing better goals and short-term objectives or benchmarks. *Teaching Exceptional Children, 34*(1), 52–58.

Maag, J. W., & Katsiyannis, A. (2006). Behavioral intervention plans: Legal and practical considerations for students with emotional and behavioral disorders. *Behavioral Disorders, 31*(4), 348–362.

Moreno, G. (2010). No need to count to ten: Advocating for the early implementation of the functional behavioural assessment in addressing challenging behaviors. *Emotional and Behavioural Difficulties, 15*(1), 15–22. doi:10.1080/13632750903512373

Nuri-Robins, K., Lindsey, D. B., Terrell, R. D., & Lindsey, R. B. (2007). Cultural proficiency: Tools for secondary school administrators. *Principal Leadership, 8*(1), 16–22.

Scott, T. M., Anderson, C. M., & Spaulding, S. A. (2008). Strategies for developing and carrying out functional assessment and behavior intervention planning. *Preventing School Failure, 52*(3), 39–50. doi:10.3200/PSFL.52.3.39–50

Shippen, M. E., Simpson, R. G., & Crites, S. A. (2003). A practical guide to functional behavioral assessment. *Teaching Exceptional Children, 35*(5), 36–44.

Van Acker, R., Boreson, L., Gable, R. A., & Potterton, T. (2005). Are we on the right course? Lessons learned about current FBA/BIP practices in schools. *Journal of Behavioral Education, 14*(1), 35–56.

Chapter 11 References

Byiers, B. J., Reichle, J., & Symons, F. J. (2012). Single-subject experimental design for evidence-based practice. *American Journal of Speech-Language Pathology, 21*(4), 397–414. doi:10.1044/1058-0360(2012/11-0036)

Etscheidt, S. (2006). Behavioral intervention plans: Pedagogical and legal analysis of issues. *Behavioral Disorders, 31*(2), 223–243.

Horner, R. H., Carr, E. G., Halle, J., Odom, S., & Wolery, M. (2005). The use of single-subject research to identify evidence-based practice in special education. *Exceptional Children, 71*(2), 165–179.

Horner, R. H., Swaminathan, H., Sugai, G., & Smolkowski, K. (2012). Considerations for the systematic analysis and use of single-case research. *Education and Treatment of Children, 35*(2), 269–290.

Katz, E., & Girolametto, L. (2013). Peer-mediated intervention for preschoolers with ASD implemented in early childhood education settings. *Topics in Early Childhood Special Education, 33*(3), 133–143. doi:10.1177/0271121413484972

Maag, J. W., & Katsiyannis, A. (2006). Behavioral intervention plans: Legal and practical considerations for students with emotional and behavioral disorders. *Behavioral Disorders, 31*(4), 348–362.

McDougall, D., Hawkins, J., Brady, M., & Jenkins, A. (2006). Recent innovations in the changing criterion design: Implications for research and practice in special education. *Journal of Special Education, 40*(1), 2–15.

Nolan, J. D., & Filter, K. J. (2012). A function-based classroom behavior intervention using non-contingent reinforcement plus response cost. *Education and Treatment of Children, 35*(3), 419–430.

Shabani, D. B., & Lam, W. Y. (2013). A review of comparison studies in applied behavior analysis. *Behavioral Interventions, 28*(2), 158–183. doi:10.1002/bin.1361

Skerbetz, M. D., & Kostewicz, D. E. (2013). Academic choice for included students with emotional and behavioral disorders. *Preventing School Failure, 57*(4), 212–222. doi:10.1080/1045988X.2012.701252

Chapter 12 References

Artiles, A. J., Bal, A., & King Thorius, K. A. (2010). Back to the future: A critique of response to intervention's social justice views. *Theory into Practice, 49*(4), 250–257. doi:10.1080/00405841.2010.510447

Barnes, A. C., & Harlacher, J. E. (2008). Clearing the confusion: Response-to-intervention as a set of principles. *Education and Treatment of Children, 31*(3), 417–431.

Bradley, R., Danielson, L., & Doolittle, J. (2005). Response to intervention. *Journal of Learning Disabilities, 38*(6), 485–486.

Calderón, M., Slavin, R., & Sánchez, M. (2011). Effective instruction for English learners. *Future of Children, 21*(1), 103–127.

Education for All Handicapped Children Act of 1975, Pub. L. No. 94–142, 89 Stat. 773 (1975).

Fairbanks, S., Sugai, G., Guardino, D., & Lathrop, M. (2007). Response to intervention: Examining classroom behavior support in second grade. *Exceptional Children, 73*(3), 288–310.

Ferri, B. A. (2012). Undermining inclusion? A critical reading of response to intervention (RTI). *International Journal of Inclusive Education, 16*(8), 863–880.

Fuchs, D., & Fuchs, L. S. (2006). Introduction to RTI: What, why and how valid is it? *Reading Research Quarterly, 41*(1), 93–99.

Fuchs, D., Fuchs, L. S., & Compton, D. L. (2012). Smart RTI: A next generation approach to multilevel prevention. *Exceptional Children, 78*(3), 263–279.

Gresham, F. M., Hunter, K. K., Corwin, E. P., & Fischer, A. J. (2013). Screening, assessment, treatment, and outcome evaluation of behavioral difficulties in an RTI model. *Exceptionality, 21*(1), 19–33. doi:10.1080/09362835.2013.750115

Hammond, R. K., Campbell, J., & Ruble, L. A. (2013). Considering identification and service provision for students with autism spectrum disorders within the context of response to intervention. *Exceptionality, 21*(1), 34–50.

Hernández Finch, M. E. (2012). Special considerations with response to intervention and instruction for students with diverse backgrounds. *Psychology in the Schools 49*(3), 285–296. doi:10.1002/pits.21597

Hill, D. R., King, S. A., Lemons, C. J., & Partanen, J. N. (2012). Fidelity of implementation and instructional alignment in response to intervention research. *Learning Disabilities Research & Practice, 27*(3), 116–124.

Individuals with Disabilities Education Improvement Act of 2004, Pub. L. No. 108–446, 20 U.S.C. § 300 *et seq.*

Johnson, E., Melard, D. F., Fuchs, D., & McKnight, M. A. (2006). *Response to intervention (RTI): How to do it.* Lawrence, KS: National Research Center on Learning Disabilities.

Kamei-Hannan, C., Holbrook, M. C., & Ricci, L. A. (2012). Applying a response-to-intervention model to literacy instruction for students who are blind or have low vision. *Journal of Visual Impairment and Blindness, 106*(2), 69–80.

Klingner, J. K., & Edwards, P. A. (2006). Cultural considerations with response to intervention models. *Reading Research Quarterly, 41*(1) 108–117. doi:10.1598/RRQ.41.1.6

Linan-Thompson, S., Cirino, P. T., & Vaughn, S. (2007). Determining English language learners' response to intervention: Questions and some answers. *Learning Disability Quarterly, 30*(3), 185–195.

Lindstrom, J. H., & Sayeski, K. (2013). Identifying best practice in a shifting landscape: Making sense of RTI in the context of SLD identification. *Exceptionality, 21*(1), 5–18.

Mastropieri, M. A., & Scruggs, T. F. (2005). Feasibility and consequences of response to intervention: Examination of the issues and scientific evidence as a model for identification of individuals with learning disabilities. *Journal of Learning Disabilities, 38*(6), 525–531.

McKinney, E., Bartholomew, C., & Gray, L. (2010). RTI and SWPBIS: Confronting the problem of disproportionality. *NASP Communique, 38*(6), 1–5.

National Association of State Directors of Special Education. (2008). *Response-to-intervention: Blueprint for implementation—district level.* Alexandria, VA: Author.

National Association of State Directors of Special Education & Council of Administrators of Special Education. (2006, May). *Response to intervention: NASDSE and CASE white paper on RTL.* Alexandria, VA: Author.

No Child Left Behind Act of 2001, Pub. L. No. 107–110, § 115, Stat. 1425 (2002).

Orosco, M. J., & Klingner, J. (2010). One school's implementation of RTI with English language learners: "Referring into RTI." *Journal of Learning Disabilities, 43*(3), 269–288.

Reynolds, C. R., & Shaywitz, S. E. (2009). Response to intervention: Prevention and remediation, perhaps. Diagnosis, no. *Child Development Perspectives, 3*(1), 44–47.

Sanger, D., Friedli, C., Brunken, C., Snow, P., & Ritzman, M. (2012). Educators' year long reactions to the implementation of a response to intervention (RTI) model. *Journal of Ethnographic and Qualitative Research, 7*(2), 98–107.

Stecker, P. M. (2007). Tertiary intervention: Using progress monitoring with intensive services. *Teaching Exceptional Children, 39*(5), 50–57.

Sugai, G., & Horner, R. H. (2009). Responsiveness-to-intervention and school-wide positive behavior supports: Integration of multi-tiered system approaches. *Exceptionality, 17*(4), 223–237.

Sugai, G., O'Keeffe, B. V., & Fallon, L. M. (2012). A contextual consideration of culture and school-wide positive behavior support. *Journal of Positive Behavior Interventions, 14*(4), 197–208. doi:10.1177/1098300711426334

Sulkowski, M., Joyce, D., Storch, E. (2012). Treating childhood anxiety in schools: Service delivery in a response to intervention paradigm. *Journal of Child and Family Studies, 21*(6), 938–947.

Vaughn, S., & Fuchs, L. (2003). Redefining learning disabilities as inadequate response to instruction: The promise and potential problems. *Learning Disabilities Research & Practice, 18*(3), 137–146.

Vujnovic, R. K., & Fabiano, G. A. (2011). Supporting students with attention-deficit/hyperactivity disorder within a response to intervention framework. *ADHD Report, 19*(3), 1–6. doi:10.1521/adhd.2011.19.3.1

Xu, Y., & Drame, E. (2008). Culturally appropriate context: Unlocking the potential of response to intervention for English language learners. *Early Childhood Education Journal, 35*(4), 305–311.

Chapter 13 References

Algozzine, K., & Algozzine, B. (2007). Classroom instructional ecology and school-wide positive behavior support. *Journal of Applied School Psychology, 24*(1), 29–47.

Anderson, J. A., Wright, E. R., Smith, J. S., & Kooreman, H. E. (2007). Educational profiles of students at enrollment in a system of care. *Remedial and Special Education, 28*(1), 9–20.

Bandura, A. (1986). *Social foundations of thought and action: A social cognitive theory.* Englewood Cliffs, NJ: Prentice-Hall.

Bandura, A. (1997). *Self-efficacy: The exercise of control.* New York: W. H. Freeman.

Bradshaw, C. P., Mitchell, M. M., & Leaf, P. J. (2010). Examining the effects of school-wide positive behavioral interventions and supports on student outcomes: Results from a randomized controlled effectiveness trial in elementary schools. *Journal of Positive Behavior Interventions, 12*(3), 133–148. doi:10.1177/1098300709334798

Bronfenbrenner, U. (1979). *The ecology of human development: Experiments by nature and design.* Cambridge, MA: Harvard University Press.

Bruns, E. J., Walrath, C. M., & Sheehan, A. K. (2007). Who administers wraparound? An examination of the training, beliefs, and implementation supports for wraparound providers. *Journal of Emotional and Behavioral Disorders, 15*(3), 156–168.

Burke, M. D., Davis, J. L., Lee, Y.-H., Hagan-Burke, S., Kwok, O., & Sugai, G. (2012). Universal screening for behavioral risk in elementary schools using SWPBS expectations. *Journal of Emotional and Behavioral Disorders, 20*(1), 38–54. doi:10.1177/1063426610377328

Burns, M. K., & Coolong-Chaffin, M. (2006). Response to intervention: The role of and effect on school psychology. *School Psychology Forum: Research in Practice, 1*(1), 1–13.

Carter, D. R., Carter, G. M., Johnson, E. S., & Pool, J. L. (2013). Systematic implementation of a Tier 2 behavior intervention. *Intervention in School and Clinic, 48*(4), 223–231. doi:10.1177/1053451212462879

Chitiyo, M., May, M. E., & Chitiyo, G. (2012). An assessment of the evidence-base for school-wide positive behavior support. *Education and Treatment of Children, 35*(1), 1–24.

Coffey, J. H., & Horner, R. H. (2012). The sustainability of schoolwide positive behavior interventions and supports. *Exceptional Children, 78*(4), 407–422.

Crone, D. A., Hawken, L. S., & Horner, R. H. (2010). *Responding to problem behavior in schools: The Behavior Education Program* (2nd ed.) New York: Guilford Press.

Debnam, K. J., Pas, E. T., & Bradshaw, C. P. (2012). Secondary and tertiary support systems in schools implementing school-wide positive behavioral interventions and supports: A preliminary descriptive analysis.

Journal of Positive Behavior Interventions, 14(3), 142–152. doi:10.1177/1098300712436844.

Dowdy, E., Chin, J. K., Twyford, J. M., & Dever, B. (2011). A factor analytic investigation of the BASC-2 Behavioral and Emotional Screening System parent form: Psychometric properties, practical implications, and future directions. *Journal of School Psychology, 49*(3), 265–280.

Dowdy, E., Doane, K., Eklund, K., & Dever, B. V. (2011). A comparison of teacher nomination and screening to identify behavioral and emotional risk within a sample of underrepresented students. *Journal of Emotional and Behavioral Disorders, 21*(2), 127–137.

Dowdy, E., Twyford, J. M., Chin, J. K., DiStefano, C. A., Kamphaus, R. W., & Mays, K. L. (2011). Factor structure of the BASC-2 Behavioral and Emotional Screening System student form. *Psychological Assessment, 23*(2), 379–387. doi:10.1037/a0021843

Drummond, T. (1994). *The Student Risk Screening Scale (SRSS)*. Grants Pass, OR: Josephine County Mental Health Program.

Eber, L., Breen, K., Rose, J., Unizycki, R. M., & London, T. H. (2008). Wraparound as a tertiary level intervention for students with complex emotional/behavioral needs and their families and teachers. *Teaching Exceptional Children, 40*(6), 16–22.

Eber, L., Hyde, K., & Suter, J. C. (2011). Integrating wraparound into a schoolwide system of positive behavior supports. *Journal of Child and Family Studies, 20*(6), 782–790. doi:10.1007/s10826-010-9424-1

Epstein, M. H., Nordness, P. D., Gallagher, K., Nelson, R., Lewis, L., & Schrepf, S. (2005). School as the entry point: Assessing adherence to the basic tenets of the wraparound approach. *Behavioral Disorders, 30*(2), 85–93.

Feuerborn, L., & Chinn, D. (2012). Teacher perceptions of student needs and implications for positive behavior supports. *Behavioral Disorders, 37*(4), 219–231.

Fries, D., Carney, K. J., Blackman-Urteaga, L., & Savas, S. A. (2012). Wraparound services: Infusion into secondary schools as a dropout prevention strategy. *NASSP Bulletin, 96*, 119–136.

Gresham, F. M., Hunter, K. K., Corwin, E. P., & Fischer, A. J. (2013). Screening, assessment, treatment, and outcome evaluation of behavioral difficulties in an RTI model. *Exceptionality, 21*(1), 19–33. doi:10.1080/09362835.2013.750115

Hallinan, M. T. (2008). Teacher influences on students' attachment to school. *Sociology of Education, 81*(3), 271–283.

Handler, M. W., Ray, J., Connell, J., Their, K., Feinberg, A., & Putnam, R. (2007). Practical considerations in creating school-wide positive behavior support in public schools. *Psychology in the Schools, 44*(1), 29–38.

Hawken, L. S., & Horner, R. H. (2003). Evaluation of a targeted group intervention within a school-wide system of behavior support. *Journal of Behavioral Education, 12*(3), 225–240.

Hawken, L. S., O'Neill, R. E., & MacLeod, K. S. (2011). An investigation of the impact of function of problem behavior on effectiveness of the Behavior Education Program (BEP). *Education and Treatment of Children, 34*(4), 551–574.

Horner, R. H., Sugai, G., Todd, A. W., & Lewis-Palmer, T. (2005). School-wide positive behavior support. In L. Bambara & L. Kern (Eds.), *Individualized supports for students with problem behaviors: Designing positive behavior plans* (pp. 359–390). New York: Guilford Press.

Jones, C., Caravaca, L., Cizek, S., Horner, R. H., & Vincent, C. G. (2006). Culturally responsive schoolwide positive behavior support: A case study in one school with a high proportion of Native American students. *Multiple Voices, 9*(1), 108–119.

Kalberg, J. R., Lane, K. L., & Menzies, H. M. (2010). Using systematic screening procedures to identify students who are nonresponsive to primary prevention efforts: Integrating academic and behavioral measures. *Education and Treatment of Children, 33*(4), 561–584.

Kamphaus, R. W., & Reynolds, C. R. (2007). *BASC-2 Behavioral and Emotional Screening System (BESS)*. Bloomington, MN: Pearson.

Kelm, J. L., & McIntosh, K. (2012). Effects of school-wide positive behavior support on teacher self-efficacy. *Psychology in the Schools, 49*(2), 137–147. doi:10.1002/pits.20624

Lane, K. L., Menzies, H. M., Oakes, W. P., Lambert, W., Cox, M., & Hankins, K. (2012). A validation of the Student Risk Screening Scale for Internalizing and Externalizing Behaviors: Patterns in rural and urban elementary schools. *Behavioral Disorders, 37*(4), 244–270.

Lassen, S. R., Steele, M. M., & Sailor, W. (2006). The relationship of school-wide positive behavior support to academic achievement in an urban middle school. *Psychology in the Schools, 43*(6), 701–712. doi:10.1002/pits.20177

Lee, Y., Patterson, P. P., & Vega, L. A. (2011). Perils to self-efficacy perceptions and teacher-preparation quality among special education intern teachers. *Teacher Education Quarterly, 38*(2), 61–76.

Lewis, T. J., & Sugai, G. (1999). Effective behavior support: A systems approach to proactive school-wide management. *Focus on Exceptional Children, 31*(6), 1–24.

Lynass, L., Tsai, S., Richman, T. D., & Cheney, D. (2012). Social expectations and behavioral indicators in school-wide positive behavior supports: A national study of behavior matrices. *Journal of Positive Behavior Interventions, 14*(3), 153–161.

McIntosh, K., Campbell, A. L., Carter, D. R., & Dickey, C. R. (2009). Differential effects of a Tier Two behavior intervention based on function of problem behavior. *Journal of Positive Behavior Interventions, 11*(2), 82–93.

McIntosh, K., Filter, K. J., Bennett, J. L., Ryan, C., & Sugai, G. (2010). Principles of sustainable prevention: Designing scale-up of school-wide positive behavior support to promote durable systems. *Psychology in the Schools, 47*(1), 5–21.

McIntosh, K., Predy, L. K., Upreti, G., Hume, A. E., Turri, M. G., & Mathews, S. (2013). Perceptions of contextual features related to implementation and sustainability of school-wide positive behavior support. *Journal of Positive Behavior Interventions, 15*(1), 31–43. doi:10.1177/1098300712470723

Mitchell, B. S., Stormont, M., & Gage, N. A. (2011). Tier Two interventions implemented within the context of a tiered prevention framework. *Behavior Disorders, 36*(4), 241–261.

Montalvo, G., Mansfield, E. A., & Miller, R. B. (2007). Liking or disliking the teacher: Student motivation, engagement, and achievement. *Evaluation and Research in Education, 20*(3), 144–158.

Muscott, H. S., Mann, E. L., & LeBrun, M. R. (2008). Positive behavioral interventions and supports in New Hampshire: Effects of large-scale implementation of school-wide positive behavior support on student discipline and academic achievement. *Journal of Positive Behavior Interventions, 10*(3), 190–205. doi:10.1177/1098300708316258

Painter, K. (2012). Outcomes for youth with severe emotional disturbance: A repeated measures longitudinal study of a wraparound approach of service delivery in systems of care. *Child and Youth Care Forum, 41*(4), 407–425. doi:10.1007/s10566-011-9167-1

Safran, S. P. (2006). Using the effective behavior supports survey to guide development of schoolwide positive behavior support. *Journal of Positive Behavior Interventions, 8*(1), 3–9.

Scheuerman, B. K., & Hall, J. A. (2012). *Positive behavior supports for the classroom*. Boston: Pearson.

Shepherd, T. L. (2013). Enthusiasm, humor, and optimism. In R. L. Smith & D. Skarbek (Eds.), *Professional teacher dispositions: Additions to the mainstream* (pp. 25–35). Lanham, MD: R&L Education.

Shields, C., & Gredler, M. (2003). A problem-solving approach to teaching operant conditioning. *Teaching of Psychology, 30*(2), 114–116.

Skaalvik, E. M., & Skaalvik, S. (2007). Dimensions of teacher self-efficacy and relations with strain factors, perceived collective teacher efficacy, and teacher burnout. *Journal of Educational Psychology, 99*(3), 611–625.

Slavin, R. E. (2004). Built to last: Long-term maintenance of Success for All. *Remedial and Special Education, 25*(1), 61–66. doi.org/10.1177/07419325040250010701

Stambaugh, L. F., Mustillo, S. A., Burns, B. J., Stephens, R. L., Baxter, B., Edwards, D., & DeKraai, M. (2007). Outcomes from wraparound and multisystemic therapy in a center for mental health services system-of-care demonstration site. *Journal of Emotional and Behavioral Disorders, 15*(3), 143–155.

Sugai, G., & Horner, R. H. (2006). A promising approach for expanding and sustaining school-wide positive behavior support. *School Psychology Review, 35*(2), 245–259.

Sugai, G., Horner, R. H., Algozzine, B., Barrett, S., Lewis, T., Anderson, C., & Simonsen, B. (2010). *School-wide positive behavior support: Implementers' blueprint and self-assessment.* Eugene: University of Oregon.

Todd, A. W., Campbell, A. L., Meyer, G. G., & Horner, R. H. (2008). The effects of a targeted intervention to reduce problem behaviors: Elementary school implementation of check in–check out. *Journal of Positive Behavior Interventions, 10*(1), 46–55. doi:10.1177/1098300707311369

Vincent, C. G., Randall, C., Cartledge, G., Tobin, T. J., & Swain-Bradway, J. (2011). Toward a conceptual integration of cultural responsiveness and schoolwide positive behavior support. *Journal of Positive Behavior Interventions, 13*(4), 219–229. doi:10.1177/1098300711399765

Walker, B., Cheney, D., Stage, S., Blum, C., & Horner, R. H. (2005). Schoolwide screening and positive behavior supports: Identifying and supporting students at risk for school failure. *Journal of Positive Behavior Interventions, 7*(4), 194–204.

Walker, H. M., & Severson, H. (1992). *Systematic Screening for Behavior Disorders: User's guide and technical manual.* Longmont, CO: Sopris West.

Chapter 14 References

Bandura, A. (1997). *Self-efficacy: The exercise of control.* New York: W. H. Freeman.

Bronfenbrenner, U. (2005). Interacting systems of human development. Research paradigms: Present and future. In U. Bronfenbrenner (Ed.), *Making human beings human: Bioecological perspectives on human development* (pp. 67–93). Thousand Oaks, CA: Sage.

Cartledge, G., Singh, A., & Gibson, L. (2008). Practical behavior-management techniques to close the accessibility gap for students who are culturally and linguistically diverse. *Preventing School Failure, 52*(3), 29–38.

Chan, J., Lang, R., Rispoli, M., O'Reilly, M., Sigafoos, J., & Cole, H. (2009). Use of peer-mediated interventions in the treatment of autism spectrum disorders: A systematic review. *Research in Autism Spectrum Disorders, 3*(4), 876–889.

Cook, C. R., Gresham, F. M., Kern, L., Barreras, R. B., Thorton, S., & Crews, S. D. (2008). Social skills training for secondary students with emotional and/or behavioral disorders: A review and analysis of the meta-analytic literature. *Journal of Emotional and Behavioral Disorders, 16*(3), 131–144. doi:10.1177/1063426608314541

Cook, K. E., Earles-Vollrath, T., & Ganz, J. B. (2006). Bibliotherapy. *Intervention in School and Clinic, 42*(2), 91–100.

Crozier, S., & Tincani, M. (2007). Effects of social stories on prosocial behavior of preschool children with autism spectrum disorders. *Journal of Autism and Developmental Disorders, 37*(9), 1803–1814.

Dole, S., & McMahan, J. (2005). Using videotherapy to help adolescents cope with social and emotional problems. *Intervention in School and Clinic, 40*(3), 151–155.

Goldstein, A. P. (1999). *The Prepare Curriculum: Teaching prosocial competencies.* Champaign, IL: Research Press.

Goldstein, A. P., & McGinnis, E. (1997). *Skillstreaming the adolescent: New strategies and perspectives for teaching prosocial skills* (rev. ed.) Champaign, IL: Research Press.

Green, V. A., Drysdale, H., Boelema, T., Smart, E., van der Meer, L., Achmadi, D., . . . Lancioni, G. (2013). Use of video modeling to increase positive peer interactions of four preschool children with social skills difficulties. *Education and Treatment of Children, 36*(2), 59–85.

Gresham, F. M., & Elliott, S. N. (1990). *The Social Skills Rating System.* Circle Pines, MN: American Guidance Service.

Gresham, F. M., & Elliott, S. N. (2008). *Social Skills Improvement System: Rating Scales.* Bloomington, MN: Pearson Assessments.

Gresham, F. M., Elliott, S. N., & Kettler, R. J. (2010). Base rates of social skills acquisition/performance deficits, strengths, and problem behaviors: An analysis of the Social Skills Improvement System–Rating Scales. *Psychological Assessment, 22*(4), 809–815. doi:10.1037/a0020255

Gresham, F. M., Elliott, S. N., Vance, M. J., & Cook, C. R. (2011). Comparability of the Social Skills Rating System to the Social Skills Improvement System: Content and psychometric comparisons across elementary and secondary age levels. *School Psychology Quarterly, 26*(1), 27–44. doi:10.1037/a0022662

Gresham, F. M., Van, M. B., & Cook, C. R. (2006). Social skills training for teaching replacement behaviors: Remediating acquisition deficits in at-risk students. *Behavioral Disorders, 31*(4), 363–377.

Hall, J. D., Jones, C. H., & Claxton, A. F. (2008). Evaluation of the Stop & Think Social Skills Program with kindergarten students. *Journal of Applied School Psychology, 24*(2), 265–283.

Hebert, T. P., & Sergent, D. (2005). Using movies to guide: Teachers and counselors collaborating to support gifted students. *Gifted Child Today, 28*(4), 14–25.

Hemmeter, M. L., Fox, L., Jack, S., & Broyles, L. (2007). A program-wide model of positive behavior support in early childhood settings. *Journal of Early Intervention, 29*(4), 337–355.

Hsu, N., Hammond, H., & Ingalls, L. (2012). The effectiveness of culturally-based social stories to increase appropriate behaviors of children with developmental delays. *International Journal of Special Education, 27*(1), 104–116.

Hutchins, T. L. (2012, January 17). What's the story? What does the research say about how best to use social stories to help children with ASDs? *ASHA Leader.*

Kam, C., Greenberg, M. T., & Kusche, C. A. (2004). Sustained effects of the PATHS curriculum on the social and psychological adjustment of children in special education. *Journal of Emotional and Behavioral Disorders, 12*(2), 66–78.

Knoff, H. M. (2001). *The Stop & Think Social Skills Program.* Longmont, CO: Sopris West.

Kokina, A., & Kern, L. (2010). Social story interventions for students with autism spectrum disorders: A meta-analysis. *Journal of Autism and Developmental Disorders, 40*(7), 812–826. doi:10.1007/s10803–009–0931–0

Lane, K. L., Wehby, J. H., & Cooley, C. (2006). Teacher expectations of students' classroom behavior across the grade span: Which social skills are necessary for success? *Exceptional Children, 72*(2), 153–167.

Lo, Y., Mustian, A. L., Brophy, A., & White, R. B. (2011). Peer-mediated social skill instruction for African American males with or at risk for mild disabilities. *Exceptionality, 19*(3), 191–209. doi:10.1080/09362835.2011.579851

Maag, J. W. (2006). Social skills training for students with emotional and behavioral disorders: A review of reviews. *Behavioral Disorders, 32*(1), 5–17.

McGinnis, E., & Goldstein, A. P. (1997). *Skill-streaming the elementary school child: New strategies and perspectives for teaching prosocial skills* (rev. ed.) Champaign, IL: Research Press.

McGinnis, E., & Goldstein, A. P. (2003). *Skill-streaming in early childhood: New strategies and perspectives for teaching prosocial skills* (rev. ed.) Champaign, IL: Research Press.

Miller, M. J., Lane, K. L., & Wehby, J. (2005). Social skills instruction for students with high-incidence disabilities: A school-based intervention to address acquisition deficits. *Preventing School Failure, 49*(20), 27–39.

Pinar, E. S., & Sucuoglu, B. (2013). The outcomes of a social skills teaching program for inclusive classroom teachers. *Educational Sciences: Theory and Practice, 13*(4), 2247–2261. doi:10.12738/estp.2013.4.1736

Plavnick, J. B., Sam, A. M., Hume, K., & Odom, S. L. (2013). Effects of video-based group instruction for adolescents with autism spectrum disorder. *Exceptional Children, 80*(1), 67–83.

Riney, S. S., & Bullock, L. M. (2012). Teachers' perspectives on student problematic behavior and social skills. *Emotional and Behavioural Difficulties, 17*(2), 195–211.

Sansosti, F. J., & Powell-Smith, K. A. (2006). Using social stories to improve the social behavior of children with Asperger syndrome. *Journal of Positive Behavior Interventions, 8*(1), 43–57.

Scattone, D., Tingstrom, D. H., & Wilczynski, S. M. (2006). Increasing appropriate social interactions of children with autism spectrum disorders using social stories. *Focus on Autism and Other Developmental Disabilities, 21*(4), 211–222.

Shepherd, T. L. (2007). Infinite diversity in infinite combinations: Portraits of individuals with disabilities in *Star Trek*. *Teaching Exceptional Children Plus, 3*(6), article 1. Retrieved from http://escholarship.bc.edu/education/tecplus/v013/iss6/art1

Sheridan, B. A., MacDonald, D. A., Donlon, M., Kuhn, B., McGovern, K., & Friedman, H. (2011). Evaluation of a social skills program based on social learning theory, implemented in a school setting. *Psychological Reports, 108*(2), 420–436.

Skinner, B. F. (1953). *Science and human behavior*. New York: Free Press.

Spencer, V. (2006). Peer tutoring and students with emotional behavioral disorders: A review of the literature. *Behavioral Disorders, 31*(2), 204–222.

Vanderborght, B., Simut, R., Saldien, J., Pop, C., Rusu, A. S., Pineta, S., . . . David, D. O. (2012). Using the social robot Probo as a social story telling agent for children with ASD. *Interaction Studies, 13*(3), 348–372.

Van Vugt, E. S., Dekovic, M., Prinzie, P., Stams, G. J. J. M., & Asscher, J. J. (2013). Evaluation of a group-based social skills training for children with problem behavior. *Children and Youth Services Review, 35*(1), 162–167.

Walker, H. M., & Holmes, D. (1983). *The ACCESS program: Adolescent curriculum for communication and effective social skills*. Austin: Pro-Ed.

Walker, H. M., McConnell, S. R., Holmes, D., Todis, B., Walker, J., & Golden, N. (1983). *ACCEPTS: A children's curriculum for effective peer and teacher skills*. Austin: Pro-Ed.

Walton, K. M., & Ingersoll, B. R. (2013). Improving social skills in adolescents and adults with autism and severe to profound intellectual disability: A review of the literature. *Journal of Autism and Developmental Disorders, 43*(3), 594–615. doi:10.1007/s10803–012–1601–1

Wilson, K. P. (2013). Incorporating video modeling into a school-based intervention for students with autism spectrum disorders. *Language, Speech, and Hearing Services in Schools, 44*(1), 105–117. doi:10.1044/0161–1461(2012/11–0098)

Photo Credits

Chapter 1 Opener	Digital Vision/Thinkstock
Chapter 2 Opener	Pixland/Thinkstock
Chapter 3 Opener	Digital Vision/Photodisc/Thinkstock
Chapter 4 Opener	Digital Vision/Photodisc/Thinkstock
Chapter 5 Opener	Jupiterimages/Stockbyte/Thinkstock
Chapter 6 Opener	Comstock Images/Stockbyte/Thinkstock
Chapter 7 Opener	Stockbyte/Thinkstock
Chapter 8 Opener	Brand X Pictures/Stockbyte/Thinkstock
Chapter 9 Opener	Ableimages/Photodisc/Thinkstock
Chapter 10 Opener	Creatas/Thinkstock
Chapter 11 Opener	Comstock Images/Stockbyte/Thinkstock
Chapter 12 Opener	Digital Vision/Photodisc/Thinkstock
Chapter 13 Opener	Katy McDonnell/Photodisc/Thinkstock
Chapter 14 Opener	Jupiterimages/Stockbyte/Thinkstock

INDEX

Page reference followed by (figure) indicate an illustrated figure; followed by (table) indicates a table.

ABOUT THE AUTHORS

Terry L. Shepherd has been a department head and associate professor of special education at Indiana University South Bend since 2007. Prior to that, he was an associate professor of special education at Texas A&M International University, a teacher for children with emotional and behavior disorders in the public schools, and a teacher at a residential treatment center for troubled teenagers. He received his EdD in special education at Ball State University. He has published numerous professional papers in emotional and behavior disorders, international special education, and teacher education. He is the author of *Working with Students with Emotional and Behavior Disorders: Characteristics and Teaching Strategies* (Pearson-Merrill, 2010), and "Enthusiasm, Humor, and Optimism" in R. L. Smith & D. Skarbek (Eds.), *Professional Teacher Dispositions: Additions to the Mainstream,* (R & L Education, 2013). He has been a member of the Council for Exceptional Children since 1998. His hobbies include songwriting, model building, genealogy, and American history.

Diana Linn is associate professor of special education and department chair at Texas A&M International University in Laredo, Texas. Prior to that, she was a teacher in general education and special education classrooms in Mexico and South Texas. Dr. Linn received her PhD from Texas A&M University-College Station. She has several published articles concerning the disproportionality of English language learners in special education and the use of cultural autobiographies in preservice teacher education programs. She is a member of the American Educational Research Association, the Council for Exceptional Children and the National Association for Multicultural Education.

⑤SAGE research**methods**

The essential online tool for researchers from the world's
leading methods publisher

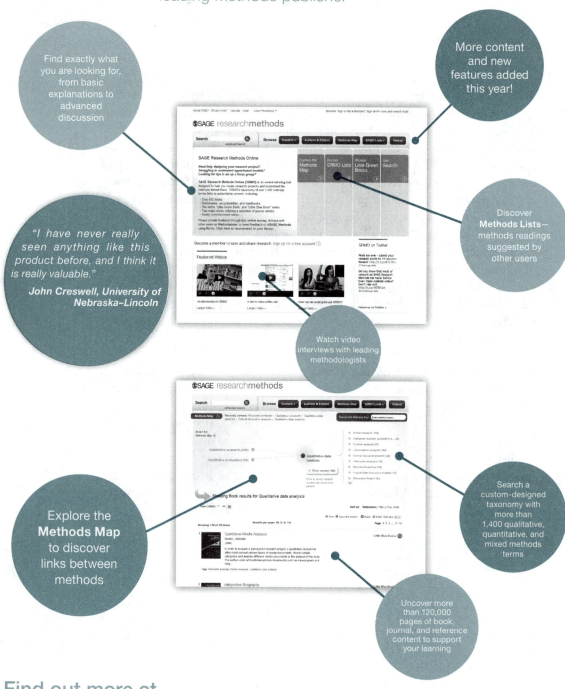

Find exactly what
you are looking for,
from basic
explanations to
advanced
discussion

More content
and new
features added
this year!

*"I have never really
seen anything like this
product before, and I think it
is really valuable."*

**John Creswell, University of
Nebraska–Lincoln**

Discover
Methods Lists—
methods readings
suggested by
other users

Watch video
interviews with leading
methodologists

Explore the
Methods Map
to discover
links between
methods

Search a
custom-designed
taxonomy with
more than
1,400 qualitative,
quantitative, and
mixed methods
terms

Uncover more
than 120,000
pages of book,
journal, and reference
content to support
your learning

Find out more at
www.sageresearchmethods.com